For the past three decades Professor A. A. Long has been at the forefront of research in Hellenistic philosophy. In this book he assembles a dozen of the articles on Stoicism he has previously published in journals and conference proceedings. Although one of the papers dates from 1971, the collection is biased in favour of Professor Long's more recent studies of Stoicism. It is focused on three themes: the Stoics' interpretation of their intellectual tradition, their ethics and their psychology. While each chapter is self-standing, the contents of the book reflect the peculiarly holistic and systematic features of Stoicism. Most chapters make reference to material found elsewhere in the book, and no main topic of the philosophy, including logic and physics, is omitted altogether. The papers are printed here in their original form for the most part, but the author has made some minor corrections and stylistic or bibliographical changes. He has also added a postscript to three papers whose topics have been the subject of much discussion during the years since they first appeared.

STOIC STUDIES

STOIC STUDIES

A. A. LONG

Irving Stone Professor of Literature, in the Department of Classics,
University of California at Berkeley

Published by the Press Syndicate of the University of Cambridge
The Pitt Building, Trumpington Street, Cambridge CB2 1RP
40 West 20th Street, New York, NY 10011-4211, USA
10 Stamford Road, Oakleigh, Melbourne 3166, Australia

First published 1996

Printed in Great Britain at the University Press, Cambridge

A catalogue record for this book is available from the British Library

Library of Congress cataloguing in publication data

Long, A. A.
Stoic studies / A. A. Long.
p.   cm.
Includes bibliographical references and indexes.
ISBN 0 521 48263 1 (hardback)
1. Stoics.   1. Title.
B528.L65 1996   95-38497
188 – dc20   CIP

ISBN 0 521 48263 1 hardback

H. C. and G. V.
in memoriam

Contents

Preface

This volume collects a dozen of the papers on Stoicism I have previously published in journals and conference proceedings. The articles are printed here without substantial revision in most cases, but I have taken the opportunity to make minor corrections and stylistic or bibliographical changes. I have also added a postscript to three papers whose topics have been the subject of much discussion during the intervening years. In assembling the papers together in this form, I hope to make them more accessible to the growing number of people who are seriously interested in Hellenistic philosophy.

I am not a Stoic, for more reasons than are stated or hinted at in this book. But their philosophy has fascinated me now for thirty years. Of all the Greek schools, Stoicism was the most ambitious in its quest for a system that would explain how human nature fits into the world at large. That project, which has beguiled many subsequent philosophers, seems to me to be vulnerable to the evidence of history, cultural diversity and our continuing ignorance of the kind of animals we are. It is, none the less, a noble error. If the Stoics were too eager, as I think they were, to make *cosmic* order relevant to *human* values, they advanced numerous theories and concepts that are a continuing challenge to thought.

Although one of the papers dates from 1971, the majority were written a decade or more later. Given the need to produce a book of manageable length and price, I decided (with helpful advice from a Cambridge University Press reader) that a selection concentrated on my more recent work would be the most useful. Hence I have omitted a good many of my older papers, including those I contributed to *Problems in Stoicism* and other papers whose findings are partly incorporated in two of my later books, *Hellenistic Philosophy* and *The Hellenistic Philosophers*, co-authored with David Sedley.

(Details of this other work are included in the bibliography of
the present volume.) Apart from issues of length and topicality, I
wanted to select papers that would make for a reasonably coherent
volume. I have tried to achieve these objectives by focusing on
three themes: the Stoics' appropriation and interpretation of their
intellectual tradition (chapters 1–4), their ethics (chapters 5–9),
and their psychology (chapters 10–12). If the length of the volume
had been no concern, I should also have included papers dealing
with sceptical criticism of the Stoics and Stoic responses to that
criticism. That important theme, which has been well recognised
in modern scholarship, is one that I hope to include in a subsequent book.

Although each chapter is self-standing and can be read as such,
many chapters make reference to at least one of the others. Readers
who are primarily interested in Stoic ethics will find something
relevant to that topic in every chapter, and chapters 6–8 may be
read in sequence as three successive attempts to clarify the central
concepts of their moral thought. Written as they were at different
times, these chapters also differ from one another in their perspectives and emphases (see the postscripts to chapters 6 and 7), but I
have let the differences stand because they seem to me to reflect
the complexity of Stoic ethics and the difficulty of assessing it from
a monolithic point of view. Retrospectively, I can see chapters 6
and 7 as preparatory to chapter 8, which is my most ambitious
attempt to justify the coherence of Stoic ethics in terms of its exponents' psychological and theological assumptions. As for logic
and physics, which are the other two official divisions of Stoic
philosophy, some aspects of logic are treated in chapter 4, and
physics is a major topic of several chapters, especially 2, 9 and 10.
Although the book does not seek to give a comprehensive account
of Stoicism, its content reflects the fact that this was a peculiarly
holistic and systematic philosophy. Trying to do justice to this fact
is the main principle that has guided all of my work on Stoicism.

Apart from the corrections and updating mentioned above, I have
frequently substituted words like 'human being' or 'persons' for
'man' or 'men' in the original publications. This is not because
I think that history should succumb to political correctness; it
would be absurd to convert the technical expression *ho sophos*, literally 'the wise man', to 'the wise person'. But while Stoic philos-

ophers followed convention in writing of their ethical paragon in the masculine gender, their generalisations about good and bad lives were intended to apply to persons without regard to their sex or class or ethnicity. Thus the Christian Lactantius was correct in supporting his own resistance to discrimination by referring to 'the Stoics who said that slaves and women should philosophise' (*Inst. div.* III.25), and the Roman Stoic Musonius Rufus delivered discourses proving that females have the same nature as males, so far as their minds and virtues are concerned, and that daughters should be educated in the same way as sons (Musonius, ap. Hense III, IV). The Stoics' ethical significance will be made clearer to modern readers by avoiding language that could imply their lack of interest in half of the human race. This is an instance in which the deplorably sexist language handed down to men of my generation has helped to falsify history.

Each of these papers began its life as the result of an invitation to contribute to a colloquium or to a collective volume. In the preface of *Hellenistic Philosophy* I acknowledged the great benefit I have derived from such invitations. It is a pleasure for me to repeat such thanks. Friends too numerous to single out by name have given me corrections and suggestions which I have gratefully incorporated. In preparing the book for publication, I could not have received better assistance than was given me by Pauline Hire and Susan Moore, from Cambridge University Press. I am also most grateful to James Kerr, a graduate student at Berkeley, for help with proofreading and compiling the indexes.

During the time when most of these studies were written I had the good fortune to be encouraged and helped by Harold Cherniss and Gregory Vlastos. These men were giants, both as scholars and as persons. With all its shortcomings, this book would scarcely have been written without their consistent support, and so I dedicate it to their memory.

Berkeley, July 1995   A. A. L.

Acknowledgements

The chapters of this book were published in their original form in the following publications, and we are grateful for permission to reprint them.

1 Socrates in Hellenistic philosophy: from *The Classical Quarterly* 38 (1988), 150–71.

2 Heraclitus and Stoicism: from *Philosophia* – Yearbook of the Research Center for Greek Philosophy at the Academy of Athens – 5/6 (1975/6), 132–53.

3 Stoic readings of Homer: from *Homer's Ancient Readers. The Hermeneutics of Greek Epic's Earliest Exegetes*, edd. R. Lamberton and J. J. Keaney (Princeton University Press, 1992), 41–66.

4 Dialectic and the Stoic sage: from *The Stoics*, ed. J. M. Rist (University of California Press, 1978), 101–24.

5 Arius Didymus and the exposition of Stoic ethics: from *Rutgers University Studies in Classical Humanities*. Volume I: *On Stoic and Peripatetic Ethics. The Work of Arius Didymus*, ed. W. W. Fortenbaugh (Transaction Books, Rutgers, 1983), 41–65.

6 The logical basis of Stoic ethics: from *Proceedings of the Aristotelian Society* 71 (1970/71), 85–104.

7 Greek ethics after Macintyre and the Stoic community of reason: from *Ancient Philosophy* 3 (1983), 184–97.

8 Stoic eudaimonism: from *Proceedings of the Boston Area Colloquium in Ancient Philosophy* 4 (University Press of America, 1989), 77–101.

9 The harmonics of Stoic virtue: from *Oxford Studies in Ancient Philosophy*, suppl. vol. 1991, 97–116.

10 Soul and body in Stoicism: from *Phronesis* 27 (1982), 34–57.

11 Hierocles on *oikeiōsis* and self-perception: from *Hellenistic Philosophy*, vol. I, ed. K. J. Boudouris (Athens, 1993), 93–104.

12 Representation and the self in Stoicism: from *Companions to Ancient Thought* 2: *Psychology*, ed. S. Everson (Cambridge University Press, 1991), 101–20.

Note: The original pagination of articles is indicated at the top of each page, and the original page divisions are marked in the text by a pair of vertical lines, ‖.

CHAPTER I

*Socrates in Hellenistic philosophy**

INTRODUCTION

In what sense did the Hellenistic philosophers see themselves as the heirs or critics of Socrates? Was Socrates, in their view, a philosopher on whom Plato was the decisive authority? What doctrines or strategies of Socrates were thoroughly alive in this period? These are the principal questions I shall be asking in this paper, particularly the third. To introduce them, and to set the scene, I begin with some general points, starting from two passages which present an image of Socrates at the beginning and at the end of the Hellenistic era. Here first are three lines from the *Silloi* of the Pyrrhonean Timon of Phlius:

From these matters [i.e. the inquiry into nature] he turned aside, the people-chiselling moralising chatterer, the wizard of Greece, whose assertions were sharply pointed, master of the well-turned sneer, a pretty good ironist.[1]

Next Epictetus (*Discourses* IV.5.1–4):

The honourable and good man neither fights with anyone himself, nor, so far as he can, does he let anyone else do so. Of this as of everything

---

* The original version of this chapter was first read to a meeting of the Southern Association for Ancient Philosophy, held at Cambridge University in September 1986; further versions of it were given at the University of Washington, at Cornell and at Berkeley. I am grateful for the discussion that took place on all these occasions, and particularly to Myles Burnyeat, who also gave me written comments. My principal indebtedness is to Gregory Vlastos, both for the stimulus of his published work and for the time we spent together discussing issues raised in the later part of the chapter. I also gratefully acknowledge the award of a fellowship from the John Simon Guggenheim Memorial Foundation, which gave me the leisure to work on this subject.
[1] D.L. II.19 = Timon fr. 799 Lloyd-Jones/Parsons 1983: ἐκ δ' ἄρα τῶν ἀπέκλινεν ὁ λαξόος, ἐννομολέσχης, | Ἑλλήνων ἐπαοιδός, ἀκριβολόγους ἀποφήνας, | μυκτὴρ ῥητορόμυκτος, ὑπαττικὸς εἰρωνευτής. For the interpretation of the opening phrase as an allusion to Socrates' disavowal of physics, cf. Sextus Empiricus, *M* VII.8 and Clem. Alex., *Strom.* 1.14.63.3. Details of the whole passage are well discussed by Cortassa 1978, pp. 140–6.

else the life of Socrates is available to us as a model (*paradeigma*), who not only himself avoided fighting everywhere, but did not let others fight. Notice in Xenophon's *Symposium* how many fights he has resolved, and again how he put up with Thrasymachus, Polus and Callicles ... For he kept utterly secure in mind the thought that no one controls another's commanding-faculty (*hēgemonikon*).

In the *Discourses* of Epictetus, Socrates is *the* philosopher, a figure canonised more regularly and with more attention to detail than any other Stoic saint, whether Diogenes, Antisthenes or Zeno. The reader who knew the history of Greek philosophy only from Epictetus would form the impression that Stoicism was the philosophy of Socrates. He would also, by Epictetus' quotations from Plato and Xenophon, learn some of the salient moments of Socrates' life – his divine mission, trial, imprisonment etc. Moreover, what Epictetus says about the elenchus (1.26.17–18, II.1.32, II.26.4), the impossibility of *akrasia* (III.3.2–4), removal of the false conceit of knowledge (II.17.1, III.14.9), and definition (IV.1.41) reveals as deep a perception or utilisation of Socrates' philosophy as we find in any ancient thinker after Plato.

Socrates' presence in Epictetus' *Discourses* – which I must pass over here – could be the topic of a monograph.[2] But, to repeat, Epictetus' Socrates is the Stoics' patron ‖ saint. He is no ironist, no sharp talker, no gadfly or sting-ray, no lover or symposiast or philosopher chiefly characterised by self-confessed ignorance (see n. 29 below). If, as I think certain, Epictetus has reflected hard on the Socratic writings of Plato and Xenophon, what he culls from those writings is an ideal of the philosophical life, as he himself conceives of it: 'Now that Socrates is dead, the memory of what he did or said when alive is no less or even more beneficial to men' (*Discourses* IV.1.169).

---

[2] See also 1.9.22–4 (paraphrase of Plato, *Ap.* 29c as in III.1.19–21), 1.12.3 (S. coupled with Odysseus), 1.12.23 (S. was not in prison since he was there voluntarily), 1.29.16–19 (Plato, *Ap.* 30c–d, as in II.2.15–18), 1.29.65–6 (Plato, *Phd.* 116d), II.1.32 (S. *did* write, for self-examination), II.12.5 (How did S. behave? He forced his interlocutor to give him testimony, and had no need of any other; cf. *Gorg.* 474a), III.24.60–1 (S. behaving as a free man, dear to the gods), IV.1.159–60 (S.'s life as a paradigm of making everything subordinate to the laws, drawing on Xen. *Mem.* 1.1.18), IV.4.21–2 (Plato, *Crito* 43d), IV.11.19–21 (S.'s toilet habits, rejecting Aristophanes, *Nub.* 103). Other refs. to Socrates in Plato and Xenophon: 1.26.18, III.12.15 (Plato, *Ap.* 38a); II.1.15 (*Phd.* 77e, *Crito* 46c); II.2.8–9 (Xen. *Ap.* 2); II.5.18–20 (Plato, *Ap.* 26e); III.1.42 (*Alc.* 1, 131d); III.22.26 (Plato, *Clitopho* 407a–b); III.23.20–6 (Plato, *Ap.* 30c, 17c, *Crito* 46b); II.24.99 (Plato, *Ap.* 28d–29a); IV.1.41 (Xen. *Mem.* IV.6.1). Döring 1979, pp. 43–79, includes a chapter on Epictetus, but misses an opportunity to deal with the subject in a searching way; cf. Long 1981.

Four hundred years of Stoicism had contributed to the preservation and interpretation of that memory. According to Philodemus, the Stoics actually wanted to be called 'Socratics'.[3] In the later part of this paper I will show, albeit selectively, how their philosophy in its earliest phase represents a self-conscious attempt to fulfil that wish. But before approaching this topic and the role of Socrates in other Hellenistic schools, let us return to Timon. His lampooning purposes do not cast doubt on the historical interest of his remarks. Timon is a caricaturist who never fails to capture one or two recognisable and dominant features of the philosophers who form his subjects. Hence his evidence is valuable both for what it includes and for what it omits – and all the more so since Timon was writing from a non-doctrinaire perspective at a time when the new Hellenistic philosophies were still in the process of fashioning their identities. His brief remarks deserve closer scrutiny.

Timon associates Socrates' concentration upon ethics with his repudiation of the inquiry into nature. This, as we shall see in more detail shortly, is the most fundamental characteristic of Socrates in the doxographical tradition. I have the impression that Xenophon, *Memorabilia* 1.1.11–16, rather than Plato's *Apology* or *Phaedo*, was the text that made this mark of Socrates so prominent. Timon's nicely coined term *ennomoleschēs* should mean not, as is standardly supposed, 'chatterer about laws', but someone who chatters in an *ennomos* way – i.e. a moralist.[4] The expression *Hellēnōn epaoidos*, 'Wizard of Greece', could owe something to Plato, *Charm.* 157a, a passage in which the soul's 'fair discourses' are described as *epōidai*; but it is probably a general reminiscence of the Aristophanic Socrates, to whom Timon is also indebted for *akribologous apophēnas*.[5] In his third line Timon focuses upon Socrates' powers of wit, censure, and irony.

The witty, sometimes caustic and ironical Socrates – Plato's Socrates, not Xenophon's – drops completely out of the early Stoic tradition.[6] The prominence of these features in Timon's vignette is interesting. As the mentor of Antisthenes, and, through him, of

---

[3] *De Stoicis* cols. 12–13, Σωκρατ[ι]κοὶ καλεῖσθαι θέ[λο]υσιν; see Giannantoni 1983–5, vol. II, Diogenes v b 126.
[4] Cf. Plato's use of *ennomos* in combination with *spoudaios*, *Rep.* IV, 424e.
[5] Cf. *Nub.* 130, where Strepsiades wonders how he will learn *logōn akribōn skindalamous*.
[6] Irony for the Stoics was exclusively a feature of the inferior man; cf. *SVF* III.630.

Diogenes and Crates, a censorious and caustic Socrates was cherished ‖ by the Cynics, with whom Timon felt some sympathy.[7] Even Epictetus, in his dialectical practice and choice of vivid metaphors, was implicitly following their lead. Unfortunately, the reliable evidence on Cynics is insufficient to provide much material for speculating on the extent to which they had any theoretical views about the connexion between Socratic irony and the way philosophical discourse should be conducted. On this, as on everything else, Socrates was attacked by the Epicureans (see below). But irony cannot be said to constitute a dominant feature of Socrates when we are considering his positive role in the main stream of Hellenistic philosophy.

From our perspective, indelibly coloured by Plato's Socrates, this is remarkable. But the irony of Socrates, together with all the other glittering characteristics of his discourse and argumentative style – what the Epicurean Colotes witheringly calls his *alazones logoi* (Plutarch, *Adv. Col.* 1117d) – was inimitable and quite inseparable from Plato's dialogues. Xenophon's often stodgy Socrates is no ironist. Though Socrates' philosophical principles clamoured for replication and interpretation, there could be no dissemination of the whole man, on the basis of all the sources, either as a paradigm on whom to model one's life or as a more abstract set of theories. Socrates was too complex, too individualistically contoured, to be appropriated in full by any single philosophical school. One of his closest approximations, Diogenes of Sinope, earned the description from Plato, 'a Socrates gone mad' (D.L. vi.54).

Timon's Socrates and that of Epictetus are composite but partial portraits, derived both from books and from Socrates' philosophical afterlife. A hundred years after Socrates' death – the time of the foundation of the Garden and the Stoa – a detailed oral tradition concerning the historical figure can probably be excluded. Even if stories about the man himself were passed on by word of mouth, the Socrates of my inquiry is the subject of the 'Socratic discourses' composed by his associates, Plato, Xenophon, Antisthenes, Aeschines. In general, it seems, neither Hellenistic philosophers with an allegiance to Socrates, nor biographers and doxographers, addressed the 'Socratic problem' of modern schol-

---

[7] I discuss Timon's Cynic leanings in Long 1978a. See also Brancacci 1981.

arship. If they were aware of discrepancies between Xenophon's accounts and Plato's dialogues, these were not regarded as any reason for having to prefer one account to the other. Control of the material, we can conjecture, was determined not by preconceptions about the superiority in historicity or philosophical sophistication of Plato to Xenophon, but by the need to derive from both of them a well-founded philosophical paradigm that would be internally coherent and consistent with the Hellenistic philosopher's own stance.

Timon's observation that Socrates concentrated on ethics and repudiated physics is the best starting-point for viewing the Hellenistic philosophers' attitude and approach to the great man. The point had already been made in similar brevity by Aristotle: 'Socrates occupied himself with ethics and not at all with nature as a whole' (*Metaph.* A 6, 987b1–2); and it would become the most commonly repeated Socratic characteristic in the doxographical tradition. Here, for instance, is the pseudo-Galenic article on Socrates:

The original philosophers opted only for the study of nature and made this the goal of their philosophy. Socrates, who succeeded them much later, said that this was inaccessible to people (for he regarded secure cognition of non-evident things as most difficult), and that investigation of how one might best conduct one's life and avoid bad things and get the greatest possible share of fine things was more useful. Believing this more useful he ignored the study of nature ... and devoted his thought to an ethical disposition that would distinguish good and bad, right and wrong ... Observing that authorities in these matters would need to be persuasive and would ‖ achieve this if they were evidently good at using dialectical arguments in dealings with their interlocutors, he elaborated dialectic.[8]

The incorporation of dialectic in this account will concern us later. For the present I call attention to the passage from Xenophon, *Mem.* 1.1.11–16, which by the Hellenistic period had become

---

[8] Ps.-Galen, *Hist. phil.* ap. Diels 1879, p. 597, 1–17: τῶν ἐξ ἀρχῆς φιλοσοφησάντων φυσιολογεῖν μόνον προελομένων καὶ τοῦτο τέλος τῆς κατ' αὐτοὺς φιλοσοφίας πεποιημένων ἐπιγεγονὼς πολλοῖς ὕστερον χρόνοις Σωκράτης τοῦτο μὲν ἀνέφικτον ἔφησεν ἀνθρώποις ὑπάρχειν (τῶν γὰρ ἀδήλων κατάληψιν βεβαίαν λαβεῖν τῶν χαλεπωτάτων ἐνόμισε), τὸ δὲ ζητεῖν ὅπως ἄμεινον διάγοι τις, καὶ τῶν μὲν κακῶν ἀποτραπείη τῶν δὲ καλῶν ὡς πλείστων μετάσχοι, τοῦτο μᾶλλον συνοίσειν. καὶ τοῦτο νομίσας χρησιμώτερον τῆς μὲν φυσιολογίας ἠμέληκεν ... ἠθικὴν δέ τινα διάθεσιν ἐπινενοηκὼς διαγνωστικὴν ἀγαθῶν τε καὶ κακῶν αἰσχρῶν τε καὶ καλῶν ... κατιδὼν δὲ ὅτι δεήσει τοὺς τούτων προεστησομένους εὐπειθείας μετέχειν, τοῦτο δ' ἂν ὑπάρξειεν εἰ λόγοις διαλεκτικοῖς φαίνοιντο πρὸς τοὺς προσιόντας καλῶς κεχρημένοι, καὶ τὴν διαλεκτικὴν ἐπινενόηκεν.

the principal authority for Socrates' exclusively ethical orientation. Xenophon is defending Socrates from the charge of impiety.
He supports this by saying that Socrates differed from the majority
of other philosophers in not studying the nature of everything and
showed up such people as fools. Did they come to the study of
nature thinking they had an adequate understanding of human
affairs, or did they think they were acting properly in neglecting
the human and studying the divine? Socrates found it amazing
that they did not find the indiscoverability of these things obvious,
and cited in support of this the failure of scientific pundits to
reach agreement with one another. Xenophon then develops Socrates' exploitation of discrepant opinions with a brief survey of
pre-Socratic theories and indicates his indictment of the useless-
ness of such inquiries. Finally, says Xenophon, Socrates himself
was constantly discussing human affairs, investigating the nature
of piety, justice and other ethical concepts: he regarded people
who knew them as noble and good, and thought that those who
did not would rightly be called slavish (*andrapodōdēs*).

If this passage strikes us as a travesty of the Platonic Socrates,
it possibly captures the Hellenistic Socrates more aptly than any
single text of Plato. In essence Xenophon is describing the Socrates
whom Antisthenes, Aristippus and Diogenes claimed to be following, and whom the Stoic Aristo would take as his model.[9] Probably
all of these, like Xenophon's Socrates, connected their interest in
ethics to the repudiation of any concern with physics. The sometimes hectoring tone of the passage – e.g., 'slavish' (*andrapodōdēs*) –
is redolent of Cynic moralising. Notice too the attribution to Socrates of 'disagreement' as an argumentative strategy for disposing
of the physicists' credentials; Socrates is already being represented
as a sceptic, so far as non-ethical knowledge is concerned. Ethical
expertise, however, is precisely his province. His general confession of ignorance is never mentioned by Xenophon. Nor does that
feature of Socrates seem to belong to the most basic Hellenistic
portrait. Like his dialectic, it is a characteristic to be mentioned or
omitted according to the kind of paradigm his inheritors want him
to instantiate.

Ancient writers were well aware of the fact that Socrates, as

---

[9] For Aristippus' repudiation of mathematics, dialectic and physics, cf. Giannantoni 1983–
85, vol. I, Aristippus IV A 170, 172. Antisthenes, at least as viewed by the Cynics, dis-
paraged the study of *grammata* (D.L. VI.103).

here portrayed in Xenophon, did not square well with the Socrates of Plato's later dialogues (according to modern chronology) or even with some of Xenophon's remarks elsewhere about his theological interests. By the end of the Hellenistic period it is a commonplace that Plato attributed to Socrates interests and theories which were entirely Plato's own (cf. Cicero, *Rep.* 1.15–16). The same is true implicitly as early as Aristotle. Only in late ‖ antiquity do we find Socrates credited with Platonist metaphysics (e.g., by ps.-Plutarch, *Plac.* 878b). The absence of an ancient Socratic problem on this issue will only occasion surprise or difficulty if Plato's dialogues are treated as the standard reference-point for Socrates' philosophy, taking priority over the writings of Xenophon, Antisthenes and others. In fact Plato, or what we call Plato's Socratic dialogues, appears to have been widely regarded as neither a more nor a less authentic witness to Socrates than Xenophon's writings.

The correctness of this last point, if it is correct, should not be interpreted as reducing the importance of Plato's Socrates in the eyes of pre-eminent philosophers such as Zeno, Chrysippus and Arcesilaus. In the later parts of this paper, I hope to show that it was Plato's Socrates, rather than any other, that stimulated serious philosophy, as we understand it today. But for the fourth century BC and for less demanding readers Xenophon had two advantages over Plato. First, it was easier to discover what the opinions of his Socrates were. Secondly, Xenophon's readers, in Antisthenes and Diogenes, had living embodiments of the self-mastery (*enkrateia*) which he so constantly emphasises as Socrates' dominant characteristic. No ancient writer, I think, ever regarded the *life* of Plato as emblematic of Socrates. It was not too difficult, on the other hand, to think of the Cynics as his genuine if one-sided imitators.[10]

Such a perception will have been encouraged by the activities of the Academy immediately after Plato's death and by the direction and style of Aristotle's philosophy. If Plato's later philosophy was readily seen as a considerable departure from that of Socrates, his immediate successors can hardly have struck their contemporaries as Socratic in any sense. Epictetus' Socrates, however Stoicised, is utterly recognisable as the man whose life and arguments and moral passion constituted an ethical revolution. Aristotle, by con-

---

[10] Cf. Grote 1885, vol. III, p. 505: 'Antisthenes and his disciple Diogenes were in many respects closer approximations to Socrates than Plato or any of the other Socratic companions.'

trast, is decidedly reticent on all of this. His interest in Plato of course ensures that 'our' Socrates is an important presence implicitly in the ethical treatises; and there is the well-known handful of passages which report and criticise Socrates by name. But Aristotle scarcely even hints at the moral significance of Socrates, as we moderns perceive it, or as it was perceived in the Hellenistic period. In a sense, we learn more about Socrates from this brief remark by Plutarch: 'Socrates was the first to show that life accommodates philosophy at every time and part and in all states and affairs without qualification.'[11]

Possibly Aristotle gave a more rounded account of Socrates in some of his exoteric writings.[12] Even so, the absence of anything comparable from his ethical treatises is remarkable. Did Aristotle himself help to set the tone for the hostile biographies of Socrates that Aristoxenus and other Peripatetics wrote, and that the Stoic Panaetius later contested? The question cannot be answered; but the fact that it can be posed at all is relevant to our inquiry. Socrates was not universally admired by Hellenistic philosophers. Before turning to his positive role in Stoicism and Academic Scepticism, something must be said about his detractors. ∥

CRITICISM OF SOCRATES IN HELLENISTIC PHILOSOPHY

We have no record, so far as I know, concerning any views of Theophrastus on Socrates. That silence may at least suggest substantial lack of interest.[13] Some of his fellow Peripatetics and successors were more outspoken. According to Porphyry, Aristoxenus' life of Socrates was more malevolent than the accusations of Meletus and Anytus (fr. 51 Wehrli). Most famously, it made out Socrates to be a bigamist, and also described him as the boyfriend of Archelaus. The charge of bigamy, repeated by other Peripatetics – Callisthenes, Demetrius of Phalerum and Satirus (Athenaeus XIII, 555d) – acquired sufficient currency to provoke the Stoic Panaetius into writing what Plutarch calls an adequate refuta-

---

[11] *Moral.* 796e: πρῶτος ἀποδείξας τὸν βίον ἅπαντι χρόνῳ καὶ μέρει καὶ πάθεσι καὶ πράγμασιν ἁπλῶς ἅπασι φιλοσοφίαν δεχόμενον.

[12] Cf. *On philosophy* fr. 1 Ross (Plutarch, *Moral.* 1118c), in which Aristotle reported the Delphic 'know yourself' as the starting-point of Socrates' philosophy.

[13] I have noticed only two inconsequential references to Socrates in the material collected by Fortenbaugh 1984: L 74 B, and L 106.

tion.[14] Such tittle-tattle, if it were confined to Aristoxenus, would merit no further comment. The fact that it became a common Peripatetic practice suggests a more studied attempt to undermine the ethical integrity of Socrates' life. We may probably conclude that a good many Peripatetics sought to combat the tendency of the other Socratic schools to set up Socrates as the paradigm of how a philosophical life should be lived. The more Socrates' exclusive concentration on ethics was stressed, the less at home he could be in the research environment of the Lyceum.

Socrates' repudiation of physics and theological speculation was one, but only one, of the many charges levelled against him by the Epicureans. Thanks to Knut Kleve, evidence of the range and intensity of this Epicurean criticism has now been thoroughly marshalled.[15] In the case of Epicurus himself it amounts to no more than an objection to Socratic irony.[16] Yet if Epicurus was fairly restrained in his remarks about Socrates, his immediate followers were not. From Metrodorus and Idomeneus, extending through Zeno of Sidon and Philodemus down to Diogenes of Oenoanda, a tradition of hostility to Socrates was established that is virulent even by the standards of ancient polemic. In their writings, Socrates was portrayed as the complete anti-Epicurean – a sophist, a rhetorician, a sceptic, and someone whose ethical inquiries turn human life into chaos.

Kleve (1983, pp. 249–50) explains this unmitigated hostility with the observation that Socrates and the Epicureans represent 'two different human types'. By this he seems to mean that their views of the world were diametrically opposed. However, this cannot be a sufficiently penetrating explanation. Both Socrates and Epicurus were in the business of curing people's souls. From Xenophon's Socrates especially, the Epicureans could have derived excellent support for much of their ethical practice – their concern with frugality, self-sufficiency, control of vain and unnecessary desires.[17] That they chose instead to attack aspects of Socrates' ethics, and

---

[14] Plutarch, *Aristides* 335c–d (= Panaetius fr. 132 van Straaten), which includes Hieronymus of Rhodes as another of the Peripatetic scandalmongers: πρὸς μὲν οὖν τούτους ἱκανῶς ὁ Παναίτιος ἐν τοῖς περὶ Σωκράτους ἀντείρηκεν.

[15] Cf. Kleve 1983.

[16] Cicero, *Brutus* 292 (Usener 231).

[17] Socrates' hardiness and self-control: Xen. *Mem.* 1.2.1, 1.2.14, 1.3.5, 1.5.4–6, 1.6.1–3; Socrates made those of his associates who had *ponēras epithumias* give them up: ibid. 1.2.64.

to treat him as a thoroughgoing sceptic, indicates a view of Socrates as transmitted by contemporary Stoics and Academics.

Early Epicureans wrote books against various Platonic dialogues
– *Euthyphro*, ‖ *Lysis, Euthydemus, Gorgias*.[18] The latter two, especially
the protreptic passage in the *Euthydemus*, were texts which the
Stoics seem to have particularly prized (see below). It is legitimate
to guess that much of the basis for Epicurean criticism of Socrates
should be sought in the central role he was now playing as a paradigm for their Stoic rivals. This suggestion, or rather the general
probability that Epicurean attacks on Socrates had a contemporary rather than a historical target, is confirmed by Colotes' criticism in his books against the *Lysis* and the *Euthydemus*. There he
maintained that Socrates ignored what is self-evident (*enarges*) and
suspended judgement (*epochōs prattein*).[19] Here Socrates, *au pied de la
lettre*, has been turned into a prototype of the Academic Arcesilaus. *epochē* at this date points specifically to the Academic sceptics;
and the Stoic Aristo commented on Arcesilaus' interest in arguments against *enargeia*.[20] Arcesilaus and the Cyrenaics (another Socratic school) were the two contemporary targets of Colotes' book,
Conformity to the doctrines of the other philosophers makes life impossible.[21]

The Stoics and the sceptical Academics were the Epicureans'
main professional rivals.[22] Both sets of opponents laid claim to being followers of Socrates. We have yet to see what they meant by
this claim, and how, being rivals themselves, they could appropriate a dogmatic Socrates in the one case and a sceptical Socrates
in the other. For the present it is sufficient to note their joint concern to establish their identity as Socratics. This justifies the suggestion that Epicurean criticism of Socrates be seen, at least in
part, as a means of undercutting the most obvious alternative

---

[18] For Colotes' books *Against Plato's Lysis* and *Against Plato's Euthydemus*, cf. Crönert 1906,
pp. 163–70. Colotes also wrote against the myth of Er in *Republic* x (cf. Plutarch, *Moral.*
xiv, B. Einarson and P. De Lacy (edd.), pp. 154–5). Metrodorus wrote *Against Plato's
Euthydemus* (Philodemus, *Piet.*, col. 77, 1ff.), and Zeno of Sidon, *Against Plato's Gorgias* (fr. 25,
Angeli-Colaizzo (*Cronache Ercolanesi.* 9, 1979, 80)). Nor was it just Plato's Socrates that
was attacked. In his *Peri oikonomias*, Philodemus objected point by point to the Socrates of
Xenophon's *Oeconomicus*. On all of this, cf. Kleve 1983.

[19] For the Greek text, cf. Mancini, 1976, pp. 61–6; and see also Plutarch, *Adv. Col.* 1118a.

[20] D.L. vii.162–3. Cf. my remarks in Long 1986b, p. 442.

[21] Cf. Plutarch, *Adv. Col.* 1120c.

[22] They fall outside the scope of Sedley's article (1976), which is largely concerned with the
attitude of Epicurus himself to earlier philosophers and to his elder contemporaries.

models of the philosophical life – Socrates as interpreted by Stoics and Academics.

SOCRATES IN THE ACADEMY OF POLEMO AND ARCESILAUS

Arcesilaus pinned his credentials as one who suspends judgement about everything, and his dialectical practice, on Socrates, and claimed that Plato's dialogues should be read in this light. Cicero, *De oratore* III.67, gives us this report:

> Arcesilaus, the pupil of Polemo, was the first to derive this principal point from various of Plato's books and from Socratic discourses – that there is nothing certain which the senses or the mind can grasp. He is said to have belittled every criterion of mind and sense, and begun the practice – though it was absolutely Socratic – not of indicating his own opinion, but of speaking against what anyone stated as his opinion.[23] ∥

Cicero emphasises Arcesilaus' originality in this reading of Plato and Socrates. He was probably right to do so. What, thanks to Gregory Vlastos, we are becoming accustomed to calling Socrates' 'disavowal of knowledge$_C$' – i.e., Socrates' disclaimer to possess *certainty* of any truth whatsoever – must have been chiefly associated, when it was noted at all, with the Platonic Socrates.[24] Xenophon's Socrates, like that of Aristippus and the Cynics, repudiates any interest in the inquiry into nature; and Arcesilaus will have appreciated the passage (mentioned above) from *Memorabilia* I.1.12–15 in which Socrates supports his indifference to physics by exploiting disagreement between natural philosophers. But I find little evidence that fourth-century interpreters of Socrates outside Plato, with some support from Aeschines Socraticus, attributed to him any scepticism about his capacity for knowledge in general, or that they took his ethical doctrines to involve seriously-held reservations about his certainty that they were true and demonstrable.[25]

---

[23] Arcesilas primum, qui Polemonem audierat, ex variis Platonis libris sermonibusque Socraticis hoc maxime arripuit, nihil esse certi quod aut sensibus aut animo percipi possit; quem ferunt ... aspernatum esse omne animi sensusque iudicium primumque instituisse – quamquam id fuit Socraticum maxime – non quid ipse sentiret ostendere, sed contra id quod quisque se sentire dixisset disputare. Cf. also *Fin.* II.2; V.10.

[24] Vlastos (1985) argues, with great force and originality, that Plato's Socrates disavows certain or infallible knowledge of anything (knowledge$_C$), but avows elenctic or fallible knowledge of propositions arrived at and tested by his elenctic method (knowledge$_E$).

[25] Two fragments of Aeschines Socraticus should be mentioned. In fr. 3 Krauss, Socrates says he would convict himself of considerable *mōria* if he attributed any help he had been

Antisthenes said that happiness needs nothing in addition to virtue except Socratic strength; virtue pertains to actions, and needs neither a quantity of arguments nor lessons.[26] That this strength included anything like Socrates' disavowal of certainty, as elucidated by Vlastos, is a refinement we may surely exclude.

Other pieces of evidence point in the same direction. Aristotle, once and very briefly, mentions Socrates' 'confession of ignorance', in explaining why he asked questions but did not answer them (*Soph. el.* 34 183b7–8). The complete absence of the same point from all the ethical contexts in which Aristotle discusses Socrates' theses on virtue and knowledge suggests that he did not regard the confession of ignorance as a constitutive feature of Socrates' philosophy, or as something which cast any doubt on the certainty Socrates attached to these doctrines.

Timon, as we saw, makes Socrates into a non-physicist, but he does not treat him as a proto-sceptic. His readiness to praise Xenophanes, Democritus and Protagoras for their sceptical leanings suggests that he would have enrolled Socrates too, if his self-confessed ignorance was already being treated as a fundamental characteristic.[27] In fact, outside the Academy the tradition of the ignorant Socrates never seems to have been taken very seriously. It is mentioned late, and inconsequentially, in Diogenes Laertius' life of Socrates (II.32), and forms no part of the pseudo-Galenic doxography (cited above). Writers from later antiquity, if they mention this feature at all, generally follow the lead of Antiochus, who had removed Socrates from Arcesilaus' list of sceptical predecessors by treating his confession of ignorance as ironical.[28] ‖

My final reason for making Arcesilaus the effective creator of the totally sceptical Socrates is a belief that this feature must post-

---

to Alcibiades to any *technē* rather than to 'divine dispensation'; and in fr. 4, he says he has no knowledge of any *mathēma* which he could teach a man and thereby help him. According to Demetrius, *De eloc.* 297, the properly Socratic method of instruction, convicting the interlocutor of ignorance, was especially imitated by Aeschines and Plato.

[26] Antisthenes ap. D.L. vi.11: αὐτάρκη δὲ τὴν ἀρετὴν πρὸς εὐδαιμονίαν, μηδενὸς προσδεομένην ὅτι μὴ Σωκρατικῆς ἰσχύος· τὴν τ' ἀρετὴν τῶν ἔργων εἶναι, μήτε λόγων πλείστων δεομένην μήτε μαθημάτων.

[27] See Lloyd-Jones/Parsons 1983 fr. 779 (Protagoras), fr. 820 (Democritus), and for Timon's praise of Xenophanes, Sextus Empiricus, *PH* 1.223.

[28] Cicero, *Acad.* ii.15 (cf. Quintilian ix.2.46, Dio Chrysost. xii.14, Themistius 21, 259b). In *Acad.* 1.16, however, Varro (speaking for Antiochus) reports Socrates' practice of 'saying that he knew nothing except that very thing', and says that he surpassed everyone else in thinking that he knew nothing – an opinion in which he consistently persisted. This

date the beginnings of Stoicism. It seems to me most unlikely that Zeno and Aristo would have modelled their philosophy so closely on Socrates if his confession of ignorance was already a dominant part of the standard characterisation. At the beginning of the Hellenistic period, what Socrates most prominently stood for, I think, was the thesis that virtue is knowledge and vice is ignorance. Or, as Diogenes Laertius' doxography states (II.31), drawing on Plato, *Euthydemus* 281e, 'he said that only one thing is good, knowledge, and only one thing is bad, ignorance'. The Socratic literature, taken as a whole, must have made it extraordinarily difficult to apply these propositions to a completely ignorant Socrates, who would thus by implication be vicious and in possession of all that is bad.[29]

In accounting for Arcesilaus' scepticism, we do best to take Cicero's report seriously. Read literally, it tells us that what drew Arcesilaus powerfully in this direction was in fact his own original interpretation of the Platonic Socrates – the Socrates who, even at the moment of concluding an ethical argument in the *Gorgias* 508e6–509a7, which he describes as 'clamped down and bound by arguments of iron and adamant', confesses that he does not speak as one who has knowledge.[30] Arcesilaus' scepticism, on this view, was actually the outcome of his reading of Plato's Socrates – a fundamentally new reading – and not something he foisted on Socrates and Plato because he was already a sceptic. This tallies with the well-known passage from Cicero's *Academica* I.44–5, where Cicero treats Arcesilaus' scepticism as a response to the obscurity of the things that led Socrates and earlier philosophers to a *confessio ignorationis*. In that context, Arcesilaus, according to Cicero, took Socrates to have had knowledge of just one

---

passage, unlike *Acad.* II.15, seems to reflect Antiochus' sympathy for Arcesilaus' interpretation of Socrates (*Acad.* 1.45); which, of course, he will have fully endorsed during his own sceptical phase; cf. the report of Socrates' total disapproval of an *ars quaedam philosophiae et rerum ordo et descriptio disciplinae* (ibid. 17), which is hard to reconcile with Antiochus' own mature conception of philosophy, or his bracketing of Plato and Socrates in *Acad.* II.15.

[29] Epictetus' Socrates *knows* various moral principles, yet 'never said that he knew or taught anything' (*Discourses* III.5.17; cf. III.23.22). Andrea Nightingale has suggested to me that this may be read as an alternative both to the sceptical Academics' Socrates and to the ironically ignorant Socrates of Antiochus. Epictetus interestingly differentiates Socrates from Diogenes and Zeno, viewing Socrates' special province as the elenchus, Diogenes' as reproof, and Zeno's that of instruction and doctrine (*Discourses* III.21.18–19).

[30] For the interpretation of Socrates' procedure here, cf. Vlastos 1985, pp. 20–2.

thing – his own ignorance. The nearest the Platonic Socrates comes to saying this is *Apology* 21b4–5: 'As for myself, *I am not aware* of being wise in anything, great or small.' The expression he uses, σύνοιδα ἐμαυτῷ, probably means only that Socrates does not think of himself as wise in anything (cf. *Ap.* 21d3–6). But Arcesilaus, we can suppose, interpreted Socrates as making the strong cognitive claim that he *knew* that he knew nothing (for this interpretation of Socrates, see also Antiochus, in n. 28 above), and then denied that he himself knew even this much.[31]

My suggestion about a genuine causal connexion between Arcesilaus' scepticism and his interpretation of Socrates seems to be novel in modern scholarship. But is it correct? I have given the external reasons for taking it to be so – the absence of any clear evidence of a rigorously sceptical Socrates prior to Arcesilaus. What makes me ‖ more confident of its correctness is the belief that virtually everything we know about Arcesilaus indicates his singleminded intent to model himself on the Platonic Socrates – his declining to write books, what Diogenes Laertius (IV.33) calls his 'excellence at stating propositions and deriving conclusions from them, his concern for linguistic precision in conversation, his hard-hitting rejoinders and frankness',[32] his playing the role of questioner rather than answerer, his elenctic practice, and, quite generally, a life devoted to discussion with anyone he thought it worth talking to. According to Epiphanius – not the most trustworthy witness – Arcesilaus said that 'truth is accessible only to god and not to man'.[33] Does this reflect a tradition that Arcesilaus said something analogous to Socrates' disparaging contrast in the *Apology* (23b) between the worthlessness of human wisdom and the wisdom of god?

Elsewhere I have argued that Arcesilaus' Socratic character was first formed by his encounters with his elder Platonists, Polemo, Crates and Crantor.[34] They presumably had not discovered the sceptical Socrates, but the little that we know about their philoso-

---

[31] *Acad.* 1.45: *itaque Arcesilas negabat esse quidquam quod sciri posset, ne illud quidem ipsum, quod Socrates sibi reliquisset.* For this thesis, Arcesilaus could cite the authority of Metrodorus of Chios, mentioned by Cicero at *Acad.* II.73.

[32] ἦν [Arcesilaus] δὲ καὶ ἀξιωματικώτατος καὶ συνηγμένος καὶ ἐν τῇ λαλιᾷ διαστατικὸς τῶν ὀνομάτων, ἐπικόπτης θ' ἱκανῶς καὶ παρρησιαστής.

[33] *Adv. Haeres.* III.29 (Diels 1879, p. 592.6): Ἀρκεσίλαος ἔφασκε τῷ θεῷ ἐφικτὸν εἶναι μόνῳ [Diels: μόνον codd.] τὸ ἀληθές, ἀνθρώπῳ δ' οὔ.

[34] In Long 1986b, pp. 440–1.

phy suggests (if I may quote myself) that they 'were already stressing the Socratic side of Plato in contrast with the systematic and theoretical tendencies of Speusippus and Xenocrates'. One of the few substantive reports about Polemo not only points in this direction, but is also remarkably similar to testimonies for Antisthenes and the Stoic Aristo: 'Polemo was in the habit of saying that people should be trained in practical matters and not in dialectical theorems, like someone who has absorbed some musical expertise and does not practise, and so being admired for their argumentative powers but inconsistent with themselves in their character.'[35]

I think the mature Arcesilaus would have endorsed these educational precepts. Two aphorisms attributed to him are warnings against dialectic and dialecticians.[36] If these refer, as they surely do, to the professional school of Dialecticians, no conflict arises with his own dialectical practice.[37] Like Socrates, he uses argument not for argument's sake, but to subject the opinions of his interlocutor to critical scrutiny.

Reflection along these lines suggests that we should start to think of Arcesilaus as a sceptical Socrates, where the proper name carries its full resonance – commitment to a life in which nothing can countervail the claims of intellectual integrity. In reporting Arcesilaus' scepticism in the *Academica*, Cicero on two occasions attaches the highest moral commendation to suspension of judgement. For Arcesilaus, he maintains, opining nothing was not simply the rational response to the impossibility of knowledge, but the only right and honourable response (*Acad.* II.77). And he insists on Arcesilaus' complete consistency in refraining from all assertion (*Acad.* I.45). He might just as well have said Arcesilaus' 'Socratic strength'.

There is, of course, a further tradition concerning Arcesilaus' emergent scepticism, ‖ which does not undermine anything I have been saying – his opposition to Zeno's epistemology. If Zeno, an older pupil of Polemo, was both representing himself as a Socratic,

---

[35] D.L. IV.18: ἔφασκε δὲ ὁ Πολέμων δεῖν ἐν τοῖς πράγμασι γυμνάζεσθαι καὶ μὴ ἐν τοῖς δια-λεκτικοῖς θεωρήμασι, καθάπερ ἁρμονικόν τι τέχνιον καταπιόντα καὶ μὴ μελετήσαντα, ὡς κατὰ μὲν τὴν ἐρώτησιν θαυμάζεσθαι, κατὰ δὲ τὴν διάθεσιν ἑαυτοῖς μάχεσθαι.

[36] Stobaeus II.22,9 Wachsmuth: Ἀρκεσίλαος ... ἔφη, τοὺς διαλεκτικοὺς ἐοικέναι τοῖς ψηφοπαίκταις, οἵτινες χαριέντως παραλογίζονται. II.23,13: διαλεκτικὴν φεῦγε· συγκυκᾷ τἄνω κάτω. I am grateful to David Blank for suggesting that the second passage may be a reminiscence of Plato, *Phd.* 101e: ἱκανοὶ γὰρ ὑπὸ σοφίας ὁμοῦ πάντα κυκῶντες.

[37] For the Dialectical School, cf. Sedley 1977.

and also advancing doctrines inconsistent, in Arcesilaus' opinion, with that posture, we obtain a further motive for his advertising Socrates' sceptical tendencies. At this point, then, we may leave Arcesilaus, the discoverer of the sceptical Socrates, and turn to Socrates in early Stoicism.

SOCRATES IN EARLY STOICISM

From Zeno to Epictetus, that is to say throughout the history of the Stoa, Socrates is the philosopher with whom the Stoics most closely aligned themselves. The importance of Socrates to the Stoics is regularly acknowledged, but it has never been studied in any detail.[38] One reason for this neglect, I suspect, is a prejudice concerning Plato. We tend to regard Socrates as Plato's special property, and find it difficult to accept the idea that the early Stoics, who are often hostile to Plato, could have reached independent interpretations of Socrates that deserve a serious place in the history of philosophy.

The Stoics' use of Socrates is too large a subject to be studied in all its aspects in a single article. What I will do here is, first, expand my introductory remarks on his unique importance to the Stoa; then, I will argue that divergent interpretations of Socratic ethics help to explain Aristo's disagreement with Zeno over the value of *ta adiaphora*.

Socrates' name crops up a good many times in the fragments of early and middle Stoicism. Passing for the moment over Zeno's biography, we find that his follower Sphaerus wrote a work in three books *On Lycurgus and Socrates* (*SVF* 1.620). The association of these two names must indicate an interest in Socrates' attitude to law and society.[39] Cleanthes, in Book II of his *On pleasure,* said that Socrates on every occasion taught that the same man is just and happy, and that he put a curse on the man who first distinguished justice from utility (*SVF* 1.558). Chrysippus commented on Socrates' devotion to dialectic in a list of philosophers which includes Plato, Aristotle and their successors down to Polemo and Strato (*SVF* II.126). Antipater, the fifth Head of the Stoa, reported one of Socrates' sayings (*SVF* III Antipater, 65), and in his work *On proph-*

---

[38] For such acknowledgements, cf. Dyroff 1897, p. 320; Maier 1913, p. 610.

[39] Note that Sphaerus, who spent time with the Spartan reformer Cleomenes, also wrote a book *On the Spartan constitution* (loc. cit.).

ecy included 'very many instances of amazing Socratic proph-
ecies' (Cicero, *De div.* 1.123; cf. 1.6). Panaetius defended Socrates
against Peripatetic detraction (see above), and also restricted the
'truthful' accounts of Socrates to the writings of Plato, Xenophon,
Antisthenes and Aeschines, raising doubts about those of Phaedo
and Eucleides, and condemning all the rest.[40] His effort to establish a canon of the reputable Socratica was combined, if Pohlenz
is right, with his responsibility for authorising the doxographical
tradition that Socrates, as the ‖ founder of ethics, was the ancestor
of all the post-Socratic schools.[41] Posidonius cited Socrates, Diogenes and Antisthenes as examples of moral progress (D.L. vii.91).

From Cicero we can infer that Stoic philosophers were in the
practice of attaching Socrates' name to some of their central ethical theses. For instance, they took from Socrates the view that 'all
who lack wisdom are insane' (*Tusc.* iii.10), or supposed that 'everything goes well for great men if the statements of our school and
the leader of philosophy Socrates are adequate concerning the
bounty and resources of virtue' (*ND* ii.167).

Material such as this indicates Socrates' authority within the
Stoic school, but it does not take us beyond surface impressions. In
order to approach the subject in a more penetrating way, we need
to reflect on the origins of Stoicism and the various lines its
founding fathers developed. According to the biographical tradition, Zeno's decision to devote himself to philosophy was generated by his reading about Socrates. In one version of the story,
his merchant father brought the young Zeno books about Socrates
from Athens (D.L. vii.31). In another, he started to read Xenophon's *Memorabilia*, Book ii, in an Athenian bookshop, and began
to associate with the Cynic Crates because the shopkeeper told
him that Crates was a man like Socrates (D.L. vii.2–3). In a third
version, what brought Zeno to Athens from Citium was his read-

---

[40] D.L. ii.64: πάντων μέντοι τῶν Σωκρατικῶν διαλόγων Παναίτιος ἀληθεῖς εἶναι δοκεῖ
τοὺς Πλάτωνος, Ξενοφῶντος, Ἀντισθένους, Αἰσχίνου· διστάζει δὲ περὶ τῶν Φαίδωνος
καὶ Εὐκλείδου, τοὺς δὲ ἄλλους ἀναιρεῖ πάντας. Does ἀληθεῖς mean 'authentic', in the
sense that Panaetius accepted Plato, Xenophon, Antisthenes and Aeschines as the authors of the Socratic works ascribed to them? Or does it mean that he regarded their
works as genuine or truthful accounts of Socrates? The latter is more likely. ἀληθής does
not appear to be Diogenes' normal word for describing a work's authenticity, for which
he uses μόνος with the genitive, e.g. Σωτίων ... ταῦτα μόνα φησὶ Διογένους εἶναι, vi.80
(cf. vii.163), or γνήσιος as distinct from νοθεύονται (iii.57, iii.62). At ii.105 he contrasts
γνησίους with διστάζόμενον.

[41] Pohlenz 1959, vol. i, pp. 194–5; vol. ii, pp. 10, 98.

ing of Socrates' *Apology* (*SVF* 1.9); whether Plato's or Xenophon's, we are not told.

The literal truth of these stories is unimportant. What they attest to is a tradition, which Zeno's followers must have encouraged, that Socrates was the primary inspiration of his philosophy. The next step is to consider this tradition in relation to Zeno's studies with the Cynic Crates and the Academic Polemo.[42] If I was right in my earlier remarks about Polemo, his view of Socrates, though strongly tinged by Plato, may not have differed in many essential points from what was being propagated by the Cynics. In any case, it may be misleading to think of Zeno's philosophical formation as a Cynic phase, followed by an Academic orientation, leading finally to his own independent position. We should perhaps view him as a Socratic throughout, who looked to the Cynics and the Academy for interpretations of Socrates' philosophy which he could develop or reject according to his own independent reflections. So I proceed to test this hypothesis.

From the Cynics Zeno is likely to have acquired an account of Socrates' philosophy that did not differ essentially from ethical doctrines attributed to Antisthenes (D.L. vi.10–13). In advancing such propositions as the following – 'the same men are noble and virtuous', 'virtue is sufficient for happiness', 'the wise man is self-sufficient', 'virtuous men are friends', 'prudence (*phronēsis*) is the most secure fortification', 'what is good is honourable (*kala*) and what is bad is disgraceful (*aischra*)' – Antisthenes, we can assume, took himself to be representing Socrates' philosophy. Zeno's agreement to all these propositions, which he could, of course, check against Xenophon, Plato etc., shows the extent to which he appropriated the Cynic Socrates.

Beginning with Antisthenes, a Cynic tradition of hostility to Plato developed. It must in large part have been motivated by a wish to detach Socrates from Plato, and, so far as the early Stoics are concerned, the Cynics were successful. Zeno's *Republic* seems to have been overtly anti-Platonic. In his physics he sided with the materialist Giants of Plato's *Sophist* (246a); he reduced Platonic Forms to mere conceptions; he ‖ denied the immortality of the soul; and he denied any value to pleasure. I am not maintaining

---

[42] For Zeno's studies with Polemo and Crates, cf. D.L. vii.2, Suda s.v. Ζήνων, Numenius, fr. 25 des Places; and with Polemo in particular, Cicero, *Acad.* 1.35, *Fin.* iv.3.

that Zeno owed nothing to Plato as distinct from Plato's Socrates. But in general the early Stoics' acknowledged relationship to Plato's own philosophy, as distinct from Plato's Socrates, was critical and often hostile.[43]

Such Stoic divergences from Plato as I have mentioned were no barrier to the Stoics' presenting themselves as Socratics. Antisthenes' anti-Platonic claim that he could see a horse but not 'horseness' could be interpreted as an anticipation of Zeno's reduction of universals to mere thoughts.[44] It is reasonable to suppose that Antisthenes took himself to have Socratic support for rejecting Plato's independently existing 'Forms'. As for ethics, the Socrates of Cicero, *De finibus* II.90, rules pleasure completely out of account. This is in line with Antisthenes and Stoicism, and against Plato.[45]

But Zeno made physics and theology indispensable to ethics, and an entirely Cynic Socrates should abjure the study of nature. Or, to put the point more strongly, was Zeno in a position to represent himself as a Socratic when the doxographical tradition, drawing on Xenophon and Plato, insisted that Socrates was purely a moral philosopher? At this point we should return briefly to the Academic Polemo. In discussing Arcesilaus, I suggested that his Socratic leanings may have been stimulated by the work of his Academic seniors, especially Polemo. From Polemo, according to Cicero (*Fin.* IV.45; cf. IV.14ff.), Zeno acquired the concept of 'primary natural things' – objects to which we are inclined by our nature – which he, following Polemo's lead, incorporated in his doctrine that the ethical end is a life in agreement with nature. There are problems, to be sure, about accepting Cicero's report at face value since it depends upon Antiochus' distorted account of the continuity between the philosophies of Plato, Aristotle and Zeno. Still, I side with the majority of scholars in finding it im-

---

[43] For evidence and discussion of these anti-Platonic points, cf. Long/Sedley 1987, vol. 1, p. 435 (Zeno's *Republic*), 181–2, 274 (metaphysics and physics), 272, 318 (soul's corporeality and destructibility), 421 (pleasure). A more positive attitude towards Plato himself seems to begin with Chrysippus, who drew heavily on the *Timaeus*; cf. Long/Sedley 1987, vol. 1, p. 278.

[44] Cf. the anachronistic introduction to this account of Antisthenes' point, fr. 50c Caizzi: ὁ τοίνυν Ἀντισθένης ἔλεγε τὰ γένη καὶ τὰ εἴδη ἐν ψιλαῖς ἐπινοίαις εἶναι λέγων ὅτι ἵππον μὲν ὁρῶ, ἱππότητα δὲ οὐχ ὁρῶ, and compare it with *SVF* 1.65. For the Stoic view of universals, cf. Long/Sedley 1987, vol. 1, pp. 179–82.

[45] For the various versions of Antisthenes' dictum, 'madness is preferable to pleasure', cf. fr. 108 Caizzi.

probable that Antiochus completely fabricated the influence of Polemo on Zeno's ethics.[46] If this has some historical foundation, it allows us to think that Polemo encouraged Zeno to interpret Socrates' philosophy less restrictively than was the Cynic practice.

However, the Polemo connexion is highly speculative, and Polemo was a Platonist. Did Zeno also have access to an account of Socrates' philosophy, independent of Plato, which made ethics depend upon certain truths about nature?

The answer, if we attend to two passages of Xenophon's *Memorabilia*, is so strongly positive that one scholar has argued that these passages are interpolations based on the *Timaeus* and even on Stoicism itself![47] In I.4.5–18 Socrates demonstrates god's benevolence to human beings, by detailing their special advantages over the other animals in sensory equipment, hands, intelligence, and sociability. He concludes with the ‖ observation that the divine is all-seeing, all-hearing, omnipresent and universally providential. In IV.3.2–18 the theme is the same, only this time some attention is given to cosmology and to technology through human ability at manipulating fire. Socrates here maintains that the other living creatures were created for mankind's sake. At section 11, he says:

Since there is abundance of fine and beneficial things, but they differ from one another, the gods provided human beings with senses suitable to each type of thing, through which we enjoy all goods. Further, they have engendered intelligence in us, by means of which, calculating and recalling what we perceive, we learn the mode of each thing's utility, and make many contrivances through which we enjoy good things and ward off bad ones. They have also given us language, through which we give one another a share of goods, by instruction and association, and establish laws and social life.[48]

This is certainly high-flying stuff for Xenophon. Yet it contains nothing that an early fourth-century writer could not have written

---

[46] On the positive side, see especially von Fritz 1952, pp. 2524–9, and Brink 1956, pp. 123–45; and on the negative, Pohlenz 1959, vol. I, pp. 249–51.

[47] Cf. Lincke 1906, pp. 673–91. Among the many things which vitiate his argument is a chronology of Zeno which places his birth, and the origin of the Stoa, far too early.

[48] τὸ δ', ἐπειδὴ πολλὰ μὲν καλὰ καὶ ὠφέλιμα, διαφέροντα ἀλλήλων ἐστί, προσθεῖναι [sc. τοὺς θεοὺς] τοῖς ἀνθρώποις αἰσθήσεις ἁρμοττούσας πρὸς ἕκαστα, δι' ὧν ἀπολαύομεν πάντων τῶν ἀγαθῶν· τὸ δὲ καὶ λογισμὸν ἡμῖν ἐμφῦσαι, ᾧ περὶ ὧν αἰσθανόμεθα λογιζόμενοί τε καὶ μνημονεύοντες καταμανθάνομεν ὅπη ἕκαστα συμφέρει, καὶ πολλὰ μηχανώμεθα, δι' ὧν τῶν τε ἀγαθῶν ἀπολαύομεν καὶ τὰ κακὰ ἀλεξόμεθα· τὸ δὲ καὶ ἑρμηνείαν δοῦναι, δι' ἧς πάντων τῶν ἀγαθῶν μεταδίδομέν τε ἀλλήλοις διδάσκοντες καὶ κοινωνοῦμεν καὶ νόμους τιθέμεθα καὶ πολιτευόμεθα.

and believed to be Socratic. For my own part, I believe it was part of Xenophon's text by the time of Zeno and Polemo.[49] If so, its implications for the Stoic Socrates are considerable. We now have a source, independent of Plato, which credits Socrates with doctrines fundamental to Stoicism – thoroughgoing teleology, divine providence, the gods' special concern for man, and cosmic underpinning for law and society. But we have still more. Reflection on Socrates' remarks here about the structure of the senses, and their capacity, in concert with reason, to enable human life to proceed according to a divinely ordered plan, could have served Zeno well. Not only could it have helped to shape his conception of a life in agreement with nature; it could also have stimulated his efforts to find an account of sense-perception and knowledge which might be given Socratic endorsement.

The Epicureans were not slow to point out that Xenophon was inconsistent in his remarks about Socrates' interest or lack of interest in theological speculation (Cicero, *ND* 1.31). By appeal to such passages as the two I have just discussed, Zeno, if I am right, thought he could combine a Socratic identity with the development of other aspects of his philosophy. I am not suggesting, by way of a rather mindless source criticism, that these two passages from Xenophon were sufficient to shape the impulse of his overall philosophy. Their coherence with Stoicism, however, is sufficiently suggestive to provide further support for my hypothesis concerning the importance to Zeno of finding Socratic support for his doctrines.

Next, dialectic. If Socrates was to be securely distanced from sophists and eristics, his interest in adversary argument had to be carefully interpreted. Plato's *Euthydemus* is the classic text. As dialectic began to take on a life of its own during the early Hellenistic period, with logical paradoxes being eagerly debated, it became the more urgent for philosophers who claimed allegiance to Socrates to insist that he was no supporter of skilful disputation for its own sake. (Recall my earlier remarks about Polemo and Arcesilaus.) As the Cynics seem to have interpreted it, the purpose of ‖ Socrates' verbal virtuosity was not argument in any formal sense but purely moral exhortation and instruction.

---

[49] Antisthenes has often been suggested as Xenophon's source, but on the flimsiest of grounds; cf. Caizzi 1964, pp. 65–9.

Zeno, we can see, thought otherwise. If he did little to anticipate Chrysippus' great contribution to logic, he undoubtedly
regarded the subject as an integral part of philosophy. He wrote
two books of *Elenchoi* (D.L. vii.4), and his follower Sphaerus was
famous for his 'definitions' (*SVF* 1.628). To Epictetus, at any rate,
both these interests were explicitly Socratic (see p. 2 above). I
cannot cite any text which proves that Zeno invoked Socrates in
support of his logic, but there is negative evidence to point that
way – his disagreements with his follower Aristo.

Bearing in mind what I have been saying about the dominant
image of the Hellenistic Socrates, consider the following testimonies concerning Aristo.

First, he confined the scope of philosophy to ethics, urging that
physics is beyond human powers, and that dialectic is irrelevant
since it does not contribute to the correct regulation of life (*SVF*
1.352). In a text of Eusebius (*SVF* 1.353) which mentions Socrates'
repudiation of physics, Aristippus and Aristo are referred to as
later philosophers who went the same way.

Second, Aristo is reported to have denied that god's form can
be known. One of the sources of his thesis – Minucius Felix
(*Octavius* 19.13) – appends it to his previous observation that
'Xenophon's Socrates denies the visibility of god's form and
therefore says it should not be investigated.'[50]

Third, Aristo accounted for the unity of the virtues in a manner
which many scholars take to be the correct interpretation of Socrates' thesis in the *Protagoras*. He regarded the several virtues as
alternative characterisations of a single state of mind, knowledge
of good and bad, holding that their differences are only accidental
differentiations of this state, relative to circumstances. Malcolm
Schofield has argued persuasively that Aristo's doctrine should be
regarded as a criticism of Zeno: the master, Aristo held, was committed to the Socratic unity of the virtues, and yet misleadingly
also spoke as if he believed in a plurality of distinct virtues.[51]

These three points are sufficient to establish Aristo's strong Socratic leanings. But they offer us a further and more exciting suggestion. Aristo, having totally embraced the Socratic identity of
the school, as directed by Zeno, becomes disquieted. He sees Zeno,

[50] A somewhat garbled conflation of *Memorabilia* iv.3.14–15 and i.1.13–15.
[51] Cf. Schofield 1984.

in his support for physics and logic, backtracking on his true Socratic inheritance, and also misrepresenting Socrates on a crucial ethical doctrine. It has been customary to treat Aristo as a Stoic whose deviance is constituted by his Cynic proclivity, and undoubtedly his Socrates is closer than Zeno's to the hero of Antisthenes and Diogenes. But rather than calling Aristo a Cynicising Stoic, it would be better, I propose, to regard him as a Stoic who thought that the Cynic tradition of Socrates was truer to the spirit of the philosopher than tendencies which Zeno was initiating.[52]

ZENO, ARISTO AND SOCRATES IN PLATO, *EUTHYD.* 278e3–281e5

I have omitted what is undoubtedly Aristo's most famous heresy – his insistence that unqualified indifference extends to everything except virtue and vice.[53] Zeno held the ‖ following propositions to be true. First, that nothing is good except virtue and what participates in virtue. Second, that nothing is bad except vice and what participates in vice. Third, that of everything else, which is indifferent, some indifferent things have negative or positive value, while others are absolutely indifferent. Fourth, that the value or disvalue of indifferent things is constituted by their accordance or lack of accordance with nature. Fifth, that those which have positive value give us good reason to prefer them whenever we are faced with choosing between them and their opposites; our happiness and virtue require us to make good use of these materials. Aristo accepted the first two of these propositions, rejected the third and fourth, and thereby eliminated the need for the fifth. In his doctrine, there is no reason in the nature of, say, health or sickness, why one of these should be preferred to the other. Considerations of the relative worth of such things play no part in a virtuous agent's decisions about what he should do. He does just whatever it occurs to him to do, on the basis of his ethical knowledge (*introduxit, quibus commotus sapiens appeteret aliquid, quodcumque in mentem incideret et quodcumque tamquam occurreret,* Cicero, *Fin.* IV.43).

---

[52] Anna Maria Ioppolo, in her fine book (Ioppolo 1980), though well aware of Socrates' importance to Aristo, does not, I think, suggest this point anywhere. For passages in her book which discuss Aristo's relation to Socrates, see pp. 70, 76, 79, 86–9, 104, 136, 196, 208.

[53] *SVF* 1.351, 361–9. For the Stoic doctrine of value, and the heresies of Aristo and Herillus, cf. Long/Sedley 1987, vol. I, pp. 354–9.

Could both Zeno and Aristo invoke Socratic support for their divergent doctrines of value? Diogenes Laertius II.31, a passage I have mentioned before (above p. 13), attributes to Socrates the statement that one thing alone is good, knowledge, and one thing alone is bad, ignorance. In the next sentence Socrates is alleged to have also said that wealth and noble birth have no high standing (οὐδὲν σεμνὸν ἔχειν), but, quite the reverse, are bad.[54] Substitute 'utterly indifferent' for the doxographer's absurd 'bad', and we have in effect Aristo's doctrine. Substitute 'second-rank value' for 'bad', and we get Zeno's position.

The basis for the doxographer's garbled account is the conclusion of Socrates' argument with Cleinias in the protreptic passage of Plato's *Euthydemus* (278e–281e5). The first part of the argument may be summarised as follows:

A   Everyone wishes to fare well.
B   Faring well requires the possession of many goods.
C   These goods include (1) wealth, health, beauty, other bodily advantages, noble birth, power, honour; (2) temperance, justice and courage; (3) wisdom; (4) good fortune.
D   But wisdom *is* good fortune, since it never fails to make men act and acquire correctly.
E   The goods enumerated in C cause us to fare well because they benefit us.
F   They benefit us not by being possessed but by being used.
G   The correct use of C(1) goods is knowledge, which guides action and makes it correct.
H   Therefore knowledge not only provides men with good fortune in every action and acquisition but also with faring well.
I   Without prudence and wisdom C(1) goods harm rather than benefit men.[55]

The last part of the argument needs to be presented in full:[56] ‖

J   'In sum', I said, 'it would appear, Cleinias, that in the case of all those things which we first said were good, our account is

---

[54] ἔλεγε [Σωκρ.] δὲ καὶ ἓν μόνον ἀγαθὸν εἶναι, τὴν ἐπιστήμην, καὶ ἓν μόνον κακόν, τὴν ἀμαθίαν· πλοῦτον δὲ καὶ εὐγένειαν οὐδὲν σεμνὸν ἔχειν, πᾶν δὲ τοὐναντίον κακόν.

[55] The inclusion of courage and temperance as examples within this section of the argument, 281b4–c9, should not be taken to imply that they, as distinct from C(1) goods, could ever be detached from wisdom; cf. Vlastos 1984, p. 210 n. 84. It is a pleasure to acknowledge my indebtedness to this outstanding article.

[56] Translation (modified) of Vlastos 1984, p. 199.

that (i), it is not their nature to be good just by themselves, but the position, it seems, is as follows: (ii) if ignorance controls them, they are greater bads than their opposites to the extent of their greater power to serve their bad leader; while if they are controlled by prudence and wisdom they are greater goods, though in neither case do they have any value just by themselves.' 'Evidently, as it seems', he said, 'it is just as you say'. 'What, then, follows from what has been said? Is it anything but this: that of the other things, none is either good or bad, but of these two things, one – wisdom – is good, and the other – ignorance – is bad?' He agreed.[57]

Diogenes' garbled doxography is an indication of the importance of this passage for those who wanted a clear and authoritative statement on Socrates' ethics. Consider it now in relation to Zeno and Aristo. (The assumption that they knew the text intimately will, I hope, be fully justified by my following remarks.) They both accepted its conclusion: 'Of the other things, none is either good or bad, but of these two things, one – wisdom – is good, and the other – ignorance – is bad'.[58] Socrates arrived at this conclusion by arguing (J(i)), that health, wealth etc. are not of a nature to be good just by themselves (αὐτὰ καθ' αὐτά); and (J(ii)), that such so-called 'goods' are actually greater bads than their opposites in cases where both of them are controlled by ignorance, and greater goods in cases where both of them are controlled by wisdom, but in neither case do they have any value just by themselves.[59]

---

[57] *Euthyd.* 281d2–e5; Ἐν κεφαλαίῳ δ', ἔφην, ὦ Κλεινία, κινδυνεύει σύμπαντα ἃ τὸ πρῶτον ἔφαμεν ἀγαθὰ εἶναι, οὐ περὶ τούτου ὁ λόγος αὐτοῖς εἶναι, ὅπως αὐτά γε καθ' αὐτὰ πέφυκεν ἀγαθά, ἀλλ' ὡς ἔοικεν ὧδ' ἔχει· ἐὰν μὲν αὐτῶν ἡγῆται ἀμαθία, μείζω κακὰ εἶναι τῶν ἐναντίων, ὅσῳ δυνατώτερα ὑπηρετεῖν τῷ ἡγουμένῳ κακῷ ὄντι, ἐὰν δὲ φρόνησίς τε καὶ σοφία, μείζω ἀγαθά, αὐτὰ δὲ καθ' αὐτὰ οὐδέτερα αὐτῶν οὐδενὸς ἄξια εἶναι. – Φαίνεται, ἔφη, ὡς ἔοικεν, οὕτως, ὡς σὺ λέγεις. – Τί οὖν ἡμῖν συμβαίνει ἐκ τῶν εἰρημένων; ἄλλο τι ἢ τῶν μὲν ἄλλων οὐδὲν ὂν οὔτε ἀγαθὸν οὔτε κακόν, τούτοιν δὲ δυοῖν ὄντοιν ἡ μὲν σοφία ἀγαθόν, ἡ δὲ ἀμαθία κακόν; – Ὡμολόγει. Cf. *Meno* 87e–89a for a strikingly similar argument.

[58] Cf. 292b, where Socrates reminds Cleinias of their agreement that only ἐπιστήμη τις is good.

[59] I take it that τῶν ἐναντίων in 281d6 must mean 'the opposites of health etc. when these opposites are controlled by ignorance', and μείζω ἀγαθά, 281d8, 'greater goods than the opposites of health etc. when these opposites are controlled by wisdom'. This is what the argument requires, and it receives support from 281b6–8: 'Would a man be benefited who had acquired much and does much without intelligence, or rather one who had [acquired and does few things] with intelligence?' The upshot of what immediately

Before discussing the two Stoics' interpretation of these premises, a word must be said about Socrates' conclusion. Gregory
Vlastos argued that it is misleadingly formulated.[60] It should be
read, he proposes, not as an unequivocal assertion to the effect
that nothing at all is good except wisdom, and nothing at all is
bad except ignorance, but rather as follows: 'None of those other
things is either good or bad [just by itself], while wisdom alone is
good [just by itself] and ignorance alone is bad [just by itself].'
The '[just by itself]' interpolations are necessary, he argues, in
order to make the conclusion square with Socrates' views about
non-moral goods elsewhere in Plato; they are also necessary on the
logical ground that the conclusion stated at 281e2–5 only makes
sense if it is treated as a deduction from what is explicit at 281d4–
9: 'no non-moral good is good *just by itself*, and no non-moral evil
is bad *just by itself*'.[61] ‖

Putting aside for the moment the matter of consistency with
Socrates' views elsewhere, I tend to think that the suggested inter-
polation is a weakening, and not a logical improvement, of the
argument.[62] To be sure, Socrates has allowed a so-called 'good'
of the C(1) type, such as health, in conjunction with wisdom to be
a greater good than sickness in conjunction with wisdom. But he
combines this thought with the proposition that such a so-called

---

follows this question is that opportunities for doing wrong and thereby faring badly are
diminished the less the wrongdoer has or does. Sickness provides less of an opportunity
for doing wrong or for doing right than health.

[60] Vlastos 1984, pp. 199–201.

[61] Vlastos (1984) writes (n. 90, p. 211): 'From "x is F only in conjunction with W" it would
be crazy to infer "x is not F". The sober inference from that premise would be "x is not
F in disjunction from W", i.e., "x is not F just by itself".' For my response to this, see
main text below and n. 62.

[62] Vlastos 1984, p. 200, argues that this is how Socrates' conclusion must be read, in order
that (*a*), 'none of those other things is either good or bad', should be entailed by the
previous claim that no non-moral good is good 'just by itself'; and (*b*), consistency be
secured with the trichotomy of *Gorgias* 467e1–468b4, in which health is classified as a
'good'. With regard to (*b*), see main text below and n. 70. (*a*), on Vlastos' reading, turns
out to be not a significant inference, but a repetition of what it is said to follow from. In
281d3–5, Socrates has already asserted that 'the things we first said were good are not
good just by themselves'. If this is all that he is asserting in the first part of his conclusion, 'none of these other things is either good or bad', his ostensible conclusion is reduced to a summary, which contributes nothing new. I find it more plausible to suppose
that Socrates takes the non-goodness / total valuelessness of health, wealth etc., just by
themselves, together with the claim that what confers value on them (if anything does) is
wisdom alone, to sanction the conclusion that wisdom, strictly speaking, is the only good.
I.e. wisdom alone is good, because all other so-called 'goods' like health, in cases where
they can be truly called good, owe all their goodness to wisdom.

'good' in conjunction with ignorance is a greater bad than sickness so conjoined. What, then, is his view about the goodness of health where health is treated universally or without any indication from the context of how it is being used? If health, considered simply as health, is not good by its nature, and health can under one condition be better than sickness and under another condition be worse than sickness, it seems that health in general is no more good than it is bad. Goodness is not a property that can pertain to health, in virtue of anything that health is. Health can be better than sickness, but its superiority in such cases is entirely to be chalked up to the credit of wisdom.

If this is the point for which Plato's Socrates is arguing here, I think it would be misleadingly redundant to include the words 'just by itself' in his conclusion (last lines of J above). What he takes himself to have established is that so-called 'goods' such as health, and so-called 'bads' such as sickness, strictly speaking are neither good nor bad. Strictly speaking, goodness pertains solely to wisdom and badness to ignorance.

The Stoics welcomed this conclusion. In addition, the reasoning by which it was deduced seems to have decisively influenced their doctrine of the 'indifference' of such things as health and sickness. Thus, at Diogenes Laertius VII.103 the non-goodness of wealth and health is inferred from the propositions (1) that they no more benefit than they harm, and (2) that they can be used well and badly. On this point, there was no disagreement between Zeno and Aristo. Returning now to the section of the *Euthydemus* immediately preceding the conclusion, I want to ask how they responded to J(i), so-called 'goods' such as health are not of a nature to be good just by themselves; and J(ii), such things when controlled by wisdom are greater goods than their opposites, though in neither case do they have any value just by themselves.

I suggest that Aristo fully accepted J(i), and interpreted J(ii) simply as the justification for Socrates' conclusion concerning the sole goodness of wisdom. I.e., he did not take Socrates to be attributing even conditional value to such things as health. It was Zeno's doctrine, on the other hand, that health is naturally preferable to sickness, and that it does possess value (*axia*) 'just by itself'.[63] He

---

[63] I am assuming that Stobaeus, II.82,20–83,4 represents a position Zeno pioneered: health is *kath' hauto lēpton*. This is in line with Stobaeus II.84,18–85,11, where the *proēgmena* (Zeno's original term) are likened to courtiers whose rank is second to that of the King.

could agree to ‖ J(i), the non-goodness of health just by itself, but not to the second part of J(ii), its lack of all value 'just by itself'. How did Zeno react to J(ii) taken as a whole? Socrates maintains that health is better than sickness if and only if it is used wisely. Zeno would say that health has value (*axia*), however it is used, but is never something good. In his ethics, 'value' is the genus of which 'good' (*agathon*) and 'preferred' (*proēgmenon*) are two distinct species. Does this mean that Zeno has to reject the first part of J(ii), in which Socrates makes the greater *goodness* or *badness* of the so-called 'goods' over their opposites depend upon wisdom or ignorance respectively?

It would certainly be un-Stoic to maintain that someone who uses health wisely will be happier than someone who uses sickness wisely. If that is Socrates' point here, Zeno was bound to disagree. Quite probably, as Vlastos has argued, it was Socrates' point. Yet, given the final clause of J(ii), the conclusion of the whole argument, and basic Stoic doctrines, we can see why Zeno may have been less troubled by the comparatives *meizō agatha* and *meizō kaka* than he ought to have been.

According to Diogenes Laertius' summary of Stoic ethics (VII.104), the indifference of such things as health and wealth consists in the fact that they do not contribute to happiness or unhappiness; for one can be happy even without them. He then adds the following qualification: 'the kind of use made of them is constitutive of happiness or unhappiness' (τῆς ποιᾶς αὐτῶν χρήσεως εὐδαιμονικῆς οὔσης ἢ κακοδαιμονικῆς).

For a gloss on this passage, we may go to Seneca, *Ep.* 92.11–13. He is clarifying the relationship between the thesis that virtue is the only good and the value of such things as health. His imaginary interlocutor asks: 'If good health, rest and freedom from pain are not going to thwart virtue, will you not pursue them?' Seneca answers:

Of course I will. Not because they are good, but because they are in accordance with nature, and because they will be taken on the basis of my good judgement. What then will be good in them? Just this – being well selected. For when I put on the right sort of clothes, or walk as I should, neither the dining nor the walking nor the clothes are good, but the intention I display in them by preserving a measure, in each thing, which conforms with reason ... So it is not elegant clothes which are a *bonum per se*, but the selection of elegant clothes, since the good is not in the thing but in the quality of the selection.[64]

Socrates, in his summation of the argument from the *Euthydemus*, stated that only wisdom's control confers any degree of goodness or positive value on such things as health. The orthodox Stoics, following Zeno's lead, maintained that the wise use or wise selection of health etc. is good *per se*. They agreed with Socrates that the mere possession of health is not something good. Is there, then, any disagreement between them on the relation between goodness, wise use and health? Socrates is committed to the proposition *p*: 'Health is good – a constituent of happiness – if and only if it is wisely used'. Zeno endorses proposition *q*: 'The wise use of health is a *per se* good – a constituent of happiness.'

I think Zeno thought there was no material difference between these propositions. He took Socrates' denial of any intrinsic goodness to health etc., together with Socrates' conclusion, 'wisdom is the only good', to confirm his own view that health as such could never merit the predicate 'good'. Hence he interpreted Socrates' implicit claim that wisely used health is good as a judgement not about health as such but about its wise use. Socrates, however, just before his conclusion, had indicated his assent to the following proposition: 'health etc., wisely used, is a greater good than sickness, ‖ wisely used'. Hence, Zeno reasoned, Socrates was misleading in denying any intrinsic value to health and such like things (αὐτὰ δὲ καθ' αὑτὰ οὐδέτερα αὐτῶν οὐδενὸς ἄξια εἶναι, *Euthyd.* 281d8). Only a value properly predicable of health as such could account for Socrates' immediately preceding judgement that the wise use of something like health is a *greater* good than the wise use of its opposite. Treat health as such as naturally 'preferable' to or more 'valuable' than sickness, but not as 'better' or 'more constitutive of happiness', and Socrates' confusing remarks could be satisfactorily interpreted. In Zeno's view, the person who uses health wisely does have more of what is valuable than the wise user of sickness. Thus the Stoic doctrine of 'preferred indifferents' would allow Socrates to keep his stated conclusion that wisdom is

---

[64] Translation by Long/Sedley 1987, text 64J. The notion of 'good selection' reflects formulations of the ethical end by Diogenes of Babylon and Antipater (see our commentary *ad loc.* and Long 1967). But there is no reason to think that these depart in substance from the spirit of Zeno's philosophy.

the only good, while also making sense of his claim that the wise user of health has more of what is good (Stoically reinterpreted as 'valuable') than does his sick counterpart.

More could be said about this argument from the *Euthydemus*. In particular, a reader who thinks my interpretation of it assimilates Socrates too closely to Stoicism will find a powerful ally in Vlastos.[65] What I hope to have shown is an ambiguity in its closing lines which helped to feed the disagreement between Zeno and Aristo, while enabling each of them to think he was being faithful to Socrates' basic ethical doctrine. For Zeno, Socrates could be pressed into support for his own view that, while only virtue and what participates in virtue is good, there is a real difference of value between health and its opposite, attention to which is essential to any moral agent. Aristo, on the other hand, could urge against Zeno Socrates' statement that, just by themselves, health and such like things have no value whatsoever.

At *Crito* 48b8–9, Socrates secures Crito's agreement to the proposition that living well is the same as living virtuously.[66] Vlastos has argued that 'is the same as' should not be interpreted as positing identity between virtue and happiness.[67] Rather, we should take it to signify that 'virtue and happiness are necessarily interentailing'. So interpreted, the proposition allows Socrates to acknowledge the existence of non-moral goods, such as health, which, if virtuously used, make a tiny increment to happiness that it lacks without them. Vlastos has two principal reasons for crediting Socrates with the thesis that virtue is sufficient for happiness rather than identical to it. First, he finds the latter outlandish.[68] Secondly, he thinks

---

[65] See Vlastos 1984.
[66] Τὸ δὲ εὖ καὶ καλῶς καὶ δικαίως ὅτι ταὐτόν ἐστιν, μένει ἢ οὐ μένει; – Μένει.
[67] Vlastos 1984, pp. 191–201.
[68] This paper is not the place to deal adequately with Vlastos' detailed arguments, but one issue must be mentioned. Vlastos (1984) writes, pp. 196–7: 'If the Identity Thesis were true, we would have no rational ground for preference between alternatives which are equally consistent with virtue – hence *no rational ground for preference between states of affairs differentiated only by their non-moral values*. And if this were true, it would knock the bottom from eudaimonism as a theory of rational choice. For most of the choices we have to make throughout our life have to be made between just such states of affairs, where moral considerations are not in the picture at all: Shall I walk to my destination or ride the bus? Shall I have my hair cut today or next week? ... We do make such choices all the time ... and the grounds on which we have to make them are clearly non-moral: hedonic, economic ... or whatever. This being the case, if the Identity Thesis were true it would bankrupt the power of eudaimonism to give a rational explanation of *all* our deliberate actions by citing happiness as our final reason for them. On that theory, if

that the Platonic ‖ evidence for Socrates' views about goods – especially *Gorgias* 467e, *Lysis* 218e – indicates Socrates' lasting commitment to the existence of non-moral as well as moral goods. In order to bring the argument from the *Euthydemus* into line with the sufficiency thesis, he interprets its conclusion not as a statement denying the existence of any non-moral goods *simpliciter*, but as a denial that anything non-moral is good 'just by itself'.

I suggest that the Stoics reflected on Plato's statements in very similar ways, but arrived at the conclusion that what Socrates was really after was the Identity Thesis. This, they could say, was the obvious sense of the passage from the *Crito* and of *Euthydemus* 281e4–5. True, Socrates elsewhere included moral and non-moral items in a single list of 'goods'. But the import of his discussion in the *Meno* 87e–88d, like that of the *Euthydemus*, was that only virtue or wisdom bears the necessary relation to benefiting that anything good, properly speaking, must have: i.e., always benefiting and never harming.[69] In the *Gorgias* 467e1–468b4, Socrates had introduced an 'intermediate class' – things neither good nor bad, which partake now of the one now of the other and at times of neither; they are exemplified by sitting, walking, running, sailing, stones and logs. In terms of the arguments from the *Meno* and the *Euthydemus* the intermediate class should include things like health, which in the *Gorgias* are assigned to the class of goods.

happiness were identical with virtue, our final reason for choosing anything at all would have to be our concern for our virtue; so the multitude of choices that have nothing to do with that concern would be left unexplained.' Zeno's doctrine of the *proēgmena*, I would respond, was formulated precisely to reconcile the Identity Thesis with the need to have rational grounds for preference between states of affairs differentiated only by their non-moral values. (Contrast the position of Aristo.) A Zenonian wise man will make happiness = virtue the only ground for any choice he makes. But, unlike Vlastos, he takes non-moral differences of value to form the very material (*hylē*) to which the virtuous agent must attend. His concern for happiness = virtue involves a concern for every detail of his life. (Was not this also Socrates' concern (cf. n. 11 above)?) Given the choice, he prefers health to sickness, not because he would be less happy *if he could not avoid* sickness, but because, if he can be healthy, he *should* prefer health because of its naturalness to the human condition. So although, considered just by itself, health is not a constituent of happiness for Zeno, he would expect anyone concerned for happiness in his sense to prefer health to sickness etc. *for the sake of happiness*. Vlastos (1984), n. 77, p. 209, thinks the Stoics would have done better to adopt 'the multicomponent model of happiness' he attributes to Socrates. For what can be said for and against the Stoic position in general, cf. Long/Sedley 1987, vol. i, commentary on 64.

[69] Cf. the Stoics' use of following proposition as a premise in an argument concluding to the non-goodness of wealth and health: ὡς γὰρ ἴδιον θερμοῦ τὸ θερμαίνειν, οὐ τὸ ψύχειν, οὕτω καὶ ἀγαθοῦ τὸ ὠφελεῖν, οὐ τὸ βλάπτειν, D.L. VII.103.

There are, then, as Vlastos too acknowledges, at least surface inconsistencies in statements put forward by Socrates on the value of things like health.[70] They are spoken about (1) as goods in a list that includes wisdom (*Gorg.* 467e; cf. Glaucon at *Rep.* 11, 357c); (2) as sometimes good and sometimes harmful (*Meno* 88d); (3) as good solely in consequence of virtue (*Ap.* 30b 2–4); (4) as without value just by themselves (*Euthyd.* 281d); (5) as falling outside the class of what is good (*Euthyd.* 281e). I am not out to challenge Vlastos' impressive thesis that (3) was actually Socrates' position, and that his other formulations can be brought into line. My interest here is in what Zeno took Socrates to be searching for.

The answer, I propose, was the Zenonian distinction between moral and non-moral value. Assign the former to virtue and the latter to things like health, and the true spirit of Socrates' position became plain. Socrates, Zeno reasoned, was right to suppose that non-moral so-called 'goods' can be used well or badly. Two conclusions, true to the spirit of Socrates' philosophy, were to be drawn from this: (1) goodness properly speaking, which is exclusively moral, can never be predicated of something ‖ valuable but non-moral; (2) the *use* of such a thing (as distinct from its mere possession) can be good and a constituent of happiness. Socrates found himself speaking of health etc., sometimes as good, and sometimes as totally without intrinsic value. The inconsistency could be resolved, and the significant insight of Socrates' thought clarified, if health, just by itself, were accorded non-moral value, promoted above the position set out in the *Euthydemus* but below what it is apparently assigned in the *Gorgias* and *Lysis*.

If my approach is correct, it will not show that Zeno's analysis of these Platonic passages should be preferred to Vlastos' interpretation of Socrates. What I hope to have proved is that Zeno (and Aristo) did read and reflect on them carefully, and that their own ethical theory should be viewed as an actual elucidation of Socrates' philosophy. In other words, what the Stoics made of Socrates remains an option that anyone interested in reconstructing his thought should take seriously.

---

[70] I say 'statements put forward by Socrates', since the question of his assent to such statements must be distinguished from the role they play in his arguments. Thus it is surely evident that the status of the 'goods' initially proposed to Cleinias at *Euthyd.* 279a–b is radically altered by the conclusion of the argument at 281d–e; and the same is true if we compare *Meno* 78c with 88d.

CONCLUSION

By applying similar methods of analysis, I think it would be possible to show that the Stoics thought of their moral psychology, with its pronounced differences from Plato and Aristotle, as a development of Socrates' purely intellectualist account of virtue and vice. The Peripatetics took Socrates' thesis, 'virtue is knowledge', to commit him to an implicit denial of the irrational part of the soul since it treated the virtues (so they put it) as exclusively resident in the soul's rational faculty, and thereby ignored *pathos* and *ethos*.[71] It would be worthwhile to consider how the orthodox Stoics welcomed this interpretation of Socrates, and fully developed its implications in their own account of the mind's faculties and moral states.

But, to conclude the present paper, let my last word pass back to Arcesilaus. We should not suppose that Plato was the only author who shaped his view of the sceptical Socrates. Let us suppose, for the sake of argument, that Arcesilaus was fully cognisant of the way Zeno and Aristo wanted to interpret the *Euthydemus* passage as a guide to Socrates' and their own ethics. To cast doubt on the legitimacy of attaching Socrates firmly to any conclusions, he had only to set Xenophon, *Memorabilia* IV.2.31–5 against the other text. Xenophon is reporting Socrates' refutation of Euthydemus. The latter claims that he knows what sort of things are good and bad, if he knows anything at all. He cites as instances health and sickness. Forced to admit that such things are no more good than bad, since health can be harmful and disease beneficial, he offers first wisdom and then happiness as unequivocal goods. Socrates disposes of wisdom by arguing that it ruined figures such as Daedalus and Palamedes. As for happiness, its claims are wrecked by enumerating various of its possible constituents, any one of which can bring unhappiness to people.

This is an *ad hominem* argument, strictly intended to show up Euthydemus' false conceit of knowledge. None the less, it stands as a warning against committing Socrates' assent to any firm conclusions he elicits by means of propositions assented to by his interlocutor. ‖

---

[71] *MM* I 1182a15–17: γίνονται οὖν αἱ ἀρεταὶ πᾶσαι κατ' αὐτὸν ἐν τῷ λογιστικῷ τῆς ψυχῆς μορίῳ· συμβαίνει οὖν αὐτῷ ἐπιστήμας ποιοῦντι τὰς ἀρετὰς ἀναιρεῖν τὸ ἄλογον μέρος τῆς ψυχῆς, τοῦτο δὲ ποιῶν ἀναιρεῖ καὶ πάθος καὶ ἦθος.

POSTSCRIPT 1995

The foregoing text was written in 1986. Its principal findings concerning the Stoics' Socratic orientation have now been confirmed and extended by several scholars. David Sedley (1993) shows that the Stoics drew upon Plato's portrayal of Socrates in the *Crito* and *Phaedo* as a way of illustrating the wise man's assent to the rationality and providence of nature. In *The Socratic Movement* (cf. Vander Waerdt 1994a), convincing reasons are given for linking Stoic thought on natural law to reflections on Socrates, both Xenophon's Socrates (cf. DeFilippo and Mitsis 1994) and Plato's (cf. Vander Waerdt 1994b). In my paper I drew attention (p. 20) to Xenophon, *Mem.* 1.4 as a salient influence on the Stoics' Socrates, and that point is well developed by DeFilippo and Mitsis. Like myself, though without reference to my paper, Gisela Striker (1994) proposes that the Stoics thought hard about Socrates' arguments in the *Euthydemus* concerning the relation between virtue = knowledge and other so-called good and bad things. *The Socratic Movement* (Vander Waerdt 1994a) also includes a useful treatment of Socrates in the early Hellenistic period, written by the editor. In the same volume the role of Socrates in early scepticism is interestingly tackled by Annas (1994) and by Shields (1994).

Further attention to the Stoics' appropriation of Socrates may help to throw light on the vexed question of their knowledge and utilisation of Aristotle's ethics (see chapter 8 below, p. 185 n. 7). I make this observation because there is no reason to treat Socrates and Aristotle as mutually exclusive influences on the Stoics. When I argued years ago (see Long 1968b) that the Stoics reflected seriously on Aristotle's ethics, I made it clear at the time that I regarded their possible attention to Aristotle as additional to the indubitable influence of Socrates and the Academy. Then as now I took Socrates to be their dominant inspiration, but I still think (in spite of Sandbach 1985) that the hypothesis of some Aristotelian influence on Zeno and his followers is probably correct (cf. Long 1996).

CHAPTER 2

*Heraclitus and Stoicism**

As a young man, Zeno of Citium is said to have consulted an oracle about what he should do to live best: the god told him 'to be in
close contact with the dead' (εἰ συγχρωτίζοιτο τοῖς νεκροῖς) and
Zeno understood this discouraging advice to mean 'read the works
of the ancients' (D.L. vii.2).[1] We are not told who the ancients
were whom Zeno read, but apart from Homer and Hesiod it is
tempting to see an allusion to Heraclitus in the anecdote.[2] To the
best of my knowledge there is only one piece of evidence which
associates Zeno, as distinct from other Stoics or the Stoics in general, with Heraclitus explicitly.[3] Indeed, evidence which enables us
to distinguish Zeno's ideas from those of later Stoics is regrettably
slight. But if some uncertainty attaches to Zeno's indebtedness to
Heraclitus we reach firmer ground with his successor, Cleanthes.
Cleanthes was well acquainted with Heraclitus and reflects his
influence both in thought and in language. The importance of
Heraclitus to the later Stoics is evident most plainly in Marcus
Aurelius (see p. 56), and while this may reflect both the personal

---

* This chapter is based upon the text of a lecture which I was privileged to give at the
 Research Center for Greek Philosophy at the Academy of Athens on 30 March 1976. It is
 a pleasure to express my thanks to Professor J. N. Theodprakopoulos, Dr L. Benakis and
 Dr M. Dragona-Monachou for their kindness in arranging the lecture and for offering to
 publish it in Φιλοσοφία.
[1] On the oracle cf. von Fritz 1972, cols. 85–6.
[2] Zeno wrote 5 books of *Problēmata Homērika*, D.L. vii.4, and his interest in Hesiod is
 attested in *SVF* 1.103–5; see chapter 3 of this volume, pp. 65, 76–81.
[3] Numenius ap. Euseb. *Praep. evang.* xiv.5.11 (*SVF* 1.11), after citing Xenocrates, Polemo and
 Crates as philosophers with whom Zeno associated, proceeds: νυνὶ δὲ αὐτῷ λελογίσθω
 ὅτι καὶ Στίλπωνός τε μετέσχε καὶ τῶν λόγων τῶν Ἡρακλειτείων. He then remarks
 that Zeno took Heraclitus, along with Stilpo and Crates, as an ally in his controversy with
 Arcesilaus. Whether these remarks have any biographical value, independently of learned
 inference from Stoic doctrine, is difficult to say. But the report scarcely entitles Hicks
 1910, p. 10, to speak of 'strong and explicit testimony that Zeno [and Cleanthes] studied
 Heraclitus'; similarly, Arnold 1911, p. 70.

interest of the emperor and the general philosophical taste of the
early Christian period, there is no reason to regard Marcus' pre-
dilection for Heraclitus as unusual in a later Stoic. The influence
of Heraclitus on ‖ Stoicism is a commonplace of ancient philosophical commentators and epitomists.

But what did that influence really amount to? There seems to be
no general agreement among those who have discussed the subject
during the last hundred and fifty years. Already in 1911 R. D. Hicks
had drawn attention to exponents of the two extreme positions –
minimal influence, on the one hand, and on the other hand, Stoicism as diluted and distorted Heracliteanism – and adopted a
middle course himself.[4] Until recently, perhaps, it might be said
that Hicks' standpoint, which allowed Stoicism to differ substantially from Heraclitus, while granting important conceptual affinities between both philosophies, was accepted by the most reliable
interpreters of the Stoics.[5] But at the present time there is a clear
tendency among scholars to return to the view that Heraclitus'
impact upon the early Stoics was relatively insignificant. The reasons for this are closely bound up with the long overdue recognition that Stoicism was not an *ad hoc* and retrogressive system of
dogmatic postulates but an important new development in Greek
philosophy. It is now generally accepted that the early Stoics were
strongly influenced by the Academy and also by the Lyceum,
whether directly from the writings of Aristotle, or through the
work of Theophrastus and other Peripatetics.[6] Add to this the well
known indebtedness of Zeno to the Cynics and to the Megarians,
and it becomes clear that the Stoa was founded by a man deeply
familiar with the main currents of thought in his time.

As the sphere of influence on early Stoicism has been enlarged
so the interest of scholars in Heraclitus' imprint appears to have
declined. The case against Heraclitus was briefly stated in 1961 by
Friedrich Solmsen, who asked: 'Are contemporary scholars, who
treat the Stoic exegesis of Homer and Hesiod with a smile or a
shrug of the shoulders, well advised if they accept the Stoic inter-

---

[4] Cf. Hicks 1911, cols. 944–5. Hicks' examples for the two extremes were Siebeck 1873 who
    minimised Heraclitus' influence and Lassalle 1858 who exaggerated it. The latter position
    goes back to Hegel 1971, pp. 263, 266.
[5] Cf. especially Pohlenz 1959, vol. I, pp. 23, 34–5, 68, 160 and Bréhier 1951, pp. 141–51,
    176–7.
[6] So I wrote in 1976. I am now doubtful about whether Zeno paid much heed to the work
    of Theophrastus; cf. Long 1996.

est in Heraclitus as basis for their own appraisal of Stoicism and its place in the history of Greek thought?"[7] Solmsen argues ‖ that the Stoics' fundamental debts in cosmology were to Plato, Aristotle and medical writers such as Diocles and Praxagoras. A complementary study of the four-element theory in Stoicism, based on Solmsen's assumptions, has been made by J. Longrigg in a recent article.[8] Such positive arguments against the influence of Heraclitus are supported in a negative way by those scholars who allude to him merely *en passant* or omit any reference to his general influence.[9]

We have reached a curious position, which would have amused Hegel. Having been frequently regarded as the decisive influence on the early development of Stoic cosmology, Heraclitus is now being pushed into the background or quietly allowed to drop out of the discussion. Solmsen himself admits that 'the early Stoics recognized Heraclitus as their ἀρχηγέτης and made the most strenuous efforts to find their doctrines ... anticipated in his utterances' (loc. cit). But he recommends modern historians not to take their efforts very seriously. This is an odd prescription, especially when Solmsen offers no clear reasons for the Stoics' attribution to Heraclitus of ideas which, he thinks, were rooted in contemporary physics. His valuable work of tracing Stoic indebtedness to those ideas does not in the least rule out a serious historical link between Heraclitus and the Stoics. It is merely an accident that the thesis of Heraclitus' dominating influence was often accompanied in the past by a failure to locate Stoicism adequately within its contemporary intellectual milieu. The Stoics' importance as philosophers is not diminished if they were strongly influenced by Heraclitus *as well as* by the Academy and the Lyceum.

The purpose of this paper is to reconsider and to illustrate Heraclitus' influence on the Stoics, especially Cleanthes. It is a large subject and I make no claim to treat it exhaustively here. But I hope to prove that the present tendency to reduce Heraclitus' influence on early Stoicism is not well grounded. It should be emphasised that I do not intend my thesis to cast doubt upon the Stoics'

[7] Cf. Solmsen 1968a, p. 456.
[8] Cf. Longrigg 1975.
[9] Cf. Rist 1969; Graeser 1975; Sandbach 1975. See also however, Watson 1966, pp. 10–11, 82 and Long 1986a, pp. 131, 145–6.

close attention to positions taken up by other philosophers of their own time. I shall not suggest that Heraclitus was their starting-point in cosmology. But his importance, especially to Cleanthes, so I shall argue, ‖ was fundamental. In attempting to demonstrate this, one is faced with a series of questions, all of which seem to be interesting and worth posing for their own sake. What knowledge of Heraclitus did the early Stoics possess? Was their method of interpretation their own or did it derive from the work of others, especially Aristotle and Theophrastus? Did the Stoics merely twist Heraclitus' views to suit their preconceived needs, or has their interpretation, in some cases, a valid basis in Heraclitus' thought? Above all, why did they take an interest in this remote and extraordinarily difficult thinker?

The process by which Heraclitus' words were transmitted to the fourth century is an unsolved problem. But it is reasonable to assume that the early Stoics had access to a series of texts, known as Heraclitus' book, which gave them as authoritative a record of his work as the sources available to Aristotle and Theophrastus. This point has to be stressed since some scholars argue that the Stoic interpretation of Heraclitus was heavily dependent on Theophrastus. I shall consider this point in some detail shortly, but even if it is true, it does not prove that the Stoics derived their knowledge of Heraclitus from Theophrastus. G. S. Kirk has drawn attention to the fact that Theophrastus' enormous list of writings includes no specific work on Heraclitus.[10] He suggests that Theophrastus' interpretation of Heraclitus, so important to the later doxographical tradition, was close to Aristotle's and may have been based not on Heraclitus' so-called book but on 'a mechanically-arranged selection of the odder sayings'.[11] It does not seem to me necessary to suppose that the Peripatetic interpretation of Heraclitus rested on such inadequate source material. Aristotle and Theophrastus depreciated and misunderstood Heraclitus, but they had their own reasons for doing so.[12] In any case, it is inconceivable that the very

[10] Cf. Kirk 1955, p. 37. Theophrastus' *Physikōn doxai* of course included an account of Heraclitus (cf. Diels 1879, p. 163) but he also devoted separate works to many early Greek philosophers – Anaxagoras, Anaximenes, Archelaus, Democritus, Empedocles (D.L. v.42–9).

[11] Loc. cit. Kirk's conjecture (1954, p. 7), expressed more guardedly in the 1962 reprint of his book, that Heraclitus 'wrote no book, in our sense of the word', has not won general acceptance, cf. Marcovich 1965, col. 257; Mondolfo 1972, p. xxxiv.

[12] Cf. especially Cherniss 1935 passim and McDiarmid 1953, pp. 93–6.

close ‖ links between Cleanthes' *Hymn to Zeus* and Heraclitus were mediated to the Stoic through the doxography of Theophrastus (see below).

But one of Aristotle's own Academic contemporaries, with a strong interest in the Presocratics, did write at length on Heraclitus. This was Heracleides of Pontus, who is said to have written four books of 'commentary' (ἐξηγήσεις) on him.[13] It is possible that Heracleides, who was an independent-minded thinker, played a key part both in disseminating knowledge of Heraclitus' recorded sayings and in giving them philosophical respectability. He may also have initiated methods of interpretation which attracted the Stoic interest in Heraclitus. We can only speculate about Heracleides' sources but there is no reason to think that any later figure was in a better position to read Heraclitus' own words.[14]

At some point in his career Cleanthes imitated Heracleides in writing his own 'four books of commentary on Heraclitus', Τῶν Ἡρακλείτου ἐξηγήσεων τέσσαρα (D.L. vii.174 = *SVF* 1.481). The number four is an interesting coincidence and tempts me to conjecture that Cleanthes took Heracleides' work as his own basis, amplifying and amending it in accordance with Stoic doctrine. However that may be, the early Stoic interest in Heraclitus is strongly confirmed by the record of Sphaerus' writings, which includes 'five books of conversations on Heraclitus', Περὶ Ἡρακλείτου πέντε διατριβῶν (*SVF* 1.620). Sphaerus, who was subordinate to Cleanthes in the Stoic hierarchy, may be presumed to have had his attention to Heraclitus stimulated by Cleanthes if not already by Zeno.[15]

It cannot be proved that the early Stoics were in a better position to read Heraclitus than were the Peripatetics; indeed this seems unlikely. Members of both schools in all probability had indepen-

---

[13] D.L. v.88 (= fr. 39 Wehrli, *Die Schule des Aristoteles* vii), probably confirmed by Athenaeus iv 134b (= fr. 10 Wehrli) which implies some notoriety for his commentary.

[14] If D.L. ix.15 is to be trusted, Heracleides' work was preceded by commentary on Heraclitus' σύγγραμμα by Antisthenes. Not much should be built upon a bald notice of this kind but the links between Antisthenes and Zeno of Citium are sufficiently strong (cf. von Fritz 1952, cols. 93–5) to suggest him as a further possible link between Heraclitus and the Stoics.

[15] The Aristo whose work *Peri Hērakleitou* is quoted by D.L. ix.5 has been identified with the Peripatetic philosopher of that name and not the dissident Stoic (Wehrli, *Die Schule des Aristoteles* vi², s.v. *Ariston von Keos*, fr. 28) but this is far from certain. The work is not included in the Stoic's list of writings at D.L. vii.163 but that does not disprove his authorship.

dent access to copies of his book, or collections of his sayings, which included most of the extant fragments and some other texts that are now lost. Heracleides' work shows ‖ that the Stoics were not the first philosophers to attempt detailed interpretation of Heraclitus; and we may presume that when they were developing their own ideas they were in a position to supplement their reading of Heraclitean texts with the interpretation of Heracleides (and Antisthenes, cf. n. 14) as well as Theophrastus. We may now look rather more closely at Theophrastus' interpretation.

Simplicius gives us this report on Heraclitus which he drew from Theophrastus:[16]

Hippasus of Metapontum and Heraclitus of Ephesus ... made fire the principle, and out of fire by condensation and rarefaction they make the things that exist and resolve them again into fire, since fire is the single underlying nature; for Heraclitus says that all things are an exchange for fire. He also assigns a certain regularity and limited time to the world's change according to a predetermined necessity.

(Ἵππασος δὲ ὁ Μεταποντῖνος καὶ Ἡράκλειτος ὁ Ἐφέσιος ἓν καὶ οὗτοι καὶ κινούμενον καὶ πεπερασμένον, ἀλλὰ πῦρ ἐποίησαν τὴν ἀρχήν, καὶ ἐκ πυρὸς ποιοῦσι τὰ ὄντα πυκνώσει καὶ μανώσει καὶ διαλύουσι πάλιν εἰς πῦρ, ὡς ταύτης μιᾶς οὔσης φύσεως τῆς ὑποκειμένης· πυρὸς γὰρ ἀμοιβὴν εἶναί φησιν Ἡράκλειτος πάντα. Ποιεῖ δὲ καὶ τάξιν τινὰ καὶ χρόνον ὡρισμένον τῆς τοῦ κόσμου μεταβολῆς κατά τινα εἱμαρμένην ἀνάγκην.)

The principal points to notice in this account are first, that fire is treated as an Aristotelian substrate, the material cause of all change; secondly, that the method of generating other things out of fire is condensation and rarefaction; thirdly, that the universe itself is regarded as subject to regular change, beginning as fire and ceasing as fire.[17]

It is improbable that Heraclitus would have accepted any of these three points, though the third – the periodic dissolution of everything into fire, called *ekpyrōsis* by the Stoics – has been regarded as his own view by many scholars.[18] But this Theophrastean interpretation largely determined the representation of Heraclitus by

---

[16] *Phys.* 23.33 (= DK 22 A5).

[17] For a full discussion cf. Kirk 1954, pp. 303, 318–19, 327 and also McDiarmid 1953, with whom I am inclined to agree (against Kirk 1962, p. 304) that κατά τινα εἱμαρμένην ἀνάγκην reflects Stoic influence on the doxography. But Mondolfo 1972 defends the substance, if not the terminology, of the doxographical tradition on Heraclitus.

[18] The most recent defender is Mondolfo 1958, pp. 75–82 answered by Kirk 1959, pp. 73–6, with further comments by Mondolfo 1972, pp. clxxx–cxciii. For Mondolfo's predecessors and arguments against them cf. Burnet 1930, pp. 158–63.

the doxographers.[19] Diels conclusively proved the dependence of Diogenes Laertius' detailed summary of Heraclitus' doctrine (ix.8–11) on Theophrastus, and the same holds good for Aetius and others.[20] ||

But what does this tell us about early Stoic interpretation? Jula Kerschensteiner asserted that the Stoics did not go back to the original Heraclitus but rather took over and developed the picture presented by Theophrastus.[21] Kirk adopted a similar view and offered more evidence to support it than Kerschensteiner.[22] His main argument is a summary of Zeno's cosmogony by Arius Didymus (*SVF* 1.102). Kirk rightly sees a connexion between Zeno's doctrine, as reported here, and Heraclitus fr. 31. But he thinks that the Stoic use of this fragment has been strongly influenced by Theophrastus' misinterpretation, which is the source of Diogenes Laertius ix.8–9.

Heraclitus fr. 31 runs as follows: 'Turnings of fire: first sea, and of sea one half earth, and the other half lightning flash' (πυρὸς τροπαί· πρῶτον θάλασσα, θαλάσσης δὲ τὸ μὲν ἥμισυ γῆ, τὸ δὲ ἥμισυ πρηστήρ). Some comments by Clement of Alexandria, the source of the fragment (ii.396 Stählin), separate this part of it from the next: 'Earth is poured forth as sea and is measured in the same ratio as it was before it became earth' (⟨γῆ⟩ θάλασσα διαχέεται, καὶ μετρέεται εἰς τὸν αὐτὸν λόγον, ὁκοῖος πρόσθεν ἦν ἢ γενέσθαι γῆ). Clement then concludes by saying: 'The most renowned of the Stoics have similar doctrines to this in their assumptions concerning the *ekpyrōsis* and the organization of the world.'

When we compare Arius Didymus' text with the Theophrastean treatment, it seems to me far from clear that Zeno's cosmogony, as described by Arius, 'is developed out of Theophrastus' extension of Heraclitus fr. 32'.[23] The Stoic text says this:

Of such a kind the organization of the world out of substance will periodically have to be – when the turning from fire into water through air takes place, one part underlies and is composed as earth. From the rest,

---

[19] Whether Aristotle attributed the concept expressed by *ekpyrōsis* to Heraclitus is too large a question to be discussed briefly. Cherniss 1935, p. 29 n. 108, argues that he did not, but cf. Kirk 1962, pp. 319–22.

[20] Diels 1879 *ad loc.* Cf. Deichgräber 1938–9, pp. 12–30, Kerschensteiner 1955, pp. 385–411, both of whom find Theophrastus more influential on D.L. ix.7 than did Diels.

[21] Cf. Kerschensteiner 1955, p. 411.

[22] Kirk 1962, pp. 327–9; cf. also pp. 318–19.

[23] Kirk 1962, p. 328, who concedes that 'there were, of course, some non-Heraclitean elements in Stoic cosmogony'.

one part persists as water, and from this as it evaporates air is generated. From some of the air fire is kindled, and blending takes place by the interchange of the elements since one body interpenetrates another through and through.

(τοιαύτην δὲ δεήσει εἶναι ἐν περιόδῳ τὴν τοῦ ὅλου διακόσμησιν ἐκ τῆς οὐσίας, ὅταν ἐκ πυρὸς τροπὴ εἰς ὕδωρ δι' ἀέρος γένηται, τὸ μέν τι ὑφίστασθαι καὶ γῆν συνίστασθαι, ἐκ τοῦ λοιποῦ δὲ τὸ μὲν διαμένειν ὕδωρ, ἐκ δὲ τοῦ ἀτμιζομένου ἀέρα γίνεσθαι, ἐκ τινὸς δὲ τοῦ ἀέρος πῦρ ἐξάπτεσθαι, τὴν δέ κρᾶσιν γίνεσθαι τῇ εἰς ἄλληλα τῶν στοιχείων μεταβόλῃ, σώματος δι' ὅλου τινὸς ἑτέρου διερχομένου.)

Compare with this the relevant parts of the Theophrastean account:

The world is alternately generated from fire and resolved into fire according to definite cycles throughout eternity ... for fire by condensing liquefies, and when compacted becomes water; and water when it has congealed turns into earth. This is the downward path. Then again earth dissolves and from it water arises, and from water the remainder come to be.

(γεννᾶσθαί τε αὐτὸν ἐκ πυρὸς καὶ πάλιν ἐκπυροῦσθαι κατά τινας περιόδους ἐναλλὰξ τὸν σύμπαντα αἰῶνα ... πυκνούμενον γὰρ τὸ πῦρ ἐξυγραίνεσθαι, συνιστάμενόν τε γίνεσθαι ὕδωρ, πηγνύμενον δὲ τὸ ὕδωρ εἰς γῆν τρέπεσθαι· καὶ ταύτην ὁδὸν ἐπὶ τὸ κάτω εἶναι, πάλιν τε αὖ τὴν γῆν χεῖσθαι, ἐξ ἧς τὸ ὕδωρ γίνεσθαι, ἐκ δὲ τούτου τὰ λοιπά. (D.L. ix.8–9)

As Kirk notes, the Stoic text differs from Heraclitus in introducing air, ‖ and there are other differences he does not discuss. The Stoic text, unlike Theophrastus (ap. D.L.), does not incorporate anything corresponding clearly to the second part of the fragment (cf. however *SVF* ii.413), but it is closer than Theophrastus to the first half. Heraclitus' noun τροπή is used, and the Stoic text reflects his ἥμισυ in its use of τὸ μέν and τὸ λοιπόν. These points are indications that Zeno, or whoever it is that Arius records, had a text of fr. 31 available to him. Whether condensation (πύκνωσις) and rarefaction (ἀραίωσις) are implied by συνίστασθαι and ἀτμιζομένου I am not sure; but these concepts are certainly not made fully explicit as they are in the Theophrastean interpretation of Heraclitus (D. L. ix.8).[24] I conclude that Theophrastus is at most

---

[24] They do occur unambiguously in some accounts of Stoic cosmogony, cf. D.L. vii.142, Plutarch, *Stoic. rep.* 1053a (= *SVF* ii.579): but in as much as these are interpretations of

one possible intermediary between Heraclitus and the passage from Arius Didymus, the beginning and end of which have no connexion with Theophrastus. How far Arius Didymus represents a valid account of Zeno's cosmogony need not concern us here, though it is worth noting that his passage needs to be considered alongside other accounts of Stoic cosmogony.[25]

This becomes particularly clear when Arius Didymus' evidence for Zeno is compared with that which he gives for Cleanthes (*SVF* 1.497, see further p. 52). Theophrastus, as we have seen, regarded Heraclitus' fire as a material substrate whose changes of density account for water and earth. In Cleanthes' cosmogony as described by Arius, where the links with Heraclitus are quite unmistakable, fire is presented not only as the material starting-point of cosmogony but also as the organising agent of the universe (ἄρχεσθαι διακοσμεῖν τὸ ὅλον). That point is not made plain in the Zenonian account, but there is every reason to regard it as the orthodox early Stoic view. The early Stoics distinguished between fire, the eternal active principle (πῦρ τεχνικόν), and πῦρ ἄτεχνον, which is one of the four elements generated by the creative fire in its association with the eternal passive principle (ὕλη).[26] It is highly probable that they thought Heraclitus supported this distinction, and virtually certain that they did not interpret his fire simply as a material substrate along the lines of Theophrastus.[27] ‖

Why then did Kirk (1962, p. 328) find it so obvious, on the basis of this text, that 'the Stoics accepted Theophrastus' extension of Heraclitus fr. 31 as a legitimate one, and developed out of it their own cosmogony'? It is due to the fact that they, like Theophrastus, interpreted fr. 31 as referring to stages of world-formation – the 'turnings of fire', repeated in regular cycles following the absorp-

Heraclitus they need not derive exclusively, or even partially, from Theophrastus. Mondolfo 1972, pp. 36–7 defends Theophrastus' historicity in attributing to Heraclitus processes which may be described as condensation and rarefaction.

[25] Cf. Lapidge (1973), pp. 265–7.

[26] Cf. *SVF* 1.120, 504, with discussion by Lapidge 1973, pp. 267–73.

[27] The Stoic distinction between an eternal κόσμος and a perishable κόσμος (*SVF* ii.526–9), well explained by Kirk 1962, pp. 307–10, in relation to Heraclitus fr. 30, is closely related to the distinction between two kinds of fire, and both could be partly inspired by the difficulty of reconciling πῦρ ἀείζωον with ἁπτόμενον μέτρα καὶ ἀποσβεννύμενον μέτρα. Clement of Alexandria, the source of Heraclitus fr. 31, gravely misrepresents the Stoic position by treating fire as material organised ὑπὸ τοῦ διοικοῦντος λόγου καὶ θεοῦ. For Theophrastus' distinction between two kinds of fire, and its possible influence on the Stoics, cf. Longrigg 1975, pp. 219–22. Mondolfo 1972, p. cxxvii, thinks that Plato *Tht.* 153a attributes a directive function to 'fuoco eracliteo'.

tion of each world into fire. Kirk regards this interpretation of the fragment as demonstrably false since it refers, in his view, not to cosmogony but to changes which go on continuously within an eternal world-order. There can be little doubt that Kirk is right about this; successive worlds periodically created and destroyed were probably not part of Heraclitus' philosophy, but it does not follow from this that the Stoics misunderstood their predecessor as a result of reading Theophrastus. Many modern scholars have followed their lead, and it may well have been Aristotle's view too. It has taken a very large amount of scholarly discussion to establish the distinctive nature of Heraclitus' cosmology, and agreement on many issues has not been reached. Neither the misattribution of *ekpyrōsis* to Heraclitus – if such it is by Theophrastus and the Stoics – nor other details of Stoic cosmogony suffice to show that the Stoics' interpretation of Heraclitus was largely based on Theophrastus.

The later doxographical tradition incorporates Stoic features into the Theophrastean interpretation. This seems to have led some scholars into thinking that the early Stoics merely added to or modified his views. But this is unlikely in principle and not demonstrable in fact. Stoic elements in the doxography of Heraclitus are due to the general influence which Stoicism exercised on the later philosophical tradition and to the specific interest of the Stoics in Heraclitus. They are not the best evidence for telling us what Cleanthes and other early Stoics thought about Heraclitus. Modern research has concentrated on disentangling Heraclitus' ideas from the views of later philosophers. In this process Stoic approaches to Heraclitus have too readily been regarded as only a link in the chain of Theophrastus' influence on the doxographical tradition. ∥

My paper up to this point has been largely concerned with clearing the ground in order to examine some aspects of the Stoics' relationship with Heraclitus. I turn now to consider these in more detail.

From Zeno onwards the Stoics denied the eternity of the phenomenal world. That thesis, so dear to the Peripatetics, seemed to them inconsistent with the empirical evidence of natural change (cf. *SVF* 1.106) and in place of it they adopted a belief in a regular and ceaseless succession of similar worlds. Unlike Plato and Aristotle they confined existence to bodies, but they agreed with these philosophers that the orderliness of nature points to the existence of a source of motion which is eternal and rational. Cosmogony, change within the world, orderliness and rationality, and materialism, were all accounted for in Stoicism by the postulation of an active and a passive *archē*. Often called *theos*, the active principle of eternal substance in early Stoicism is a *pyr technikon*, corporeal, rational and self-moving.[28] The early Stoics' choice of fire as their eternal, active principle which persists throughout the succession of worlds was influenced by a variety of considerations. Chief among these were the associations between fire and the life-force of living things, the fiery nature of the heavenly bodies and the creative power of fire in technology.[29] The early Stoics could have no better candidate than fire if they were to posit a single material principle as the active power in the universe.

Neither the early Stoics' basic assumptions about the universe, nor their choice of fire as the active principle, are likely to have been derived directly from Heraclitus. I agree with Zeller that the Stoics' (he says Zeno's) Weltanschauung was the ground of their Heracliteanism, not the consequence of it.[30] The general basis of Stoic cosmology is best explained as a critical reaction to the Academy and the Lyceum.[31] But something of profound ‖ importance to the Stoics influenced their attitude to contemporary philosophical positions and stimulated their interest in Heraclitus. What was this?

The goal of Stoicism was to create a picture of the world which would be completely coherent. They wanted to explain natural events, human conduct and the apprehension and description of reality (physics, ethics and logic) as manifestations of an all-pervading rationality or *logos*. At bottom the Stoics, for all their distinction between two basic principles, were monists. 'The universe is one', said Zeno (*SVF* 1.97) and it was a desire to maintain

---

[28] For the evidence and an excellent discussion cf. Lapidge 1973. In Chrysippus' cosmology, *pneuma* replaces *pyr* as the active *archē*, with important consequences for the earlier Stoic distinction between fire as an eternal *archē* and fire as one of the four derived *stoicheia*. When referring to the 'early Stoics' over the next few pages I do not include Chrysippus.

[29] On the first two points, with arguments that develop from biology to cosmology, cf. Cic. *ND* II.23–8, who drew them from Cleanthes. Cf. Solmsen 1968a, pp. 436–45. On fire as a craftsman, cf. its description as *technikon* or *artificialis SVF* 1.171, II.422, 1133–4, and Zeno's explanation of Vulcan (i.e. Hephaestus) as fire, *SVF* 1.169.

[30] Zeller 1892–1909, vol. III.1, pp. 126–7, 'seine eigentümliche Weltanschauung war nicht die Folge, sondern der Grund seines Heraklitismus'.

[31] As is well shown by Solmsen 1968a and Longrigg 1975.

unity at all costs which helps to explain many features of Stoicism – their restriction of existence to body, their refusal to accept an irrational faculty in the human soul, their denial of Plato's degrees of reality or of Aristotle's distinction between celestial movements and the sublunar sphere, their strict determinism. Of course the early Stoics admitted the existence of plurality and diversity within the world, but they explained the multiplicity of things as impermanent transformations and products of their eternal rational principle or creative fire.

No doubt this sketch of Stoic aspirations is oversimplified. But I would maintain that it is essentially correct. In the interests of explaining all experience and providing human beings with an attitude to the world which was proof against all circumstances, the Stoics claimed that the rational principle in man, his *logos*, is part of the rational principle which governs the world at large. Thus man and nature are fundamentally at one, or should be. The Stoics recognized that human beings can and do fail to accord with their own rationality and that of the world. But by expedients which are ingenious rather than convincing they maintained that such failures are compatible with and even necessary to the good order of the universe as a whole.[32]

Unity within apparent diversity, unity in change, a controlling *logos* manifested in fire, and common to man as well as the universe, exhortations to follow this wise directive power, in Heraclitus the Stoics could find these and other ideas related to their own basic assumptions; which is not to say that they formulated all their own conceptions independently of him. We simply cannot relate the formative stages of Stoicism to their interest in Heraclitus. But we can see that in Cleanthes the links between Stoicism and Heraclitus had definitely been forged. His use of Heraclitus, I shall suggest, shows a much deeper understanding of the other philosopher's work than we find in Plato, Aristotle or Theophrastus.

Cleanthes' *Hymn to Zeus* falls into three main sections:[33] lines 1–14 ‖ praise Zeus for the power which he exercises throughout all nature, animate and inanimate alike; lines 15–31 describe human folly and mistaken conceptions of the good life and also assert

---

[32] For the evidence cf. n. 44 below.

[33] Stobaeus 1.25.4 (= *SVF* 1.537). The text of the *Hymn to Zeus* is notoriously difficult, but my interpretation here does not turn upon any controversial passages. For a recent discussion see Dragona-Monachou 1971 and the works cited by her in her n. 36 p. 349.

Zeus's capacity to unite good with bad in a harmonious unity; lines 32–9 are a prayer to rescue human beings from their lack of insight into the true nature of things, which Zeus directs by reason, justice and law. The tone and style of the poem owe much to the epic tradition, but to understand its individual ideas and total effect we have to consider it in relation to Heraclitus.[34]

In the first section verbal echoes are prominent. Cleanthes addesses: 'Most majestic of immortals, many-titled, ever omnipotent Zeus, prime mover of nature, who with your law steer all things' (Κύδιστ᾽ ἀθανάτων, πολυώνυμε, παγκρατὲς αἰεί, Ζεῦ, φύσεως ἀρχηγέ, νόμου μέτα πάντα κυβερνῶν, 1–2). The whole universe obeys Zeus willingly. In his hands he holds the 'double-edged, fiery, ever-living, thunderbolt' (ἀμφήκη, πυρόεντα, ἀειζώοντα κεραυνόν, 10), at whose 'stroke' (πληγή) all the works of nature are accomplished. It is the instrument by means of which he directs 'the universal reason' (κοινὸς λόγος) that passes through everything (12–13). For Heraclitus, 'The wise, one thing alone, is willing and not willing to be called by the name Zeus' (ἓν τὸ σοφὸν μοῦνον λέγεσθαι οὐκ ἐθέλει καὶ ἐθέλει Ζηνὸς ὄνομα, fr. 32). This sentence may be reflected in Cleanthes' epithet for Zeus, 'many-titled' (πολυώνυμε), but more significant is the fact that Cleanthes incorporates two statements by Heraclitus about the thunderbolt, the instrument of Zeus's power: 'The thunderbolt steers all things' (τὰ δὲ πάντα οἰακίζει κεραυνός, fr. 64), and 'Every beast is driven to pasture by a blow' (πᾶν γὰρ ἑρπετὸν πληγῇ νέμεται, fr. 11).

In Heraclitus the cosmic role assigned to fire or thunderbolt cannot be separated from the functions he attributes to *logos, nomos*, 'the wise' and 'the divine'.[35] So it is with Cleanthes. As Heraclitus speaks of a *logos* which is 'common' (*koinos*) and a single divine law which fosters all human laws (fr. 114), so Cleanthes stresses the obedience of nature to Zeus, writes of a *koinos nomos* and treats the thunderbolt as the means by which Zeus directs the *koinos logos* permeating everything.[36] ‖ Heraclitus, for his part, refers to 'the plan

---

[34] This is well appreciated by Meerwaldt 1951 and 1952, who observes (1951, p. 46), that the 'Hymnus in Iovem singulis paene versibus vestigia exhibet Heraclitea', and cf. the (incomplete) list of parallels cited by Marcovich 1967, p. 637 and by Zuntz 1958, pp. 290–28 discussed below. Most studies, where one would expect the close connexion to be noted, are either completely reticent, e.g. Pohlenz 1959 and Verbeke 1949, or misleadingly selective, e.g. Pearson 1891.

[35] Cf. Kirk 1962, pp. 402–3; Guthrie 1962, p. 434.

[36] Lines 2, 7–8, 12–13, 39.

by which all things are steered through all things' (... γνώμην,
ὅτέη κυβερνᾶται πάντα διὰ πάντων, fr. 41).[37]

So much for the first section of Cleanthes' *Hymn to Zeus*. In the
second part he asserts that nothing is done in the world apart from
Zeus:

> Save what the bad do in their folly. But you know how to
> make things crooked straight and to order things dis-
> orderly. You love things unloved. For you have so welded
> into one all things good and bad that they all share in a
> single everlasting reason. It is shunned and neglected by
> the bad among mortals ...

> (πλὴν ὁπόσα ῥέζουσι κακοὶ σφετέραισιν ἀνοίαις·
> ἀλλὰ σὺ καὶ τὰ περισσὰ ἐπίστασαι ἄρτια θεῖναι,
> καὶ κοσμεῖν τἄκοσμα καὶ οὐ φίλα σοὶ φίλα ἐστίν.
> ὧδε γὰρ εἰς ἓν πάντα συνήρμοκας ἐσθλὰ κακοῖσιν,
> ὥσθ' ἕνα γίγνεσθαι πάντων λόγον αἰὲν ἐόντα,
> ὃν φεύγοντες ἐῶσιν ὅσοι θνητῶν κακοί εἰσι)

> (17-22)

Cleanthes then analyses the failure of the bad to observe or listen
to the 'universal law' (*koinos nomos*). Obedience to this principle is
the formula for a good life, but human beings who lack this insight
pursue such inappropriate goals as fame, possessions, leisure and
sexual pleasure (23-31).

It is immediately evident that we have further indebtedness to
Heraclitus in these lines. The eternal *logos* and the unity of all
things are verbatim citations of Heraclitus (cf. λόγου τοῦδ' ἐόντος
ἀεί, fr. 1 and ἓν πάντα εἶναι, fr. 50). Cleanthes' Zeus harmonises
and unifies moral opposites; in Heraclitus god is a series of opposites – day night etc. (fr. 67), and 'To god all things are fair and
good and just, but human beings have supposed some things to be
unjust and other things just' (fr. 102). But the connexion between
the two philosophers goes deeper than verbal parallelism. Cleanthes develops the moral consequences of obedience to and recognition of the 'common' *logos* or *nomos*. So too does Heraclitus. He exhorts his hearers to follow the common *logos* (fr. 2) instead of living
idiosyncratically, and Cleanthes' constant imperative is similar.
Charles Kahn has written that Heraclitus' real subject is not the

---

[37] ὅτέη κυβερνᾶται Deichgräber for the various transmitted corruptions. In favour of
γνώμη = 'divine guiding principle' cf. Marcovich 1967, pp. 451-2 with bibliography pro
and contra.

physical world but the human condition.[38] If this over-emphasises the moral element, consider also Kirk's observation that 'Heraclitus made it far clearer than his immediate predecessors that man himself is a part of his surroundings; in him, too, the Logos is operative, and his effective functioning depends upon action in accordance with it – and so upon his understanding of it.'[39] Heraclitus does not, in so many words, list the false goals which the unknowing aim at, but ‖ his insistence on the need to follow the common *logos*, and his diagnosis of most people's failure to do so, has probably inspired much of this section of Cleanthes' poem. Heraclitus uses the contrasts between sleeping and wakefulness, and between private and common understanding,[40] but the implication is the same as that of Cleanthes: only a life based upon the *logos* common to all things can have a proper grounding. So far as our evidence goes, Cleanthes grasped the moral significance of Heraclitus' thought in ways which Plato, Aristotle and Theophrastus either ignored or misunderstood.

But someone could object that I have so far established no more than surface parallels between Heraclitus and Cleanthes' *Hymn*. Heraclitus' logos, the argument might run, was not that of the Stoics. He meant by it 'the formula which connects opposites into a unity'; they meant 'reason or rationality pervading and directing the world as a whole'. I do not myself think it is possible to characterise *logos* either in Heraclitus or in the Stoics as simply as this. But for the present let that pass, for the kind of objector I have in mind can be illustrated by some comments of Günther Zuntz on the middle section of Cleanthes' poem.[41]

Zuntz thinks that Cleanthes has *unconsciously* combined here two totally irreconcilable concepts of *logos*, the Stoic and the Heraclitean. Before and after lines 18–21 we have the Stoic concept, a positive directing power present in everything, which guides things to the good; but in lines 18–21, 'like a bomb from another world' (p. 297), the harmony of the Stoic cosmos is shattered by the Heraclitean λόγος, a 'formula of being, the union of opposites', whereby Zeus harmonises good and bad into a unity. This, Zuntz asserts, is not a moral but a metaphysical principle, the *logos* of Heraclitus,

---

[38] See Kahn 1964, p. 194. See also Marcovich, col. 295.
[39] Kirk 1962, p. 403.
[40] Cf. frs. 1, 2, 17, 28, 89.
[41] See Zuntz 1958, pp. 296–8.

according to which all things happen. 'How could a fugitive lay this aside?', asks Zuntz, as Cleanthes in line 22 says that the bad do. Zuntz means that no-one could do so, and that Cleanthes moves imperceptibly from a Heraclitean *logos* which accounts for all that happens to a Stoic *logos* which is a moral imperative that human beings can coherently disobey.

For Cleanthes' alleged failure to recognise this juxtaposition of incompatible *logos* concepts, Zuntz draws attention to his echo of the Heraclitean pun, ξυνός – ξὺν νόῳ (frs. 2 and 114) in the supposedly transitional lines, 24–5, κοινός – σὺν νῷ. Zuntz is right to draw attention to the importance ‖ of Heraclitus in Cleanthes' poem, but his attempt to analyse and separate the two *logos* concepts does not seem to me successful.

Let me offer three points for consideration: 1. The Stoics, like Heraclitus, held that everything in the world accords with *logos*.[42] 2. This applies for the Stoics to the behaviour of the bad as well as the good; from the perspective of the individual bad person such behaviour is seen as a consequence of his own *logos* being 'at fault' *para ton orthon logon*, but it is still attributable to *logos*.[43] From the perspective of cosmic *logos* or universal law, the behaviour of the bad was regarded by the Stoics as necessary to the economy of the universe as a whole: without bad good could not exist.[44] We may well feel that this attempt to reconcile bad in the part with good and harmony in the whole is unsatisfactory, and that it raises substantial difficulties for Stoic ethics.[45] But it is certain that the Stoics incorporated the co-existence of moral opposites in their concept of cosmic order and saw the good and harmony of cosmic *logos* as compatible with the existence of bad in individual people.[46] If then we find difficulty in reconciling the harmony of good and bad with the imperative, 'be good', that is not due to Cleanthes' lack of sensitivity to different *logos* concepts. The Stoics, as monists, required the harmony of moral opposites in order to reconcile

---

[42] Many texts could be cited: cf. Chrysippus ap. Plutarch, *Stoic. rep.* 1050a (*SVF* II.937) οὐθὲν γὰρ ἔστιν ἄλλως τῶν κατὰ μέρος γενέσθαι οὐδὲ τοὐλάχιστον, ἢ κατὰ τὴν κοινὴν φύσιν καὶ κατὰ τὸν ἐκείνης λόγον; Chrysippus' description of ὁ τοῦ Διὸς λόγος as the same as εἱμαρμένη ibid. 1056c (*SVF* II.997). For Zeno cf. *SVF* I.160–2, and for Cleanthes, outside the *Hymn to Zeus*, *SVF* I.531, 533.

[43] *SVF* III.445, 459, etc. Cf. Rist 1969, pp. 22–36; Gould 1970, pp. 181–96; Long 1986a, pp. 175–8.

[44] Cf. Plutarch, *Stoic. rep.* 1050e–1051d, *Comm. not.* 1065b–1066d. *SVF.* II.1168, 1186.

[45] Cf. my remarks in Long 1986a, pp. 181–4.

[46] Apart from the passages cited in n. 44 cf. Epictetus, *Discourses* I.12.16.

their belief in universal providence with their knowledge of the existence of bad people. 3. It is thoroughly misleading to label Heraclitus' *logos* 'metaphysical' and that of the Stoics *moral*. In both systems *logos* is a principle of being *and* a principle of morality. Such 'naturalism' was precisely what attracted the Stoics to Heraclitus. In him, as in the Stoics, all things are determined by *logos* but the many fail to recognise this and thus seek to organise their lives on alien principles. In calling their own active power in the universe *logos* the Stoics were expressing the closest affinity with Heraclitus.[47] ‖

I do not wish to imply that the Stoic *logos* was simply adopted without change from that of Heraclitus. My point is rather that the two concepts are sufficiently close to rule out Zuntz's notion of an unrecognized juxtaposition of alien notions on Cleanthes' part. Heraclitus' concept of *logos* as the unification of opposites was used by Cleanthes to provide the orthodox Stoic reduction of 'partial evil to universal good'. But in these lines (18–21), which Zuntz regards as Heraclitean, the thought is Stoic and an important modification of Heraclitus. The earlier philosopher does not speak of Zeus or his cosmic principle making the crooked straight or harmonising the bad with the good so that the resulting unity is good, and obeyed by all save the bad. Cleanthes regards the *logos* as an objective power of good which, through Zeus, can accommodate those exceptionally recalcitrant parts of the cosmos which are bad. Heraclitus has a more radical and paradoxical conception. He reduces opposites to the constituents of harmony. Human beings distinguish good from bad, but to god all things are good (fr. 102). This is not what Cleanthes says. He recognizes objective evil in the world but asserts that Zeus can make it blend with the good. The thought of Cleanthes is closely modelled on Heraclitus; but it is not the same.

The final short section of the *Hymn*, with its prayer to Zeus to enlighten people, is not directly modelled on Heraclitus. But the content of the prayer keeps him closely before our minds. In Cleanthes' epithets for Zeus the thunderbolt is repeated (line 32), and when in the next line Cleanthes begs Zeus to rescue people from 'pitiful incompetence' (ἀπειροσύνης ἀπὸ λυγρῆς), he again echoes Heraclitus' assessment of his own audience (ἀπείροισιν ἐοί-

---

[47] Cf. Pohlenz 1959, vol. I, pp. 34–5.

κασι, fr. 1). Cleanthes asks Zeus to 'grant us the power of judgement by trusting in which you steer all things with justice' (δὸς δὲ κυρῆσαι γνώμης ᾗ πίσυνος σὺ δίκης μέτα πάντα κυβερνᾷς, 34–5). This is a clear allusion to Heraclitus' statement that the 'one thing that is wise is to know the plan by which all things are steered through all things' (fr. 41, cf. n. 37).

Cleanthes' *Hymn to Zeus* is not a summary of Stoic thought, nor do its very strong links with Heraclitus constitute a comprehensive interpretation ‖ of that philosopher. What we have here is a remarkably interesting example of the constructive use of one thinker's work by another where the borrower, as I have tried to show, proves to have a deep understanding of his creditor's ideas without being slavishly bound by them. One would give much to have Heraclitus' own verdict on Cleanthes' hymn. If its teleology, piety and moral emphases are thoroughly Stoic, it is also true that Cleanthes' insight into Heraclitus' own thought is closer to the historical views of modern critics than it is to the ancient doxographical tradition.

There is further evidence which confirms Cleanthes' close reading and positive use of Heraclitus. Arius Didymus' report of his cosmogony (Stobaeus 1.17.3 = *SVF* 1.497) includes three items which are particularly noteworthy. First, the earliest clear reference by a Stoic to *tonos*, 'tension', which 'does not cease in the substance of the universe' as fire continuously goes about its periodic constitution of the cosmos.[48] It has often been suggested that the Stoics found support for their concept of 'tension' and 'tensional motion' (*tonikē kinēsis*) in Heraclitus' 'back-turning' or 'back-stretched harmony' (*palintropos* or *palintonos harmoniē*, fr. 51), and that Cleanthes was the first Stoic to develop the concept in detail.[49] The context of this passage tends to confirm both suggestions, for it includes two further unmistakable echoes of Heraclitus.

Cleanthes proceeds to illustrate the periodic growth and decline of the world, under the direction of fire and its persistent 'tension', by analogy with organic parts, which come together in a seed and are subsequently separated from it:

---

[48] Καὶ τοιαύτην περίοδον ἀεὶ καὶ διακόσμησιν ποιουμένου [sc. πυρός] τὸν ἐν τῇ τῶν ὅλων οὐσίᾳ τόνον μὴ παύεσθαι. For discussion of the whole passage cf. Hirzel 1882, vol. II, pp. 128–31, von Arnim 1924, cols. 563–4, Meerwaldt 1951, pp. 44–53.

[49] Cf. Hirzel 1882, vol. II, pp. 158–9, Pohlenz 1959, vol. I, p. 74, Marcovich col. 315. Both Marcovich 1967, pp. 125–6, and Kirk 1962, pp. 211–15, prefer παλίντονος to παλίντροπος. But even the latter reading does not preclude a connexion, in Stoic eyes, with τόνος.

Just as all the parts of a single thing grow from seeds at the proper times, so too the parts of the world, which include animals and plants, grow at their proper times. Further, just as the particular formulae (*logoi*) of the parts, coming together in a seed, mingle and in turn separate as the parts are generated, so all things arise from one thing and from all things one thing is composed, as the cycle proceeds systematically and harmoniously.

In this passage Cleanthes adapts the Heraclitean *logos*, meaning 'divine measure or ratio,' to the Stoic concept of 'seminal formulae' (*spermatikoi logoi*), which are probably to be construed as 'measures' or 'proportions' of the creative fire and its tensional motion. That Cleanthes intends his thought to be construed with allusion to Heraclitus is made certain by the fact that the cosmic truth ‖ he is illustrating concerning the alternation of one and many is expressed in the words of his Ephesian predecessor: ἐκ πάντων ἓν καὶ ἐξ ἑνὸς πάντα (fr. 10).

As in the *Hymn to Zeus* Cleanthes' use of Heraclitus here is neither mere imitation nor wilful misinterpretation. Heraclitus may not have likened the universe to a living thing, as Cleanthes does, and 'tension' is too important a concept in Stoicism to be derived from misreading Heraclitus. Tension is a property of the divine fire or fiery breath which is also the *logos* pervading and maintaining the universe. But accounts of *tonikē kinēsis* as simultaneous motion in contrary directions (*SVF* II.451), or alternation of two opposite movements (*SVF* II.450, 458), show why the Stoics found it proper to associate their concept with Heraclitus. He had repeatedly stressed that harmony is of opposites and this seems to be implicit in the Stoics' doctrine that the stability of the universe is constituted by the tension of the active principle – its contrary movements which unite the centre of the cosmic sphere with the circumference.[50] By calling 'tension' a 'blow of fire' (*plēgē pyros, SVF* 1.563) Cleanthes may be presumed to have deliberately echoed Heraclitus' fire whose balanced changes maintain order in the universe.[51]

Heraclitus' psychology and its connexions with fire and *logos* also influenced the Stoics, but that subject is much too large to

---

[50] Cf. my remarks in Long 1986a, pp. 156–7. In the Stoic evidence referred to above, it is the *tonos* of *pneuma* and not just that of *pyr*. This reflects Chrysippus' doctrine, whereas Cleanthes speaks explicitly of *pyr*, cf. *antitypēsantos* (as well as *tonos*) in Arius Didymus above, perhaps reflecting *plēgē* in Heraclitus (fr. 11).

[51] The context of *SVF* 1.563 is ethical, but its description of *tonos* is quite consistent with Arius Didymus' evidence.

pursue in detail now. Instead we may conclude this treatment of Cleanthes' relationship to Heraclitus by glancing at a most interesting and controversial text. Once again it comes to us from Arius Didymus[52]:

Citing Zeno's doctrines on the soul, for comparison with the other natural philosophers, Cleanthes says that Zeno, like Heraclitus, calls the soul a sentient exhalation. For Heraclitus, who wanted to show that souls are always becoming intelligent by exhalation, likens them to rivers in these words: 'On those who step into the same rivers a succession of different waters flows', and 'Souls are exhaled from moisture.' So Zeno like Heraclitus declares the soul to be an exhalation.

(περὶ δὲ ψυχῆς Κλεάνθης μὲν τὰ Ζήνωνος δόγματα παρατιθέμενος πρὸς σύγκρισιν τὴν πρὸς τοὺς ἄλλους φυσικούς φησιν, ὅτι Ζήνων τὴν ψυχὴν λέγει αἰσθητικὴν ἀναθυμίασιν, καθάπερ Ἡράκλειτος. βουλόμενος γὰρ ἐμφανίσαι, ὅτι αἱ ψυχαὶ ἀναθυμιώμεναι νοεραὶ ἀεὶ γίνονται, εἴκασεν αὐτὰς τοῖς ποταμοῖς λέγων οὕτως "ποταμοῖσι τοῖσιν αὐτοῖσιν ἐμβαίνουσιν ἕτερα καὶ ἕτερα ὕδατα ἐπιρρεῖ" καὶ "ψυχαὶ δὲ ἀπὸ τῶν ὑγρῶν ἀναθυμιῶνται". ἀναθυμίασιν μὲν οὖν ὁμοίως τῷ Ἡρακλείτῳ τὴν ψυχὴν ἀποφαίνει Ζήνων.)

This text provides us with most valuable information about Cleanthes' ‖ methodology. As Kirk says (1962, p. 367), 'it is almost certainly Cleanthes and not Zeno who quotes from Heraclitus'. Cleanthes, we may infer, looked for views similar to Zeno's in other thinkers and found them in Heraclitus. While Arius speaks here specifically of Zeno's psychology, it is highly likely that Cleanthes cited parallels from Heraclitus in his other comments on Zeno's philosophy. This passage supports the idea that Cleanthes went to Heraclitus in particular for strengthening the foundations of Zeno's philosophy (cf. Kirk *ad loc.*); and such a motive helps to explain both his interest in Heraclitus and innovations in Stoicism which Heraclitus may partly have inspired.

The validity of Cleanthes' interpretation of the river and the soul is controversial. As a severe sceptic Kirk may be cited.[53] He argues that Heraclitus used the river to illustrate the stability in change of *all* things and therefore its restriction in this case to an image of psychology is mistaken. He suggests that Cleanthes was misled by his source – a superficial arrangement of Heraclitus' sayings in which the river was wrongly juxtaposed to a statement

---

[52] Ap. Eusebium *Praep. evang.* xv.20 = *SVF* 1.519.
[53] See Kirk 1962, pp. 367–80.

giving the gist of our fr. 36, to the effect that the source of souls is the moist. But one is reluctant to posit an inadequate source for Cleanthes. Why should he not have had access to a version of Heraclitus' book which was generally authoritative? Since Kirk, several scholars have defended the main lines of Cleanthes' quotation.[54] Heraclitus may have used the river image in more than one context, and he certainly held that the dry, fiery substance of souls at their best is a transformation of moisture (cf. fr. 36). Probably he did not use the word *anathumiasis* but there are good reasons for thinking that it represents his belief.[55] Thus the continuity of the river by the flow of different waters would be like the soul which owes its continuing (or renewed) existence to the flow of vaporising moisture.

Cleanthes at least found sufficient resemblance between this doctrine and Zeno's psychology to claim that they agreed in calling the soul an *aisthētikē anathumiasis*. Zeno probably held that the soul as *pneuma* is principally nurtured from the blood and his use of *anathumiasis* to describe the process of vaporisation may well owe more to Aristotle and medical theory ‖ than to Heraclitus.[56] We may accept that Cleanthes is responsible for linking Zeno with Heraclitus, but if his interpretation of the latter is defensible his attempts to identify the views of Zeno and Heraclitus are less plausible. In this case Cleanthes helped to promote misinterpretation of Heraclitus by trying to associate him with Stoicism.

Cleanthes' understanding and utilisation of Heraclitus raise many problems. He was not a historian of philosophy and his own preconceptions affected his reading of his predecessor's work. In cosmogony and psychology he certainly read into Heraclitus unwarranted anticipations of Stoicism, but when due allowance is made for these points we are still left with general conceptual affinities which are of great importance to both systems. The Stoic cosmos of Cleanthes has far more in common with Heraclitus than it shares with other systems. Hirzel argued that Cleanthes was chiefly responsible for the Heraclitean features of Stoicism, and

---

[54] Cf. Vlastos 1955, pp. 338ff., especially n. 2 p. 338, Guthrie 1962, pp. 491–2, Kahn 1964, p. 199. Meerwaldt's emendation of νοεραί to νεαραί in the fifth line of Arius Didymus' citation, printed above, strengthens an authentic link with Heraclitus' own thought (cf. Meerwaldt 1951, pp. 53–4).

[55] Cf. Kirk 1962, pp. 273, 334, 368, Guthrie 1962 and Kahn 1964.

[56] *SVF* I.135, 139, 140, cf. Solmsen 1968a, pp. 452–3.

this seems to be correct.[57] It gains probability if we assume that Zeno did not argue in detail for many of his views and that Cleanthes sought to give them further support by linking them to the most appropriate philosopher of earlier times. Nor should we overlook the possibility that Cleanthes' interest in Heraclitus and other past writers was stimulated by the need to protect Stoicism against attack from the Academic sceptics. By associating Heraclitus with his own views he could present a more united front against scepticism.

Cleanthes' influence on the development of Stoicism was most conspicuous in physics and theology. He elaborated Zeno's doctrines here and established an orthodoxy for Chrysippus and later Stoics, which is not to say that they agreed with him on everything. His interest in Heraclitus, probably stimulated by Zeno, was so strongly imprinted in what he wrote that later Stoics inevitably accepted Heraclitus as a precursor of comparable stature to Socrates and Diogenes of Sinope. Thus the Stoics themselves helped to propagate that confused amalgam of Stoic and Heraclitean notions which permeates the later Greek tradition of the history of philosophy. Chrysippus may have contributed to this, but it does not seem that he shared ‖ Cleanthes' special regard for Heraclitus. In developing Stoic logic and ethics, as he did with such success, Chrysippus looked to the Academy and Lyceum rather than to Heraclitus.[58]

There is, however, a later Stoic on whose writings Heraclitus has left a remarkable impression – Marcus Aurelius. In conclusion, it is appropriate to mention some features of his indebtedness[59].

Marcus Aurelius refers to Diogenes, Heraclitus and Socrates as models of enlightenment and contrasts them with Alexander, Julius Caesar and Pompey (VIII.3). He regards Heraclitus as one of the

[57] Cf. Hirzel 1882, vol. II, pp. 115–82, unreasonably criticised by Pearson 1891, p. 22, though Hirzel overstated his argument. His work still deserves consultation, especially for links between Cleanthes' astronomy and Heraclitus. Kirk 1962 gives a well-balanced account of Cleanthes' relation to Heraclitus, pp. 367–8, and considers many aspects of the Stoic interpretation which I have not attempted to deal with here.

[58] So I wrote in 1976. Skilful detective work by Malcolm Schofield (1991, pp. 74–84) shows that I did not search hard enough for Heraclitean influence on Chrysippus. Schofield finds extensive allusion to Heraclitus by Chrysippus in the latter's book *On nature*, a fact explicitly noted by Philodemus, *Piet.* cols. vii.12–viii.4.

[59] For further details cf. Farquharson 1944. The importance of Heraclitus in Marcus' *Meditations* is not adequately covered in standard books on Stoicism and deserves detailed study. Cf. Dragona-Monachou 1976, p. 241, and Long 1992, pp. 275–7.

great sages, and in an interesting passage exhorts himself to remember Heraclitus' maxims, four of which he then quotes (IV.46).
But his implicit references to Heraclitus are much more numerous.
He repeatedly uses the 'river' as an image of universal flux and
also the cycle 'up and down' (e.g. II.17, IV.43, V.23, VI.17, IX.28). He
reflects Heraclitus' emphasis on the relativity of human judgements (VI.57) and observes that 'nothing is bad for things which
are in process of change, as nothing is good for things which exist
in consequence of change' (IV.42). Like Heraclitus, he dwells on
the hidden nature of things (V.10, X.26) and on the reciprocal
process of change which absorbs a thing's parts and then redis-
tributes them (IV.36, V.13). Even when he is not apparently allud-
ing to Heraclitus, he uses word-play which Heraclitus would have
approved (e.g. V.36–7, VII.27).

Like Cleanthes, Marcus Aurelius reflects Heraclitus at many
points. In this paper I have concentrated on the earlier Stoic, for
when considering Marcus we enter a quite different period, by
which time Heraclitus' influence has become diversified through
Hippocratic writings, apocryphal letters and the revival of Pyr-
rhonian scepticism. The interpretation of Heraclitus' role in Stoicism remains open for discussion. But can we deny that it was of
decisive importance both in its acknowledged influence and in its
formative effect?

CHAPTER 3

Stoic readings of Homer*

I

How did the Stoics read Homer? Common sense suggests that the
question must be complex. The evidence confirms this. Are we
asking about Zeno or Posidonius? Should one mention Aristo's
brilliant parody of Homer's line about the Chimaera (*Iliad* vi.181)
to mock the Academic philosopher Arcesilaus (Diogenes Laertius
iv.33)? Or Strabo's ingenious efforts to demonstrate Homer's geo-
graphical expertise? Or Epictetus' remark that the *Iliad* is nothing
but an idea (*phantasia*), because it would not have occurred if Paris
and Menelaus had not made their respective mistakes in regard
to Helen (*Discourses* 1.28.10)? Stoic philosophers, like all educated
Greeks, knew Homer intimately and could use him as they saw fit.
Were they also, however, united in their acceptance of a general
theory about the meaning and interpretation of the epics and the
philosophical value of these poems from a Stoic viewpoint? The
question cannot be settled decisively from the surviving words of
the early Stoics, but modern scholars are not deterred from arriv-
ing at a virtual consensus about how it should be answered. Their

* In drafting and revising this paper, I have been helped by many people. It would not
have become even an embryonic idea but for the invitation from Bob Lamberton to write
on this topic. Before the paper was read to the conference on 'Homer's ancient readers'
held at Princeton University in 1989, Tom Rosenmeyer gave me detailed criticisms and
encouraged me in my heresies. Like all the conference participants I benefited from the
excellent discussions our work received. Subsequently, Alan Bowen, Denis Feeney and
Jim Porter sent me further comments, all of them trenchant and helpful, which I have
tried to absorb and answer, and I learned much from further discussion of the paper by
audiences at the Universities of Leiden, Utrecht and the Free University of Amsterdam. I
am also grateful to Glenn Most, who gave me a copy of his fine study, 'Cornutus and
Stoic allegoresis', before it appeared as Most 1989. Finally, I thank the classical fraternity
at Leiden University for housing me graciously during the final work of revision, and the
National Endowment for the Humanities, which provided me with a fellowship at that
time.

theory, generally asserted as a fact, is that Stoic philosophers, beginning around 300 BC with Zeno, the founder of the school, interpreted Homer himself as a crypto-Stoic. In ‖ this chapter I shall cast doubt on this theory and offer a different interpretation of the Stoics' generic interests in Homer.

According to this received opinion the Stoics took Homer (and other early Greek poets, especially Hesiod) to have a correct understanding of the world – its physical structure and processes, its god(s), its basic causes and purposes – a correct understanding because it coincided with the Stoics' own philosophy of nature.[1] Thus, so the theory goes, the Stoics interpreted certain episodes in Homer, for instance the story at the beginning of *Iliad* xv that Zeus punished Hera by hanging her from the sky by a golden chain, as deliberately *disguised* references to astronomy and other natural phenomena. Crucial to this theory is the supposition that Homer often *means* something other than he *says*. Homer, the Stoics are supposed to have thought, really understood the world in the Stoics' way; but because he was a poet, he does not express Stoicism directly. He composed, in other words, on two levels: on the surface he offers an epic narrative about the deeds of gods and heroes, but what he is *really* talking about, and understands himself to be talking about, is the physical world in a sense acceptable to Stoic philosophers.

We can sum up this theory by the term 'allegory', taking allegory in its standard ancient definition: 'saying what is other – i.e. saying or meaning something other than what one seems to say'.[2] The Stoics, we are asked to believe, took Homer to be an allegorist; they interpreted the epics 'allegorically' because of assumptions that they made concerning the poet's philosophical understanding and methods of composition. That is the theory I propose to contest, but its proponents have never, to the best of my knowl-

---

[1] Because the theory, as I call it, has been taken to be a fact, no publication that I know of seeks to prove it, and I have to confess to endorsing it myself in Long 1980, pp. 165–6. Characteristic statements of it can conveniently be found in De Lacy 1948, pp. 241–4, esp. 256–63, and in Pfeiffer 1968, p. 237, which I discuss below. Some qualified dissent is offered by Steinmetz 1986, pp. 18–30; cf. also, Tate 1930, pp. 7–10. The other studies that I have found most helpful are Most 1989 and Wehrli 1928. For further references see the bibliographical citations given by Steinmetz and Most.

[2] Cf. Heraclitus, *Quaest. Hom.* 5.2, and Anon., Περὶ ποιητικῶν τρόπων under ἀλληγορία in *Rhetores Graeci* III.207, 18–23 Spengel. In the second passage, allegory is exemplified by the 'idea of devil' as signified by the word *snake*.

edge, made its implications fully explicit. Part of the difficulty of understanding what the Stoics were doing arises from the vagueness of the modern claim that they allegorized Homer. ‖

Allegory is a very complex notion. Some preliminary clarification of it can be reached once we recognise that a text might be called allegorical in a strong sense or in a weak sense.[3] A text will be allegorical in a *strong* sense if its author composes with the intention of being interpreted allegorically. Familiar examples of such texts are Dante's *Divine Comedy*, Spenser's *Faerie Queen*, and Bunyan's *Pilgrim's Progress*. Such texts require their reader to take them allegorically; they are composed as allegories. A text will be allegorical in a *weak* sense if, irrespective of what its author intended, it invites interpretation in ways that go beyond its surface or so-called literal meaning. Examples include the stories of Pandora's box in Hesiod and Adam and Eve in Genesis. Such stories, as we today read them, seem to signify something general about the human condition which is quite other than their narrative content; but they are weak allegories because, in these cases, the allegorising is a contribution by us, the readers, and not something that we know to be present in the text as originally constructed. In some sense, all literary interpretation is weak allegorising – our attempt to say what a narrative *means*.[4] As we shall see in detail later, Heraclitus, the author of *Homeric problems*, interpreted Homer as a strong allegorist. Yet even Heraclitus did not take Homer to be the author of an 'allegory'. As a literary genre, allegory is scarcely attested in antiquity before Prudentius (fourth century AD). Medieval and later allegories need to be put on one side in considering the scope of allegorising in classical antiquity.

According to the theory I propose to reject, the Stoics as a school took Homer to be a strong allegorist in the way just explained. Instead, I shall argue, it is doubtful whether they even took themselves to be allegorising *Homer's* meaning, i.e. interpreting the epic

---

[3] The distinction is my own, but influenced by the work of others, especially Quilligan 1979, pp. 25–6, where she acutely distinguishes allegorical narrative from allegoresis, 'the literary criticism of texts'. See also Dawson 1992, pp. 3–5. For good remarks on the Greek terminology and recognition of how it may differ from 'allegory in the modern sense', cf. Richardson 1975, pp. 65–81.

[4] Cf. Frye 1967, p. 89, and Lamberton 1986, p. 20, who observes that allegorical interpretation 'can comprehend virtually the whole of what we call "interpretation" beyond mere parsing'.

narratives, in a weak sense. As the chapter develops, I will offer a different account of the Stoics' generic interest in Homer, and also, by the way, in Hesiod. Before we come ‖ to grips with the details, something needs to be said about why the question matters: what is at stake in our asking how the Stoics read Homer?

II

Homer was *the* poet for the Greeks. Children learned large parts of the *Iliad* and *Odyssey* by heart as part of their primary education. All Greek literature and art, and just about all Greek philosophy, resonate against the background of Homer. Throughout classical antiquity and well into the Roman Empire, Homer held a position in Mediterranean culture that can only be compared with the position the Bible would later occupy. The comparison is important if we are to understand why, from as early as 500 BC, the status and meaning of Homer were central questions for philosophers. Like the Bible for the Jews, Homer offered the Greeks the foundation of their cultural identity. Such texts, however, can only remain authoritative over centuries of social and conceptual change if they can be brought up to date, so to speak – I mean they must be capable of being given interpretations which suit the circumstances of different epochs.[5] When read literally, Homer was already out of date – physiologically and ethically unacceptable – for the early Ionian thinkers Xenophanes and Heraclitus. It was probably their criticism that evoked the first so-called 'allegorical' defence of Homer. In the fifth century, Metrodorus of Lampsacus (frs. A3–4 DK) 'interpreted the heroes of the *Iliad* as parts of the universe, and the gods as parts of the human body. Agamemnon represented the *aether*, Achilles the sun, Helen the earth, Paris the air, Hector the moon.'[6] Crazy though this kind of allegorising seemed to many in antiquity, Metrodorus was not alone in his style of interpretation. Plato a few decades later (*Theaetetus* 153c) makes Socrates refer ironically to a proposal that the golden chain (with which Zeus challenges the other Olympians to a tug-of-war, *Iliad* VIII.18–27,) is 'nothing else but the sun'.

---

[5] The point is well stated by Henrichs 1968, p. 439.
[6] Cf. Richardson 1975, p. 69. Tatian (Metrodorus fr. A3 DK) describes Metrodorus as 'converting everything to allegory' (πάντα εἰς ἀλληγορίαν μετάγων).

Metrodorus and his like seem to have taken Homer to be a strong allegorist – a poet who was really *au courant* with scientific theories, but who chose to disguise them in a misleading narrative. Why would anyone ‖ suppose that a poet would do such a thing? Plato (*Protagoras* 316d) makes Protagoras say that Homer, Hesiod and Simonides were really sophists – possessors and teachers of practical wisdom – who used poetry as a 'cover' for their real purposes in order to avoid unpopularity. Plato is probably ironical again here, but the kind of explanation he ascribes to Protagoras is essential to anyone who proposes, against the evidence of historical change, that an ancient author actually *intends* to give a contemporary message or a message that differs from the literal sense of his text. The message must be covert, esoteric, allegorical in the strong sense – and yet, somehow or other, open to the expert interpreter to disclose.

Later antiquity reveals many examples of such allegorical readings. One of the most famous is that of the Neoplatonists who interpreted the *Odyssey* as a spiritual journey through the Neo-Platonic universe. Another example is the Jew Philo of Alexandria's interpretation of whole episodes in the Pentateuch, for instance Noah's construction of the Ark, by means of Stoic and Platonic concepts. The author I want to focus on is the Heraclitus (not the famous Ephesian philosopher) who wrote a work called *Homeric problems – Homer's allegories concerning the gods*.[7] Nothing is known about this man's life or background or precisely when he wrote. His work probably dates from the first or second century AD.

Heraclitus announces his purpose very clearly at the beginning of his book. He intends to rescue Homer from the charge that his account of the gods is blasphemous. He states his primary point in his second sentence: 'If Homer was no allegorist, he would be completely impious.'[8] That is to say, if Homer's apparent meaning is his real meaning, his gods are violent, sexually corrupt, the very reverse of moral exemplars. As Heraclitus knows very well, Plato had banned Homer from his ideal state for just this reason. By interpreting Homer as a strong allegorist, Heraclitus sets out to save Homer from Plato's criticism (and also from Epicurean dis-

---

[7] The text has been excellently edited in the Budé series by Buffière 1962.
[8] [Ὅμηρος] πάντα ἠσέβησεν, εἰ μηδὲν ἠλληγόρησεν.

paragement). He proceeds systematically through the epics, book by book, to illustrate Homer's 'allegorisations concerning the gods'. One example will suffice because Heraclitus' methods are monotonously similar. The 'theomachy' – the battle between the gods in *Iliad* XXI – is not to be taken literally; rather, the warring gods are to be ‖ interpreted as natural elements and heavenly bodies: Apollo is the sun, Poseidon is water, Hera is air, etc. What Homer is really talking about in this passage is cosmology.

For Heraclitus, allegory is not an importation by the interpreter; it is not the interpreter's reading of a text, but central to the text's, or rather, to the author's intent. He characterises allegory as 'a trope that consists in saying one thing but meaning something different from what one says' (5.2), or a disjunction between 'what is said' (*legomenon*) and 'what is thought' (*nooumenon*, 5.16). As justification for applying it to Homer, he gives examples from other poets – Archilochus' use of a storm at sea to signify the perils of war, and Anacreon's image of a frisking horse as a way of insulting a girl-friend (5.3–11). These examples, from our point of view, are cheating. They are metaphors, not allegories; or, if you want to say that all metaphors are allegories, then Homer is an allegorist (because he uses metaphors), but not the kind of allegorist Heraclitus needs to prove. However, Heraclitus is not interested in Homer's metaphors, but in his supposedly deliberate treatment of the gods as veiled references to natural phenomena. This is evident, for instance, in the following quotations: 'Homer conceals his philosophical mind', 'the hidden truth in [Homer's] words', and '[Homer] has signified to us the primary elements of nature.'[9] Heraclitus knows there are obvious objections to reading Homer in this way. He defends his position by alleging that philosophers such as Heraclitus, his Ephesian namesake, and Empedocles use allegory, and so there should be nothing surprising if the poet Homer does so too (24.8).

Heraclitus' allegorical reading of Homer can rest there for the present. We now come to the Stoics. Scholars have generally supposed that Heraclitus was a Stoic or that he at least followed Stoic precedent in his allegorisation of Homer.[10] If that were so, and if (as was also supposed), Heraclitus was transmitting a Stoic reading

---

[9] ὑποκρύπτεταί τις Ὁμήρῳ φιλόσοφος νοῦς (26.3); τὴν ὑπολελησμένην ἐν τοῖς ἔπεσιν ἀλήθειαν (6.5); ὑπεσήμηνεν ἡμῖν τὰ πρωτοπαγῆ στοιχεῖα τῆς φύσεως (23.14).

[10] This is particularly evident in the influential study of De Lacy 1948.

of Homer that had been orthodox for centuries, there would be nothing to argue about: the Stoics will have interpreted Homer as a strong allegorist. Why does correctness on this point matter? If the standard theory is correct, the Stoics will have been primarily responsible for authorising the allegorical interpretations of literature that we find in Philo, the Neoplatonists, and others because the Stoics were far and away the most influential philosophers during the ‖ Hellenistic and early Roman period. In that case, we learn something very important concerning both Stoicism and the interpretation of Homer. However, to anyone who respects the Stoics as serious philosophers this finding should be unwelcome. The Stoics were rationalists and they were also empiricists. They don't talk nonsense, and it is frankly nonsensical to suppose that Homer was a crypto-Stoic. In addition, what motivation could the Stoics have for such an enterprise as Heraclitus is engaged in? Why should it matter to them to save Homer's theological credit at the cost of claiming, against all reason, that he is a strong allegorist?[11]

However, if Heraclitus were an orthodox Stoic, that would seem to settle the question. In fact, as Félix Buffière, the latest editor of Heraclitus has carefully argued, there are no good grounds for thinking that Heraclitus was a Stoic.[12] Although he often draws on Stoic physics for the cosmology that his allegories ascribe to Homer, that alone does not make him a Stoic; by this date Stoicism has become a lingua franca for technical writers who are not themselves Stoics. In addition, Heraclitus includes doctrines that are non-Stoic and inconsistent with orthodox Stoicism.[13] Buffière concludes that Heraclitus was not affiliated with any specific

---

[11] No satisfactory answer to this question has been proposed, as Most 1989, pp. 2018–23, recognises in a careful discussion of the 'motivations' of Stoic 'allegoresis'. The favourite answer is that the Stoics wanted Homer's support for their own philosophy. If, however, they had to allegorise Homer in order to make him appropriately Stoic, their procedure was egregiously circular, as Most points out. There is no evidence that the Stoics took Homer to be a philosopher or a Stoic sage. Indeed, Seneca, *Ep.* 88.5, pokes fun at the whole idea of Homer's being a philosopher of any persuasion, including a Stoic. The joke would be in bad taste if the school of his allegiance had allegorised the poet in the way commonly proposed, though Seneca's position is compatible with the Stoics' taking Homer's poetry to be a *philosophēma*, which Strabo (1.2.7) takes to be universally accepted.

[12] Cf. Buffière 1962, pp. xxxi–xxxix. Buffière's detachment of Heraclitus from Stoicism is unknown to or ignored by Hilgruber 1989, who (p. 22) invokes Heraclitus in order to support his claim that Dio Chrysostom's account of Zeno *ad loc.* refers to Zeno's allegorisation of Homer.

[13] E.g., he invokes Plato's tripartite psychology (17.4–18.8) in order to explain various lines in the *Odyssey* and, unlike the Stoics, locates rationality in the head (19.1–19). The

philosophical school, and his arguments seem to me utterly convincing.[14] ||

There is a further crucial point which he does not make. If Heraclitus were simply drawing upon Stoic orthodoxy, his whole essay would be redundant and disingenuous. Because he does not support his approach to Homer by any appeal to the Stoics or, for that matter, to other authorities, the obvious implication is that he takes himself to be doing something not readily accessible in the way the standard theory would have us suppose. We are in no position, then, to infer from the work of Heraclitus that official Stoics interpreted Homer in his manner. He offers no confirmation for the theory that the Stoics took Homer to be a strong allegorist.

Unquestionably, Homer was important to the Stoics. The founding fathers of Stoicism – Zeno, Cleanthes, Chrysippus, none of whom were from mainland Greece – developed a philosophy that would appropriate, as far as possible, traditional Greek culture. Contrast the Athenian Epicurus, who rejected Homer as part of his radical programme to abandon all *paideia* (*Epicurea* 228–9 Usener). The Cypriot *arriviste* Zeno could not have been more different. He wrote five books of *Homeric problems* (D.L. vii.4), perhaps his most extended work on any subject.

Zeno's work on Homer is totally lost. The one thing we can say about it for certain is that he discussed standard philological cruxes, which reminds us that Homeric philology had just become extremely fashionable through the work of scholars in Alexandria.[15] In the case of Chrysippus, some few generations after Zeno,

---

Stoic doctrines that he uses he takes over without acknowledgement, or attributes to 'the greatest philosophers' (22.13; cf. 25.2), citing Stoics only once by name (33.1) for their interpretation of Herakles.

[14] Cf. Buffière 1962, who notes that many of Heraclitus' allegories recall interpretations current before the Stoics – 'Les Stoiciens ne sont donc qu'un des derniers chaînons de la grande chaîne' (p. xxxvii) – and sums up Heraclitus' relation to Stoicism by saying (p. xxxix): 'La teinte de stoicisme qu'il offre par endroits, n'est rien de plus, chez lui, qu'un vernis récent sur un meuble ancien.' Because Buffière accepts the traditional doctrine on Stoic allegoresis, he has no vested interest in detaching Stoicism from Heraclitus. For further study of Heraclitus, cf. Dawson 1992, pp. 38–51.

[15] For the evidence, cf. *SVF* i.275 (Zeno's proposal to emend καὶ Ἐρεμβούς to Ἄραβάς τε, *Od.* iv.84), and *SVF* iii.769–77 (von Arnim's collection of passages documenting Chrysippus' interpretations of Homer). For discussion, cf. Steinmetz 1986, pp. 19–21, 26–7. A recently published papyrus of a commentary dealing with passages from *Odyssey* xi probably includes Chrysippus' name; cf. *Corpus dei papiri filosofici greci e latini* vol. i, 421 (Chrysippus 5T) (Florence, 1989).

there survive eight examples of his work on Homer (cf. n. 15). They are all emendations to the text or grammatical explanations. In none of them does he draw upon doctrinaire Stoicism. He contributes intelligent philology, and the Homeric scholia record this, mentioning his name alongside the famous grammarian Aristarchus. Like all educated Greeks, of course, the Stoics had lines of Homer and other poets in their heads which they could use to make an ethical point and to show that their philosophy accorded with 'the common ‖ conceptions' of people. Although the voluminous writings of Chrysippus have not survived, we possess fragments of them in which some seventy lines of Homer are quoted. In all of these, Chrysippus cites Homer in order to support a Stoic doctrine – for instance the mind's location in the heart – and in all cases he takes Homer literally, not allegorically.[16]

For what reason, then (apart from the misconception concerning Heraclitus), have scholars propagated the belief that the Stoics took Homer to be a strong allegorist? The principal reason is that they have misleadingly focused upon just one text, to the neglect of all evidence that tells a rather different story. I will illustrate the point by reference to Rudolph Pfeiffer in his highly influential *History of Classical Scholarship. From the Beginnings to the End of the Hellenistic Age* (= Pfeiffer 1968).

Pfeiffer (p. 237) writes as follows: 'Orthodox Stoics were necessarily allegorists in their interpretation of poetry.' He does not explain what he means by 'allegorist', though without elucidating the terms he writes of 'genuine allegory' and 'true allegorist'. Pfeiffer justifies his claim about the Stoics with a selective quotation in Latin from Cicero's *De natura deorum* 1.41: [*Chrysippus*] *volt Orphei Musaei Hesiodi Homerique fabellas accommodare ad ea quae ipse ... de deis immortalibus dixerat, ut etiam veterrimi poetae ... Stoici fuisse videantur*. As translated, this says: 'Chrysippus ... wanted to fit the stories of Orpheus, Musaeus, Hesiod and Homer to his own statements about the immortal gods [namely in his first book *On the nature of the gods*] in order that even the most ancient poets ... might seem to have been Stoics.' Pfeiffer leads his readers to sup-

---

[16] The point is made by Steinmetz 1986, p. 27: 'Alle diese Verse werden nicht anders als die Zitate aus den Lyrikern und aus den Tragikern im Wortsinn verstanden. Kein einziger Vers wird in einer irgendwie gearteten Allegorese ausgelegt.'

pose that this is a totally objective remark about the Stoics. But it is not. Actually, it is a piece of anti-Stoic polemic by the Epicurean spokesman in this Ciceronian book, and we know Cicero's source for it. Cicero got the remark from the Epicurean philosopher Philodemus, but Cicero himself has subtly altered the original. What Philodemus said is this: 'Chrysippus just like Cleanthes tries to harmonise the things attributed to Orpheus and Musaeus, and *things* in Homer, Hesiod, Euripides and other poets' with Stoic doctrine.[17] The 'things' in question, as Philodemus ‖ indicates, were divine names and myths *transmitted by the poets*. Philodemus, hostile to Stoicism though he is, does not imply that Chrysippus took Homer and the other poets to be crypto-Stoics or strong allegorists. This is an addition by Cicero on behalf of his Epicurean critic.

Cicero, or his source, also adds to Philodemus a very damning clause which Pfeiffer omits: the full Latin text reads ... 'in order that even the most ancient poets, *who did not even suspect this* (*qui haec ne suspicati quidem sunt*) might seem to have been Stoics'.[18] There, in a nutshell, we have the principal basis for the modern theory about the Stoics' allegorical interpretation of Homer – a text that, in reality, is a Ciceronian distortion of Epicurean polemic.[19]

Still, one may retort, there must be some foundation to the Epicurean criticism. There is, as we shall see, but ancient philosophical polemic did not operate with any rules of fair play. Before taking the Epicurean critique of the Stoics at face value, we should let the Stoics speak for themselves. Cicero himself provides us with one means of doing so in a passage he writes for the Stoic Balbus in book II of his *De natura deorum*. As we shall see, this passage does

---

[17] Philodemus, *Piet.* col. VI (ed. in A. Henrichs, *Cronache Ercolanesi* 4 (1974), 5–32): ἐν δὲ τῷ[ι] δευτέρ[ωι] τὰ εἰς Ὀρφέα [καὶ] Μουσαῖον ἀναφερ[όμ]ενα καὶ τὰ παρ' ['Ο]μήρῳ καὶ Ἡσιόδῳ[ι] καὶ Εὐριπίδη καὶ ποιητα[ῖ]ς ἄλλοις [ὡ]ς καὶ Κλεάνθης [πει]ρᾶται σ[υ]νοικειοῦ[ν] ταῖς δόξ[αι]ς αὐτῶ[ν]. This passage is often overlooked when the Cicero text is cited, and Cicero's divergence from it has never, to the best of my knowledge, been noted.

[18] I read *sunt* rather than *sint*, which would most naturally make the relative clause a comment by Chrysippus. *sunt* is reported as a reading of some MSS by the Loeb editor of Cicero's *De natura deorum*, though it is not recorded in the Teubner edition or that of A. S. Pease *ad loc.*

[19] For other examples of unqualified reliance on Cicero's comment here, cf. Tate 1929, p. 42; Weinstock 1927, p. 137; Steinmetz 1986, p. 27; Hilgruber 1989, p. 19 n. 33; De Lacy 1948, p. 263, actually referring to Cicero, *ND* 1.36.

not sit well with the traditional account of Stoic allegoresis, and it
is generally ignored in discussions of the subject. Before setting it
alongside the Epicurean critique just examined, we need to consider what is unambiguously attested concerning the Stoics' attitude to early Greek poetry.

III

So far as Homer is concerned, the Stoics' interest in his poems was
plainly complex. As I have mentioned, Zeno and Chrysippus contributed to Homeric philology; and we also know that Zeno had
views about the whole || corpus of Homeric poetry since he judged
the *Margites* to be a youthful work by the poet (*SVF* 1.274). But
our central question is the Stoics' approach to early Greek poetry
generically. For if they interpreted Homer allegorically, they also
approached Hesiod in the same way. The question of how, in general, the Stoics interpreted passages in Homer is a question about
what they thought early Greek poetry could contribute to the history of ideas.

Contexts in which we learn about this are not philological or
literary, but theological and cosmological.[20] Like the Epicureans,
the Stoics were much concerned with the anthropology and aeti-
ology of religion. Both schools found elements of truth in traditional Greek religion but saw them as overlaid by superstition and
myth. The Epicureans thought people were right to picture the
gods in human form, but wrong to involve them in the world.
Stoics took the opposite view. They rejected anthropomorphic
gods, but retained a divine presence throughout nature. As theo-
logians and cosmologists, they took on the task of studying Greek
mythology for traces of their own views. This prompted them to
investigate the factors that led people to conceive of gods in the
first place. A doxographical summary shows the role they assigned
to poetry in this study.[21]

The author attributes to the Stoics three 'forms' which have
mediated reverence for the gods:

---

[20] This point is well taken by Most 1989, pp. 2025–6.
[21] Ps.-Plutarch, *De placitis philosophorum* 879c–880d = Aetius, *De placitis* 1.6 = *SVF* II.1009.
   The importance of this neglected testimony was brought to my attention by Wehrli 1928,
   pp. 52–3.

The physical is taught by philosophers, the mythical by poets, and the legislative is constructed by each city.[22] The entire discipline has seven divisions. The first one deals with phenomena and the heavens. People got a conception of god from the sight of the stars; they observed that these are responsible for great harmony, and they noticed the regularity of day and night, winter and summer, risings and settings, and the earth's production of animals and plants. Therefore they took the sky to be a father and the earth a mother ... father because the outflow of waters is the same type of thing as sperms, and mother because of her receiving the waters and giving birth ... To the second and third topic they [the Stoics] distributed gods as ‖ benefactors and agents of harm – as benefactors Zeus, Hera, Hermes, Demeter, and as agents of harm Poinai, Erinyes, Ares ... The fourth and fifth topics they assigned to things and to passions, as passions Eros, Aphrodite, Pothos and as things Hope, Justice, Eunomia. As the sixth topic they included the poets' inventions (τὸ ὑπὸ τῶν ποιητῶν πεπλασμένον). For Hesiod, because he wanted to construct fathers for the generated gods, introduced such progenitors for them as ‘Koios and Krios and Hyperion and Iapetos’ [*Theog.* 134];[23] hence this topic is also called myth. The seventh topic is [here I summarise] apotheosised men who were great benefactors, such as Herakles.

In this sophisticated and perceptive passage, myth and poetry are mentioned as just one of many sources of theological notions. The text does not say that Hesiod – the one poet named – really understood the gods to be different from what he said they were. It simply registers the fabricated character of his account, and his wish to construct divine genealogies.

A much fuller statement of the same topics is to be found in Cicero, *De natura deorum* ii.63–72. After dealing with the apotheosised humans, Cicero's Stoic spokesman Balbus turns to myth and poetry, and he adds a central point omitted by the doxographical text. Stories such as Hesiod tells, for instance the castration of Ouranos by Kronos and the fettering of Kronos by Zeus, are utterly erroneous and stupid. However, that story is actually a fictional and superstitious perversion of an intelligent and correct

---

[22] Dio Chrysostom xii.44 adopts a version of this tripartite division, substituting *emphyton* for *physikon* and then adding a fourth category in order to accommodate the plastic arts.

[23] I translate the received text, Ἡσίοδος γὰρ βουλόμενος τοῖς γενητοῖς θεοῖς πατέρας συστῆσαι εἰσήγαγε τοιούτους αὐτοῖς γεννήτορας, "Κοῖον κτλ." Von Arnim in *SVF* ii.1009 prints θεούς, an emendation of the transmitted text by Diels 1879, p. 296, and also accepted by J. Mau in the Teubner edition of Plutarch, *Moralia* v, fasc. 2 Pars i (Leipzig, 1971), but sense and flow of the Greek are against this. The Titans named are from the first generation of gods, and are sires of gods themselves; cf. Hesiod, *Theogony* 404.

understanding of certain natural phenomena (*physica ratio non inelegans inclusa est in impias fabulas*): that the highest entity, the aether,
does not need genitals in order to procreate, and that Kronos, i.e.
chronos ('time'), is 'regulated and limited'.[24]

Cicero's Stoic spokesman is not interested in saving the veracity
of poets including Homer. He dismisses anthropomorphic gods –
and their involvement in the Trojan war – as absurd (*ND* II.70).
What he ‖ commits himself to is a theory of cultural transmission,
degeneration and modification. At some time in the remote past,
on this view, certain people intuited basic truths about nature.
They expressed these, however, in a symbolical mode that was
easy to misinterpret as independently valid.[25] Hence the emer-
gence of misleading myths. The task of the Stoic interpreter of
religious history is to identify and articulate the correct beliefs that
directly gave rise to such myths but are not evident in their superficial narrative content. Far from suggesting that Homer and
Hesiod were proto-Stoic cosmologists, this passage implies that
the poets propagated misleading myths as if they were truths.

Cicero's Balbus, giving the official Stoic view, does not match
well with the Epicurean account in *De natura deorum* 1.41, the passage on which Pfeiffer and others chiefly rely for their theory about
the Stoics' allegorisation of Homer. Here, in the Stoics' own account, nothing is said about what *Homer or Hesiod themselves meant*.
The Stoics are interested in their poems as *sources* of pre-existing,
pre-philosophical views of the world – what we may call 'true
myths', which in the later poems take on a narrative life of their
own and are thus misunderstood.[26]

The two pieces of evidence I have just analysed give a clear and
coherent account of the Stoics' generic interests in early Greek
poetry. However, they can be supplemented by something else,
which, until recently, had been curiously neglected in the discus-

---

[24] Cicero twice uses *voluerunt* in *ND* II.64 to refer to the meaning intended by those who developed the *physica ratio non inelegans*. He does not imply that this meaning was understood
by those who told the *impias fabulas*.

[25] *Videtisne igitur ut a physicis rebus bene atque utiliter inventis tracta ratio sit ad commenticios et fictos
deos? Quae res genuit falsas opiniones* ...

[26] When referring back to these Stoic activities, the Academic critic of the Stoics (*ND* III.63)
does not refer to their 'allegorisation' of the *poets* but to their pointless efforts 'to ratio-
nalise the mendacious stories and explain the reasons for the names by which each thing
is so called' (*commenticiarum fabularum reddere rationem, vocabulorum cur quidque ita appellatum sit
causas explicare*).

sion of this whole topic.[27] From the first century AD there survives
an entire book by the Stoic philosopher Cornutus, entitled *Compendium* [Ἐπιδρομή] *of the tradition of Greek theology*. Cornutus wrote this
work, as he remarks, for young students. His topic is the transmitted names, epithets, cults and myths pertaining to particular
divinities. He draws on poetry, especially Hesiod's, simply because
poetry is a primary vehicle for the transmission of theology.

Cornutus has a methodology for analysing his data. It is not
allegory ‖ (to which he never refers) but etymology. He assumes
(as the earliest Stoics had also assumed) that the Greek gods have
the names and epithets that they do – 'earth-shaking Poseidon',
etc. – because in their original usage these names represented the
way people understood the world. Etymology, that is, analysis of
the original meaning of names, enables the Stoic philosopher to
recover the beliefs about the world held by those who first gave
the gods their present names. From our modern perspective, Stoic
etymologies often seem fantastic. From the same perspective, we
have to say that the Stoics were far too bold in relying on etymology as they did and in presuming a coincidence between the original meaning of divine names and aspects of their own philosophy
of nature. More on this point later. What I want to emphasise now
is that etymology is not the same as allegory, although allegories
may make use of etymology. Etymology offers explanations of
single names and phrases – atomic units of language as it were.
But to have allegory, it seems, we need a whole story, a narrative
– Pandora's box, The Garden of Eden, etc.[28] Only rarely does
Cornutus offer an interpretation of any extended episodes in early
Greek poetry. He is an etymologist, not an allegorist.[29]

Cornutus' etymologies are based upon the same cultural assumption that we found just now in Cicero. Greek poetry is not the
bottom line for recovering primitive beliefs about the gods and

---

[27] Cf. Most 1989, whose work has ensured that Cornutus will not be neglected in future.
Although Most endorses the notion of Stoic 'allegoresis', what he understands by this
seems to be largely compatible with the thesis of this paper. Most's and my own findings
concerning Cornutus have been usefully supplemented by Dawson 1992, pp. 24–38.

[28] The points I have just made are well developed by Dawson 1992, pp. 3–7, 42–3.

[29] Contrasting Cornutus' methodology with Heraclitus', Buffière 1962, p. xxxi, notes: 'Cornutus ne s'attarde guère aux allégories proprement dites et ne se limite point aux don-
nées d'Homère, pour les dieux qu' il étudie.' An interesting feature of Cornutus' etymological analysis is his frequent mention of and refusal to choose between alternative
etymologies; cf. Most 1989, pp. 2027–8.

cosmology. Behind the earliest Greek poetry, and distortedly present in it, are ways of understanding the world whose basic correctness the Stoic interpreter, through etymology, can reveal. Cornutus' principal source is Hesiod, and he also refers to Homer a number of times. Fortunately for our purposes he is explicit about his approach to poetic texts and his methodology. In section 17 (Lang) Cornutus begins by noting the number and variety of myths generated among the ancient Greeks and other peoples. As an example he takes two stories from Homer: Zeus's suspending Hera by the golden chain (*Iliad* xv.18–24), and Thetis' support of Zeus against rebellion of the other Olympians (*Iliad* 1.396–406). Of the first of these he writes: 'The poet seems to cite [or, possibly, pervert, *parapherein*] this fragment of an ancient myth, according to which Zeus was fabled to have suspended Hera from the sky with golden chains, since the stars have a golden appearance, and to have ‖ attached two anvils to her feet, i.e., evidently earth and sea, by means of which the air is stretched down and cannot be removed from either of them.' Cornutus bases his interpretation on the traditional etymology of *aēr*, 'air', as Hera.[30]

Cornutus then adduces the second myth, that of Thetis, and says: 'Clearly each of these gods was privately plotting against Zeus continuously, intending to prevent the world's origin. And that would have happened if the moist had prevailed and everything had become wet, or if fire had prevailed and everything had become fiery, or if air had prevailed. But Thetis, who disposes everything properly, positioned the hundred-handed Briareus against the gods mentioned – Briareus, who perhaps controls all exhalations from the earth.' For this interpretation Cornutus relies on etymologies of the names Thetis (*tithēmi*) and Briareus (*bora* and *airein*). Thus he finds germs of Stoic cosmogony in Homer's story, but he does not suggest that Homer himself did so.[31]

---

[30] Cosmological readings of this passage are ancient. For the view that they may go back to the time of Anaximenes, cf. Buffière 1956, pp. 115–17. Socrates cites a version in Plato, *Tht.* 153c, and the etymology of Hera as *aēr* is found in *Crat.* 404c. Heraclitus (40) elaborates the interpretation along the same lines as Cornutus but conjoins it (41.1) with an allegorisation of Hera's oath (*Il.* xv.36–7), where he also locates the four elements: thus he thinks himself entitled to say: 'Homer continuously allegorises them' (41.12).

[31] Heraclitus (25) explains this story as an allusion to the eventual destruction of the world by deluge or conflagration, which are, of course, Stoic ideas.

Immediately following this passage, Cornutus gives the following instruction: 'One should not conflate myths, nor should one
transfer names from one to another; and even if something has
been added to the transmitted genealogies by people who do not
understand what the myths hint at (*ainittontai*) but who handle them
as they handle narrative fictions, one should not regard them as
irrational.'[32] Cornutus is addressing would-be students of the history of religion. Not unlike a modern ethnographer or cultural
anthropologist, he warns against tampering with the recorded data.
He recognises that the data, as transmitted, may distort the original beliefs which he takes to underlie existing ‖ myths, but the
problems of transmission are not sufficient to rule out recovery of
the myths' original rationale. In the next part of this section, he
turns to Hesiod's 'mythical' cosmogony, and interprets its details
in terms of Stoic physics. He concludes with these remarks: 'I could
give you a more complete interpretation of Hesiod's [genealogy].
He got some parts of it, I think, from his predecessors, and added
other parts in a more mythical manner, which is the way most of
the ancient theology was corrupted.'[33] Reading this passage in the
light of Cornutus' previous instructions, we can see that Hesiod is
one of the people who made inappropriate additions through his
failure to see the theological physics implicit in his inherited material. For Cornutus neither Homer nor Hesiod is a crypto-Stoic.
Both are the transmitters of myths.

In his interpretation of those myths. Cornutus intends to elucidate neither the scientific acumen of Homer and Hesiod nor their
poetic intentions. He is interested in what we might call proto-
myth, myth detached from narrative context in a poem, myth as
interpretable evidence of pristine cosmological beliefs. At the
end of his book, he tells its young addressee to realise that 'the
ancients were not nobodies but competent students of the world,

[32] Cornutus 27.19 Lang: δεῖ δὲ μὴ συγχεῖν τοὺς μύθους μηδ' ἐξ ἑτέρου τὰ ὀνόματα ἐφ'
ἕτερον μεταφέρειν μηδ' εἴ τι προσεπλάσθη ταῖς παραδεδομέναις κατ' αὐτοὺς γενεαλο-
γίαις ὑπὸ τῶν μὴ συνιέντων ἃ αἰνίττονται, κεχρημένων δ' αὐτοῖς ὡς καὶ τοῖς πλάσ-
μασιν, †ἀλόγως† τίθεσθαι. Tom Rosenmeyer has convinced me that the sense requires
ἀλόγους (referring to μύθους) and I translate the text accordingly. Cornutus, as he noted
in written comments he gave me, is 'talking about methods of looking at myth, not about
the mentality of the one who looks at the myth'.
[33] I give the Greek of the concluding parts of this translation, Cornutus 31.14–17: Lang: τὰ
μέν τινα, ὡς οἶμαι, παρὰ τῶν ἀρχαιοτέρων αὐτοῦ παρειληφότος, τὰ δὲ μυθικώτερον
ἀφ' αὐτοῦ προσθέντος, ᾧ τρόπῳ καὶ πλεῖστα τῆς παλαιᾶς θεολογίας διεφθάρη.

and well equipped to philosophise about it via symbols and riddles' (Cornutus 76, 2–5 Lang).[34] Does Cornutus take the wise ancients to have been deliberate allegorists – practitioners of indirection – and to be identical with the early Greek poets? Surely not. He is saying that proto-myth, in the sense just explained, is the form in which the ancients expressed their serious thoughts about the world. The Stoic exegete seeks to recover these by removing the veneers created by poetic fictions and superstitions.

The evidence of Cornutus, an official Stoic, tells decisively against the ‖ evidence of Heraclitus, a contemporary perhaps but a dubious Stoic at best. Thus far we have found no shred of evidence from unimpeachable Stoic sources to suggest that Stoics in general interpreted Homer allegorically or took Homer himself to be an allegorist. They had many interests in Homer; in so far as they asked themselves what cosmological truths he expressed, they took themselves to be interpreting pre-Homeric myths within the poem, not the poem's narrative content or Homer's own knowledge or purposes.[35]

At this point, however, an obvious question arises. It may seem that my account of the Stoics' interpretative interests in Homer and Hesiod has merely pushed matters one stage further back. The new theory saves the Stoics from taking Homer to be a crypto-Stoic, but it does so at the cost of positing crypto-Stoics prior to Homer – the original enlightened ancients whose names for the

---

[34] Cornutus 76.2–5 Lang: οὐχ οἱ τυχόντες ἐγένοντο οἱ παλαιοί, ἀλλὰ καὶ συνιέναι τὴν τοῦ κόσμου φύσιν ἱκανοὶ καὶ πρὸς τὸ διὰ συμβόλων καὶ αἰνιγμάτων φιλοσοφῆσαι περὶ αὐτῆς εὐεπίφοροι. It is not necessary to take Cornutus' words to endorse Posidonius' controversial position on the existence of full-fledged philosophers in the Golden Age (Seneca, *Ep.* 90.4ff.). For discussion of Stoic views on cultural history, cf. Most 1989, pp. 2020–3, and Frede 1989, p. 2088. Strabo (x.3.23) makes a similar point to Cornutus, but he also emphasises the difficulty of extracting primary theological truths from mythical material that is not internally consistent. The passage is mentioned by Lamberton 1986, p. 26.

[35] The thesis I am advancing has affinities with the positions of both Steinmetz 1986 and Most 1989, though I differ from both of them in my view of the Stoics' attention to myth rather than poetry. Most (pp. 2023–6) criticizes Steinmetz for attacking a straw-man, 'allegorical interpretation of poetry as poetry'; but Steinmetz has good reason to do this within the context of the traditional theory, since it enables him to shift the focus of the Stoics' interests to the myths incorporated by the poets. However, Steinmetz continues to think (see p. 23 of his article), incorrectly I believe, that the Stoics took themselves to be uncovering via etymology the poet's meaning. Most, though he writes of the Stoics' allegoresis of poetry, comes close to my position when he notes (p. 2026 n. 80): 'The figures of mythology ultimately have an explanation in terms of physical allegoresis which is their ἀλήθεια; but in many details this has been misunderstood, presumably already by the poets themselves, and the result is the δόξα of superstition.'

gods display their correct understanding of nature. That challenge demands an answer and I will give it at the end of the paper. For the present, I want to leave it in abeyance because some further evidence requires consideration.

IV

So far, my case against the standard theory of the Stoics as allegorists of poetic meaning has largely rested on the following points: rejection of Heraclitus as an official Stoic, rejection of the polemical evidence of the Epicurean in Cicero, and reliance on the three witnesses who explain the Stoics' interest in the myths expressed in poetry. This material is all relatively late within the history of Stoicism. What reason do we have for thinking that it correctly represents the views of the earliest Stoics, the founders of the school? Is it not possible that they, or some of them, were ‖ allegorists as the standard doctrine proposes, and that it is the anonymous doxographer, Cicero's Stoic spokesman and Cornutus who are aberrant?[36] I cannot decisively disprove this suggestion because what we know of Zeno, Cleanthes and Chrysippus on this matter is so fragmentary, but the evidence we have seems to offer nothing unambiguously in its favour.

First Chrysippus. It was he, above all, who represented orthodoxy for later Stoicism. As I have already said, his eight recorded contributions to Homeric exegesis are all philological. I also pointed out that in all cases where he cites Homer in support of a doctrine he takes Homer's text at its surface or literal meaning. The only cosmological allegory he is known to have advanced concerns not a text but a painting. There was a famous and obscene painting at Argos which showed Hera fellating Zeus (*SVF* II.1071–4). Chrysippus explained this (Do we know he was utterly serious in doing

---

[36] This is the view of Tate 1929, but only so far as Cornutus is concerned since Tate overlooks Cicero, *ND* II.63–72. Tate claims that earlier Stoics believed ‘Homer and Hesiod to have been original thinkers, who expressed sound doctrine in the mythical style proper to the primitive times in which they lived’. The evidence he cites to support this is our old favourite, Cicero, *ND* I.41, and other indirect testimonies – Strabo I.1.10, 1.2.9, Dio Chrysost. LV.9ff., and Heraclitus. Yet Cornutus himself, apart from his coherence with the other Stoic evidence discussed above, says that his book is only a summary of works by earlier philosophers (Cornutus 76.6–8 Lang).

so?) as an interaction between the two Stoic principles, Zeus/god and Hera/matter. Interestingly enough, this interpretation does not invoke the standard Stoic etymology, Hera/*aēr*.

When it was a question of choosing between interpretations of a myth, Chrysippus was skilful at exploiting the literal sense of a passage. He wanted to show that Hesiod's account of Athena's birth from the head of Zeus does not contradict the Stoic doctrine of the heart as the mind's centre.[37] 'Some people', he says, 'take this story to be a symbol of the mind's location in the head'; but they fail to attend properly to Hesiod's text. Chrysippus notes that Hesiod gives two versions of Athena's birth and that a common feature of both is Zeus's swallowing of Metis.[38] So Athena is generated from Metis, present in the belly of Zeus, and not *simpliciter* from the head of Zeus. Therefore, the myth in Hesiod confirms Chrysippus' view on the central location of the mind. This piece of exegesis ‖ may be over-ingenious, but it approaches the text in ways that are scrupulous, closely argued and even, perhaps, ironical.

Galen characterises Chrysippus' practice here in language that modern scholars conventionally call allegorising.[39] But Galen has correctly seen that what interests Chrysippus is the interpretation of a myth, and *interpretation* is a much better term than *allegorisation* for what Chrysippus is doing. Chrysippus does not take himself to be identifying a gap between surface meaning and hidden meaning. His interpretation demythologises Hesiod but it does so in ways that retain the obvious link in the text between Metis as goddess and *mētis* as a word signifying 'intelligence.'

Next Zeno. In his fifty-third oration, 'On Homer', Dio Chrysostom speaks briefly about Zeno's judgement of the poet. Dio's context is this: most philosophers and grammarians are unequivocal in their admiration of Homer. Plato, however, while sensitive to Homer's charm, criticises the poet severely for his myths and statements about the gods. This is not an easy matter to assess. Did Homer err, or did he merely 'transmit certain physical doc-

---

[37] Galen, *De plac. Hipp. et Plat.* III.8.1–28 = *SVF* II.908–9.
[38] Chrysippus' text of the *Theogony* included lines that modern scholars excise; cf. fr. 343 Merkelbach–West.
[39] Cf. *De plac. Hipp.et Plat.* III.8.34 on Chrysippus' concern to explain the *hyponoiai* of myths.

trines present in the myths according to the custom of his time'?[40]
Dio seems to allude to the Stoic theory of cultural transmission,
and not to Heraclitus' treatment of Homer as an allegorist. He
then observes that Zeno wrote on both Homeric poems, and found
nothing to criticise in them. Zeno's object, according to Dio, was
to save Homer from the charge of self-contradiction. He did this
by showing in detail that Homer wrote 'some things in accordance
with opinion (*doxa*) and other things in accordance with truth
(*alētheia*)'.[41] Dio then notes that Antisthenes anticipated Zeno in
this approach to Homer. It was Zeno, however, and others including Zeno's follower Persaeus, who expounded Homer in this way,
point by point. Unfortunately Dio gives no example of Zeno's
procedure. We are left to infer what apparent inconsistencies he
sought to remove and how he did so. ‖

Given Dio's context, the inconsistencies should above all include
apparently incongruent statements in Homer about the gods. If
Zeno harmonised these by distinguishing 'opinions' from 'truths',
he presumably wanted to show that Homer's treatment of the
gods is epistemologically complex, containing both identifiable
truths and identifiable fables or falsehoods. Coherence would be
established by distinguishing these two modes of discourse, and by
appropriately assigning passages to (false) opinion or to truth.
There is good reason to attribute this procedure to Antisthenes.
He distinguished, as the Stoics later did, between the many gods
of popular religion and a single divinity in nature (Cicero, *ND*
1.32). Ethically impeccable passages in Homer about the gods collectively or about Zeus in particular could seem to justify the
application of this distinction to the poet.

There is no good evidence that Antisthenes offered physicalist
allegories of the Homeric gods in the manner of Metrodorus of
Lampsacus.[42] His well-known interest in the figures of Odysseus,
Ajax and Herakles was ethical. Is allegory implied by or consonant
with Zeno's use of the distinction between truth and opinion?

---

[40] Dio Chrysostom LIII.3: πότερον Ὅμηρος ἥμαρτε περὶ ταῦτα ἢ φυσικοὺς ἐνόντας ἐν τοῖς μύθοις λόγους κατὰ τὴν τότε συνήθειαν παρεδίδου τοῖς ἀνθρώποις. Cf. Cicero, *ND* II.64, *physica ratio non inelegans inclusa est in impias fabulas.*
[41] Dio Chrysostom LIII.4 (*SVF* I.274): ὁ δὲ Ζήνων οὐδὲν τῶν Ὁμήρου ψέγει, ἅμα διηγούμε-νος καὶ διδάσκων ὅτι τὰ μὲν κατὰ δόξαν, τὰ δὲ κατὰ ἀλήθειαν γέγραφεν, ὅπως μὴ φαίνηται αὐτὸς αὐτῷ μαχόμενος ἔν τισι δοκοῦσιν ἐναντίως εἰρῆσθαι.
[42] Cf. Wehrli 1928, pp. 65ff.; Richardson 1975, pp. 77–81; Hilgruber 1989, pp. 15–18.

Many have thought so,[43] but there are strong reasons for doubt. Fritz Wehrli states the obvious objection: 'It is false to take this as evidence for allegory since allegory creates truth out of everything mythical.'[44] His point is that Antisthenes and Zeno would not have distinguished between Homer's true and opining statements if they had taken the opining ones to express covert truths.

Peter Steinmetz goes a step further than Wehrli: 'It is unclear how physico-cosmological allegory or psychological-ethical allegory could help in resolving inconsistencies between two Homeric passages.'[45] Steinmetz interprets Zeno's concern as philological. On this view, Zeno was primarily interested in close textual analysis of Homer – in resolving apparent inconsistencies such as the description of Ithaca as 'low' and 'very high' in adjacent words (*Odyssey* IX.25).

It is highly likely that Zeno's five books of *Homeric problems* did address such points. We have no evidence that this work included allegorisation, and Steinmetz could have helped himself to an additional point. Cicero ‖ tells us, on Stoic authority, that the separation of proto-science from legend and superstition was treated more fully by Cleanthes and Chrysippus than by Zeno (*ND* II.63). It can hardly, then, have formed a major part of his *Homeric problems*. However, Steinmetz's strictly philological reading of Dio's testimony will not do. That interpretation does not fit Zeno's distinction between 'truth' and 'opinion', nor does it chime with Dio's theological context.

The most obvious point was made by J. Tate in an article written sixty years ago: the distinction between 'truth' and 'opinion' or fiction was a commonplace in the interpretation of Homer.[46] Strabo uses it (1.2 etc.) to save Homer's credit as a geographer

---

[43] Cf. Hilgruber 1989, who is the latest to take Dio's text to refer to Zeno's allegorising, but in my opinion he fails to overturn the arguments of Tate (cf. n. 46 below). He adduces no new evidence for the thesis, and saddles himself with a view of the passage which makes Zeno, but not Antisthenes, an allegorist of Homer.

[44] Cf. Wehrli 1928, p. 65.

[45] Steinmetz 1986, p. 20.

[46] Cf. Tate 1930, pp. 7–10, whose view is summed up in these remarks of his *ad loc.*: 'As spokesman for the multitude [Homer] may contradict the truths he knew and expressed elsewhere. But this contradiction is only apparent, for in this case it is not Homer who is wrong but the multitude whose views he is expressing.' Diogenianus criticises Chrysippus for his selective quotations from Homer, which obscure the fact that Homer does not consistently support Chrysippus' doctrine that everything is fated; cf. the citation of Diogenianus by Eusebius, *Praep. evang.* VI.8.1–7.

against Eratosthenes' opinion that the poet is entirely concerned with fiction. According to Strabo, Homer regularly combines truth and falsehood (1.2.7–9; 1.2.19, etc.). In addition, the poet sometimes overlays truths with a mythical covering to flavour his style and enchant his audience. Strabo is confident, too confident, that he can remove Homer's mythical accretions and exhibit the kernel of his factual knowledge. He treats Homer as fully in control of his (Strabo's) distinction between truth and falsehood; perhaps Zeno did so too. However, Strabo does not maintain, as Heraclitus does, that Homer's myths are regularly reducible to covert truths.[47]

Another author who can illuminate Zeno's approach to Homer is Plutarch. In his essay *On how to study poetry*, Plutarch rejects astrological and cosmological allegory as the way to clear Homer from the charge of representing the gods immorally (19e–20a). In this context he is clearly talking about the likes of Heraclitus, but he does not name the Stoics. For Plutarch one correct response to this charge is to recognise that Homer includes 'healthy and true theological doctrines' and others 'that have been fabricated to excite people' (20f). Setting the former against the latter enables the poet's own voice to be distinguished. This comes as close as possible to the simplest interpretation of Zeno's distinction between 'truth' and 'opinion'.

A second recommendation of Plutarch is also relevant to the Stoics' ‖ procedures. He emphasises the importance of recognising how poets use the names of the gods (23a). Sometimes a divine name is to be taken as a direct reference to the god himself. Frequently, however, poets use the names of gods, by metonymy, to refer to impersonal states of affairs – for instance, Zeus to denote fate or fortune, Ares to signify war, Hephaestus to signify fire. Plutarch does not call this allegory, and nor would I. The second kind of usage does not invoke a hidden meaning. It is a transparent application of names, and one that belongs to the Greek language from its recorded beginnings. Plutarch offers it as a way of 'correcting' most of the seemingly out-of-place statements made in Homer about Zeus (24a).

Plutarch may have drawn heavily on Stoicism in his writing of this essay. However that may be, Zeno could certainly have availed himself of Plutarch's two procedures in his process of removing

---

[47] For a well-balanced account of Strabo's treatment of Homer, cf. Schenkeveld 1976.

apparent inconsistencies from Homer. Unlike allegory, these procedures clearly fit his distinction between truth and opinion, and
both are set by Plutarch within a theological context, as Dio's
citation of Zeno requires.

Before leaving Plutarch, a further word on his approach to
Homer is in order. He has no time for allegorical euhemerism, as
we have seen. Yet, as far as I know, Plutarch never launches any
attack on allegorical interpretation of poetry by the Stoics.[48] Since
his knowledge of Stoicism was second to none, and since he uses
every opportunity to make fun of Stoic extravagances, his silence
on this point should embarrass proponents of the standard theory
about the Stoics, represented by Pfeiffer, as 'necessarily allegorists
in their interpretation of poetry'.

V

However Zeno read Homer, he certainly sought to demythologise
Hesiod by means of etymology.[49] What survives of Zeno's work
on the *Theogony* has close affinities with Cornutus. Zeno interpreted Hesiod's *chaos* as 'primal water', deriving the word from
chysis or *cheesthai* (*SVF* 1.103–4), meaning 'pouring'. He identified
four of Hesiod's Titans (children of Earth and Heaven) with cosmic powers, justifying this by etymology, ‖ and treated the names
of the Cyclopes similarly (*SVF* 1.100, 118). Above all, he set a pattern for later Stoics in explaining the names of the Olympians as
primary allusions to the physical elements – Hera/air, Zeus/aether,
Hephaestus/fire, etc. Like Cornutus, Zeno seems to have focused
on divine names and epithets rather than the extended episodes of
the poem.

It seems quite credible that Zeno applied this approach to
Hesiod, as he is said to have done (Cicero, *ND* 1.36), but not to
Homer.[50] Unlike Homer, Hesiod has an explicit cosmogony. His
divine genealogies include many items that we today would call
abstract powers or that have a straightforward reference to physical phenomena. His narratives are much simpler than Homer's.

---

[48] Plutarch does complain (*De aud.* 31e) about the 'childishness' or 'irony' Cleanthes exhibits
  in his physicalist etymology of *ana Dōdōnaie* (see main text below). Immediately after, he
  criticises Chrysippus for an implausible, but not physicalist, etymology of *Kronidēs*.
[49] Cf. Steinmetz 1986, pp. 21–3.
[50] Steinmetz makes this point, loc cit.

The whole tenor of his work is descriptive rather than dramatic. As modern studies of myth and the beginnings of philosophy have shown, Hesiod lends himself to treatment as a pioneer in speculative thought.

Homer was more hallowed and more complex. He had been interpreted allegorically long before the Stoics, but not with results that any major thinker took seriously. For Cornutus' theology Hesiod is far more significant than Homer. Cornutus does show, however, that Stoicism by his time was accommodating some cosmological interpretations of episodes in the *Iliad*. Steinmetz is probably right to give Cleanthes the credit or discredit for adumbrating these.[51] In Cleanthes' case, unlike that of Zeno, we have clear evidence of reading isolated words in Homer through Stoic eyes. Cleanthes derived *ana Dōdōnaie*, 'O lord of Dodona', an invocation of Zeus in the *Iliad*, from *anadidōmi*, and related this to the Stoic doctrine of air vaporising from the earth (*SVF* 1.535). He wanted to make Atlas' epithet in *Odyssey* 1.52 *holoophrōn*, 'mindful of everything', instead of 'malevolent', *oloophrōn*, in order to indicate Atlas' providential concern for the world (*SVF* 1.549). And he interpreted the mysterious plant *mōly* (*Od.* x.305) as signifying 'reason', deriving it from the verb *mōlyesthai*, 'to relax' (*SVF* 1.526).[52] Thus he could explain ‖ why *mōly* protected Odysseus from the passions that Circe exploited in his followers.

This is not allegory, as Heraclitus uses it, but etymology. For Heraclitus it is crucial that Homer means something different from what he says – that he intends his stories to be taken not literally but as *covert* references to natural phenomena. No such assumption is required by Zeno or Cleanthes. Their explanations of divine names are based upon etymologies whose validity is quite independent of anything Homer or Hesiod may have thought. For all we know, Cleanthes may have supposed that Homer wrote *oloophronos*. His emendation could have aimed at restoring a truth not evident to Homer but familiar to Homer's wiser predecessors.

---

[51] Cf. Steinmetz 1986, pp. 23–5.
[52] According to Apollonius Sophistes, the source of this evidence, 'Cleanthes says that reason (*logos*) is signified allegorically (*allēgorikōs*).' The absence of any official Stoic account of 'allegory' makes it likely that this is a scholiast's report of Cleanthes rather than his own verbatim statement. In any case, as I have tried to emphasise throughout, the important point is not the ancient terminology applied to Stoic interpretations but whether they should be termed *allegorical* from our perspective. Sometimes *allēgoreō* is simply synonymous with *hermēneuō*; cf. Metrodorus fr. 6 DK with Plutarch, *De Iside* 363d.

VI

The lines between poetry and myth and between poetic meaning and mythological interpretation are fine ones to draw. It would be a mistake to presume that the Stoics never overstepped them or that they always tried to keep them apart. None the less it does appear that we have failed to distinguish between the Stoics' interest in myth and their understanding of literature. They were well aware that poets combine truth *and* fiction at the surface level of meaning. As students of Hesiod, they will have known *Theogony* 27–8 where the poet himself seems to alert his audience to the fact that he is about to recite just such a combination. What passes under the name of Stoic allegorising is the Stoic interpretation of myth. The Stoics seem to have recognised that *myths are allegories*, stories told in order to explain problematic features of the physical world. They thought that elucidation of these myths could help to confirm their own understanding of nature. Interpretation of the meaning and composition of Homer or Hesiod *per se* was not their concern. As even the hostile Philodemus says (*Piet.*, col. vi), 'It was *things in* Homer and Hesiod' that Chrysippus tried to harmonise with Stoic doctrines. The things in question were divine names and myths transmitted by the poets, and not the poets' own use of these. By taking the latter to have been the Stoics' concern, we have come to believe that they advertised Homer and other early poets as proto-Stoics.

The evidence I have reviewed – drawn from Stoics and not their detractors – tells decisively against the pertinence of this assessment. Some Stoics, though perhaps not Zeno, used Homer among other poets as a ‖ source of myth pertaining to cosmology. They did this as students of natural theology, believing, most reasonably, that divine names and epithets and myths *are* serious evidence of how early people interpreted the world. They assumed, less reasonably, that etymology is the best device for recovering the beliefs of the primary users of names, and that etymology could line up those beliefs with some of their own views on nature. They had enough confidence in their own cosmology and human rationality to presume that many of their own findings were not original; this was naive perhaps, but it is an approach that should appeal to cultural historians and anthropologists. In all of this, the Stoics treated early Greek poetry as ethnographical material and not as literature in, say, an Aristotelian sense.

So – to conclude – has my revision of the standard theory merely pushed the problem one stage further back, so that instead of Homer and Hesiod being crypto-Stoics that role is now being played by the anonymous myth-makers who preceded them? I think not. For one thing, on my explanation, the ancient sages are not crypto-Stoics. They are not deliberately concealing truths about nature in misleading myths. Myth, in the theory I am offering, *is* the early people's mode of interpreting the world. Secondly, up to quite a large point, the Stoics were right about this. Many Greek myths *are* cosmological – ways of ordering the physical world. To have had the insight to see this is greatly to the Stoics' credit, and gives them a very different theory from the standard one that Homer's epic narrative is a Stoic cosmology in disguise. Many anthropologists take allegory to be central to a myth's mode of signification. The Stoics clearly had an inkling of this. They did not make the mistake of supposing that a myth's meaning is identical either to its function in a larger story (the personification of concepts) or to a secret message inscribed by the storyteller.

Allegory, so we are often told today, covers everything written. All texts are codes, no meaning is objective or stable, authorial intentions do not count, what *we* find in a text *is* what the text says. Although this modern fashion might seem to suit the Stoics, they should firmly reject it. Their hermeneutic is fundamentally historicist. That is why it depends on etymology, the search for original meanings. Independently of the Stoics the idea had developed that Homer was his own allegorist; the task of the exegete then became one of demonstrating Homer's knowledge of philosophical truths.[53] This is the position of Heraclitus, and it is also ‖ evident in that curious work, attributed to Plutarch, *On the life and poetry of Homer*.[54] Once Homer was his own allegorist, he could

---

[53] This practice seems to be well under way by the end of the fifth century, on the evidence of Metrodorus of Lampsacus, and it can also be observed in the Derveni papyrus, whose author takes Orpheus to have had access to truths about the world which he then clothed in enigmas: cf. Rusten 1985, pp. 121–40. In comments on the original draft of this paper, which he kindly sent me, Denis Feeney wrote: 'If it was possible in the fifth century to talk of Homer as someone who expressed truth in veiled ways, then the Stoics' later discretion in using him only as a source for early belief is even more striking.' I agree. But, apart from the arguments I have advanced, it would be quite unlike their philosophy in general if they had simply appropriated an earlier, but highly contentious, approach to Homer. What I am proposing has much in common with Aristotle's view of mythically clothed truths about astronomy (see especially *Metaphysics* XII 1074b1), but a comparison with Aristotle is too large a subject to be pursued here.

be turned into any philosopher one liked, as he is by pseudo-Plutarch. The scene was set for Neoplatonist allegorical readings.

The contribution of Stoicism to this was partly substantive but also accidental and indirect. It was substantive because the Stoics had shown how to give cosmological readings to certain myths by etymologising the names of their divine agents. Their philosophy of nature is a strong presence in Heraclitus. But an element of accident is also evident there. Stoicism simply was the most powerful philosophy at that time. If Heraclitus was to use philosophy as the way of exonerating Homer, he had to turn to the Stoics. *Mutatis mutandis*, the same holds for Philo's allegorical readings of Scripture. These do not make him a Stoic. The Stoic contribution is indirect for the reason I have emphasised throughout this chapter – the shift from interpreting the earliest poets' myths as sources for archaic beliefs to interpreting Homer as an allegorist.

---

[54] Until recently the most accessible edition of this work was the Teubner edited by G. N. Bernardakis (*Plutarchus Moralia VII* (1896), which contains the Plutarchan spuria). Now, however, this has been superseded by J. F. Kindstrand's new Teubner (*[Plutarchus] De Homero*). The author of *On the life and poetry of Homer* sees no difficulty in making Homer the source of contradictory doctrines, for instance Stoic *apatheia* and Peripatetic *metriopatheia* (cf. sections 134–5), and the inspiration of all the most famous philosophers. Thus he entirely fits Seneca's sarcastic critique (cf. n. 11 above).

CHAPTER 4

Dialectic and the Stoic sage

Most of the leading Stoic philosophers, from Zeno onward, divided their philosophy into three parts, logic, ethics and physics.[1] The logical part was commonly divided into two 'sciences', rhetoric and dialectic (D.L. VII.41). Matters that modern logicians would recognize as their field were included in the study of dialectic, but this subject also covered epistemology, grammar, and even, in some treatments, literary style. In the fully developed Stoic system, dialectic was the general science of rational discourse and of language, while rhetoric dealt with the organization and construction of arguments for political, forensic, and panegyric speeches (D.L. VII.42–3).

Modern logicians have largely confined their attention to that part of Stoic dialectic which corresponds to the more formal aspects of contemporary logic.[2] This is perfectly legitimate, provided that the artificiality of the restriction is acknowledged: the Stoics' treatment of modality and their analysis of propositions and methods of inference have a permanent philosophical interest, which does not apply to some of their other work in dialectic. But for the understanding of Stoicism, throughout its history, it is worthwhile to ask how they conceived of dialectic in general, where they stood in relation to other ancient philosophers, what ‖ value they attributed to it, and why, in particular, they held that 'only the wise man is a dialectician'. My purpose in this chapter is to offer some of the answers to these questions.[3]

---

[1] D.L.VII.39. This division of philosophy and the use of the term 'logic' probably go back to the Academy under Xenocrates, cf. Frede 1974, pp. 24–5.

[2] So Frede 1974, Mates 1961 and Kneale 1962.

[3] Several recent studies have touched on these topics in emphasising the close relationship between aspects of Stoic logic and the Stoic system as a whole: Watson 1966; Kahn 1969; Lloyd 1971; Long 1971b and 1986a, pp. 121–47.

THE STOIC CONCEPTION OF DIALECTIC

At the beginning of his commentary on Aristotle's *Topics*, Alexander of Aphrodisias notes the value of realising that the term *dialectic* does not have the same meaning for all philosophers: 'the Stoics define dialectic as *science of speaking well*, and make speaking well consist in speaking things that are true and fitting'. He then observes that the Stoics 'give this meaning to dialectic because they regard it as a property peculiar to the philosopher of the most perfect philosophy; and for this reason, in their view, only the wise man is a dialectician' (p. 1, 8 Wallies = *SVF* II.124). Alexander was writing at about the end of the second century AD when Stoicism was in decline. Five centuries earlier, at the origin of the Stoa, it was all the more pertinent to distinguish different senses of dialectic. The period of 300 BC was a time of great variety, vitality and rivalry in Greek philosophy. At Athens, Academics, Peripatetics, Cynics, Megarians and the newly founded schools of Zeno and Epicurus were competing for followers, and they differed from one another in their conceptions of dialectic and in their attitudes toward it. But all would have agreed that dialectic, however practised and defined, undertook the posing and solving of logical paradoxes and also the provision of relatively formal techniques of argument between a questioner and a respondent on a variety of subjects. Cynics and Epicureans condemned such activities as worthless for the advancement of human well-being. They could not completely ignore them, and they were in a minority.[4]

The Stoic conception of dialectic was not developed in isolation from its treatment by other philosophers. But before considering its historical background, we must return to Alexander of Aphrodisias and statements by Stoics themselves about this subject. When we compare his definition of dialectic in Stoicism with other sources, it may seem that he has either confused dialectic with rhetoric or given a statement that applies to both of these together, ‖ that is, to 'logical science' in general. The Stoic definition of dialectic which is most widely attested is 'the science of things true and false and neither true nor false'. It was equally standard for them to define rhetoric as 'the science of speaking well', which Alexander

---

[4] On Epicurus' method in dealing with certain Megarian sophisms, cf. Sedley 1973, pp. 71–7.

ascribes to dialectic. But before castigating Alexander too severely, it is important to take account of a passage in the introductory section of Diogenes Laertius' account of Stoic logic: '[According to the Stoics] rhetoric is the science of speaking well on arguments which are set out in narrative form; dialectic is the science of discoursing correctly on arguments in question-and-answer form; hence they also define it as the science of things true and false and neither true nor false' (D.L. VII.42).

This text suggests that 'the science of speaking well' is a truncated definition of rhetoric which might, with further explanation, fit dialectic as well; it also implies that method and style are what principally differentiate rhetorical from dialectical argument. These points are confirmed by a manual illustration attributed to Zeno: when asked how dialectic differed from rhetoric, he clenched his fist and then opened it out. The clenched fist illustrated the 'compactness' and 'brevity' of dialectic, while the open hand with the fingers spread out was intended to simulate the 'breadth' of rhetoric. (Sextus Empiricus, *M* II.7 = *SVF* 1.75). For the Stoics in general, rhetoric like dialectic is peculiar to the wise man. Neither subject is merely a skill or technique.[5] As 'sciences' both parts of Stoic logic demand, at least in theory, that infallible ability to distinguish truth from falsehood which is characteristic of the Stoic sage.

It is reasonable to suppose that Zeno and Cleanthes, as well as later Stoics, held this view. As the ideal reference of all human excellences, the wise man in Stoicism fulfils many of the functions of Platonic Forms. In rejecting these incorporeal entities, Zeno offered the wise man as the goal and standard of a perfectly rational life. But we may doubt whether the account of dialectic as 'the science of things true and false' has a Stoic history before Chrysippus or, at least, before Cleanthes. There are several reasons for regarding this conception of dialectic as a later development in Stoicism.

Diogenes Laertius gives it as an *alternative* definition to 'the science of discoursing correctly on arguments in ‖ question-and-answer form.' This account of dialectic is almost certainly the older of the two. Far from being distinctively Stoic, it describes

---

[5] Sextus Empiricus (as cited above) notes this as the difference between Xenocrates' account of rhetoric and the Stoic definition that uses the same words as Xenocrates.

dialectic in a manner that fits the general conception of the term in the early Hellenistic period. Argument by question and answer was the most characteristic philosophical connotation of dialectic, deriving from the ordinary meaning of the word 'converse' (*dialegesthai*), and from Socratic and sophistic methods of argument. The practice of this activity, however 'correctly', is not *prima facie* equivalent to 'the science of things true ...', which makes such large claims for itself.

Furthermore, the detailed summary of Stoic logic in Diogenes Laertius has nothing whatsoever to say about how 'to discourse correctly on arguments in question-and-answer form'.[6] But its subject matter is entirely appropriate to 'the science of things true ...', or, to use Chrysippus' language, 'signs and things signified' (D.L. VII.62).[7] First we are given an account of sense-impressions, the formation of concepts, and the criterion of truth – epistemology; next a discussion of dialectic under the headings of voice, elements of speech, types of style, genus, species, division and amphiboly – broadly, the sign function of language; next, we have language as meaningful ('things signified'): *lekta* (what are said or meant), propositions, and arguments, including a brief section on logical paradoxes. At the end of this section Diogenes Laertius writes:

Such then is the logic of the Stoics, which chiefly establishes their point that the wise man is the only dialectician.[8] For all things are brought to light through the study in rational utterances, both the subject-matter of physics and again of ethics (as for logic that goes without saying), and (?without logic the wise man?) would not be able to speak about correctness of names, how the laws have made arrangements for actions.[9] Of the two forms of inquiry which fall under the virtue (of dialectic), one considers what each thing that exists is, and the other what it is called. (VII.83)

---

[6] VII.49–82. This section begins with a quotation from Diocles Magnes (first century BC) which probably extends beyond chapter 49, but cf. Sandbach 1971a, p. 33.

[7] So too Diogenes' opening remarks about the contents of dialectic, VII.43–4.

[8] I follow von Arnim's text for this line (*SVF* II.39.39) and not H. S. Long in the Oxford edition with a reading: 'the wise man is always a dialectician'.

[9] The text of this sentence is very difficult and almost certainly corrupt. My question marks frame words that are absent from the Greek, but I conjecture with von Arnim (*SVF* II.130) that a subject (the wise man?) is needed for the infinitives *echein eipein*. The subsequent reference to 'considering what each thing is called' seems to imply that the wise man is an expert in the correct use of names. For a different translation, cf. Hicks in the Loeb edition, who takes 'virtue' in a general sense and not as a reference to the virtue of dialectic.

A scope and a significance are here attributed to dialectic which go far beyond argument by question and answer and which do suit the 'science of things that are true …' Diogenes Laertius speaks about a doctrine and a methodology that are not the common property of dialectic in other philosophers' usage and which may fairly be credited to Chrysippus. ‖

For it is noteworthy that Chrysippus' name figures more frequently than any other in Diogenes Laertius VII.50–82 and no Stoic prior to him is mentioned at all. This may seem to be labouring the obvious, since it is regularly acknowledged that Stoic logic was primarily the creation of Chrysippus. But this point is generally related to his achievements in elaborating logical theory. I am now suggesting that he may have been the first Stoic to develop dialectic beyond argument by question and answer into a science that made epistemology, language and logic together an integral part of Stoic philosophy as a whole.

Here a few words are needed about his Stoic predecessors. The material has recently been examined by Michael Frede and I shall limit myself to points that bear on the history of dialectic in the early Stoa.[10] I agree with Frede that we have little reason to think that Zeno's strictly logical interests went much beyond the kind of puzzles, such as the Liar and the Hooded Man, which he would have encountered with the Megarians.[11] Plutarch tells us that Zeno 'used to solve sophisms and recommended his pupils to take up dialectic for its capacity to do this' (*Stoic. rep.* 1034f = *SVF* 1.50). He is said to have paid two hundred drachmas, twice the price demanded, for seven forms of the puzzle known as 'the Reaper' (D.L. VII.25), and he clearly thought that an ability to handle the stock paradoxes was a necessary part of the training of any would-be philosopher. 'Knowing how to discourse correctly on arguments in question-and-answer form' suits Zeno's attested attitude to dialectic very well. He wrote a book of 'solutions' and two books of 'refutations'; his so-called *Technē* was probably a treatment of rhetoric, and some aspects of dialectic in Chrysippus' sense were

---

[10] Cf. Frede 1974, pp. 12–26. See also Rist (1978a) and Schofield (1983).

[11] Cf. the Megarian style of Zeno's argument against the proposition, 'do not pronounce judgement until you have heard both sides', Plutarch, *Stoic. rep.* 1034e. It is probable, as Frede argues (1974, pp. 23–6), that Zeno's logic was also influenced by the Academy, though the most likely date for his arrival in Athens (*c.* 311 BC) rules out the report of D.L. VII.2 (accepted by Frede, p. 23 n. 8) of lengthy study under Xenocrates.

doubtless treated in Zeno's other works, particularly *On logos* and *On signs* (D.L. VII.4, 39–40). The basic theory of *katalēpsis*, 'grasping' valid perceptual data, was Zeno's own invention; but we have no evidence that he presented his epistemology as the primary part of dialectic corresponding to the arrangement of Diogenes Laertius.

If dialectic for Zeno was largely restricted to knowing how to acquit oneself creditably in debates about logical puzzles, Aristo's attitude towards logic becomes more intelligible, as Frede observes.[12] This pupil of Zeno wrote three books *Against the dialecticians*, in which he must have advanced the position, ‖ repeatedly attributed to him, that logic is completely without value, or even positively harmful.[13] Aristo's general tendency was to emphasise the Cynic elements of Stoicism, and this suits his dismissal of logic. It is more difficult, however, to understand his contempt for dialectic if this had already been adumbrated as 'the science of things true ...' Given his Cynic inclinations, he may readily be supposed to have thought the solution of sophisms to be useless for the good life, and although Zeno saw some point in this activity, we should not overestimate the value that he himself placed on it.[14]

Of Zeno's other pupils only Sphaerus and Cleanthes are known to have written logical works. But the little that can be said about these is quite significant. Sphaerus books included two *On the art of dialectic* and also works *On predicates* and *On ambiguities*. (D.L. VII.178). Cleanthes also wrote on the first two subjects and *On sophisms* and *Forms of argument* (D.L. VII.175). He made dialectic a sixth part of philosophy and his claim that 'not everything past and true is necessary' (SVF 1.489) was a contribution to the debate about the Master argument initiated by that most famous of dialecticians, Diodorus Cronus.[15] While Frede is probably right to think that Cleanthes 'had little interest in arguments as such' (1974, p. 15), it may also be correct to see him as the Stoic who prepared the ground for the very large place that dialectic was to take in the philosophy of Chrysippus. It must have fallen to Cleanthes to de-

---

[12] Cf. Frede 1974, p. 13. I doubt whether we can learn much about Zeno's logic from Epictetus, *Discourses* IV.8.12 (*SVF* 1.51) but cf. Graeser 1975, pp. 11ff.

[13] D.L. VI.103; VII.160, 163; Sextus Empiricus, *M.* VII.12, etc.

[14] Cf. Stobaeus II.22.12 Wachsmuth (*SVF* 1.49): 'Zeno used to liken the arts of the dialecticians to the right measures which do not measure wheat or anything else worthwhile but chaff and dung.'

[15] For the evidence, bibliography and discussion, cf. Döring 1972, pp. 39–44, 132–8.

fend Zeno's doctrines against attacks from the sceptical Academy of Arcesilaus;[16] and the importance of systematising Stoic philosophy and making it competent to withstand sceptical criticism must have stimulated a greater interest in logic among some of Zeno's successors. I don't wish to overemphasise this point, but it seems to me insufficient to account for Chrysippus' conception of dialectic purely on the grounds of his personal interests.[17] Of course these must have played a major part. But if we need a Stoic who prompted the development of dialectic as a systematic science before Chrysippus, the most likely candidate is Cleanthes.

We may now return to the wise man and to Chrysippus' conception of dialectic, first recalling the relevant remarks in Diogenes Laertius. As a dialectician, the wise man knows how to investigate what each thing is and what it is called. These two ‖ functions of dialectic are hardly original to the Stoics. They associate the dialectician of Plato's *Cratylus* with his namesake from the *Republic*: in the *Cratylus* Socrates argues that only the dialectician – the man who knows how to ask and answer questions – is competent to evaluate the work of the 'legislator', the giver of names (390b-e). The influence of this dialogue is perhaps evident from Diogenes' reference to correctness of names and the laws' (*nomoi*) arrangements for actions, and more generally from the Stoics' methods of etymology.[18] But the reminiscence of the *Republic* is still more striking where (to cite just one passage) dialectic is the only 'method of inquiry which systematically attempts in every case to grasp the nature of each thing as it is in itself' (533b, trans. Cornford). Both Plato and Chrysippus (to whom we may surely attribute Diogenes' statement) assert that dialectic is the science that investigates *ti esti hekaston*, 'what each thing is'.

I do not believe that these verbal similarities are accidental or insignificant, which is not to say that Chrysippus set out to reveal

---

[16] This is a valid inference from the chronology: when Cleanthes succeeded Zeno as Head of the Stoa in about 261 BC Arcesilaus was already Head of the Academy and Chrysippus hardly more than twenty years old. Cleanthes may have had little competence in logic (cf. Frede 1974, pp. 26-7), but not much credence should be rested on the ancient biographical tradition, cf. Hirzel 1882, vol. II.1, pp. 85-8. D.L. VII.182 reports that Chrysippus diverted a dialectician's attack from Cleanthes to himself.

[17] The same point is made by Gould, 1970, p. 9 and by Frede 1974, pp. 26-7.

[18] Cf. Steinthal 1890 vol. I, especially pp. 334, 344. Stoic principles of etymology and the grammatical part of their dialectic fall outside the scope of this article; for two recent discussions that raise points about their general philosophical position, cf. Lloyd 1971 and my remarks in Long 1986a, pp. 131-9.

his allegiance to Plato explicitly. He certainly did not harness dialectic to the ideal metaphysics of Plato's Forms nor, as I shall argue
later, did he assign an important heuristic function to discussion
by question and answer. But he agreed with Plato that dialectic is
the science indispensable to all philosophical inquiry, and this is
important. It gives to logic or dialectic, whatever this connotes in
practice, an independent scientific or epistemological status that it
did not possess for Aristotle. This is indicated in Stoic sources by
two points: first, the rejection of the Peripatetic term *organon* as the
designation of logic and the substitution of 'nor contingent portion
but part' (of philosophy) (*SVF* II.49); second, the use of the term
'dialectic' with 'knowledge of demonstrative procedures' given as
its goal (*SVF* II.49.31). Both these points are totally incompatible
with Aristotle's official description of dialectic, which is sharply distinguished from *apodeixis*, 'demonstration' or 'deductive proof'.[19]
(See further below.)

Both the general principles of Stoic philosophy, which Chrysippus inherited, and the destructive criticism of the sceptical Academy can help to explain parts of his conception of dialectic. Further evidence on the *values* of dialectic needs to be considered here.
We have seen that dialectic is a human excellence or virtue (*aretē*)
and it belongs, as we should expect, to those virtues that ‖ are *necessary* to the good life. Diogenes Laertius, who states this (VII.46),
continues with a list of the specific virtues of dialectic, and these
help to illuminate its general functions in Stoicism. First he mentions *aproptōsia*, which means literally 'not falling forward' and is
defined as 'knowledge of when one should give assent and not' (give
assent); next *aneikaiotēs*, 'unhastiness', defined as 'strong-mindedness
against the probable (or plausible), so as not to give in to it'; third,
anelenxia, 'irrefutability', the definition of which is 'strength in argument, so as not to be driven by it to the contradictory'; and fourth,
amataiotēs, 'lack of emptyheadedness', defined as 'a disposition which
refers impressions (*phantasiai*) to the correct *logos*'.

This catalogue of dialectical virtues may fairly confidently be
attributed to Chrysippus. All four terms are neologisms of the kind
that he liked to make, and the definition of *aneikaiotēs* uses a bogus
etymological link between *eikēi* (the adverb from which *(an)eikaiotēs*

---

[19] On the general background to Aristotelian dialectic, cf. Solmsen 1968b and Owen's
paper, 'The Platonism of Aristotle' in Owen 1986, pp. 213–16.

is formed) meaning 'at random' and *eikos*, 'probability', which is equally characteristic of Chrysippus. The four terms are all privative nouns that denote a disposition *not* to behave in a certain way, and what links them is the Stoic concept of knowledge, which Diogenes Laertius next proceeds to define: 'secure grasp or disposition in acceptance of impressions which is unchangeable by argument.' Dialectic is then asserted by Diogenes to be a necessary condition of knowledge: without it 'the wise man will not be infallible in argument', and it enables him to do three kinds of things – distinguish true and false, discriminate what is persuasive and what is ambiguous, argue methodically by question and answer.

The main points of this passage are confirmed and amplified by a papyrus from Herculaneum, which discusses dialectic in relation to the wise man (*SVF* II.131).[20] *Aproptōsia*, and *aneikaiotēs* recur, *anelenxia* is also expressed through its adjectival form *anele(n)ktos*, and much else is said about the sage: he is not subject to persuasion, he does not change, he does not err in respect of any sense organ, he does not deceive and is not deceived; as before, the wise man's dialectical qualities are expressed by negative predicates, or largely so. But what they denote are meant to be read as positive values, instances of the fact that 'the wise do all things well' (*SVF* II.41.25). As in Diogenes Laertius, the focus of the wise man's ‖ dialectical virtues is on his 'assenting correctly,' and all the nouns or adjectives that describe him pick out particular types of situation, most notably philosophical arguments, in which precipitate assent would be the mark of folly. The main emphasis in both texts is upon dialectic in the limited, argumentative sense. We seem to be closer to the science of discoursing correctly by question and answer (Zeno's probable conception of dialectic) than to the larger, epistemological activity which I attributed to Chrysippus – dialectic as knowing how to investigate what each thing is and what it is called. Yet both our passages seem to point most clearly to Chrysippus.

This problem, I would suggest, is more apparent than real. Chrysippus did not abandon dialectic's traditional associations

---

[20] Cf. von Arnim 1890. It should be emphasised that he established his readings on the basis of the Naples and Oxford apographs without inspection of the papyrus itself (cf. p. 473). That is not an adequate basis for an authoritative edition of any of the Herculaneum material, and it is virtually certain that new work on the papyrus would reveal some errors in his text, which should be regarded for the present as provisional. His attribution of the papyrus to Chrysippus is highly probable.

with formal debate and philosophical polemic. As the Stoa's chief
protagonist against the Academic Sceptics, he could not afford to
do so. But he combined what we may call the defensive function
of dialectic, as a weapon against rival philosophers, with its positive role as a systematic science of epistemology, language and
logic. Another way of putting the point would be to regard Chrysippean dialectic as incorporating both the Platonic and the Aristotelian conceptions of this term: it is Aristotelian in the sense that
it provides its practitioner with the training necessary to cope
with arguments for and against a given thesis; but it is Platonic
in the sense that its overall purpose is the discovery and demonstration of truths.

In fact both passages just discussed include hints of a wider
conception for dialectic than preservation of the wise man from
unguarded assent in argument. Diogenes Laertius observes a connexion between dialectic and ethics when he says that 'precip-
itancy in assertions extends to actual events, so that those whose
impressions are not trained tend to disorderliness and random-
ness' (vii.48). We may interpret him to mean that persons who
give their assent injudiciously, whether to a sense-impression or to
a statement, will be unable to live in a consistent, purposeful manner. The Stoic goal of 'living in agreement with nature' presupposes the ability to make correct judgements about facts and
values. So the wise man needs to possess a disposition to grasp
the truth in every situation if his moral conduct is to be infallible.
The papyrus text – as supplemented by von Arnim – includes
these interesting remarks, which follow its insistence that assent
should always be ‖ linked to *katalēpsis*, 'grasping': 'for in the first
place philosophy, whether it is (practising) correctness of *logos*, (or)
knowledge, is the (same as business) concerning *logos*; (for) by being
(within) the parts of the *logos* and their (arrangement) we shall use it
with experience; and by *logos* I mean that which belongs by (nature
to all) rational beings'.[21] Here too the writer (*SVF* ii.27–32, 41) is
stepping beyond the narrower confines of dialectic into other
wellknown Stoic territory. He appears to be saying that thorough
acquaintance with logic, 'the parts of the *logos*', is necessary for

---

[21] I have bracketed those words of which the Greek equivalents are missing or seriously
defective in the text as reported by von Arnim. But this does not imply that I have
serious doubts about the validity of his restorations or the sense of the passage.

the cultivation of human beings' rational powers, their specifically human nature.

There are other texts that indicate Chrysippus' view that dialectic has both a defensive and a creative function. Plutarch devotes the tenth chapter of his treatise *On the contradictions of the Stoics* to statements by Chrysippus about dialectic. The inconsistency that Plutarch seeks to detect has a bearing on the two functions of dialectic which I have suggested.

The main point at issue, for Plutarch, is Chrysippus' attitude towards 'arguing the opposite sides of a question'. Chrysippus recognised the value of this activity for sceptics whose aim is to promote suspension of judgement (*epochē*) in their audience (1036a). But he was at pains to qualify this approval in his advice to Stoic teachers, 'those seeking to produce knowledge according to which we shall live consistently'. Their task is not to argue with equal cogency on both sides but to 'give their pupils basic instruction and to fortify them from beginning to end'. They may, however, in appropriate circumstances, mention 'the opposing arguments' as well, their justification being to 'destroy their plausibility'. Here then Chrysippus regards arguing the opposite sides of a question purely as an educational tool that must be used with caution (*eulabeia*). Much the same general position is stated in other quotations by Plutarch: opposing arguments must be handled in such a way that the inexperienced are not taken in by a plausible refutation – 'for those who follow everyday experience in grasping perceptible things ... (i.e., accepting the cognitive value of certain sensations) easily abandon these if they are carried away by the questions of the Megarians and a greater number of other more powerful questions' (1036e). This caveat is put still more positively in a passage from Chrysippus' work *On the use* ‖ *of the logos*: '[The faculty of reason] must be used for the discovery of truths and for their organisation, not for the opposite ends, though this is what many people do' (1037b trans. Cherniss, *Moralia* Loeb. ed. XIII.2). In these texts we witness the two aspects of Chrysippus' dialectic, its defensive function, where arguing both sides of a question may have limited value, and its creative role in the discovery of truths.

Plutarch's effort to detect inconsistency is based largely on one, apparently youthful, activity of Chrysippus. Under the influence of Arcesilaus, with whom he studied as a young man, Chrysippus published arguments for and against Everyday experience (1036c,

1037a).[22] These were an investigation into the pros and cons of the conventional position that some sense experience provides demonstrably valid evidence about the world. Plutarch would have us believe that Chrysippus' arguments against the senses were far more effective than his defence of them and that his support for a position contrary to his own beliefs was grossly inconsistent with his published views about the use of contrary theses. There can be little doubt that Plutarch is here drawing upon a hostile biographical tradition, to which he himself gives the lie when he concludes his discussion with the words: 'you do yourself confess that from ambition you are showing off by using the faculty of reason in ways unprofitable and harmful' (1037c, trans. Cherniss). Possibly Chrysippus' arguments for and against Everyday experience were an exercise set him by Arcesilaus (cf. D.L. vii.184). We certainly have no ground for thinking that his views on the value of arguing both sides of a question were inconsistent during his maturity as a philosopher.

Apart from its biographical interest, Plutarch's evidence shows that Chrysippus envisaged for dialectic the two complementary functions I have indicated. Arguing both sides of a question was the dialectical method of the contemporary Academy. Stoicism needed defence against this form of attack, and the dialectical virtues which we have studied refer to the ideal armoury of the Stoic sage who knows how to acquit himself excellently in disputation. Without his irrefutability and the like, as Diogenes Laertius says, 'he will not show himself sharp and acute and generally skilful in arguments' (vii.48). The titles of Chrysippus' logical works prove that he wrote at enormous length on techniques of argument and ‖ the handling of sophisms; in this respect he may be regarded as one of the heirs of Aristotle's *Topics*.

This brings us back to the whole question of what dialectic connotes for Chrysippus and the relation of this to Plato and to Aristotle. I have already drawn attention to points of contact and difference with both earlier philosophers and it is time to try to state these more precisely. Chrysippus agreed with Plato and Aristotle that philosophical argument, formally conducted, is the only proper procedure for the demonstration of truth. Like Plato he

---

[22] It is these works that are included by Diogenes Laertius, along with their addressees Metrodorus and Gorgippides, in his catalogue of Chrysippus' writings, vii.198.

called the expert in this a dialectician, which meant, for both philosophers, not merely a skilled logician but also, most important, someone who has knowledge of reality. In his conception of reality, however, and in his theory of knowledge Chrysippus differed sharply from Plato. In place of an investigation by question and answer which has as its goal to establish relationships between Forms, supra-sensible realities, Chrysippus was interested in demonstrating the conditions that make it proper to assent to sense-impressions and propositions concerning empirical nature.

For Aristotle the scope of dialectic, argument by question and answer, is limited to subjects on which the majority of people have 'opinions'. Such matters, in Aristotle's view, not admitting of necessary truths, are appropriate for debate, which is not the case with the premises of the demonstrative syllogism that are 'true and primary' (*Top.* 100a25–b23). We do not, on Aristotle's view, demonstrate truths by engaging in dialectical discussion. But this activity has value, both for clarifying the subjects it is competent to handle, and above all, for training the intellect.

Chrysippus' attitude toward dialectic in this sense seems not to have been very different from Aristotle's.[23] He too regarded training in handling contrary theses as a useful educational device provided it is not confused with the discovery of truths or treated as an end in itself. He certainly thought the wise man should be excellent at questioning and responding in formal debates, but nothing suggests that he shared Plato's views about the cognitive value of such encounters. They form a part of dialectic, as Chrysippus conceived of this, but not its positive role for the demonstration of truths. Though using the term 'dialectic' much more broadly than Aristotle, Chrysippus agreed that in logic we should distinguish ‖ between demonstrative science and knowledge of how to conduct oneself in argument by question and answer.

DIALECTIC AND THE DISCOVERY OF TRUTH

Up to this point I have dwelt largely on statements by Stoics or Stoic sources on the nature and value of dialectic. These have helped to explain why the sage is a dialectician but not, perhaps, why he is the only dialectician. What about Chrysippus himself?

[23] Cf. Moraux 1968, p. 304, and more generally Bréhier 1951, pp. 62–5.

He made no claims to be a Stoic sage yet it was popularly said of him, 'if the gods had dialectic it would be the dialectic of Chrysippus' (D.L. VII.180). The apparent paradox is partly resolved by pointing out that in statements of the form 'only the sage is a such and such', the predicate is evaluative as well as descriptive. It refers to what we might call supreme or perfect competence but with the fundamental proviso that no one who falls short of perfect competence can even qualify for the description. The Stoics admitted no degrees of virtue or vice, so banning the use of the comparatives better or worse, and they also regarded dialectic, itself a virtue, with the same complete lack of compromise. Either a man is wise and therefore a dialectician, or he is not wise and not a dialectician.

It may be said that this treatment of the term, 'dialectician', is merely one of the innumerable examples of the Stoics' practice in confining all knowledge, skill and virtue to the wise man and that it is of no particular philosophical interest. I think this conclusion would be premature. The fact that 'dialectician', in Stoic usage, falls into the category of predicates peculiar to the wise man tells us something about the Stoic view of dialectic. Moreover, as we have seen, Stoic statements about dialectic lay great emphasis upon the wise man's unique competence.

He instantiates what dialectic is, the science of things true and false, and he is distinguished from other people, including would-be dialecticians, by his possession of truth (*alētheia*).[24] According to strict Stoic usage, truth is knowledge, a disposition of the wise man's *logos*, and it differs from 'the true' in various ways. Above all, truth is something compound or complex whereas the true is ‖ uniform and simple. Dialectic, whether treating of assent to sense-impressions or to methods of inference, deals with the conditions that make particular propositions true or false. But a person can learn to formulate true propositions without grasping a complete structure of logical relationships, an ordered system of true propositions, which constitutes dialectic as such and therefore truth as a whole. The distinction between truth and the true helps to show the systematic character of the wise man's knowledge. He represents an ideal of language and rationality at one with reality, of truth discovered.

---

[24] For evidence and discussion, see Long 1971b, pp. 98–102, and 1978b.

Chrysippus, it may be recalled, said that 'the faculty of reason must be used for the discovery of truths and for their organisation', and 'the discovery of truth' occurs in Diogenes Laertius' introductory remarks on logic (VII.42). He speaks of a (sub-)division of logic concerned with 'canons and criteria' which has discovery of truth as its function, and says that it formulates rules about the differences of *phantasiai* (impressions presented to the sense organs or the mind). He also refers to a further part of logic, to do with 'definition', saying that 'they use this in the same way for recognition of truth; for things are grasped through general concepts' (*ennoiai*).[25]

In a treatise attacking Epicureans and Academics, Epictetus charges the latter, as sceptics, with trying to case off or blind their own sense-perceptions (*aisthēseis*). He asserts that a human being has natural endowments 'for recognising the truth' (Diogenes Laertius' phrase) but fails to 'go on and take the pains to add to these (sc. measures and standards) and to work out additional principles to supply the deficiencies, but does exactly the opposite, endeavouring to take away and destroy whatever faculty he does possess for discovering the truth' (*Discourses* II.20.21, trans. Oldfather). Omitting for the present Epictetus' professed attitude to dialectic, I would suggest that this passage gives us a moral statement on the Stoic attitude toward discovering truth. Human beings are innately equipped to achieve this by reason of their own intellect and sensory faculties, but these require training in (we may interpret) the subject-matter and methodology of dialectic; hence what Epictetus calls elsewhere 'the necessity of logic' (*Discourses* II.25).

The orthodox Stoic doctrine, which he implies, takes us back to Diogenes Laertius on the discovery of truth. His 'canons and ‖ criteria' and 'definition' refer to the two primary aspects of the Stoic theory of knowledge. 'Distinguishing between *phantasiai*', the scope of 'canons and criteria', is the province of the human faculty to 'assent correctly' and to grasp (*katalambanein*) the valid content of a sense-impression or a sentence;[26] and we have noted those dialectical virtues that signify the wise man's capacity to do

---

[25] In the last sentence of VII.41 D.L. says: 'but some omit what has to do with definition'. That these did not include Chrysippus seems clear both from our general accounts of Stoic logic and from Chrysippus' list of writings.

[26] On the meaning of the terms and the Stoic doctrine they help to express, cf. Rist, 1969, pp. 133–41; Sandbach 1971b, pp. 9–21; Graeser 1975, pp. 39–55.

this. But assenting and grasping are activities of the *logos*, a human being's rational governing principle, and a fundamental fact about the *logos* is its being 'a collection of general concepts and preconceptions' (*SVF* II.841).[27] Similarly according to Diogenes' analysis of the cognitive value of 'definition', 'things are grasped through general concepts'. If we are to *know* what each thing is, we need to bring the particular percept or proposition under a valid general concept the basis of which, in Stoicism, is also sense-experience and its organisation by the intellect. As Gerard Watson has written, 'the new piece of information must fit into the so far established picture, and *katalēpsis* cannot be separated from *logos*, the particular act from the general disposition. For truth, then, there must be coherence.'[28]

This last point is clearly hinted at in the dialectical virtue of *amataiotēs* – 'a disposition which refers *phantasiai* to the correct *logos*'. But how are we to interpret *orthos logos* here? Hicks in the Loeb edition says 'right reason'. That is implied, no doubt, but it leaves the definite article untranslated. 'Right reason' describes the *logos* of the wise man (and god) and it is his *logos* that pronounces judgment on the *phantasia*. But what intellectual process does this involve? Is it not more accurate and more informative to interpret *ton orthon logon* here as '*the* correct argument'?[29] An example, which might do justice to various items of our evidence, would be this: the wise man wakes up at 9:00 a.m. in a relatively dark room and his initial impression (*phantasia*) on waking is that it is still night. But before assenting to this impression he takes stock of his surroundings and realises that it is light. His experience of the world has taught him the truth that 'if it is night, it is not light'; he therefore withholds assent from his initial impression and infers that it is not night and therefore that it is day. This example seeks to bring together particular *phantasiai*, general concepts, Stoic methods of inference, and the sense of *orthos logos* in Diogenes. To possess an *orthos logos* implies the ability to reason correctly, ‖ and while we need not suppose that the Stoics were so humourless that they thought the wise man would subject all his

[27] A quotation by Galen from Chrysippus.
[28] Cf. Watson 1966, p. 37. The importance of general concepts (*ennoiai*) in the Stoic theory of knowledge is very well argued by Watson.
[29] This also suits the other occurrences of *logos* in D.L. VII.46–7, three of which Hicks rightly translates by 'argument'.

experience to formal methods of inference, they should not be taken to regard reference to *orthos logos* as recourse to a mysterious intuition. The wise man has 'right reason' because he has an infallible disposition to reason correctly. We should not perhaps forget Chrysippus' dialectical dog which infers the correct one of three possible roads for pursuit of its quarry by smelling only at the two roads that it did not take and then, without smelling at the third, rushes off along it (Sext. Emp. *PH* 1.69)!

The wise man's possession of right reason relates him to the active principle of the universe which *is* right reason and identical with god. Consideration of this relationship can illuminate both the practical application of Stoic dialectic and the overriding imperative to live consistently in accordance with nature. This goal becomes more intelligible and practicable if it is seen to depend upon the systematic ability to grasp facts and to reason correctly. Life according to nature entails for the Stoic an attunement between his own attitudes and actions and the rational course of events. But how is someone to know whether he has achieved, or is progressing toward achieving, such a relationship? The answer is surely that the more he succeeds in grasping what is true the closer he comes to attunement with right reason in its cosmic sense.[30] For right reason (*orthos logos*) is logically equivalent to truth (*alētheia*).[31] What truth means in this connection depends upon whether we are referring to the sage or to the *orthos logos* that is god. In the sage truth refers to his rational disposition, his systematic knowledge and ability to state all that is true. In reference to god truth seems principally to denote destiny, the causal nexus that determines all things. But this is an activity of *logos*; that is to say, it is both expressible and intelligible. The sage's systematic knowledge of particular truths is the human counterpart to the divine nexus of causes.[32]

---

[30] This goes some way toward resolving the question I raise in chapter 6 of this volume, p. 150, where I suggest that the Stoics gave no satisfactory answer to the question how someone might know whether his reason accorded consistently with Nature.

[31] *Alētheia*, as 'knowledge', is a disposition of the 'governing principle' (*hēgemonikon*) or *logos* such that the *logos* is upright or correct (*orthos*); cf. *SVF* II.132 with other descriptions of the wise man. For *orthos logos* and *alētheia* as cosmic principles cf. *SVF* II.913 and III.4; Marcus Aurelius IX.2.

[32] I am not of course denying knowledge and consciousness to the Stoic deity; Cleanthes and Chrysippus are said to have claimed 'the same virtue and truth belong to man and god', *SVF* III.250.

The moral implications of the link between cosmic and human *logos* have been well understood by modern students of Stoicism. No one today would readily accept the view that logic in the mature Stoic system ranks below physics and ethics in importance.[33] But it is tempting to go further and to suggest that the study of dialectic itself, for Chrysippus at any rate, is an integral ‖ part of moral conduct. In analysing the structure of language and its function to express true propositions, the Stoics were taking as their subject-matter fundamental aspects of the human *logos*, the rationality of human nature. Language and logic are not capacities of the human *logos* which can or should be isolated from its more obviously moral dispositions. The character of the wise man is sufficient proof of this point, and it can be confirmed by a wide range of Stoic texts. Chrysippus, as we have seen, was well aware that *logos* can be misused in dialectical activities. But when applied to the genuine discovery of truth, exercise of the *logos* must be an activity that accords with human nature; and this allows the most technical details of Stoic logic, and even the solution of sophisms, to be regarded as actions that contribute to the understanding of human nature and of the rationality of the universe. Thus dialectic may be regarded as a method of self-discovery.

That Chrysippus held such a view is implied by the catalogue of his writings preserved in part by Diogenes Laertius (VII.189–202). This appears to have been arranged under the three headings, logic, ethics and physics, and only the first of these is complete. The ethical catalogue breaks off in the middle of a title, and physics is missing altogether. Now the titles of the works arranged under logic give no indication of the broad significance for dialectic that I have sought to establish for Chrysippus. They cover in enormous detail a range of topics – types of proposition, aspects of grammar and style, methods of argument and solutions to sophisms – which correspond to the summary of Stoic logic in Diogenes Laertius, with one major omission. Not one of Chrysippus' logical titles refers explicitly to epistemology, the first subject treated in Diogenes.

Then we turn to ethics (VII.199–202). Like the logical titles the ethical books are arranged by sections. The first of these is headed 'the classification of ethical concepts' and the books listed in its

---

[33] As is implied by Zeller 1892–1909, vol. III.1, pp. 60–1, and Pohlenz 1959, p. 33.

first series are mainly *Of definitions*, e.g., *Of definitions of the good man, to Metrodorus*, two books. But the most interesting item is the second main section, 'concerning the common *logos* and the arts and virtues deriving from it' (VII.201). Its first series includes one of Chrysippus' books from which I have already quoted, *On the use of the logos*, and all but one of the remaining titles concern topics that appear in Diogenes Laertius' treatment ‖ of Stoic logic: *On how we speak each thing and conceive of it, On general concepts, On supposition, Demonstrations that the wise man will not hold opinions* (i.e., that his sole cognitive state is knowledge), *On grasping (katalēpsis) and knowledge and ignorance* – four books, and *On logos*.

If we find it strange that these titles should appear under ethics, we have a further surprise in the second series of this section: I report this in full: *On the fact that the ancients admitted dialectic along with demonstrations, to Zeno* – two books; *On dialectic, to Aristocreon* – four books; *On objections brought against the dialecticians* – three books; and finally, *On rhetoric, to Dioscurides* – four books.[34]

The source of the catalogue is not known, and we cannot be certain that Chrysippus arranged his works in this way.[35] But there can be no serious doubt that the arrangement has Stoic authority. It proves that some Stoics, if not Chrysippus himself, found it appropriate to classify under ethics some of his works that dealt quite explicitly with dialectic, rhetoric and epistemology. If this appears to breach the recognised sphere of Stoic logic we should remember that 'no part [sc. of Stoic philosophy] is separate from another part', according to some, 'but they are mixed together' (D.L. VII.40). Of great interest too is the heading for this section of ethics, which I quoted above. What is meant by 'the common *logos*' from which arts and virtues are derived? Hicks translates *koinos logos* by 'common view', which I fail to understand. I cannot see how 'common view' could be a source for arts and virtues, but if we take *koinos logos* in a familiar Stoic sense the heading becomes intelligible and highly significant. The phrase should mean the community of reason which unites human beings and god. This is indeed the basis of virtue in Stoic theory and such a heading is

---

[34] Notice also that logical subjects and etymologies predominate in the later series of the first ethical section, VII.200.

[35] For bibliography on the catalogue, cf. Gigante 1976, vol. II, p. 541 n. 233. Bréhier's claim (1951, p. 22) that logical works have 'surreptitiously' contaminated the ethical catalogue raises more questions than it resolves.

fully appropriate to most of the titles of all three series in this section. But above all, it helps to explain the presence of dialectic in
the treatment of ethics. As the science that handles language and
logic, dialectic is concerned with *koinos logos* and therefore with
ethics and with physics too. On the basis of independent evidence
we have thus arrived at a conclusion already stated in Diogenes
Laertius: the interdependence of dialectic, the wise man, and pro-
ficiency in physics and ethics. ‖

THE SAGE AND DIALECTIC IN EPICTETUS

Up to the time of Chrysippus, Stoics differed in their conception
and evaluation of dialectic and they continued to do so thereafter.
It is likely that many of them, including Panaetius and Posidonius,
accepted his view of the wise man as dialectician even if few Stoics
apart from Chrysippus' immediate successors extended the study
of logic and grammar. Historians generally associate the later
Stoa with a decline of interest in logic, and up to a point this is
correct. But it is important to distinguish professional Stoic teachers, with different views, from eclectic practitioners of Stoicism
such as Seneca and Musonius Rufus. Seneca's attitude toward
logic was dismissive, recalling the Cynic approaches of Aristo (*Ep.*
45.5, 49.5, 82.19, etc.). But logic continued to form an important
part of the Stoic curriculum during the imperial period, so much
so that it was often regarded as mere pedantry and irrelevant to
practice of the good life, thus explaining, if not justifying, a standpoint like Seneca's. Between these two extremes it was clearly possible to adopt a series of intermediate positions, and we have an
interesting example of this in Epictetus. His statements about the
value of logic are particularly relevant to our main theme since no
Stoic was more insistent on the practical purpose of philosophy.[36]

Epictetus claimed no expertise as a logician and his discourses,
as recorded by Arrian, make only passing reference to the more
formal elements of Stoic dialectic. But his terminology and his
methods of argument suggest quite considerable familiarity with
logical textbooks by Chrysippus or other Stoics. Several of his discourses (1.7; 1.17; 11.12; 11.25) are specifically concerned with the
value of logic, and the subject recurs in many others. When all of

---

[36] For a well-balanced account cf. Bonhöffer 1894, pp. 122–7.

these passages are put together, they show that Epictetus' general conception of the role of dialectic was broadly in line with the position of Chrysippus. Many of his remarks on this subject are related to the two extreme positions that he rejected. Epictetus constantly attacks pretentious display of logical techniques which are unrelated to practical conduct. 'The books of the Stoics are full of quibbles. What then is the thing lacking? The man to make use of them, the man to bear witness to the arguments by what he does' (1.29.56). It is not the mark of a man making true progress ‖ to want to know 'what Chrysippus means in his books on the *Liar*' (II.17.34) or to pride himself on posing the Master argument (II.17–18.18).³⁷ A man might analyse syllogisms in the manner of Chrysippus and still be wretched (II.23.44). Taken in isolation such statements as these (and there are many more of the same kind) seem to treat logic as a trivial activity which has no function for the serious-minded. But Epictetus' purpose is different. In these statements he is not rejecting logic as such but misapplications of it and erroneous views about its intrinsic value. He is rejecting the idea that would-be Stoics who get first-class marks on Chrysippean logic have achieved anything worthwhile if this is unrelated to the structure and plan of their life as a whole; and with this Chrysippus would have agreed.

Epictetus' positive attitude to logic is quite consistent with his negative posture. 'Logic is necessary': not as an end in itself but as the 'measuring instrument' of our *logos*, our rational faculty (1.17). The faculty of reason is our innate instrument of judgement, and it is through logic alone that we can come to understand and refine this power. We should read and try to interpret Chrysippus, not for its own sake, but in order to 'follow nature' and to enlarge our understanding of ourselves. It is the interpretation, not the interpreter, which has value.

In discussing Chrysippus I suggested that he might have regarded dialectic as a means of self-discovery, but I could not prove this from any surviving quotation. In Epictetus this is stated explicitly: he compares Chrysippus' achievement in logic to that of a diviner who predicts the future from inspecting entrails (1.17.18–29). Chrysippus is someone whose analysis of *logos* has yielded true indications of human nature.

---

³⁷ Epictetus is however our principal source for the Master argument, II.19.1–5.

In this treatise Epictetus moves rapidly from an assessment of logic to psychological and ethical conclusions, and this is characteristic of his methodology. But there is one discourse that deals at some length with the theme, *On the use of equivocal premisses, hypothetical arguments and similar subjects* (1.7). Epictetus' purpose here is to show that dialectic in the more restricted sense – knowing how to argue by question and answer – is a field in which the wise man will be proficient. It is not enough to have knowledge of particular facts. 'One must learn how one thing follows as a consequence upon other things ... if a man is to acquit ‖ himself intelligently in argument ... and is not to be deceived by quibblers as though they were conducting a proof' (1.7, 10–12).

Having established the wise man's need of dialectical competence, Epictetus turns to particular problems that arise in formal debates. If the premises of an argument are equivocal, how is someone to deal with an inference that is valid but false? Or if an argument is built on hypothetical premises, under what conditions should someone give his assent to the hypothesis and how far does his acceptance of it commit him to granting all its consequences? Epictetus raises these questions, and argues that a training in formal argument to deal with them is presupposed by the Stoic conception of the wise man (1.7, 25–9). He then infers the need for ordinary persons to work at the perfection of their own reason. It is no excuse to claim that an error in reasoning is not equivalent to parricide. Reckless assent to a sense-impression and inability to follow an argument are errors in themselves and signify an untrained reasoning faculty (1.7, 30–3). We are reminded once again of Diogenes Laertius' dialectical virtues. The wise man is infallible in all respects. His dialectical prowess is both a faculty to reason correctly in debate and a means of conducting himself without error in all the occasions of life.

This discourse by Epictetus – the seventh of Arrian's first book – is the nearest thing we possess to a Stoic equivalent of Aristotle's *Topics*. It shows us that formal argument by question and answer was still being practised in the first century AD and it also recalls Zeno's interest in the ability to cope with sophisms. The Stoic sage was always a dialectician, but it is remarkable that his dialectical prowess and significance under Chrysippus have remained so prominent in Epictetus.

CHAPTER 5

Arius Didymus and the exposition of Stoic ethics

The second book of Stobaeus' *Anthology* contains the longest and most detailed surviving account of Stoic ethics (II, pp. 57–116 Wachsmuth). Much of this corresponds closely to Cicero *De finibus* III.16–76 and Diogenes Laertius VII.84–131. These are the fullest parallel accounts, and there is every reason to think that all three derive ultimately from Stoic sources of unimpeachable orthodoxy. In some places Cicero, Diogenes and Stobaeus are so close to one another that they appear like variant copies of a single tradition.[1] Their common features have been most thoroughly assembled and discussed by Michelangelo Giusta in his *I dossografi di etica*.[2] That work is packed with valuable material and insights. But it suffers, as reviewers have pointed out, from unitarian zeal.[3] Giusta was too ready to turn Eudorus of Alexandria (see n. 4 below) into the mind and method latent in *all* summary accounts of later Greek ethical philosophy. There are important differences between Cicero, Diogenes and Stobaeus which his book tends to obscure. In this chapter I want to focus attention on some of the idiosyncratic features of the Stoic material in Stobaeus. This may put us in a better position to assess the method and purposes of its compilation, and its philosophical relationship with the accounts of Stoic ethics in Cicero and Diogenes.

ARIUS DIDYMUS' AUTHORSHIP

A preliminary point needs clarification – the authorship of the material in Stobaeus. It is quite certain that this Byzantine scholar

---

[1] Cf. Covotti 1897; von Arnim 1903–5, vol. I, pp. xxx–xliii.
[2] Cf. Giusta 1964, 1967.
[3] Cf. Kerferd 1967, pp. 156–8; Boyancé 1967, pp. 246–9.

produced his anthology from previous compendia, and thus the determination of his sources is crucially important for evaluating the material he transmits. An unchallenged answer to this question was advanced in the nineteenth century by a series of German scholars – *Arius Didymus*. The significance of Arius was considerable. He was active at the time of the Roman emperor Augustus, and well known as a philosophical encyclopaedist of higher repute than most.[4] If he could be proved to be Stobaeus' author or principal source, that was a conclusion greatly to be wished.

His name was first advanced on the grounds of general probabilities, but it was given evidential support by Meineke in 1859.[5] He pointed out that a short paragraph in Stobaeus II (pp. 129–30 W.) is repeated exactly in Stobaeus IV ‖ (pp. 918–19 Hense): 'the sources of happiness'. According to one, but only one, of the manuscripts which records this second occurrence of the passage, Stobaeus prefaced it with the heading: 'from the epitome of Didymus'.[6] This was taken to show, in Zeller's words, that 'not only the whole Peripatetic section', where the first passage on the 'sources of happiness' occurs, 'but also the corresponding section on Stoic doctrine was derived from Arius' epitome'; and that 'Stobaeus probably also took from Arius the four preceding sections which begin at volume II, p. 37 W.'[7] Wachsmuth himself supplied the words 'from the epitome of Didymus' at this place in his edition of Stobaeus, supported (as he says) by Diels.

Arius is known from Eusebius to have written a handbook which contained Stoic physics, and Eusebius also included extracts from a work by Arius on Platonism.[8] It is entirely plausible that he should have written or compiled accounts of Stoic and Peripatetic

---

[4] On Arius Didymus and what is known about him, cf. Diels 1879, pp. 69–88; Fraser 1972, vol. I, pp. 489–91; Glucker 1978, pp. 94–7. Fraser and Glucker should also be consulted on Eudorus, and cf. Dillon 1977, pp. 114–35.

[5] Cf. Meineke 1859, p. 564, and Diels 1879, p. 69.

[6] According to Hense's critical apparatus, the lemma is included in S but omitted by M and A. S is a Viennese MS (Hunger I, 184 (0412.41.47)) dated to the 10th/11th centuries; cf. Wachsmuth in Wachsmuth/Hense 1884–1912, vol. I, p. xiii. However, Wachsmuth in Wachsmuth/Hense 1884–1912, vol. II, p. 129 (critical apparatus to line 19) writes *inscriptum in T*, where T = Trincavelli's ed. princeps (Venice 1536). Since the editors of Stobaeus treat T as having the status of a MS, the discrepancy between their reports is unfortunate.

[7] Cf. Zeller 1892–1909, vol. III.1, p. 637 n. 1.

[8] *Praep. evang.* xv.15.9 (vol. 2 Mras, p. 380), xi.23.2 (vol. 2 Mras, p. 51). A work *On Pythagorean philosophy* is also attributed to Arius by Clement of Alexandria, *Strom.* 1.16.80.4 (vol. 2 Stählin, p. 52).

ethics. But it is not certain that he did so, nor can the solitary reference to his epitome in Stobaeus IV, p. 918.15 conclusively establish the hand of Arius in the *whole* of the Peripatetic section, much less the whole of the Stoic section and all of vol. II, pp. 37–152. Superficial impressions of the style perhaps suggest a single source, and the personal tone of pp. 41–5 can hardly point to Stobaeus himself. It is also most appropriate for Arius Didymus to have an interest in Philo of Larisa and Eudorus of Alexandria, as he does in these pages. So there is good reason to speak of Arius as if he were the direct or indirect source of Stobaeus' material. But that should be done in full awareness that it is a conjecture, a good conjecture certainly, but not a fact, as the incautious reader of Wachsmuth or Diels might readily suppose.

If Stobaeus' Stoic, Peripatetic and preceding ethical material were presented on unitary organisational principles, this could seem a pedantic recommendation. Arius' authorship would satisfy economy of explanation as well as historical plausibility. But Stobaeus' text, as will be shown towards the end of this chapter, shows considerable internal discrepancies. One of these is so important that it can bear repetition. The Peripatetic section, as has long been recognised, is heavily contaminated with Stoicism, and this points to the eclecticism associated particularly with Antiochus of Ascalon.[9] But the Stoic section appears to be as accurate a summary of Stoic doctrine in Stoic diction as we possess. It does not seem therefore as if 'Arius' has presented the two schools according to a common eclectic viewpoint. Yet eclecticism is strongly present in the preliminary definitions of terms (II, pp. 37–9, 45–57) with more explicit interest being taken in Plato and Aristotle than in the Stoics.

If such points are not sufficient to disturb the conjecture of Arius' principal authorship throughout, they certainly raise questions about his methods of work and doxographical intentions. For

---

[9] Madvig 1876, p. 848, was so impressed by the similarities between Stobaeus' section on Peripatetic ethics and the Antiochean material in Cicero, *Fin.* v, that he proposed Antiochus as their author. Zeller 1892–1909, vol. III.1, pp. 637–9, accepted the point, taking Arius to be the intermediary between Antiochus and Stobaeus. Hirzel 1882, vol. II, pp. 694ff., affirmed the link between Antiochus and Stobaeus, but without committing himself to Arius' transmission of the material. But Diels 1879, p. 72, who had a strong interest in resuscitating Arius, insisted that Stobaeus' material showed too much difference from Antiochus to support an Antiochean compendium as Arius' source. See further, n. 44 below.

the purpose of this chapter I will assume that he is the main source for both ethical sections in Stobaeus, together with the preliminary material, and I will suggest a hypothesis to reconcile the discrepancies without abandoning Arius or carving him up into two or more people. Any methodological contribution of his own is likely to have consisted in the framework he adopts for ‖ presenting the first part of his Stoic section. For that, as will be seen, has some interesting features which are without parallel in Cicero or Diogenes Laertius. As for the Peripatetic section, such few traces as we may conjecture concerning Arius' trademark seem still harder to detect. I would hazard the guess that he has taken over a Stoicising account, like that of Antiochus, without attempting to make it more than loosely similar in structure to his cast of the Stoic material.

THE 'DIVISION' PROCEDURE AND SUBJECT HEADINGS

Arius' presentation of Stoic ethics is best known through the many passages excerpted from it by von Arnim for his *Stoicorum Veterum Fragmenta*. Placed, as they are, alongside a mass of parallel texts these excerpts from Stobaeus give few indications of any organisational principles in Arius' work, and even those who have studied his entire exposition find nothing to praise in its procedure. Diels, following Madvig, complained about the lack of order and apparently random juxtaposition of subjects; and he noted fifteen topics as the headings for discussion between pages 57 and 93 after which repetitions and inconsequentialities seem to become still greater.[10] Unfortunately Diels' censure was quite inadequately grounded. There are certainly a good many inconcinnities in this section of Stobaeus, taking it as a whole. But they coexist within a pattern of exposition which shows a definite system of arrangement. This deserves careful detection and analysis.

Arius himself promises a coherent procedure: he says that he will make a record of the headings of the essential doctrines of Zeno and the other Stoics (p. 57.15).[11] In order to assess his fulfil-

---

[10] Cf. Diels 1879, p. 71. My more positive assessment of Arius is confirmed and complemented by Kahn 1983 and Hahm 1983, although White 1983 continues to voice scepticism.

[11] After a lemma referring to 'the doctrines of Zeno and the other Stoics on the ethical part of philosophy', the Greek runs: περὶ δὲ τῶν ἠθικῶν ἑξῆς ποιήσομαι τὸν ὑπομνημα-

ment of this promise we may best begin by studying the opening sections (pp. 57–79).

The first and most important step is to follow the guidance of his first two sentences: 'Zeno says that these are the things which participate in existence; and of existing things some are good, others bad, and others indifferent' (p. 57.18–20). The first sentence refers to something said by Zeno outside the context reported by Stobaeus, presumably to the effect that only corporeal things exist. In the second sentence Arius divides the class of existing things into the three specified subclasses. This division, and subdivisions dependent upon it, provide the main framework for his exposition.[12] That this is so can be seen particularly clearly on pages 79 and 85 where he gives explicit instructions to his reader:

Having dealt adequately with goods and evils and things to be chosen and avoided, and with the goal and happiness, we think we should expound in proper order the doctrines on indifferents. (P. 79)[13]

His treatment of 'indifferents' includes, as it should in Stoic ethics, an account of 'preferred things' (*proēgmena*). Having completed that, he writes:

The subject of the appropriate (*kathēkon*) follows on from the doctrine concerning preferred things. (P. 85) ‖

Arius can expect his attentive reader to observe that everything from pp. 57 to 85 has been developed out of his opening division into goods, evils and indifferents: pp. 57–79 handle goods and evils, while pp. 79–85 deal with indifferents. *All* that material, including much detail on virtue and the goal, prepares the ground for a new topic, the 'appropriate'.

τισμὸν τὰ κεφάλαια τῶν ἀναγκαίων δογμάτων ἀναλαβών. In my original version of this chapter I took ἑξῆς to qualify ποιήσομαι, and reported Arius as saying that he would 'make an orderly shopping list'. Thus I would respond to White 1983, p. 67, who objects that 'the author of the Stoic section does not actually *say* that his account will be coherent or orderly'. It may be better to interpret ἑξῆς as meaning merely 'next', with Kahn 1983, p. 6; cf. Aristotle, *EN* IV 1119b22. Even so, the general usage of ὑπομνηματισμός (note the definite article) and κεφάλαια seems to justify my original comment.

[12] For an excellent treatment of Arius' diaeretic methodology, cf. Hahm 1983. He proposes that the governing principle is a division into 'things, actions and men', into which Arius interpolates his treatment of 'topics.'

[13] I take 'things to be chosen and avoided' and 'happiness' as amplifications respectively of 'goods and evils' and 'goal', and not as independent subjects; cf. pp. 72.19–21, 77.16. Wachsmuth (*ad loc.*) suggests that 'things to be chosen and avoided' is a spurious addition, or alternatively, that p. 75.1–6 = B3 is a correctly placed fragment of a missing section on this theme: cf. n. 16 below.

Diels (above, n. 10) proposed that the material down to 'indifferents' covers nine topics, but that suggestion completely distorts Arius' procedure. He thinks of himself as having handled two principal topics – goods and evils, and the goal – and that is a just statement of what he has done. For analytical purposes, however, it is better to distinguish three topics which govern the organisation of his opening material: goods and evils, virtues and vices (strictly a subdivision of goods and evils) and the goal. It will be helpful to exhibit and label these divisions (down to p. 85) in a table.

A	Existing things consist of Goods, Evils, and Indifferents	pp. 57–8
B1	Goods and Evils	p. 58
	c1–6 Virtues and Vices	pp. 58–64
B2	Goods	p. 64
	c7–8 Virtues and Vices	pp. 64–8
B3–13	Goods and Evils	pp. 68–75
	D1–5 Goal and Happiness	pp. 75–8
E1–11	Indifferents	pp. 79–85

In what follows reference will be made to a more detailed 'Table of Ethical Theses in Stobaeus' (appended to this chapter), which sets out all the principal theses of these pages, using the same system of lettering and numeration.

As these tables show, Arius uses his division procedure in order to isolate one species of good, viz. virtues which are 'sciences and skills' (c1.i.1, pp. 58–9). These are in turn divided into 'primary' (the four cardinal virtues) and 'subordinate', which comprise further similarly describable virtues falling under the cardinal ones. He next (p. 62.7–14) appends a brief argument, the significance of which can be easily overlooked. First the conclusion is stated:

All these virtues have life in accordance with nature as their goal, and they each make man possess this goal through their own characteristics.[14]

---

[14] It may seem odd to write of 'the goal of the virtues'. Usener proposed to delete τὸ before τέλος, and it would be possible, as Gisela Striker suggested to me, to take τέλος here to mean 'result'. But I take the point to be that life in accordance with nature is brought about by or realised by the cardinal virtues. The chief ethical problem facing the Stoics was to show why the human goal is entirely constituted by living virtuously. Their answer, as suggested here and at p. 65.8–9 (cf. D.L. vii.87), is that virtue comprises the full content of a person's natural life, that to which human beings are impelled by their nature as human. This point is well stressed by White 1983, pp. 68–9, in his comments on my paper; and cf. my discussion on pp. 141–5 of this volume.

This claim is justified by what follows:

> For he has from nature impulses for discovering what is appropriate, for the stable condition of his impulses, for acts of endurance, and for acts of distribution. Each virtue, by harmoniously performing its own function, makes man live in accordance with nature.[15]

If it were not for this important section, Arius' opening material would be radically different from Cicero, *De finibus* III and Diogenes Laertius VII. In both of these accounts the discussion of Stoic ethics starts from *oikeiōsis*, a consideration of an animal's ‖ *natural impulse* to pursue what is appropriate to its constitution and to avoid the opposite. There is every reason to suppose that this was standard Stoic practice. Arius, as we have seen, begins his account quite differently. But in the brief argument translated above, together with his preceding material, he has provided the means of formulating the following thesis:

1. One of the constituents of reality is goods.
2. Goods include all the virtues.
3. Some virtues are sciences and skills.
4. Four of these virtues are primary: wisdom, moderation, courage, justice.
5. Man is impelled by nature to attain these virtues, and he lives in accordance with nature by each of these virtues' performing its function harmoniously.
6. The goal of these virtues is life in accordance with nature.

The last two propositions in this thesis correspond very closely with Diogenes Laertius VII.87: 'Zeno ... said that the goal is life in agreement with nature, that is life in accordance with virtue; for nature directs us towards virtue.' But Diogenes arrives at this specification of the goal by a different route. Unlike Arius his starting-point is impulse (*hormē*), common to all animals, and he then marks out rationality (impulse shaped by reason) as the distinctive characteristic of human nature. In his opening procedures (and the same holds for Cicero, *Fin.* III.16–21) no general claims about goods and virtues are involved. Arius on the other hand has told us nothing at this stage about the relationship between rationality and human

---

[15] Wachsmuth follows Usener in adding κατά before τὸ σύμφωνον, but there is no reason to alter the text. Take τὸ σύμφωνον and τὸ ἑαυτῆς as compound objects of πράττουσα. The meaning is hardly affected.

nature or virtue. These points will only emerge much later, when he has concluded his analysis of goods and evils, and passes on to consider the goal in detail (D1, D2, D5).

We should probably suppose then that Arius' brief remarks about the goal and human nature, at this early stage, are an interim summation which anticipates later sections but fits well into a detailed account of the cardinal virtues, where it is placed. Possibly he knows that Stoics regularly began their ethical disquisitions with an account of the primary impulse and human nature. For reasons we have yet to consider he is proceeding differently, providing a taxonomy of goods and virtues, evils and vices, before treating of the goal. But he is familiar enough with other procedures to give some satisfaction to readers who want to be told, pretty early, about the connexion between goods, virtues, impulses and the goal.

His main focus at this stage, however, is on the virtues. Having indicated that the cardinal virtues have life in accordance with nature as their goal, Arius amplifies their teleological significance from several points of view. Taking up what I have called his interim summation he repeats the claim that the cardinal virtues (and here he includes their subordinates too) are 'constitutive of life's goal', and adds the new point that they consist of 'rational principles' (*theōrēmata*, p. 62.15 = C5). Lest, however, we should think that this holds for all virtues, he explains the different status of the 'non-technical virtues' such as mental health, which are 'powers acquired by practice' and supervenient on the others (C1.i.2). Then, with a backward reference to his interim summation (p. 63.7), he shows how the ‖ cardinal virtues are both inseparable, owing to their *common* principles and goals, and at the same time distinguishable through their specific targets and subject-matter (C6.1, C6.2).

So far, it should now be plain, Arius has proceeded fairly clearly and coherently. The virtues have been firmly located within the class of goods, their specific differentiae have been stated, and we are well informed about their relationship to the goal of life. Formally speaking, the *telos* or goal has yet to be treated in its own right, but given Arius' division procedure, or any other procedure for that matter, he cannot deal with everything at once. If he is responsible for the next four theses in their present position – B2 and C7.1–7.3 – his credit for orderliness goes down. Thesis B2 seems

out of place,[16] c7.1 repeats c1.1; and c7.2 and c7.3 read like after-
thoughts, albeit legitimate ones. There is little point in speculating
about the history of these passages. Worse incongruities and repetitions occur later. But even if Arius himself let them pass, they do
not do much to disturb his exposition, and all are germane to an
account of the Stoic virtues.

There follow four pages (65–9) which, according to Diels, present a quite new subject: 'the character of the wise man'.[17] That is
certainly an accurate description of their contents, but it misrepresents the coherence of Arius' exposition by implying that he has
anticipated the subject of his final section. What he actually does
here is to set out a series of theses concerning *virtuous and vicious
dispositions* which simply continues his treatment of virtues and
vices. The wise and the inferior man enter his discussion at this
point because they illustrate a new and fundamental claim: 'There
is nothing intermediate between virtue and vice' (c8.1). This thesis
helps to sanction c8.2: 'The inferior are imperfect, and the good
are perfected', and it prepares for c8.3: 'The wise man always acts
according to all the virtues.' That proposition is inferred from the
fact that 'his every action is perfect, and so he falls short in no
virtue' (p. 65.13–14). The adverbs which now follow are no random description of the wise man's actions (c8.4). They are explicitly stated to 'follow from' c8.1–8.3 (p. 65.15). 'The wise man
does everything well' (c8.5) is partly based on his doing everything
in accordance with virtue (cf. c8.3).[18] So, contrary to Diels, these
pages continue and conclude the development of the virtues,
which have been consistently classified as a subdivision of goods.

[16] B2 = p. 64.13–17 explains Diogenes of Babylon's two senses of the phrase 'intrinsically
choiceworthy'. I include this passage as a B thesis because it applies to goods in general
and not only to the virtues. But it does refer to those virtues which are 'choiceworthy in
relation to the goal' (*telikōs haireta*), with a backward reference to pp. 62–3; and the virtues are being presented as a subdivision of 'goods'. Moreover, the position of B2 is paralleled in the Antiochean section of Cicero, *Fin.* v.67–8, where it also follows Cicero's
equivalent to c6.1–6.3. Stobaeus has three further sections on 'choiceworthy', all of
which are oddly placed: pp. 75.1, 78.7, 97.15. Cf. Giusta 1964, 1967, vol. I, pp. 43ff. for
suggestions about their original position.

[17] Cf. Diels 1879, p. 71

[18] It is also based upon his acting in accordance with 'right reason' (*orthos logos*), p. 66.19–
20. The justification and importance of this fundamental concept are not made clear in
Stobaeus, though he later records a brief account of it in the context of 'law' (p. 96.10–
12), repeated at p. 102.4–6. On this point D.L. vii.86–8 is much superior, bringing 'right
reason' into an analysis of virtue and the goal.

They provide, indeed, more than a catalogue. The wise man's sympotic and erotic activities are not merely asserted to be virtuous, but defined as instances of 'understanding' (*epistēmē*, p. 66.3–9). His 'doing everything well' (c8.5), though related to c8.3, is clarified by the assertion that 'virtue is an art embracing the whole of life' (p. 66.20–67.2). Arius does include, to be sure, certain 'professional skills' of the wise man (the so-called *epitēdeumata*) which are not, strictly speaking, virtues. They are 'goods', defined by reference to virtue (p. 67.12), and wholly appropriate to be mentioned here as being present in 'good tenors', i.e. virtuous dispositions (p. 67.8). They are followed, moreover, by piety, which is a virtue (pp. 67–8). ‖

After briefly applying the same procedures to the inferior man (p. 68), Arius (B3.i) returns in effect to his initial general thesis concerning all goods (B1.i): 'Goods comprise virtues and not-virtues.' That is the neatest explanation of the sequence of B theses which he now provides down to p. 74. Nor is it difficult to justify his procedure for ourselves, as readers and students. Having exhaustively treated the most important species of goods, the virtues, he can now assume an understanding of virtue and particular virtues in these subsequent classifications. Having also introduced the wise and the inferior man, he can refer to these without further explanation, as he does in his first new B theses (B3.i and B3.ii). Other concepts which have been briefly mentioned hitherto, e.g. non-essential goods and 'professional skills' (*epitēdeumata*), are also taken up and amplified. Thus these further B theses provide us with both fuller understanding of anything good, and more particularly, a framework to classify types of good and specific goods. By the end of p. 74 we can answer such questions as 'What is courage?' or 'What is joy?' and supply very detailed answers.

Regarding joy (*chara*) we can say that it is:

1. A good of the species not-virtue (B1.i.2).
2. It does not belong to all wise men, or to any of them all the time (B3.i).
3. It is beneficial, etc. (B4.i).
4. It is a final good (B7.i.1).
5. It is in motion (B10.1).

Or, regarding 'musicality,' we can say that it is:

1. A good of the species not-virtue (B10.2.b).
2. It does belong to all wise men (c8.5).
3. It is beneficial, etc. (B4.i).
4. It is a psychic good of the type 'tenor' (*hexis*) (B6.i.1.2).
5. It is at rest (B10.2.b).

The traditional moral virtues, together with a vast range of other 'good' qualities and skills, have now been suitably mapped. A quick glance at Diogenes Laertius (VII.89–101) will be sufficient to show how much more minutely and methodically Arius has done his Stoic cartography.

Now at last he turns to a new topic, the goal (pp. 75–8). Its relatively late appearance can be justified by at least two reasons. First, there is good evidence that the Stoics regularly discussed the goal (*telos*) after their treatment of virtue.[19] Secondly, according to Arius (p. 76.17–18), the first sense of the term *telos* which they distinguished was 'the final good', following 'philological practice', and this makes it appropriate to expound the goal after a full exposition of 'goods'. In Diogenes Laertius VII and in Cicero, *De finibus* III the main treatment of the goal arises early, in connexion with the doctrines of *oikeiōsis* and *primary* impulse. Arius, as we have seen, is anomalous in paying no attention to these. But he may ‖ reflect Stoic practice accurately in the fact that he reserves his detailed discussion of the goal to these later pages, while anticipating it in his brief remarks at c4 (cf. c8.1) on the relationship between living in accordance with nature, virtue, impulse and the goal.

The Stoic goal is happiness (*eudaimonia*), and it is the elucidation of this newly mentioned concept with which he is chiefly concerned in D1–5. This accounts for two theses concerning goods and evils (D3, D4) which would seem out of place if Arius were thought to be merely wandering back to his earlier topic (B). But they are placed here because he is concerned with distinguishing between those goods and evils which are necessary to happiness and unhappiness and those which are not.

Thesis D6 concludes with the sentence: 'And so the Stoic goal is equivalent to life in accordance with virtue' (p. 78.5). That would be a fitting end to the whole treatment of goods and the goal, which

---

[19] Cf. D.L. VII.84, which is discussed below.

is formally concluded half a page later (p. 79.1–2). In between, our text continues inconsequentially with B14, a thesis about goods as 'choiceworthy' and their difference from 'benefits' (*ōphelēmata*) as 'things to be chosen'. As Wachsmuth noted, B14 seems quite out of order, and would fit better along with B13, which in turn interrupts the transition from goods in general to the goal. I doubt whether the placing of either of these theses can be confidently assumed to fit Arius' original design. But they are a small blemish in an otherwise coherent account.

The next four sections run:

E theses	Indifferents (*adiaphora*)	pp. 79–85
F theses	Appropriate acts (*kathēkonta*)	pp. 85–6
G theses	Impulse (*hormē*)	pp. 86–93
H theses	Lives (*bioi*)	pp. 93–116

The first three need little discussion for the purpose of elucidating the structure of Arius' presentation. His E section was promised by his opening division (A) of existing things into goods, evils and indifferents. We have already seen how he announces his progression to the third of these. The substance and order of his treatment of indifferents agree closely with Diogenes Laertius (VII.104–7). But Arius is much the fuller, and there are differences over details.

Both doxographers conclude their treatment of indifferents with an account of those important *adiaphora* which have non-moral value and disvalue, the so-called 'preferred and rejected things' (*proēgmena* and *apoproēgmena*). The 'preferred' indifferents form the material of 'appropriate acts' (*kathēkonta*), and an understanding of the connexion between the two concepts is vital to a rudimentary grasp of Stoic ethics.[20] It is therefore helpful for Arius to preface his treatment of 'appropriate acts' (F) by observing that this topic follows on from the doctrine of preferred things (p. 85.12–13). Diogenes Laertius fails to bring out that link, which is further elucidated in Arius by his noting that 'appropriate acts' have 'certain ∥ indifferents' as their measuring stick (p. 86.12–13). Cicero makes the same point at greater length (*Fin.* III.58ff.).

'What sets impulse in motion is nothing else, they say, than an impression which directly impels the appropriate act' (p. 86.17–

---

[20] Cf. Kidd 1971, especially p. 155. A curious omission in D.L.'s treatment of 'appropriate' acts is all reference to their 'perfect' form (*katorthōmata*). However, he does include some material (VII.108) that is absent from Stobaeus.

18). This is the first sentence of Arius' section G on 'impulse', and it is clearly intended to indicate the doctrinal connexion between 'appropriate acts' (F) and 'impulse'. That connection emerges in Cicero explicitly and in Diogenes implicitly in their opening accounts of the natural objects to which animals are attracted from their birth onwards.[21] Arius, as we have already noted, has dispensed with their material on *oikeiōsis*, and impulse has previously figured only briefly in his comments on the cardinal virtues and their goal (C4).[22] What the present section offers is a set of definitions, by genus and species, of impulse considered normatively, concentrating on the species of 'practical impulse', and then passing to the deviant species, 'passion' (*pathos*). Arius' procedure is utterly methodical, but it raises interesting questions about his difference from Cicero, *De finibus* III and Diogenes Laertius VII. On 'passion' Diogenes corresponds to Arius closely,[23] but the little that he says on normative impulse is stated quite differently: only traces of Arius' opening matter are included, and they are placed as an appendix to 'passion' in a discussion of 'good emotional states' (*eupatheiai*), a term completely absent from Arius.[24] Cicero has just one short paragraph on 'passion' (*Fin* III.35), and does not connect it at all with any discussion of 'impulse'.[25] But both these writers show an interest, not shared by Arius, in connecting the concept of impulse with an animal's primary consciousness of values and the development of moral awareness.

It seems likely that Arius (or his sources) is more concerned with the systematic classification of concepts than with such questions as the justification or grounding of Stoic ethics.[26] He has given a detailed account of impulse. But he has not made it primary, as appears to have been the Stoic practice. This then, as was noted above, is a problem demanding elucidation. It may be postponed until our general survey of his material has been completed.

---

[21] *Fin.* III.20–5; D.L. VII.85–6.

[22] It also plays a part in his account of 'indifferents', pp. 79.8, 82.5.

[23] Cf. his VII.110–15 with Stobaeus pp. 88.8–93.13.

[24] D.L. VII.116 lists joy (*chara*), watchfulness (*eulabeia*) and well-wishing (*boulēsis*) as the three *eupatheiai*. That list is standard, cf. *SVF* III.431–42, but there is no trace of it in Stobaeus. Arius includes well-wishing as one of the species of 'practical impulse' (p. 87.16ff.) but joy is treated by him under 'goods', and he has nothing to say about watchfulness. Cicero knows of the *eupatheiai*, citing them in *Tusc. disp.* IV.12–14 but not in the *De finibus*.

[25] His cursory treatment of 'passion' may be due to his having already dealt with it fully in *Tusc. disp.* IV.10–32.

[26] 'A sort of glossary or lexicon', White 1983, p. 69.

The case for a coherent plan concerning section H in Stobaeus (pp. 93.14–116.10) is harder to make. As Wachsmuth notes (p. 93), this section presents miscellaneous material and considerable repetition. Yet, as he also points out, one theme does predominate, 'the character of the wise man'.

Section H starts abruptly with a thesis concerning 'perfectly appropriate acts' (*katorthōmata*) and 'faults' (*hamartēmata*, p. 93.14–18). It is given a cross-reference to the previous discussion of 'appropriate acts' (p. 85.19). So either Arius or Stobaeus or an intermediary is aware of the position of this material. Next, linked on by 'and' (*te*), comes a thesis concerning the community of goods possessed by good people, and the mutual hostility of inferior people (pp. 93.19–94.6). The next three pages seem to follow on quite coherently, dealing as they do with the social and political characteristics of the two classes of people. If this is their theme, there is good reason for them to juxtapose treatments of justice, politics, education, friendship, business activities, forgiveness, punishment, law – and to ‖ amplify the thesis concerning the community of goods (p. 95.3–8). The opening thesis of the section, on 'perfectly appropriate acts' and 'faults', gains point as the preface to this list of actions, presented normatively as characteristic of the wise or inferior man. Some actions, however, such as talking and walking, are morally neutral taken by themselves, so Arius suitably rounds off this passage by a three-part classification of actions (*energēmata*): 'perfectly appropriate acts', 'faults' and 'neither' (pp. 96.18–97.14).

The remainder of the whole piece continues the description of the two classes of human beings. Principal differences between them are outlined (pp. 98.14–100.14). Then, after paragraphs on the different predicates applicable to virtue (pp. 100.15–101.4) and a reminder concerning the exclusive possession by good persons of goods and by inferior persons of evils (pp. 101.4–102.3), we get a lengthy description of the epithets and actions which characterise the two classes of people, punctuated by occasional irrelevant paragraphs in the manner of the earlier sections.[27] The main intention, if marred at times by inept execution, is plain. On the basis of the ethical concepts outlined in the previous sections Arius is

---

[27] E.g. p. 113.18–23, where a short account of the equality of all faults has no connexion with its surrounding contexts on the behaviour of the wise.

indicating that this is what a good human being is like in Stoicism
and how an inferior one differs. As before, he offers us a map
which will enable us to locate the principal concepts of Greek
social life and moral character on a Stoic interpretation of them.

Arius' treatment of Stoic ethics appears then to be based upon
the following plan:

A   Goods, evils, and indifferents
B/C   Goods and evils: virtues and vices
B   Goods and evils more generally
D   Goal
E   Indifferents
F   Appropriate acts
G   Impulse
H   Lives (good and inferior human beings)

How does this scheme compare with the accounts of Diogenes
Laertius and Cicero? Like Arius, Diogenes passes from G (restricted by him to 'passion') to H. At VII.117 he begins a characterisation of the wise man which persists up to 124 with an interruption in 120 concerned mainly with the equality of all faults.[28] His
final chapters (129–31) are a sketchy collection of material on the
wise man's social behaviour which corresponds broadly to Arius'
treatment. These are preceded by a lengthy and ill placed discussion of virtue (125–9), which handles points presented by Arius
within his discussion of goods.[29]

Minor differences apart, Arius and Diogenes agree in moving
from the exposition of ethical concepts to a characterisation of the
wise man and the good life, focusing particularly on social behaviour. Cicero's treatment in *De finibus* is similar. He too deals in his
final chapters (from III.62) with social conduct and the wise man.
Like Arius and Diogenes he includes within this material a section
on ethical concepts, justifying mention of them at this place by
their relevance to 'the preservation of ‖ human society' (III.69).[30]

---

[28] So too Stobaeus; see previous note.
[29] But Stobaeus himself includes a passage on the predicates of virtue, p. 100.15ff., within
his final section, which corresponds to an early part of D.L.'s account of the predicates
of good, VII.99. Such common disorder suggests confusion probably subsequent to Arius
in the transmission of the material.
[30] *Ut vero conservetur omnis homini erga hominem societas, coniunctio, caritas, et emolumenta et detrimenta*
(*quae* ophelemata *et* blammata *appellant*), *communia esse voluerunt.* Similarly Stobaeus,
p. 101.5–13 within his last section.

We may conclude therefore that Arius' procedure in his final section had the authority of the sources used by Diogenes and Cicero.

As for the earlier sections of Arius, Diogenes agrees with him in the order of treating virtues and vices, goods and evils, indifferents, appropriate acts, and passions (C, B, E, F, G). The main procedural differences between them have already been mentioned: Diogenes begins with impulse and goal; Arius handles these later, and starts from the division into goods, evils and indifferents. Diogenes, it should be noted, knows of this division, but uses it only to conclude his discussion of goods and evils and to introduce indifferents.[31] It plays no structural part in his narrative, and its presence in Cicero is even more tenuous (*Fin.* III.50).

Cicero proceeds less systematically than Arius or Diogenes. He agrees with Diogenes against Arius in starting with impulse, and this determines his early treatment of the goal and virtue (III.12–26). But his manner of presenting goods and evils, indifferents and appropriate acts is sufficiently similar to theirs to indicate a common background. One oddity is the brevity and placing of his section on passions (see n.25 above).

The distinctive features of Arius' exposition appear to be:

1. His opening division into goods, evils and indifferents.
2. His lack of interest in 'impulse' as a primary ethical concept.
3. The amplitude, system and exhaustive nature of his mapping of ethical concepts.

Would we be justified in attributing any of these characteristics to his own initiative rather than to Stoic or other sources?

THE BACKGROUND AND FUNCTION OF ARIUS' EXPOSITION

Diogenes Laertius reports a division of the topics of ethics which was adopted, he says, by all the leading Stoics from Chrysippus down to Posidonius (VII.84): 'They divide the ethical part of philosophy into: (1) the topic of impulse, (2) that of goods and evils, (3) that of passions, (4) of virtue, (5) of the goal, (6) of primary value and actions, (7) of appropriate acts, (8) of suasions and dissuasions.'

---

[31] As Charles Kahn pointed out in the discussion of the original paper, this sentence of Diogenes is wrongly punctuated in the modern editions. It goes with what follows, and should thus begin a new paragraph.

The interpretation of these headings is an unsolved problem. Most of them are familiar enough, and fit Arius' exposition with minor adjustments: 1 and 3 = G, 2 = B, 4 = C, 5 = D, 6 = E (in part), 7 = F. If 'suasions and dissuasions' (8) corresponds to his final section 'Lives (good and bad human beings)' (H), which seems plausible, the only misfit (and the same holds good for Cicero and Diogenes Laertius) is 'actions' (the second part of 6). What seems to be needed in place of 'actions' is a reference to 'indifferents' (*adia-phora*).

More problematical is the ordering of the topics. Why are 'passions' placed so early in the list? They are treated relatively late in all three of our authors, and that seems obviously where they should come. It has been suggested that the first three ‖ topics are generic; and if this is right, it would allow topics 4 to 7 to be treated under 2 (or 1 and 2), leaving 'passions' till later.[32] But that solution is rather forced, since 6 and 7 are regularly expounded after the discussion of goods and evils has been completed. Rather than offering a general interpretation of the division, I propose to consider what light it may shed on the special features of Arius' exposition.

The first and basic observation is the support it gives to the opening procedures of Cicero and Diogenes against Arius. They both begin their treatment of Stoic ethics with 'impulse', the first topic of the division. In Arius 'impulse' plays a modest part in the treatment of C, D, E and F, but it is not discussed in its own right until he reaches G, his seventh topic. There, moreover, as we saw, it subsumes the treatment of 'passions', yet these are treated independently by Cicero and Diogenes, and their methodology has the support of the division attributed to Chrysippus and his successors. Arius' different procedure is much too sharp to be accounted for by disturbance to his text in the transmission to Stobaeus.[33] Otherwise, however, he agrees so closely with Cicero and Diogenes in his ordering of subjects that a common Stoic tradition appears to be at work.

---

[32] This was argued by Dyroff 1897, pp. 4–7. Cf. Zeller 1892–1909, vol. III.1, pp. 210–12, who accepted the generic interpretation of the first three topics but rejected Dyroff's attempt to classify the remainder accordingly.

[33] I do not exclude considerable tampering with Arius' text, to account for minor displacements and incongruities; cf. Giusta 1964, 1967, vol. I, pp. 43–5, for suggestions about some of these.

Stoic interest in the systematic exposition of ethics received its chief stimulus from Chrysippus.[34] In the list of his ethical writings, partially preserved in Diogenes Laertius (VII.199–202), several works are mentioned which may bear directly or indirectly on Arius' account. In his final words Arius notes that 'Chrysippus has discussed all the paradoxical doctrines in many different works' and he singles out two of these: *On doctrines* and *Outline of the theory*. The second of these is probably the first item listed in Diogenes' catalogue of Chrysippus' ethical books (VII.199); and the first section of the catalogue includes other works whose titles recall material in Arius and the other summary treatments of Stoic ethics: *Ethical theses, Definitions of the good human being, Definitions of the inferior human being, On the qualities of the virtues*, etc.

From a comparison of Arius, Cicero and Diogenes, von Arnim concluded that there existed a standard compendium of Stoic ethics, going back to Chrysippus, which was revised by later generations of Stoics.[35] What was common to all three authors, he suggested, could be explained by their recourse to this book by Chrysippus. Their deviations were due to 'a later time' – by which I take von Arnim to mean differently annotated later editions of the book, or different use of the annotations it contained. This is an economical and plausible suggestion. But its plausibility is compatible with a different explanation of the principal differences between Arius and the others; it does not readily explain those differences, which are matters of procedure rather than details of doctrine.[36]

Cicero is distinctive in devoting the greatest space to *oikeiōsis* and the acquisition of moral understanding. Diogenes actually quotes Chrysippus on this subject (VII.85), but his own exposition is more perfunctory than Cicero's. Arius, if he is the author of Stobaeus pp. 47–8 and the Peripatetic section (pp. 118–23), knows all about *oikeiōsis*, but omits it completely from his Stoic section. Cicero and Arius agree ‖ against Diogenes in presenting the main doctrines as a derived sequence of theses, coherently related together; but Cic-

---

[34] In the catalogue of Chrysippus' works, a whole section is devoted to 'the articulation of ethical concepts' (D.L. VII.199); and the earlier Stoic Sphaerus had written a work *On the arrangement of ethics* (D.L. VII.177).

[35] Cf. von Arnim in *SVF* I p. xli.

[36] White 1983, pp. 69–70, expresses this point more forcefully. For a good account of significant differences between Cicero and Diogenes, cf. Hirzel 1882, vol. II, pp. 574ff.

ero makes no use of the division into goods, evils and indifferents. Arius is distinctive in the sheer quantity of information he provides, his systematic use of the division procedure, and his very sparse references to the attested views of individual Stoic philosophers. His theses are frequently presented in the form of inferences, unlike the bald summaries of Diogenes. But they are not inferences which carry the reader forward in an evolving progression, as Cicero attempts to do.

How much can we learn about the basis of Arius' procedure by considering further material in Stobaeus?

If it is correct to supply his name before the definitions of ethical terms given on pp. 37–9, he was strongly influenced in these by Peripatetic and later Platonic theory. An orthodox Stoic would not define 'moral character' (*ēthos*) by reference to 'training the irrational part of the soul to be subordinate to reason' (p. 38.3–4), and Arius attributes this and his other opening definitions to 'the Platonists'. An interest in 'the irrational' is the dominant factor in this set of definitions, which continues with 'passion' (*pathos*), 'defined by Aristotle as irrational excessive motion of soul' (p. 38.19–20). The material attributed to Aristotle is in fact contaminated with Stoicism, an indication of the eclecticism we could expect from Arius. He does make explicit reference to Stoic definitions in this section, but they are subordinate to the purportedly Platonic and Aristotelian doctrines.

Next we are given the divisions of ethics worked out by Philo of Larisa and Eudorus of Alexandria (pp. 39–45). The Philonian division appears to have had no influence on Arius' presentation of Stoic and Peripatetic ethics. After expounding it, he says: 'If I were lazier, I should be content with it and now unfold the doctrines, supported by his six-part outline. But since I think I should above all study the substance (*ousia*) of a subject, and then its quality and quantity, and following these, its relation, I believe I must make the further effort of studying some other people's views as well, not all of them, but those which differ on these points' (pp. 41.26–42.6).[37] So he now outlines Eudorus' division of ethics. Following that, he says he must 'start with the main topics (*pro-*

---

[37] This showy parade of Aristotle's 'categories' plays no apparent part in the succeeding exposition.

blēmata), prefacing them with the headings (*genē*) according to my own arrangement, which I am convinced is conducive to clarity in division' (p. 45.8–10).

These elaborate statements of procedure are peculiar and interesting. It sounds as if Arius is setting out acknowledged methods of division before settling upon a practice of his own. 'My own arrangement' may refer both to the summary analysis of terms and topics which precedes the exposition of Stoic ethics (pp. 45–57), and to that exposition itself (pp. 57–116). But first we have to ask how Arius stands in regard to Eudorus' division.

That scheme had three principal sections (p. 42.13–15): (1) study of the value of each thing, (2) impulse, (3) action. The second section, impulse, is subdivided into (a) the species of impulse, (b) passion (p. 44.3–4). Here at last we have found authority for Arius' idiosyncratic handling of impulse in his Stoic exposition. Both ‖ Eudorus and Arius agree in removing impulse from the primary position for ethical topics. They also agree in dividing the topic of impulse, so that it includes both a list of its species and a treatment of passion. That too has no support in Chrysippus' division or in the accounts of Cicero and Diogenes.

Eudorus' third section, 'action', matches Arius less well (pp. 44.6–45.6). It includes 'appropriate acts' (*kathēkonta*); but these were treated by Arius in their own right according to regular Stoic practice. Material in Arius' own final section (H) on lives and social behaviour found its place in Eudorus here, but under 'action'. Eudorus also treated moralising advice and other topics which appear in Arius, if at all, only by implication from his descriptions of the wise and inferior human being.[38]

Eudorus' first section is difficult to ascertain in detail owing to the defective state of Stobaeus' text.[39] From a summary it would appear that 'goods and evils' served as a generic heading for the whole section (p. 43.15–17, 44.1–2), which treated of goals, virtues and also 'the so-called preferred things' (*proēgmena*), such as fame

---

[38] But the eighth topic in D.L. VII.84, 'suasions and dissuasions', well describes much of Eudorus' subject-matter.

[39] I must briefly indicate that Wachsmuth's understanding of this passage, and the supplement he prints, seem to me quite mistaken. He takes it that 'goods and evils' and 'virtues and vices' were treated as quite distinct topics. That seems to be due to a misreading of p. 43.1–4. The conclusion of the passage makes the 'most generic' status of 'goods and evils' perspicuous, and it need be no objection that virtues and vices are not restated as an example of 'the many divisions' of goods and evils, p. 43.17ff.

and good appearance. If that is correct, this section of Eudorus will have embraced the material located by Arius in his sections B, C and D, but it will also have been extended to take in the treatment of 'indifferents' (Arius' section E), which necessarily falls outside Arius' sections on goods and evils.

That conclusion should not surprise us. Eudorus must have intended his division to cover the exposition of all ethical systems. His terminology and practice were influenced, as they were bound to be in the mid first century BC, by the dominant place of Stoicism. But if he wanted his division to fit all ethical systems of the time, it had to be flexible enough to accommodate divergent doctrines. The Stoics were out on a limb in confining goods and evils to virtues and vices. Other schools were happy enough to treat the Stoics' 'so-called preferred things' as goods of a certain kind.[40] Anyone like Arius, intent on expounding Stoic ethics *per se*, would have to make a sharp break between goods and indifferents, of which the 'preferred things' are a species.

Given the general suitability of Eudorus' first section, the precise agreement between him and Arius on impulse and the loose compatibility between them in regard to Eudorus' third section, it seems probable that Arius used Eudorus in working out his own division of Stoic ethics. But he used him discriminatingly, drawing also upon the standard divisions of Stoic philosophers, and contributing something of his own.

Before attempting to finalise this last point, I must say a word about two other passages of Stobaeus: the summary analysis of terms and doctrines which comes between Eudorus and the Stoic section (pp. 45–57), and the Peripatetic section.

The summary analysis comes immediately after Arius' remarks on his 'own arrangement of division'. It appears to be an elucidation of the key terms which would figure in the first section of a Eudorean division: goal and target (cf. Eudorus p. 43.2–3), subordinate goal (*hypotelis*), happiness, virtue, goods and evils. The sources of the material, acknowledged or unacknowledged, are eclectic in the highest degree. As in the introductory pages of definitions (37–9), the supposed views of ‖ Plato and Aristotle have pride of place. But Stoics, and even Epicureans, get a mention. The most curious feature of this summary analysis is the treatment of 'subordinate

---

[40] Cf. the Peripatetic section, p. 124.15ff.

goal', *hypotelis*, a term which seems to originate with the early Stoic, Herillus.[41] No school of philosophy is mentioned in the account of 'subordinate goal'. But the doctrine reported, and nearly all the terminology, are pure Stoicism. We are given an entirely clear and accurate account of the Stoic doctrine of *oikeiōsis*, with reference to the primary impulse of living creatures and a list of 'the primary things in accordance with nature' (pp. 47.12–48.5). The purpose of the passage however is not to expound Stoicism as such, but to show that 'the subordinate goal' accommodates all possible candidates, taking in all philosophical positions, for the object of the primary impulse. That catholic procedure is well known for its use by Carneades and Antiochus.[42] It suits our expectations of Eudorus or Arius very well.[43]

But if Arius is the author of this material, he has behaved very curiously in excluding it from his treatment of Stoic ethics. All the more so, if he is the author of the Peripatetic section. For that presents a most detailed exposition of this very doctrine in its opening (pp. 118.5–123.27). Other problems about Arius come to the surface once the Stoic and Peripatetic sections are compared. If he had the eclectic interests which are manifest in Stobaeus' introductory sections, we should expect these to be reflected in like manner in his expositions of the two ethical systems. We should also expect that his methods of dividing the topics of ethics would be similar in these two sections. Yet neither of these expectations is satisfied. The division procedure of Eudorus has only the loosest approximation to the methodology of the Peripatetic section, but it fits the Stoic section fairly closely. The Peripatetic section offers a glaring contamination of Stoic and Peripatetic material.[44] But the account of Stoic ethics, if largely indifferent to distinguishing

---

[41] *SVF* I.411. Cf. Dyroff 1897, pp. 49ff.

[42] Cf. Cicero, *Fin.* v.16ff., and Zeller 1892–1909, vol. III.1, p. 635 n. 1.

[43] Dillon 1977, p. 116, thinks Arius' list of *problēmata* (pp. 45–7) is taken from Eudorus. That may be so, but the preface to these (p. 45.8–10) seems to refer in the first person to Arius himself. For further treatment of Eudorus, and support for his influence on Arius, cf. Kahn 1983, p. 10, and Hahm 1983, pp. 27–30. See also p. 250 of this volume.

[44] See n. 9 above. In making this assessment of the Peripatetic section, I recognise that it contains some genuine reminiscence of Aristotle and Theophrastus. But the famous comment by Diels 1879, p. 71, remains valid: *Stoicae disciplinae non guttae sed flumina immissa sunt.* Wachsmuth's critical apparatus collects the obvious references to Stoic doctrine. Antiochus, of course, maintained that those doctrines were largely derived from the Platonic/Peripatetic tradition, so that their presence would not represent contamination in his eyes. The evidence for Stoic material in this section is not restricted to the occurrence

between material from different periods of the system, does not appear to be infected with doctrines from any other school.

At this point it would be prudent to drop any pretence that we know Arius as the author of the Stoic section, especially when our sole *evidence* for his presence in Stobaeus comes from the treatment of Peripatetic ethics. But it may just be possible to devise a hypothesis to salvage his joint authorship, though its lack of economy will reveal its frailty.

We have to assume, I think, that Arius was largely content to transmit the principal sources he used without intruding his own contributions. In the case of the Peripatetic section he followed a handbook by Antiochus, or someone like him, which viewed Aristotelian doctrines through the strongly tinted glasses of Stoicism. For the Stoics Arius used a reliable Stoic compendium of the kind suggested by von Arnim. For his introductory sections he compiled material from standard handbooks so as to give a representative account of basic terms in common use in the different schools. But this unoriginal man had one or two ideas of his own about the right way to present summaries of doctrine. He tells us as much (p. 45.8), and his greatest idea was to structure his division of Stoic philosophy around the stock classification: ‖ goods, evils, indifferents. There is no evidence that Eudorus did this, and Arius did not do it for the Peripatetics but it seemed to him right for the Stoics.

The division had to be bought at a price, and the price was high. Arius decided he would have to jettison the Stoics' standard practice of beginning their ethics with the 'primary impulse' and *oikeiōsis*.[45] But he paid that price, justifying himself by Eudorus' division in which impulse arises second to goods and evils. He attempted, with only moderate success, to graft brief mentions of impulse onto his treatment of the goal. Fortunately for our understanding of Stoicism, Cicero and Diogenes Laertius were unaffected by Arius'

---

of terminology (e.g. *kathēkonta*), and the opening treatment of *oikeiōsis* (for which it was once fashionable to claim a Peripatetic origin). Quite distinctively Stoic doctrines are frequently included, e.g. selection of natural advantages, p. 119.16; justified suicide, p. 126.6; moral progress (*procopē*) p. 131.17.

[45] Cf. Kahn 1983, p. 11, for the intriguing suggestion that Arius 'having treated this theory briefly in his introduction [pp. 44–8] and at length in his account of the Peripatetics, saw no need to repeat it in the concluding section on Stoic ethics'. Kahn makes the good point that Arius may have regarded *oikeiōsis* as a commonly held doctrine about human nature generally. But that still fails to explain his total reticence about it in his main treatment of Stoic ethics.

procedure. But it may have been influential. Sextus Empiricus regards the division into goods, evils and indifferents as character- istic of the Old Academy, Peripatetics and Stoics,[46] and by begin- ning his ethical discussion with it he implies its logical priority. The division itself of course was utterly hackneyed. But Arius may have been original in using it as the structure for classifying the first topics of Stoic ethics.

If all this turns Arius into something of a hack, we should not complain. His detailed material in the Stoic section is probably more accurate and certainly fuller than anything else we possess. He could have followed the substance, if not the order, of a Chry- sippean handbook very closely. Unlike Diogenes Laertius, he rarely names individual Stoics, and the latest whom he does name is Panaetius.[47] Unlike Diogenes again, he refers only once to specific books by Stoics, and those are the works of Chrysippus mentioned in his conclusion. Their titles suggest the sobering reflection that we may be reading a good deal of Chrysippus in Arius Didymus, or whoever he is.[48] ‖

APPENDIX: Table of ethical theses in Stobaeus II, pp. 57–85

A	Existing things comprise: 1. goods 　　　　　　　　　　　2. evils 　　　　　　　　　　　3. indifferents	p. 57.19–58.4	D.L. VII.101 (cf. Cic. *Fin.* III.50)
BI.i	Goods (A1) comprise: 1. virtues 　　　　　　　　2. not-virtues, e.g. joy	p. 58.5–9	D.L. VII.102
BI.ii	Evils (A2) comprise: 1. vices 　　　　　　　　2. not-vices, e.g. grief	p. 58.14–18	D.L. VII.102
CI.i	Virtues (BI.i.1) comprise: 1. sciences and skills 　　　　　　　　　　2. not-sciences or not- 　　　　　　　　　　skills	p. 58.9–14	(cf. D.L. VII.93)
CI.ii	Vices (BI.ii.1) comprise: 1. ignorances and lacks 　　　　　　　　　　of skills 　　　　　　　　　　2. not-ignorances or 　　　　　　　　　　not-lacks of skills	p. 58.18–59.3	(cf. D.L. VII.93)

[46] *M* XI.3ff.

[47] The complete absence of *eupatheiai* from Arius' treatment of impulse (cf. n. 24 above) may suggest that this ill-attested doctrine was posterior to Chrysippus.

[48] The only significant change I have made to the original version of this paper is the addi- tion of references to the work of Hahm 1983, Kahn 1983 and White 1983, who were co- contributors with me at the conference on Arius Didymus organised by Bill Fortenbaugh at Rutgers University in 1981.

c1.i.1 are cardinally exemplified	p. 59.4–11	
c1.ii.1 are cardinally exemplified	p. 59.11–60.5	
c2 Virtue generically defined	p. 60.7–8	D.L. vii.89
c3 Virtues comprise: 1. primary (= c1.i.1) 2. subordinate (= c1.i.1)	p. 60.9–62.6	D.L. vii.92, 126
c4 The goal of all c1.i.1 virtues is life in accordance with nature	p. 62.7–14	(cf. D.L. vii.87, Cic. *Fin.* iii.22)
c5 All c1.i.1 virtues are constitutive of life's goals and consist of rational principles	p. 62.15–17	D.L. vii.90
All c1.i.2 virtues are supervenient on them and acquired by practice	p. 62.17–63.5	D.L. vii.90
c6.1 All c1.i.1 virtues have common rational principles and goal; inseparable	p. 63.6–64.12	D.L. vii.125–6
c6.2 All c1.i.1 virtues differ in their subject-matter		
c6.3 All c1.i.1 virtues review their subordinate and each other's subject-matter		
B2 ⟨goods as⟩ choiceworthy for their own sake comprise: 1. virtues = c1.i.1 (choiceworthy as goals) 2. all goods (intrinsically choiceworthy)	p. 64.13–17	D.L. vii.127, Cic. *Fin.* iii.36
c7.1 Virtues are plural and inseparable (cf. c6.1, c6.2)	p. 64.18–20	
c7.2 Virtue is corporeal	p. 64.20–23	
c7.3 Virtue is a living thing	p. 65.1–6	
c8.1 Nothing between virtue and vice	p. 65.7	D.L. vii.127
c8.2 Inferior are imperfect, good are perfect	p. 65.8–11	(cf. D.L. vii.128)
c8.3 Wise man always acts in accordance with all the virtues	p. 65.12–14	(cf. D.L. vii.125, 128, Cic. *Fin.* iii.32)
c8.4 Wise man's loving etc. is acting in accordance with virtue	p. 65.15–66.13	(cf. D.L. vii.122–4)
c8.5 Wise man does everything well	p. 66.14–68.3	D.L. vii.125 (cf. Cic. *Fin.* iii.75)
c8.6 Contrary theses concerning the inferior man	p. 68.3–23	
B3.i Goods comprise: 1. those which always belong to all wise men 2. those which do not	p. 68.24–69.4	
B3.ii Evils comprise: 1. those which always belong to all fools 2. those which do not	p. 69.5–10	

B4.i   All goods are beneficial, etc.   p. 69.11–14   D.L. VII.98 (cf.
                                                                         Cic. *Fin.* III.33)

B4.ii All evils are harmful, etc.

B5.i   3 senses of the good   p. 69.17–70.3   D.L. VII.94

B5.ii 3 senses of the evil   p. 70.3–7

B6.i   Goods comprise: 1. psychic   p. 70.8–14   D.L. VII.95
                        2. external
                        3. neither

B6.ii Evils comprise: same division   p. 70.14–20

B6.i.1 Goods comprise: 1. 'invariant conditions'   p. 70.21–71.6   D.L. VII.98
                          (*diatheseis*) – virtues
                        2. 'tenors' (*hexeis*) –
                           e.g. prophecy

B6.ii.1 Evils comprise: same division   p. 71.6–14

B7.i   Goods comprise: 1. final – e.g. joy (cf. B1.i.2) p. 71.15–72.6   D.L. VII.97, Cic.
                        2. efficient   *Fin.* III.55
                        3. both – virtues

B7.ii Evils comprise: same division   p. 72.6–13

B8   Goods comprise: 1. intrinsically choiceworthy   p. 72.14–18
                        2. efficient

B9.i   Every good is choiceworthy (cf. B2)   p. 72.19–25   D.L. VII.98

B9.ii Every evil is to be avoided

B10   Goods comprise: 1. moving – e.g. joy   p. 73.1–15
                        2. stationary: a. in disposition
                                          (*schesis*) only
                                        b. also in tenor
                                          (*hexis*)

B11   Goods comprise: 1. absolute   p. 73.16–74.14
                        2. relative

B12   Goods comprise: 1. unmixed   p. 74.15–20
                        2. mixed

(The differentiae of B10–12 apply similarly to vices   p. 74.21–2)

B13   ⟨good as⟩ choiceworthy distinguished from   p. 75.1–6   Cic. *Fin.* III.21–2
       'takable'

D1   Virtue and happiness described   p. 75.7–10   D.L. VII.88, Cic.
                                                                         Fin. III.28

D2   Definitions and senses of goal   p. 75.11–77.5   D.L. VII.87–8,
                                                                         Cic. *Fin.* III.21,26

D3   Goods comprise: 1. necessary to happiness   p. 77.6–15
                        2. not necessary to happiness

D4   Evils comprise: 1. necessary to unhappiness   p. 77.10–15
                        2. not necessary to unhappiness

D5	Happiness as goal	p. 77.16–27	D.L. VII.88
D6	Equivalence of goal to life in accordance with virtue	p. 78.1–6	D.L. VII.87, Cic. *Fin.* III.21
B14	⟨good as⟩ 'choiceworthy' distinguished from benefit 'to be chosen'	p. 78.7–12	
E1	Indifferents defined in reference to: 1. good and evil 2. impulse	p. 79.1–17	D.L. VII.104–5
E2	Indifferents (E1.1) comprise: 1. in accordance with nature 2. contrary to nature 3. neither 1 nor 2		cf. D.L. VII.107, Cic. *Fin.* III.20, 51
E3	Indifferents (E1.1) comprise: 1. small/great worth 2. intrinsic/efficient 3. preferred/rejected/ neither	p. 80.14–21	Cic. *Fin.* III.56, D.L. VII.107, D.L. VII.105, Cic. *Fin.* III.51
E4	'Preferred' indifferents comprise: 1. psychic 2. corporeal 3. external	p. 80.22–81.6	D.L. VII.106
	(E4 classifications applied to 'rejected' and 'neither' indifferents	p. 81.7–18	D.L. VII.106)
E5	E4.1 'preferred indifferents' of more worth than E4.2 and 3	p. 81.19–82.4	
E6	Indifferents (E1) comprise: 1. rousing impulse towards 2. rousing impulse away from 3. neither 1 or 2	p. 82.5–10	
E7	Indifferents (E2.1) comprise: 1. primary 2. by participation	p. 82.11–19	
	(Similarly applied to E2.2 indifferents)		
E8	All indifferents (E2.1, E2.2) are takable/not-takable	p. 82.20–83.9	
E9	Three senses of worth/non-worth	p. 83.10–84.17	D.L. VII.105
	(E10 repetition of E3.1, E3.3, etc.	p. 84.18–85.3)	
E11	Clarification of the term 'preferred'	p. 85.3–11	Cic. *Fin.* III.52

CHAPTER 6

The logical basis of Stoic ethics*

The Stoics said the goal of human beings is to live consistently
with or according to nature.[1] They also said that the goal can be
described by other expressions all of which are, perhaps, equally
valid: in particular, 'life according to reason', 'life according to
virtue', and 'happiness' or 'the attainment of happiness'.[2] All these
expressions have the same denotation, and cumulatively they may
give the impression that the central principles of Stoic ethics are
a series of vicious circles: one should live according to nature because this accords with reason; one should live rationally because
this accords with nature, etc. In this paper I shall argue that Stoic
ethics is not based upon a series of vicious circles. 'Accordance
with Nature' (I use this capitalised form to distinguish nature in
its cosmic sense from human nature) expresses what is right or
good in itself, and all other things have value if and only if they
accord with Nature. I recognise that Nature and 'right reason' are
often used as apparent synonyms by Stoic writers, but I claim that
Nature is not logically equivalent to 'right reason', but is that
which has 'right reason' as a necessary property.

In the modern literature I have found little enlightenment on
this subject. It seems now to be assumed that we all understand
the basic principles, but it is just these which I have found most
puzzling. There is need for a new description of Stoic ethics, a

---

* The original version of this chapter was a paper delivered to a meeting of the Aristotelian
  Society in London in 1971.
[1] By 'Stoics' in this chapter I refer to the early Greek Stoics, Zeno, Cleanthes and Chrysippus. Some of the evidence on which I draw is not attributed to any one of them by
  name, but I shall not make use of material which is conventionally regarded as a product
  of later Stoicism.
[2] It would usurp too much space to explain why 'virtue' and 'happiness' are only approxi-
  mate translations of *aretē* and *eudaimonia* respectively. 'Virtue' and 'happiness' are the conventional translations. For further discussion of these terms, see chapters 8 and 9.

task well beyond the scope of a single chapter. Here I want to make a start by offering first some general observations on ‖ Nature, then a short discussion of the other concepts mentioned above, and finally an analysis of Diogenes Laertius VII.85–8, a text which places reason, virtue and human nature in an argument concerned to establish the goal of human life.

NATURE AND ITS IMPLICATIONS

At the beginning of his discussion of 'naturalistic ethics' in *Principia Ethica* (pp. 41–2) G. E. Moore wrote:

And, first of all, one of the most famous of ethical maxims is that which recommends a 'life according to nature'. That was the principle of the Stoic Ethics; but, since their Ethics has some claim to be called metaphysical, I shall not attempt to deal with it here.

Moore returns to the Stoics in his chapter on 'metaphysical ethics'. He groups the Stoics with Spinoza and Kant, observing (p. 113):

A 'Metaphysical Ethics' is marked by the fact that it makes the assertion: That which would be perfectly good is something which exists, but is not natural; that which has some characteristic possessed by a supersensible reality. Such an assertion was made by the Stoics when they asserted that a life in accordance with Nature was perfect. For they did not mean by 'Nature', what I have so defined, but something supersensible which they inferred to exist, and which they held to be perfectly good.

Moore, then, denies that the Stoics, with the expression 'life in accordance with Nature', meant something 'which is the subject-matter of the natural sciences and also of psychology ... that has existed, does exist, or will exist in time' (p. 40).

     At face value Moore's remarks about the Stoics are fundamentally wrong, but they are none the less illuminating. Moore is wrong because he ascribes to the Stoics metaphysical principles which they strenuously denied.[3] The Stoics confined existence to bodies, meaning that only those things can be said to exist which have threefold extension together with resistance (*SVF* II.381). Under bodies they included both material objects, as we would understand that expression, and also the dispositions or properties

---

[3] For the main evidence on which this paragraph is based see Long 1971b, pp. 75–6, 88–90.

of material objects. These latter are held to be the *pneuma* (fiery breath), the active principle which holds each material ‖ object together, 'in a certain state of tension'; and *pneuma* describes an aspect of Nature. Objects of thought which have no bodily reference in either of these senses do not 'exist in some supersensible reality' (Moore's phrase, p. 111). They are 'mere ideas', parasitic upon our thinking or speaking of them. The Stoics however did not regard 'the good' as a mere idea, nor did they understand Nature to refer to 'something supersensible which they inferred to exist'. Both the good and virtue are said to be bodies, in the secondary sense. These terms have a common denotation, a particular disposition of the matter which constitutes the mind; and empirical arguments were used to prove the perceptibility of the good.[4] Further, one of the alternative definitions of the ethical goal is 'living according to experience of Natural events', where there is no question that this is compatible with 'living according to virtue' and no question that 'Natural events' refers to (though it also evaluates) a sensible reality.

Why then did Moore classify the Stoics under metaphysical ethics in his sense of metaphysical? This is a large question. Out of a number of possible answers I select two which seem to me to be significant.

The Stoics certainly held that from propositions asserting how things really are we can derive propositions concerning what is good. Propositions about Nature in Stoicism are often, perhaps always, to be construed as propositions about how things really are. Consider the following statement by Chrysippus: 'There is no possible or more suitable way to approach the subject of good and bad things, the virtues and happiness than from universal Nature and the management of the universe' (Plutarch, *Stoic. rep.* 1035c). This proposition means that some knowledge of reality is necessary as a premiss for correct conclusions as to what ought to exist. Now Moore seems to hold that this is the meaning of basing ethics upon metaphysics if and only if the term 'supersensible' precedes the word 'reality' in the last assertion. In fact, the Stoics had nothing to say about metaphysics as such. They sought to derive ethics from physics, the inquiry into the Nature of sensible objects. ‖ Moore however may have thought that what the Stoics sought to

---

[4] Plutarch, *Stoic. rep.* 1042e–f; Seneca, *Ep.* 106.

do is irrelevant in this case to what they actually did. He might have argued that Nature itself cannot be an object of sense-perception, and therefore propositions which have Nature as their subject must be propositions about a 'supersensible' entity.

As a comment on Stoicism this would, I think, be interesting and important. The Stoics inferred the existence and properties of Nature by observation of particular phenomena which seemed to them to require a teleological explanation.[5] It would be tedious here to offer an exhaustive list of all the alternative descriptions and all the properties which the Stoics gave to Nature. God, craftsman, artistic fire are alternative descriptions; providence, right reason, law are aspects or properties of Nature. Now to describe Nature as divine or artistic, or to speak of Nature's providence or right-reasoning, is to set up a norm or principle of universal value. And the point I am concerned to establish is that Nature in Stoicism is first and foremost a normative, evaluative, or if you will, a moral principle.

I do not deny that Nature may stand as the subject of propositions which seem to have nothing to do with norms, standards or ethics, propositions which purport to describe merely the physical processes which have Nature as their cause. Nor am I suggesting that the Stoics recognised or would have wished to recognise the rigid distinction between judgements of fact and judgements of value which has been endemic in much modern philosophy. The Stoics would clearly want to say that the statement, 'Nature endows all creatures with a sense of self-endearment', tells us something about the world. But the fact, if it is a fact, that all creatures have a sense of self-endearment can be described without reference to Nature. My claim is that when the Stoics prefaced such an assertion with the term 'Nature', they intended to include an evaluation of the fact described. Mention of Nature makes a presumption of the purposefulness, the rightness, displayed by the fact that all creatures have instincts of a certain kind. If all events for which Nature is directly responsible are right, then any judgement about such events which lacks an evaluative ‖ component will be incomplete. I have referred to the Stoic description of the goal as 'living in accordance with experience of Natural events'. It would be incorrect to complain that the 'concept of goodness' cannot be

[5] Cf. for instance Cicero, *ND* II.33ff.

derived from experience of Natural events, on the grounds that
this makes an illicit transition from factual to moral knowledge.
For the function of the term Natural in this description is to draw
attention to the purposeful and right character of those events
the understanding of which is necessary to the goal, to virtue, to
happiness. The Stoics are fully entitled to derive the concept of
goodness by inference from events, the complete understanding of
which entails seeing why they are right, why they should occur.[6]

A second reason for Moore's categorisation of Stoic ethics as
metaphysical in his sense may be found in his comments on the
meaning of 'natural' in the advice 'live naturally' (pp. 42ff.). 'It is
obvious', he argues, 'that we cannot say that everything natural
is good, except perhaps in virtue of some metaphysical theory.'
In the absence of such a theory Moore holds that to be told to
pursue something as a natural end is to imply that 'the normal
must be good'. Now it is certain that the Stoics did not think that
'natural' and 'normal' are terms which have the same extension.
This is easily demonstrated. They took it to be a regrettable but
indubitable fact that most, if not all people, are bad. Hence whatever Nature means in the expression 'life according to Nature', the
majority of people fail to accord with. The normal condition of
human beings is not consonant with Nature. It follows therefore
that the proposition 'everything Natural is good' would not be
inconsistent in Stoicism with the proposition 'all or most human
beings are bad'. In fact the Stoics did not hold that 'everything
Natural is good' is a true proposition, for reasons I shall not discuss here. But they did claim that everything Natural has value of
some degree. The distinction, which they drew, between *agathon*
and *proēgmenon* ('the good' and 'the preferred') refers to a classification of types of Natural things. It is fully consistent with my
argument that ‖ Nature in the aggregate means 'that which possesses the properties of providence, right reason, etc.', or in
Moore's terminology 'a metaphysical entity', something 'perfectly
good'.

I have given two reasons which could explain Moore's assessment of Stoic ethics as 'metaphysical'. They help to show that

---

[6] I do not pretend that this is an adequate account of how the Stoics explained acquisition
of the concept of goodness. But I believe it does express the essence of their theory: cf.
Cicero, *Fin.* III.33, *cum enim ab iis rebus, quae sunt secundum naturam, ascendit animus collatione
rationis, tum ad notionem boni pervenit.*

Stoic ethics is fundamentally a deductive system, which appeals to empirical experience only to get off the ground. One of our most valuable sources of Stoic ethics, the third book of Cicero's *De finibus*, gives a clear idea of their methodology.

Starting from the undemonstrated fact that all animals possess from birth specific desires and aversions, the Stoic spokesman, Cato, enters upon a lengthy series of inferences which lead to conclusions about *officium* ('the appropriate' in general), the *summum bonum*, virtue, happiness, moral action and particular obligations. The quality of argument is uneven, and the order in which conclusions are reached is not always coherent. What is undeniable is the attempt to present a set of moral truths which are so related that the last is entirely consistent with the first. Cato concludes with a lofty peroration concerning the coherence of Stoicism. He observes that the system has a structure such that the whole would collapse by the omission of a single letter; yet there is nothing which can be removed (74–5).

One is reminded, as so often in Stoicism, of Spinoza. Throughout Cicero's book logical connectives abound, e.g. *consentaneum est, ex quo efficitur, cum ... necesse est, ex quo intellegitur, ex quo fit ut, si ... non sequitur ut, e quo apparet,* and the work as a whole was evidently intended to exhibit the coherence claimed for Stoicism itself. What their opponents regarded as perverse, if not absurd, the Stoics held to be difficult but true. Cato probably reports the regular Stoic answer to charges of paradox-mongering when, after reporting the view that happiness and unhappiness do not admit of degrees, he says: 'I know this seems fantastic; but since our preceding remarks are certainly well-grounded and true, and the statements about happiness are consistent with and consequences of those earlier arguments, there can be no doubt about the truth of the statements concerning happiness' (48). This defence makes it clear that we are expected to consider particular ethical propositions in the light of their logical context: logic does not ‖ make the statements more palatable, but it compels us to accept them as the conclusions of earlier arguments whose validity has been established.

The Stoics' proud commitment to consistency and their deductive methodology in ethics were prompted, I argue, by two of the properties which they inferred to be properties of Nature. (I say this without wishing to exclude the possibility of motivation by other philosophical or non-philosophical considerations.) These are: Nature as provident and right-reasoning on the one hand, and Nature as destiny on the other hand. *Qua* provident and right-reasoning, Nature is analogous to Kant's perfectly good or Divine will. Nature's acts are consistently determined by right reason, and from this is derived the ethical principle that only acts which are consistent with Nature are right.[7] But Nature is also conceived as a causal principle, pervading all things, which brings to successful fruition most of what it wills. All events, with the exception of actions purposed by bad persons, are events willed *and* brought to pass by or in accordance with Nature.[8]

Here we come up against the question how human volitions are related to the causal nexus.[9] This is a vast problem, which falls outside the main scope of this chapter; but it cannot be ignored altogether. Let me just say now that Nature is available to all people as a moral principle through the 'impulses towards virtue' which human beings have as a Natural endowment.[10] The wise man is marked out by his voluntary submission to what ‖ Nature wills; he chooses, in some sense of choice, to act according to Nature. The actions of bad persons are necessarily contrary to Nature's will, and it is tautologous to deny that Nature is responsible for them. We are probably to think of Nature (destiny) as establishing conditions which are necessary and sufficient for the will to perform good actions, and conditions which are necessary but not sufficient for the will to perform bad actions. By giving human beings reason, Nature provides the necessary conditions of good *or* bad actions; for actions are good or bad if and only if the reason of their agents accords with or fails to accord with Nature.

---

[7] This should not be taken to imply that Nature's goodness *is derived from* 'right reason'. The Stoic position, as I understand it, is the converse. The rightness of reason is a property of Nature itself. In support of this cf. e.g. D.L. vii.128 where law and right reason are described as Natural, not conventional; Cicero, *Leg.* 1.33 who writes *quibus ... ratio a natura data est, iisdem recta ratio data est.* One can write of 'the right reason of Nature', but not 'the Nature of right reason'. 'Right reason' is an expression which has a narrower extension than the term 'Nature'. The sage has right reason but this does not imply that he is provident, artistic fire etc.

[8] Cleanthes, in his *Hymn to Zeus*, says that 'nothing takes place apart from you [sc. Zeus/Nature] ... except what the bad do in their folly' (lines 11–13). For 'the will of the director of the universe' cf. D.L. vii.86; 'the will of Nature', Epictetus, *Encheiridion* 26. Later Stoics generally prefer to speak of 'the will of God', Epictetus, *Discourses* 1.17.28; iv.7.20 etc.

[9] For further discussion see Long 1971c.

[10] Cleanthes quoted by Stobaeus, *Ecl.* ii.65.8 Wachsmuth. Nature also implants in man 'seeds of knowledge', Seneca, *Ep.* 120.4.

By endowing human beings with 'impulses towards virtue' Nature provides conditions sufficient to direct them towards what accords with Nature. The sufficient conditions of bad actions are misjudgements of value caused not by Nature but by 'the persuasiveness of external things' and 'communication with acquaintances' (i.e. keeping bad company), Diogenes Laertius vii.89.

These last remarks are not intended as a solution to all the ethical problems which Stoic statements about the causal nexus bring up. Sometimes the Stoics write as if Nature determines everything, and turns even bad things to some useful purpose.[11] Such assertions can be read as undermining the claim that Nature is the criterion for distinguishing good and bad; but I think statements about Nature's reconciliationist activities are to be construed *sub specie aeternitatis*, without implying a contradiction of the basic ethical position. According to that position, 'Natural events' exclude anything which is not right. Therefore knowledge of 'Natural events' is knowledge of what ought to be. But 'Natural events' occur necessarily, as predetermined by Nature; therefore knowledge of 'Natural events' is also knowledge of what is and must be the case. To predicate Nature as the cause of an event is both to state a necessary fact and to indicate the rightness of that fact. Stoic ethics takes certain facts of this kind as its first principles.

HUMAN NATURE, REASON, VIRTUE, GOOD, HAPPINESS

I have argued that the Stoics sought to demonstrate the ‖ *summum bonum* by inferring that this is the property of Nature. By Nature is meant a supreme providential power whose right-reasoning is manifested by events and the structure of the world. The Stoics also used the same Greek word, *physis*, to refer specifically to 'human nature'; and Chrysippus took *physis* in the expression 'it is necessary (or obligatory) to live according to *physis*' to refer both to Nature in general and human nature in particular (D.L. vii.89). It is clear that 'human nature' here does not mean the normal condition of mankind, but a condition such that living in accordance with it (and with Nature) is the *summum bonum*. Since the genetic structure of all living things is determined by Nature, and Nature designs them to fulfil determinate ends, the term 'human

---

[11] See Long 1968b.

nature' is best understood as a description of the goal which Nature has designed human beings to achieve.

In this section of the chapter I am concerned to clarify this
description of the human goal by reference to reason, virtue, good
and happiness.

Stoic theories about the human goal derive, at least in part,
from three hierarchical categories which they set up to distinguish
plants, non-human animals and human beings.[12] In a manner
which cannot fail to recall Aristotle they held that the governing
principle of plants, i.e. the internal cause of their development, is
Nature; of the animals other than human beings a non-rational
soul, and of human animals a rational soul or mind. The terminology should not be taken to imply that Nature functions exclusively in plants. The Stoics mean that Nature operates directly in
plants as a bio-physical process. Animals are endowed by Nature
with a governing principle that is both responsible for metabolism,
as in plants, and also constitutive of soul. Soul is a more subtle
type of *pneuma*. It endows non-human animals with the capacity
to live as sentient beings, motivated by appetition or aversion. In
human beings, and only in them, the *pneuma* constitutes itself as
reason (*logos*), which takes over the primary faculties of soul (sensation etc.) and turns them into rational powers.[13] From this the
Stoics concluded that the human goal must be expressible in terms
of reason, and wholly in those terms. Seneca puts their position
succinctly: 'What is man's special characteristic? Reason; in virtue
of reason man has precedence over animals, he follows the gods.
Therefore a perfect reason ‖ is man's specific good; other things
he shares with the animals' (*Ep.* 76.9).

The teleological assumptions which this argument requires for
its validity are too obvious to need discussion. They are also implicit in a description of 'the good': 'the Natural fulfilment of a
rational being as a rational being'.[14] This statement is important
to my argument because it anticipates the point I shall prove later,
that 'the goodness of living according to reason' is derived from,

---

[12] See the passages in *SVF* II, p. 205.
[13] This theory is highly relevant to Stoic attempts to reconcile some degree of autonomous
action with the causal nexus; cf. Long 1971c, pp. 189–94. For further treatment of the
psychological material, see chapter 10, pp. 237–42.
[14] D.L. VII.94. He calls it a 'specific' definition, but no other source follows this, and Diogenes gives the standard 'generic' definition in his previous paragraph, which I discuss
below.

and not the grounds of, 'living according to Nature'. The following two statements are therefore mutually consistent: 'Only what accords with or is a consequence of reason is good' and 'only what accords with human nature and Nature is good'. These are basic *moral* propositions which the Stoics did not take to imply a denial of value to other things, such as the powers of sensation which man shares with animals. These too, when they function properly, accord with Nature; but they do not accord with Nature in its specifically human sense. All that accords with human nature accords with Nature; but not all that accords with Nature accords with human nature.

In confining 'good' to what accords with reason, or what accords with human nature *and* Nature, the Stoics are arguing that nothing else is the goal of human beings *qua* human beings. Hence, if a person ought to pursue the good, she ought to pursue that alone which accords with reason. Now the proposition that a person ought to pursue the good looks like a necessary truth if any moral judgements are necessary. But in Stoicism it does not seem to be an analytic proposition in the modern sense. 'That which accords with reason', 'what a human being ought to pursue', plus other expressions to be mentioned shortly, are alternative descriptions of the single thing which is good. But 'good' does not mean 'that which one ought to pursue' etc. It is not defined by reference to these terms. 'The good' is defined as 'advantage (profit, interest), or that from which advantage ... accrues'.[15] So 'acting in accordance with reason is good' means 'acting in accordance with reason is advantageous ...' ‖

By 'advantageous' the Stoics mean beneficial to the agent and all those affected by his actions. It may be doubted whether it is possible to conceive of any action which would promote the interests of all those affected by it. But the Stoics slip out of this difficulty by claiming that only like-minded people, only virtuous people, whose goals are identical (*homonoousi*), can affect each other with respect to what is advantageous.[16] They are not therefore saying that anything which any person at any time considers to be advantageous is good. We return here to the point that for human beings only one thing is good and hence advantageous. This is

[15] D.L., loc. cit.; Sextus Empiricus, *M* XI. 22; Stobaeus, *Ecl.* II.69.17.
[16] Cf. *SVF* III, pp. 160ff.

'what accords with human nature and Nature', 'what accords with reason'. These expressions may also be exchanged for a further expression which has the same reference: 'virtue and morally fine action'.

To elucidate what the Stoics meant by virtue, I will cite a definition attributed to Zeno and Chrysippus: 'a disposition and faculty of the governing principle of the soul brought into being by reason, or rather: reason itself, consistent, firm and unwavering'.[17] 'Living virtuously' means 'having as one's principle of action a reasoning faculty which is sound and consistent'. When the Stoics used the expression 'living according to reason' they intended the reader to supply the properties of soundness and consistency.[18]

If virtue and the advantageous coincide, this could imply that Stoic ethics is fundamentally utilitarian; that virtue is to be pursued not from any specifically moral motive but in order to advance the interests of oneself and others. The Stoics however asserted that virtue is something to be chosen for its own sake (D.L. vii.89). We seem to be confronted with a hybrid of Bentham and Kant. If that makes Stoic ethics appear self-contradictory, we should probe a little deeper. It would be inconsistent to assert that virtue is to be chosen just for its own sake *and* because of its advantageous consequences. But it is not inconsistent to hold that (A): virtue is to be chosen for ‖ its own sake *and* virtue is something advantageous in itself. It does not follow from this that virtue is to be chosen on account of its consequences. For the following positions are consistent with (A): 1, virtue is to be chosen solely for the sake of its intrinsic properties, and some or all of the intrinsic properties of virtue are advantageous; 2, virtue is to be chosen for its own sake *and* because it is advantageous, i.e. something valuable in itself, independently of any of its consequences (high office, reputation etc.).

The second of these positions seems to represent the Stoic attitude, and it clearly invites comparison with Plato and Aristotle. Greek philosophers, with no legacy of Kant to trouble them, did not think they were sullying the purity of morals by taking virtue to be something which brings advantages to its possessor.

---

[17] Plutarch, *Virt. mor.* 441c.
[18] I am omitting any specific discussion of 'morally fine actions'. It is clear from D.L.'s order of ethical subjects (vii.84) and his own treatment of them, that the Stoics discussed right and morally fine actions in the light of their conclusions about the *summum bonum*.

'Only the virtuous man is a happy man' is a proposition which seemed indubitable to Plato, Aristotle and the Stoics. But although all three sets of philosophers are eudaimonists, formally speaking (see chapter 8), the Stoic position is distinctive, chiefly owing to their natural theology.

The Stoics gave happiness (*eudaimonia*) as one of their descriptions of the goal. But neither this description nor the advantageous properties of virtue should lead us to conclude that Stoic ethics is basically utilitarian in the reasons it proposes for moral action. In this section of the chapter I have deliberately kept Nature somewhat in the background. I shall now relate these last observations to the earlier discussion, with the aim of demonstrating the precise connexion between human nature and Nature in the cosmic sense. The argument which I shall analyse proves that the Stoics held the pursuit of the goal referred to by the expressions 'acting according to reason', 'virtue' and 'human nature' to be a moral imperative, a command of Nature (or God). Seen in this light, the pursuit of virtue proves to be a moral obligation, independent of the fact that it is also in one's interests.

FROM IMPULSE TO VIRTUE: THE HUMAN GOAL

In the appendix to this chapter I have offered a translation of ‖ Diogenes Laertius vii.85–88, which sets down the first principles of Stoic ethics. I now proceed to make an analysis of the argument embedded in this summary. Diogenes, it should be remembered, was not a Stoic philosopher but a compiler of no great intellectual merit. I deem it appropriate therefore to abridge and adapt his text for this analysis, so that the essential features of the argument (marked by letters below) are exhibited somewhat more formally. For this reason my enterprise may be conceived as the reconstruction of an argument. However, Diogenes makes it clear that his main source is Chrysippus, and a check against the original, plus paragraphs 148–9 of Diogenes, should show that I have not taken excessive liberties with the evidence.

Nature creates all living things and provides them with the means of securing what is advantageous to them. (*T*)

That which accords with Nature is right. (*S*)

Nature directs all animals (and children) by a self-protective impulse.

> *Given* (*T*) *and* (*S*) *it follows that,* it is advantageous and right for all animals (and children) to be directed by their self-protective impulse.
>
> Nature directs all human beings to live by sound reason (self-protective impulse shaped by reason).   (*R*)
>
> *Therefore,* it is advantageous and right (accords with Nature) for all human beings to live by sound reason.
>
> To live by sound reason ≡ living in accord with human nature ≡ living according to virtue.
>
> *Therefore,* it is advantageous and right for all human beings to live in accord with human nature and according to virtue. (*Q1*)
>
> Human nature is part of Nature.
>
> *Therefore,* it is advantageous and right for all human beings to live in accord with human nature and Nature.
>
> To live in accord with Nature entails deliberate obedience to Nature's will which ≡ living by sound reason.   (*P*)
>
> *Therefore,* it is advantageous and right for all human beings deliberately to obey Nature's will.   (*Q2*)

This argument will not, I trust, seem totally opaque in view of the previous sections of the paper. I shall comment briefly on some new features and certain general points.

It is evident from other sources that Diogenes' opening remarks concerning animal impulse conform to a standard ‖ Stoic pattern.[19] This must seem a strange way to begin an argument about the foundations of ethics. Yet, 'impulse' (*hormē*) is listed as the first subject of Stoic moral philosophy. The strangeness disappears, in part at least, once we see that the Stoics are not arguing that ethical conclusions follow directly from the proposition: 'an animal has self-protection as the object of its primary impulse'. This proposition, though the first sentence in Diogenes' summary, is an interim conclusion, grounded in the claim that Nature is a creative, teleological power. These properties of Nature are invoked to sanction an explanation of the fact that animals have the power to reject what is harmful to them and pursue what is suitable. The explanation is that Nature endowed animals with a self-protective impulse, as is only consistent with the proposition cited (*T*) above. (*T*) is clearly the basis of Diogenes' first paragraph. In making it a

---

[19] *Cf.* Cicero, *Fin.* III.16ff.

primary premiss I am not only following the implications of his text, but also conforming to Chrysippus' rule that ethical statements must take their origin from statements about Nature and the direction of the universe (see p. 136).

The second primary premiss (S) is one which I take to be implicit throughout Diogenes' summary, though he does not state it overtly. We see his use of it, however, in the following passage (86): 'Since reason by way of a more perfect management has been bestowed on rational beings, to live correctly in accordance with reason comes to be accordant with nature for them; for reason supervenes as the craftsman of impulse.'[20] The 'more perfect management' refers to Nature's provision for human beings, and the human function of 'living correctly in accordance with reason' is grounded in its accordance with *their* nature. Nature, as I have already argued, is the ultimate reference of all evaluation: it is specified, in the sequel to the argument above, as 'that in accordance with which we ought to live' (φύσιν ... ἧ ἀκολούθως δεῖ ζῆν, 89). To refer, then, to the impulses of living things is to speak of gifts of Nature, endowments which it is right, as well as advantageous, for creatures to have. What holds for animals in general holds for human beings *a fortiori*. We too have impulses as a Natural endowment, but in mature people these are of a higher order – 'shaped by reason'. ‖

There is no illegitimate transition here from facts to values. Arguments which draw premisses from Nature yield conclusions which are necessarily both descriptive and evaluative; for any statement about Nature expresses both what is the case and what ought to be the case. But if what is the case and what ought to be the case are alike subsumed under Nature, the Stoics might incur the different objection of failing to draw any sharp distinction between these two kinds of statements. I am not myself convinced that it is possible to draw the distinction as sharply as some philosophers claim. But, that aside, the objection seems to misfire against the Stoics in any event. Statements about Nature do not need to be construed as assimilating facts to values, or values to facts. They can, and I think should, be construed as *combining*

---

[20] I have revised my translation of this sentence, as explained in Long/Sedley 1987, vol. II, p. 344. The original read: 'Since reason in accord with a more perfect prescription has been bestowed on rational beings, life according to reason *rightly* becomes accordant with their nature'.

statements of fact and value. The Stoics evidently thought of Nature as consistently following out the mandates of right reason. Hence there are grounds, as I suggested earlier, for taking 'according to Nature' to be primarily an evaluative expression, and secondarily a factual one. On such a view we could perhaps say that things are as they are because Nature has determined that this is how they should be.[21] Descriptions of 'Natural events' would thus be descriptions of what is and should be the case. The statement, 'Nature brings rain in the winter', will describe both an empirical fact and something right – what Nature willed to happen.

With the premiss (R) the argument moves from what is advantageous and right for animals (and children) to what is advantageous and right for human beings. Nature is the grounds of what is advantageous and right with respect to all of these. But, as (R) implies, what is advantageous and right for human beings is to live by sound reason, not self-protective impulse. The term 'human nature', which first appears in the next step of the ‖ argument, expresses this shift of Nature's reference from animals (and children) to human beings. 'Human nature' marks the point on Nature's scale of values at which what is advantageous and right becomes co-extensive with 'living by (sound) reason' or virtue.

At this point a word of explanation is needed concerning the term 'sound reason'. According to my analysis: 'to live by sound reason is logically equivalent to living in accord with human nature'. Both expressions are of identical validity as descriptions of the human goal, but neither expression explains the logical relationship between the goal and Nature itself. For this we require premiss (P), which I extract from Diogenes' explanation of the implications of the statement 'our own natures are parts of the Nature of the universe'. On my analysis this statement means that the goal of rational beings (living by sound reason) is intrinsically related to living in accord with Nature. Nature's rationality is such that to live in accord with Nature entails for rational beings living by sound reason, being deliberately obedient to Nature's will, being

---

[21] The Stoics' interest in empirical inference and divination must derive from their concern to establish the causal connexion between events, which reveals Nature's ordering. In Long 1971b, pp. 103–4, I suggest that logic gets its moral significance in Stoicism from the fact that it provides 'an analytical framework in which to place the relations between events'. In that context I was interested in explaining the moral implications of knowing Nature, in the sense of 'knowing what is really the case'.

a part of Nature. Now at one level Nature's rationality is expressed in anything, such as the flourishing of animals, which is attributable to Nature's provisions. But of course non-rational animals cannot recognise the rightness of Nature's provisions. They have no equipment to obey Nature in any deliberate sense. The proposition 'it is right for all animals (and children) to be directed by their self-protective impulse' is a moral proposition. But it does not entail that all animals (and children) are moral agents. 'It is right that ...' expresses the objective judgement that such and such a state of affairs accords with Nature. Non-rational animals do not pursue what is suitable to them *because* this is right, but because they are impelled to do so. The human being, however, has reason, and this means that she is the only creature who can act disharmoniously with Nature. Equally, she is the only creature who can deliberately act harmoniously with Nature. The human reason is a faculty which can be sound or sick, straight or perverse, where the criterion of soundness and straightness is accord with Nature. Therefore, obedience to one's own reason, if this is sound, entails obedience ‖ to Nature; and obedience to Nature entails obedience to one's own reason. A human being who acts by sound reason does what is right both objectively (since this accords with Nature) and subjectively (since she does what her own reason tells her to do).

There is no term in Stoicism which corresponds precisely to 'moral duty'. But the absence of the term does not preclude the recognition of something which comes very close to the concept; and the Stoics came very close to the concept when they said 'human beings should live according to Nature'. Certainly, it is advantageous to live according to Nature, and Nature is the source of human well-being or happiness. To say this in Stoicism is just to say that life according to Nature is good in itself, worth having for its own sake. And this provides a utilitarian reason for living according to Nature. But independently of this, life according to Nature is to be desired because it is right, morally obligatory. When animals (and children) live according to Nature they are not commendable since their lives are directed by Natural impulse. But a human being cannot live according to Nature save by a deliberate act of obedience to Nature's will. This act is morally commendable, since it requires making what is right and good in itself the determining principle of action.

CONCLUSION

In his book *Stoic and Epicurean* R. D. Hicks wrote: 'Let us ... inquire in what life according to nature consists. The answer is, in a life at one with reason, in a harmonious, consistent life ... If so, the life according to nature must be followed because it is the reasonable life or life according to reason. Here the circle is complete. It is reasonable to live according to nature and natural to live according to reason' (pp. 22–3). Hicks has manufactured this circle by introducing 'the reasonable life ...' as a ground for living according to Nature. That is a complete misrepresentation of the logical basis of Stoic ethics. Life according to reason *is entailed by* life according to Nature; but life according to Nature is not obligatory *because* it accords with reason. Nature stands to human beings as a moral law commanding us to live by rational principles, viz. those principles of ‖ thought and action which Nature, a perfect being, prescribes to itself and all other rational beings.

My purpose in this chapter has been descriptive rather than critical. The spectre of circularity has seemed to haunt the primary principles of Stoic ethics, and I have tried to dispel it by showing what they meant when they took Nature as their starting-point. This has implications which affect every particular Stoic moral doctrine, as G. E. Moore seems to have grasped; and I am surprised to find so little assessment of the significance of Nature in a book which devotes much space to ethical problems in Stoicism.[22]

But if Stoic moral theory is unintelligible when divorced from Nature, how practicable is their system when Nature is placed in its true perspective? A human being is to live as Nature wills, that is: obedient to reason. But reason here means a sound reason, reason that accords consistently with Nature. How is one to know whether one's reason meets this condition? As far as I can see, the Stoics gave no satisfactory answer to this question.[23] What they

[22] Rist 1969.
[23] In fairness to the Stoics one might argue that the question is only answerable in terms of faith, intuition etc., and what I call 'unsatisfactory' is the attempt to lay down objective criteria. The Stoics could and did invite self-examination in relation to one's attitude to external events. A man whose attitudes and desires are compatible with what actually takes place has a disposition such that what he desires to do *could* be what Nature wills. This man has satisfied a necessary condition of sound reason. But knowledge that such-and-such an action is compatible with external events does not entail complete harmony with what Nature wills. And it is just this complete harmony that is the test of sound reason.

did was to offer the sage as a paradigm. By describing characteristics of the sage they purported to be stating the properties of a
person whose reason accords with Nature. And here we do get a
circle: Nature's will is not determinable as a practical principle
independently of what the sage does; and what the sage does is
to fulfil Nature's will. But the sage is as rare as the phoenix. Hence
Nature becomes still more elusive. Unless there are sages we
cannot knowingly live according to Nature, and perhaps there are
no sages.[24] This is the dilemma of Stoic ethics. Nature promises a
destination which is approachable by no known road. Faced with
this problem Stoic philosophers erected a superstructure of moral
rules around their primary principles. It can, I think, be ‖ shown
that the rules are consistent with the theory that produces them.
But wise and humane though they are, these rules provide no
guarantee of virtue and happiness to their observers. The rules
are according to Nature, and therefore right; but to know what it
is about Nature that makes them right, to obey the rules as a
moral principle, is only possible for someone of perfect reason;
and perfect reason is something beyond the power of any rules
infallibly and willingly to bestow.[25]

APPENDIX: Diogenes Laertius, VII.85–8

The Stoics say that an animal has self-protection as the object of its primary impulse, since Nature from the beginning endears it to itself, as
Chrysippus says in his first book *On goals*: 'The first thing which is dear to
every animal is its own constitution and awareness of this; for it was not
likely that Nature estranged the animal from itself, nor that, having
made it, Nature gave it no attitude of estrangement or endearment. It
follows then that, having constituted the animal, Nature endeared it to
itself; thus it is that the animal rejects what is harmful and pursues what
is suitable (or akin) to itself.'
     The assertion that pleasure is the object of animals' primary impulse

---

[24] In a study closely based on the original version of my paper Graeser (1972, p. 223) suggests that the problem I raise for the Stoics is 'only apparent'. But in arguing, as he does,
that Nature places people in situations where they *have* to take moral decisions he misses
my point. I am talking about knowledge or unerring insight, and the Stoics are adamant
that this is the prerogative of the sage.

[25] In writing the original version of this paper I incurred two considerable debts. The first
is to Richard Sorabji, who was kind enough to criticise an earlier draft at very short
notice. The second debt is to the Institute for Advanced Study, Princeton. By electing me
to a visiting membership in 1969–70 the Institute provided an opportunity to think about
Stoicism for which I am deeply grateful.

is proved to be false by the Stoics. For pleasure, they claim, if it really exists, is a secondary product when and only when Nature by itself has searched out and adopted the things which are suitable to the animals' constitution; as such pleasure is like the flourishing of animals and the bloom of plants. Nature made no absolute distinction between plants and animals, for Nature directs plants too, independently of impulse and sensation, and in us certain processes of a vegetative kind take place. But since animals have the additional faculty of impulse, through the use of which they go in search of what is suitable to them, it is according to Nature for animals to be ‖ directed by impulse. And since reason in accord with a more perfect management has been bestowed on rational beings, to live correctly in accordance with reason comes to be accordant with nature for them; for reason supervenes as the craftsman of impulse.

Therefore Zeno in his book *On the nature of man* was the first to say that the goal is to live consistently with Nature, that is to say, according to virtue; for Nature directs us towards virtue … Again, life according to virtue is equivalent to living in accordance with experience of Natural events, as Chrysippus says in book one of his work *On goals*. For our own natures are parts of the Nature of the universe. Therefore the goal is to live in accordance with Nature, that is, in accordance with the nature of oneself and that of the universe, engaging in no activity which the common law is wont to forbid, which is the right reason pervading everything and identical to Zeus. And the virtue of the happy man and his good flow of life consist in this: always doing everything on the basis of the concordance of each man's guardian spirit with the will of the director of the universe.[26]

POSTSCRIPT (1995)

In the years since I wrote 'The logical basis of Stoic ethics' the concept of *oikeiōsis* has rightly become a major subject of discussion. Having had the benefit of reading Simon Pembroke's pioneering study of *oikeiōsis* (1971) while I was at work on this study, I should have built some of its findings into my analysis. In particular, I should have been more careful to justify my claim that cosmic Nature, as distinct from *oikeiōsis* (which I refer to here by such expressions as 'sense of self-endearment' or 'self-protective impulse'), is the *logical* basis of the early Stoics' deduction of the human goal. That claim, however, remains valid, I believe, even when we focus on the well-attested fact that the theory of *oikeiōsis* is the proper starting-point for ethics (cf. Cicero, *Fin.* III.16, and

---

[26] For philological and interpretative details of this passage, cf. Long/Sedley 1987, vol. II, pp. 343–4, 390–1. See also pp. 169, 187, 190 of this volume.

Hierocles, *Elements of ethics* col. 1). For, in beginning their ethics with *oikeiōsis*, the Stoics were implicitly or explicitly (as in D.L. VII.85 and Hierocles, ibid., col. VI.40–3) making allusion to Nature's providential interest in the self-preservation of living creatures. *oikeiōsis* is the way Nature's teleology manifests itself in animal *psychology*. In other words, the logical priority I ascribe to the goodness of Nature is actually presupposed by beginning ethics from *oikeiōsis*.

My principal thesis in the chapter is confirmed, I think, by the entirely independent arguments advanced by White (1979) and Striker (1991). White (p. 175), referring to the end of D.L. VII.86, says 'that acting in accordance with universal nature is to be identified with different sorts of behavior in different creatures, and with rational behavior in man'. Striker (p. 12) observes that 'the Stoic conception of the end does not arise as a natural continuation of one's concern for self-preservation, but rather as the result of one's reflection upon the way nature has arranged human behaviour in the context of an admirable cosmic order'. Both of these scholars, unlike myself, are primarily concerned with elucidating Cicero's account in *Fin.* III.16–21, but they ultimately rely heavily on Diogenes Laertius VII.85–88.

They are right to do so, in my opinion, because Diogenes' evidence is almost certainly our most authoritative testimony for the primary principles of Stoic ethics. Confirmation of its authority can be found in a parallel passage of Hierocles (Stobaeus, *Ecl.* IV.502) which, to the best of my knowledge, has been almost completely overlooked (the parallelism is briefly noted by Praechter 1901, pp. 72–3). It comes from an excerpt of his work *On marriage*, and runs as follows:

Now in works treating of households we have it proved that married life on the part of the wise man is preferred, but life without a wife is conditional on circumstance. Since, then, whenever we can do so, we should imitate the man with intelligence, and marriage for this man is preferred, it is clear that we too should marry unless some circumstance is in the way. This, then, is the first rule. But it seems that, even prior to the wise man, the nature which urges him too to marry presses its call on us, and that nature did not fashion us to be merely gregarious but to live as couples too, with a single and common function as the objective of our coupling. I am referring to the procreation of offspring and a well-grounded way of life. Nature is a proper teacher because the selection of appropriate things should be in harmony with one's natural constitution. Now every [non-human] animal lives consistently with its own natural constitution – and every plant indeed too according to the plants' so-called life – except that they do not make use of any calculation or counting or acts of selection that depend on testing things: plants live on the basis of bare nature, and [non-human] animals on the basis both of representations which draw them toward things appropriate and of urges that drive them away. On us, however, Nature has bestowed reason as well as everything else, and together with everything, or rather ahead of everything, with a view to reason's primarily seeing Nature itself, so that focused on Nature like a target that is bright and fixed, and selecting everything in accordance with it, reason might fashion us to live appropriately.

I have translated this passage in full, with a view to showing how its official subject, marriage, is grounded in a view of universal Nature, exactly similar to the text of Diogenes. The second part of the excerpt can be largely read as a rephrasing of Chrysippus, as reported by D.L. vii.86. Thus we get the same hierarchical division between plants, non-human animals and human beings. But in his final sentence Hierocles is more expansive than Diogenes on the role of Nature as human reason's guiding star. Diogenes says nothing about 'gazing on Nature'. Hierocles' statement is most closely paralleled by Cicero, *Fin.* iii.21, where the end of moral development is famously characterised as '*seeing* the order and harmony of conduct'. Although Cicero does not refer explicitly to Nature at this point, I agree with Striker (1991, pp. 7, 12) that his 'order and harmony' and what he later calls *consentaneum naturae* ('agreement with Nature') 'refer to the same thing', namely, the pattern for human life 'produced by rational organisation and exhibited to the highest degree by the organisation of the universe'. Seneca presupposes the same linkage between Nature and reason when he writes: 'We must use Nature as our guide; this it is that reason looks to and consults' (*natura enim duce utendum est; hanc ratio observat, hanc consulit*; *Vit. beat.* 8.1).

In two studies, which are far too complex for me to treat adequately here, Engberg-Pedersen (1986, 1990), has contested the importance of natural teleology for Stoic ethics. In the earlier of these publications (1986, pp. 147–9) he grants the correctness of my interpretation of Diogenes Laertius (vii.85–8, and 'that something like this view of Nature's role in laying the foundations of ethics is in fact old Stoic doctrine'. However, he thinks that the account in Cicero, *Fin.* III.16–21 emphasises the developing consciousness of the individual self or subject rather than natural teleology. In his later study he presses this point at length, in opposition to the teleological interpretation he attributes to me, and which, he says, 'amounts to something resembling a received view in modern scholarship' (1990, p. 41).

My summary response to Engberg-Pedersen is that there is no incompatibility between natural teleology and the normative development of the human subject's self-reflection, on which he lays such stress (see my chapter 7, p. 178, and his own remarks (1990, p. 43)). What he wants to resist is a view of the human goal which would see this as 'something set up from the outside for a man to acknowledge whether he himself wants to or not' (loc. cit.). Hence he prefers Cicero's account (ad loc.) which lacks the talk about Nature's management. In fact, as I think I have made clear in this paper and elsewhere (cf. Long 1971c, pp. 189–94), Nature's management includes the gift to each person of an individual nature or mind, which has identity in its own right. What I have strong doubts about is Engberg-Pedersen's proposal (loc. cit.) that the Stoics construct 'wholly from within practical thought itself an argument proper for their view of the human telos that nowhere relies on any premiss outside human seeing'. Such an interpretation, with its corollary (p. 44) that the *telos* 'is quite concretely anybody's individual telos', seems to me to pay insufficient regard to the physical and theological underpinnings of Stoic ethics.[27] On the other hand, I fully agree with Annas (1993, p. 160) that these underpinnings are not featured in all of the ancient sources. What that fact attests to, in my opinion, is not merely or mainly the vagaries of our evidence but the fluidity of Stoicism in the hands of its ancient interpreters. We can capture certain fundamentals of Stoic ethics without reference to Nature's providence etc., as I try to show in chapter 7 of this book. Yet, unlike Annas (loc. cit.) I think that even when we start from the eudaimonist perspective, Stoic happiness only makes real sense when it is related to their physical and theological intuitions; see my chapter 8, and Forschner (1995, pp. 246–8, 252–3, 257–8).

[27] For detailed criticism of Engberg-Pedersen's attempt to marginalise these underpinnings, cf. Tieleman 1995.

Greek ethics after MacIntyre and the
Stoic community of reason*

The language – and therefore also to some large degree the practice – of morality today is in a state of grave disorder ... Ever since belief in Aristotelian teleology was discredited moral philosophers have attempted to provide some alternative rational secular account of the nature and status of morality, but ... all these attempts ... have in fact failed, a failure perceived most clearly by Nietzsche ... Unless ... the moral tradition to which Aristotle's teaching about the virtues is central ... could be rationally vindicated. Nietzsche's stance would have a terrible plausibility.

Thus Alasdair MacIntyre sums up the two central premisses of the argument of his recent book, *After Virtue*, which lead him to pose the 'stark question': Nietzsche *or* Aristotle?[1] His answer to this question and the book's conclusion are guardedly optimistic: Nietzsche does not defeat Aristotle. 'The Aristotelian tradition can be restated in a way that restores intelligibility and rationality to our moral and social attitudes and commitments' (p. 241). On MacIntyre's analysis, the shortcomings of modern moral philosophy, manifested in its failure to reach agreement about a rational foundation for ethics, can be traced back to the rival philosophies of the eighteenth century, when the Aristotelian tradition gave way to 'liberal individualism.' Broad agreement concerning the content of moral precepts continued; but it was against a background which no longer shared the presuppositions about human nature that had previously served to justify those precepts. The language

---

* An earlier version of this chapter was read to the Nottingham meeting of the Classical Association in April 1983. Among those to whom I am grateful for encouragement I particularly thank Julia Annas and David Sedley. The present version was presented to the American Society for Ancient Greek Philosophy's Meeting in Cincinnati in December 1983.
[1] MacIntyre 1981, p. 239. MacIntyre's sympathy for Greek ethics was already evident in an earlier book (1967), though there he was much more critical of Aristotle.

of morals, while appearing largely the same, had lost the context, social and conceptual, where its terms were properly at home. Three specific mistakes, according to MacIntyre, occurred when liberal individualism began to oust the Aristotelian tradition – the abandonment of ethical teleology, the severance of the virtues from socially defined roles and the widespread belief that moral judgements cannot be treated as statements of fact.

My quotations and summary should be sufficient to indicate the remarkable range and boldness of *After Virtue*. MacIntyre's breadth of perspective has enabled him to write a book of unusual richness and urgency. My purpose in this chapter is to extend his conception of the 'Aristotelian tradition' to include the Stoics. MacIntyre ‖ appears to regard Stoicism as a different kind of moral system from 'the Aristotelian tradition' and this, I shall argue, is a mistake.² Given his requirements of a successful moral philosophy, Stoicism, in at least some of its approaches, suits his book even better than Aristotle himself. This can be shown when we bring those prevailing tendencies in Greek moral thought approved by MacIntyre together with some Stoic conceptions of human nature and 'the community of reason'.

FUNCTIONALISM AND 'THE ARISTOTELIAN TRADITION'

'The Aristotelian tradition', as MacIntyre uses this expression, is a name for that general moral scheme which 'came for long periods to dominate the European Middle Ages' (p. 50) and whose antecedents stretch back into the Greek poets and the forms and institutions of Greek social life. Aristotle himself is seen as the supreme representative and analyst of this moral scheme, whose structure is articulated in the *Nicomachean ethics*. In its fully-fledged Aristotelian form, the scheme involves three interdependent elements: 'untutored human-nature-as-it-happens-to-be, human-nature-as-it could-be-if-it-realised-its-*telos* and the precepts of rational ethics as the means for the transition from one to the other' (p. 51). Accept such a scheme, MacIntyre argues, and we cease to be troubled by problems which have bedevilled modern moral philosophy, such as the logical status and meaning of ethical judgements and the

---

² MacIntyre 1967, p. 107, also found in Stoicism a complete 'detachment of the individual from the Platonic–Aristotelian morality of social life'.

relation between 'is' and 'ought'. The gap between facts and values disappears once we adopt a teleological view of human nature. Thus the great strength of 'the Aristotelian tradition', in MacIntyre's argument, is 'the concept of *man* understood as having an essential nature and an essential purpose or function' (p. 56). Just as a watch, by reason of its function, *ought* to tell the time accurately, or be a 'good' watch; so, for Aristotle, 'a "man" stands to "good man" as "watch" stands to "good watch"'. 'Man', like 'watch', is defined 'in terms of the purpose which' [a man] 'is characteristically expected to serve' (p. 55).³ What it is 'to be a man is to fill a set of roles each of which has its own point and purpose: member of a family, citizen, soldier ... It is only when man is thought of as an individual prior to and apart from all roles that "man" ceases to be a functional concept' (p. 56).

This thesis of MacIntyre's is complex, and I have neither the space nor the knowledge to comment on its effectiveness as a contribution to contemporary moral debates.⁴ If my summary, however, has been sufficiently clear, MacIntyre's argument forces us to reflect upon the striking differences between Graeco-Roman and modern ethical theories, differences which are all the more interesting given the actual historical and conceptual connexions between them. In ancient philosophy an ethical theory typically assumes that all actions should be undertaken for the sake of a self-fulfilling *telos* (*eudaimonia*), the attainment of which is the goal of human nature. Moral precepts are not grounded in sentiment, or utility, or the autonomy of practical reason (to mention some of the obvious modern theories). They are rules based upon the virtues, that is, the perfections of human nature, what human nature would and could be if it realised its *telos*. The project of ancient moral philosophy is to teach us how to become what we essentially are.

As MacIntyre makes plain, that project involves a concept of man, and self-identity, and public and private roles which is in striking contrast to prevalent modern attitudes, whether we call them 'liberal individualism' or freedom of conscience or ‖ self-determination. We do not go to moral philosophers today for

---

³ MacIntyre seems to be drawing here upon *EN* I 1097b24–1098a17; but his one reference to the text, 1095a16 in 1981, p. 56, is not to the point.
⁴ For an entirely fair-minded review, cf. Scheffler 1983.

advice on the meaning of life or on what we should do to be happy; that is our private affair. Yet we acknowledge many of the moral obligations characteristic of ancient ethics, though the force of those obligations has no necessary connexion with how we conceive of our own personal good. Modern ethics assumes the inevitability of conflicts between egoism and altruism. According to 'the Aristotelian tradition', there must be a coincidence between what is *actually* good for me as a man and what is *actually* good for 'those others with whom I am bound up in human community' ... 'goods are not private property' (p. 213).[5]

In order to understand these different viewpoints, we need to acknowledge, with MacIntyre, that Greek philosophers developed their ethical theories within a society which already presupposed something analogous to what he calls the 'functional concept of man'. Before Plato, of course, we do not find any developed teleology or explicit focus upon man's essential nature as a rational being. These were philosophical constructions. But in their own moral arguments, Plato and his successors could assume a general acceptance of the notion that human excellence (*aretē*) is a specification of what is naturally or factually best for human beings *and* their societies, what is most conducive to their well-being. The principal ethical disagreements were concerned not with the basic elements and logic of this scheme, but with how the key terms should be filled out, what the real interests of human beings are, and how they are to be determined. Hence Greek philosophers offered little by way of detailed justification for using concepts such as nature, objective excellence, human goal and function.[6] Broadly speaking, they assumed the propriety of a conceptual scheme in which these ideas were an uncontroversial, though unsystematic, part of the cultural tradition. Their chief efforts were not devoted to proving that human beings have determinate natures or functions or interests in their own well-being, but rather to disclosing

---

[5] In this paper I am not concerned with precise details of MacIntyre's interpretation of Aristotle himself. Some of what he says lacks the sharp analysis necessary to any clear determination of Aristotle's ethical position; contrast John Cooper's excellent book (1975). But MacIntyre's characterisation of an 'Aristotelian tradition', not specific to Aristotle, is broadly acceptable, and necessary to the kind of contrast between ancient and modern on which he is engaged.

[6] Their reliance on such general presuppositions was recognised by Sextus Empiricus in his arguments against the Dogmatists' ethics, *M* 1.1, though even he argues from within the tradition.

what all of these really are, and what kind of lives are necessary to their fulfilment.

Has Stoic moral philosophy retained intelligible connexions with this tradition? Is it a philosophy which, to a recognisable extent, includes and builds upon characteristics of the 'Aristotelian' scheme, both in its more popular and its more technical concepts? Is the Stoic 'life in accordance with nature' a moral theory which someone who accepted that basic scheme could be given good reason to endorse?

MacIntyre, in a few brief comments, makes a sharp contrast between 'the Aristotelian tradition' and Stoicism. He claims that the Stoics, like Kant, severed 'all connection between what is good (morally good, as modern writers would say) and human desires' (p. 131). According to MacIntyre, the Stoics abandoned the traditional plurality of the virtues, replacing that conception with 'a simple monism of virtue' (p. 158). The Stoics, he maintains (ibid.), make the good man 'a citizen of the universe', whose standard of right action is 'the law of the cosmic order'. That law, 'one and the same for all rational beings has nothing to do with local particularity or circumstances'. (It is a great strength of the 'Aristotelian tradition', according to MacIntyre, that it grounded its conception of the virtues in social practices and needs). He sees Stoicism as a moral theory which resembles Judaism in its emphasis ‖ upon a morality of 'law'. In contrast with 'the Aristotelian tradition', the Stoics are said to have 'abandoned any notion of a *telos*', with an 'implacable law' taking the place of the previous centrality of the virtues.

Stoicism enters MacIntyre's argument only briefly (pp. 157–9). Let my response to these particular claims of his be almost as brief; the main body of this chapter is offered as a fuller rejoinder. Certain points, however, must be settled before we proceed. 'No connexion between what is morally good and human desires'? Cicero, *De finibus* III.22; 'So it could be correctly said that the object of all proper functions (*officia*) is to obtain nature's primary requirements, but not that this is the ultimate good, since right action is not present in the first affiliations of nature ... Yet it [sc. 'right action'/'the morally good'] is in accordance with nature, and *stimulates us to desire it* far more strongly than we are stimulated by all the earlier objects.'

'To do what is right need not necessarily produce ... happiness' (p. 157)? Stobaeus, ii.77.16 Wachsmuth: They [sc. Stoics] say that being happy is the end, for the sake of which everything is to be done, but it is done for the sake of nothing.' 'No notion of a *telos*'? 'This [i.e. the *telos*] consists in living in accordance with virtue' (Stobaeus ibid.)[7] 'Simple monism of virtue', 'disappearance of their [sc. the virtues'] teleological ordering in the good life' (pp. 157–8)? Stobaeus, ii.65.6–12 (reporting Panaetius): 'For just as archers make hitting the target their highest end, but propose to achieve it in different ways, so all the virtues make being happy their end, which consists in living consistently with nature, but they achieve this in different ways.' Stobaeus, ii.72.3–6: 'All the virtues are both efficient and final goods. For they both generate happiness and they complete it, since they are its parts.'

'Stoic virtue has nothing to do with local particularity or circumstance?' Diogenes Laertius, vii.121: 'They say that the wise man will participate in politics, *if nothing prevents him* ... and will even feed off human flesh *if circumstances make that appropriate*.' Diogenes Laertius, vii.109: 'They say that some proper functions (*kathēkonta*) *depend on circumstances*, but others do not. The following do not depend on circumstances: looking after one's health and one's sense organs, and such like. Proper functions which do depend on circumstances are mutilating oneself, and dispersing one's property.'

The passages I have translated are from unimpeachable Stoic sources. Baldly stated, they perhaps make little of Stoicism clear or appealing. They are none the less sufficient to show that MacIntyre is incorrect to contrast Stoicism with Aristotle by the chief criteria that he has invoked. The Stoics agreed with Aristotle that human beings have a natural *telos*, that that *telos* is perfected activity as a rational being, that both of these are essentially constituted by a *plurality* of virtues,[8] and that what the virtuous person

---

[7] For Stoic *eudaimonein* as a state of mind which is supremely satisfying to its possessor, cf. Cicero, *Tusc.* v.40–1, Seneca, *Ep.* 90.3.

[8] It was the heretical Aristo of Chios, Zeno's contemporary, who held the *essential unity* of virtue, *SVF* 1.375, and was attacked on this, as on so much else, by Chrysippus. MacIntyre's picture of Stoicism has much in common with Aristo, who defended the complete indifference of everything except virtue and vice, and whose stress on the absolute self-sufficiency of the wise man's moral knowledge was branded useless by Stoics themselves for moral choice and the conduct of life, Cic. *Fin.* iii.50.

will do requires an intelligent and appropriate assessment of the particular circumstances. Certainly, as MacIntyre observes (p. 157), 'Stoic virtue is an all or nothing matter', and nothing except virtue is a genuine good in their system. The Stoics' insistence on the latter point was a notorious difference from the Peripatetics in antiquity. It would be interesting to know whether Aristotle also thought there could be degrees of virtue, since the *phronimos* in his ethics plays a role very similar to that of the Stoic wise man.[9] But it is not my intention to explore the familiar similarities and differences between Stoic and Aristotelian moral philosophy. I will happily agree with MacIntyre that the two systems differ importantly in certain respects. My point is simply that they do ‖ share presuppositions which he himself regards as central to an effective moral theory.

In 'the Aristotelian tradition', what someone *ought* to do is anchored to nature or function – the essence and *telos* of a human being; and the function of persons is living well in society. Consider now the answers of Epictetus to the question, 'How is it possible to discover one's proper functions (*kathēkonta*) from one's descriptions (*onomata*)?' (*Discourses* ii.10).

'Study who you are. First of all, a human being (*anthrōpos*).' To be a human, he explains, is to be marked off from wild and domestic animals by the faculty of reason. As a human, that is a rational being, one's ruling principle is *prohairesis*, 'moral character'. Epictetus does not say: moral character *should* be a human's ruling principle. He advances the sovereignty of moral character as the primary identity condition of being human. The moral life, then, is not something a human, as so identified, can opt out of. In order to qualify properly as human, you have to base your life on moral principles. Vestiges of this notion persist today in our use of the term 'inhuman'. But *we* reserve that word for instances of extreme wickedness. Epictetus is saying that to be human *at all* is to acknowledge the essential character of oneself as a moral agent.[10]

His second instruction is to recognise that 'you are a citizen of

---

[9] I am puzzled by MacIntyre's emphasis upon the Stoics' practice of speaking of moral virtue in the singular, since this is common to Aristotle as well. It is also Aristotle's view that the moral virtues do not exist in separation from one another, *EN* vi 1144b32–1145a6. For this paper I am not assuming that Stoics were working from close acquaintance with the texts of Aristotle's treatises. I have considered some of the possible connexions between them in Long 1968b.

[10] Cf. Epictetus ii.10 and Diogenes the Cynic's unsuccessful quest for 'men', D.L. vi.27, 41.

the world', one of the world's 'principal parts', endowed with a capacity to understand and draw rational conclusions from its divine administration. If the amplification of 'world citizenship' presupposes acceptance of Stoic theology and providence, Epictetus offers a further specification of more general application: acting always for the good of the whole and never for exclusively private advantage, treating oneself as a member of a rationally organised structure. Once again, this is put forward as *what* a human being actually is. If Epictetus is right, as a matter of fact, you cannot combine the policies of Callicles and Thrasymachus and also be human. Any actions or goals which favour just one individual at the expense of others are incompatible with 'world citizenship', a description which, he takes it, we all essentially bear.

He proceeds to list a human's further 'professions' (*epangeliai*), son, brother, town-councillor, and so on, and the duties they require. 'Each one of these descriptions, when rationally examined, marks out its own work.' 'If you go off and depreciate your brother, you have forgotten who you are and what is your description.' Depreciation of one's brother is taken to be analogous to a blacksmith misusing his hammer. When Epictetus calls being a brother a 'profession', he means profession quite literally. Family relationships, he is saying, are jobs, activities with aims and objective excellences in line with our modern but restricted notion of profession. The job must fit the description. Fail to do the job, and, for Epictetus, you fail to qualify as a brother.

Professions are purposive activities and require expertise. In Stoicism the profession of being human is living in accordance with 'right reason' – perfecting one's essential nature as a rational being, and conforming to all of its dictates. This 'professionalism' is pointedly reflected in the early Stoic account of virtue as 'a craft concerned with the whole of life' (*SVF* III.202, 560). Stoic lists of virtues extend to knowledge of how one should behave in music, drinking-parties and sex. If virtue is the *telos* of human nature, what human nature is for, we are so constructed as rational ‖ beings that acquiring this craft is the essence of our well-being, the foundation of our true identity as people. It is not a job, moreover, that we can ever stop doing, or trying to do, if we really are human. As Epictetus says elsewhere, a man is making moral progress if he bathes 'as someone who keeps his word' and 'eats as a man of integrity' (1.4.20). An adulterer is as useless as a *man* as

a cracked saucepan (II.4.4); a coward and weakling is really only a
'corpse' (1.9.33). We tend to act as if we were 'runaway slaves'
(1.29.62); but we should consider 'who we are.'

This is the style of the street preacher, rhetorically designed to
shock the audience's complacency. But it does not abandon all
contact with traditional values. Epictetus is trading on and extending his society's acceptance of the view that certain of the terms
which identify a person – family relationships, professional activities in the mundane sense, public offices – provide an immediate
specification of what that person ought to do, in respect of those
particular identifications. The subject-matter of the discourse I
have been discussing is *kathēkonta*, the functions proper to one's
identity. As a Stoic, Epictetus goes far beyond the popular morality of antiquity in starting from a human being's essential function or identity as a rational, moral agent. But neither that identity nor a person's 'cosmopolitanism' provides specific guidance on
what is required of this individual here and now. To know who
we are, specifically, to know what we *should* do as the individuals
we *are*, our moral characters and cosmopolitanism require reference to the roles in society that we actually fill, Epictetus' 'son,
brother', and so on. MacIntyre seems to think that the 'Stoic good
man' as 'a citizen of the universe' can have only a 'secondary and
accidental relation to all other collectivities, to city, kingdom' etc.
(p. 157). That contrast is not to be found in Epictetus.[11] His 'cosmopolitanism' obliges people to see themselves as members of the
universal rational community; but this insight, it is suggested, so
far from diminishing more local identities, will provide general
principles for executing the functions of these: 'acting always for
the good of the whole'.

What lies behind Epictetus' doctrines is a multi-faceted view of
human nature. This was explored in very interesting sections of
Cicero's *De officiis* 1.107–15, probably derived from Panaetius' two
books *On proper function*.[12] Each of us, we are told, is naturally
endowed with four *personae* – roles or identities. The first one of
these is the same as Epictetus' 'first description' – our identity as

[11] The general Stoic reconciliation of radicalism and conservatism is excellently discussed
by Bonhöffer 1894, pp. 92–7. Cf. also Brunt, 1973, pp. 9–34, and my remarks in Long
1980, pp. 164–6, 172–3.

[12] Cf. De Lacy 1977, pp. 163–72, where Panaetius' doctrine is seen as a 'broadening' of
Platonic and Aristotelian functionalism.

human beings. We all share the same nature in being endowed with rationality, a status which sets us above the rest of the animal world. From this shared rational identity, as Epictetus also maintained, the foundations of moral principles are derived. Cicero, omitting here any mention of world-citizenship, passes immediately to a second 'individual' identity, which shows itself in differences of physique, appearance, aptitude and temperament. Provided that these individual characteristics are not vicious, he insists, it is our function as persons to cultivate them and so structure our lives that we harmonise the first identity with the second. The moral requirements that result from our shared nature are assumed to be entirely compatible with full recognition of people's standard idiosyncrasies. We are not expected to be jolly extroverts if we are shy and solemn by temperament. This second role, therefore, not only allows but actually requires that we should be 'ourselves', do our own thing, not try to be what we are not.

The third *persona* is defined in terms of external circumstances, what 'chance or events impose'. Since this identity is not a product of our innate endowment as ‖ individual human beings, it is said to be derived from circumstances or *fortuna*, as distinct from *natura*. But it would be wrong to conclude from this that the third *persona* is not a constituent of our identity, or that its source is ultimately distinct from Nature = God, the rational agent which determines all events in the world, internal and external to the individual. I take the thought to be an acknowledgement of the fact that we are not identified as free or enslaved, noble or wealthy, military commanders or senators, by reference to our innate *personae* as human beings with specific temperaments and aptitudes. Yet the contingencies of life are also central to defining who we are, and thus they too become part of our identity. Marcus Aurelius was not born an emperor; he found himself cast into that role. In this third *persona*, then, we find a factual basis for the familiar Stoic doctrine that people should act appropriately to their station in life. If what you are is, *inter alia*, a person who inherits or is deprived of great wealth, that circumstance introduces an aspect of your identity which will provide part of the content of your life in accordance with nature.

Finally, personal choice. All human beings are said to have a fourth *persona*, the specific profession or life-style that they *choose* to adopt. In making that choice, we acquire a further component of *our* own identity. Collectively, these four *personae* seem intended to provide a set of designations that comprehend all that each one of us is. The moral significance of this is plain: by understanding who we are and the functions that those identities embody, we should discover the common and individual aims of our lives and the actions that are appropriate to us here and now. For instance, Mary is a wealthy, excitable actress; John is a lame, musically gifted professor; Matthew is an unemployed, shy ex-steelworker. All of these *personae* are matters of fact, and the relevant facts could be greatly elaborated. In Stoicism common duties are required of these three people in virtue of their common humanity. Yet each person's life, at its fullest and best, will be one which has its own natural shape and direction, in accordance with each person's temperament, circumstances and choices. Far from being a restriction on human freedom, life in accordance with nature, in such a formulation, offers the maximum of individual development and respect for differences that is compatible with the moral requirements of being a person.

This last point defends Stoic functionalism against the objection that such a view of persons reduces them to being the artefacts or instruments of an externally determined natural plan. If the good life is supposedly defined in terms of fulfilling our natural functions, 'natural' could be represented as an arbitrary or constraining concept of human beings. In Stoic ethics, however, all we are debarred from choosing is a life of self-seeking and 'irrational' egoism. Provided that we accept our role as moral or rational agents, we are not only free to give our lives this or that shape; we are actually required to choose modes of living that suit our inclinations and aptitudes, so long as these are means of acting harmoniously with our full identity, as specified by the four *personae*.

MacIntyre objects to the modern view, as he sees it, of taking a human being to be an 'individual prior to and apart from all roles' (p. 56), a view that makes the self just 'what I myself choose to be' (p. 205), detachable from family, community, and history. The Stoic material I have presented so far is thoroughly in line with 'the Aristotelian tradition', as approved by MacIntyre. At the same time, I would argue, it comes much ‖ closer to MacIntyre's own interpretation of the strengths of that tradition than does the explicit standpoint of Aristotle himself. The Stoic concepts of *persona* and 'profession' (*epangelia*) can be read as a development of

'Aristotelian' functionalism in a fashion that articulates quite precise connexions between self-identity, self-knowledge and appropriate moral conduct. Aristotle's concept of the 'mean' that is 'relative to us' offers an approach to a view of personal identity, but he scarcely develops it in the direction of discovering just who *we* are, as moral agents. MacIntyre himself concedes limitations and blindness in Aristotle's catalogue of the virtues, with its narrow focus upon the male citizens of a Greek *polis* (p. 149). The Stoic conception of ethical roles hardly needs translation into a wider perspective, since it starts from people's generic identity as people. While plainly not a theory of 'liberal individualism', MacIntyre's anathema, its emphasis on the *persona* we choose to adopt offers something of a bridge between his apparently unbridgeable classical and modern traditions.

CHRYSIPPUS, *KATHĒKONTA* AND COSMIC ORDER

I have been writing as if it were legitimate to label passages in Arrian [alias Epictetus] and Cicero [probably derived from Panaetius] 'Stoic' without further qualification. Can we regard these as firm elements of the Stoic tradition itself? What about early Stoicism? Was this not a radical moral theory, founded upon the perfect wise man, which paid scant regard to ordinary Greek views of society and the good life? Do we not have Cicero's own word for it, that his subject-matter in *De officiis* books I and II is only what the Stoics called *secunda quaedam honesta, non sapientium modo propria, sed cum omni hominum genere communia* (*Off.* III.15)? In that case, have we any grounds for regarding the doctrine of the four *personae* as integral to the basis of Stoic ethics?

These are large questions, too large to be answered fully in the remainder of this chapter. Moreover, so far as my suggestions to MacIntyre are concerned, they are relatively tangential. The Stoicism of Cicero's *De officiis* and of Epictetus is a central part of the classical tradition of moral philosophy, overshadowing interpretation and knowledge of the fragments of Zeno or Chrysippus. Stoics could differ sharply between themselves, however, and we miss much of the interest of their thought if we assume its monolithic form too readily.[13] For all that we know, Panaetius was the

---

[13] Cf. the deviant Aristo, n. 8 above. This is what one expects to find in any richly creative philosophical movement. The earliest Stoics toyed with utopian models of a cosmopolis

first and only Stoic who specified four *personae* in the form that Cicero represents. Yet it can be shown that this approach to a functional view of human nature and identity is entirely within the main spirit of much earlier Stoicism. It is presupposed in the doctrines of *kathēkon* and *oikeiōsis*, which are central to the philosophy of Chrysippus.

Let me take *kathēkon* first. Cicero, in the Latin I have quoted above, says that he is discussing those *officia* 'which are not *only* (*modo*) characteristic of wise men, but ones that they share with human beings quite generally'. He is not, in other words, setting up a scheme of appropriate behaviour which falls outside the scope of imperfect persons. But nor is he, either, explaining and classifying types of moral action which differ in their objective content from those of wise men. Cicero's comment is entirely in line with the main evidence for *kathēkonta*, and the differences between the performance of these by wise men on the one hand and imperfect persons on the other.

All the actions of wise men are *katorthōmata*, and *katorthōmata* are 'perfect' *kathēkonta* (*SVF* iii.494, 516, Cic. *Fin.* iii.58–9). There are difficulties, too complex ‖ to be treated here, in the interpretation of some of the sources on this subject. But I am confident that Zeno, Chrysippus and their successors were all of the view that everything which a wise man does can be described under the general concept of *kathēkon*.[14] The wise man does always, and with full understanding, and on the basis of a completely virtuous disposition what his nature, as a rational being, dictates – and it characteristically dictates such things as honouring his parents, siblings and country, spending time with friends, serving on embassies, going out for exercise, paying back deposits etc. It may also dictate his giving up his property or a part of his body: such things, as I have already mentioned, are cited as examples of *kathēkonta* which depend upon 'circumstances'.

What differentiates the wise man from imperfect people is not

---

of only the wise, which dispensed with standard social institutions. But these models have left little trace on the detailed moral theory in our record. The prevailing idea, endorsed by Zeno I surmise, was to regard actual cities as imperfect microcosms of the cosmopolis shared by gods and humans, cf. Bonhöffer 1894, pp. 93ff., and 118 nn. 66ff. Given the content of Stoic ethics, this is a powerfully radical idea, leaving it open to exceptional persons, such as Epictetus' ideal Cynic, to be 'cosmopolitans' in the larger sense. *Discourses* iii.22.67ff.

[14] Cf. also Kerferd 1978a and Kidd 1978 in Rist 1978. The position taken above has been argued more fully in Long/Sedley, 1987, vol. i, pp. 365–8.

necessarily *what* he does, but the trained moral disposition with which he acts: 'the good man's function is not to look after his parents ... but to look after them on the basis of practical intelligence' (*SVF* III.516). Given the examples of *kathēkonta* which depend on 'circumstances', obviously exceptional to any general rules of behaviour, we can conclude that everything done by a wise man will be *kathēkon* in the relevant circumstances. The man who has made such progress that he falls just short of wisdom 'performs all *kathēkonta* in all respects and omits none' (Chrysippus in *SVF* III.510). What this man lacks is not a higher moral objective content to his actions, but the wise man's absolutely firm and consistently virtuous disposition.

It follows from this that *what* a wise man does is not by itself an indication of his wisdom; for imperfect people will do many of the same things. Yet plainly what the wise man does is not detachable from his virtuous disposition. His moral actions include an objective content which can be specified in terms that often, if not always, cut across the division between the two classes of people.

This glance at the Stoic wise man is sufficient to show that Chrysippus did not regard him as a being detached from the commonly accepted and approved conventions of family and social life. The wise man will marry and raise children and play his part in the community. *Kathēkonta* provide an exemplification of the functions which it falls to a rational being to fulfil, whether he is perfect or imperfect. This is not to say that the wise man's virtue is reducible to the application of moral rules, as set out in lists of *kathēkonta*. That would be a travesty of the Stoics' deeper moral intuitions. The wise man, to return to MacIntyre (p. 157), conforms his disposition and behaviour to 'the law ... embodied in nature itself ... the cosmic order'. Does this however introduce an ethical principle which completely transcends that interest in local particularities which I have been attributing to Stoicism? My answer to this question is negative, for reasons already given. But it is still necessary to consider the practical moral significance, in Stoicism, of the wise man's concern with cosmic law and order.

Here is a summary or quotation of Chrysippus' doctrine of the human *telos*. Diogenes Laertius VII.87–8:

Living in accordance with virtue is equivalent to living in accordance with experience of what happens by nature ... for our own natures are parts of the whole. Therefore, living consistently with nature comes to be the *telos*, which is in accordance with the nature of oneself and that of the universe, engaging in no activity (*energountas*) ‖ which the common law is wont to forbid (*apagoreuein eiōthen*), which is the right reason pervading everything and identical to Zeus, who directs the organisation of reality. And the virtue of the happy man and his good flow of life consist in this: always doing everything on the basis of the concordance of each man's guardian spirit (*daimōn*) with the will of the director of the universe.

In this text we are invited to view the world as a cosmopolis or eco-system of which each person is an integral part. By paying regard to this system, we shall discover rational principles which work for the good of the whole. Our goal as individuals is to accommodate ourselves to these principles, taking them as moral precepts to which we willingly assent, as the particular rational beings that we are. Chrysippus does not exemplify an 'activity which the common law is wont to forbid'. But we can supplement his text with the concept that best fits its language and tenor – *kathēkon*.

Here is the proof. We need a concept which does justice to the providential order of nature in general. The Stoics regarded life quite generally as naturally structured to suit the needs of living beings, and were prepared to speak of *kathēkonta* in reference to animals and even plants (D.L. VII.107). We need a concept which picks up the notion of 'activity' (*energountas*) and relates that notion to the nature of rational beings. Diogenes Laertius at VII.108 reports: '*kathēkon* is an activity (*energēma*) appropriate to constitutions (i.e. the structures of animals) in accordance with nature'; and a little later he defines *kathēkonta* as 'everything which reason dictates our doing, such as honouring parents, brothers, country, spending time with friends'. The negations of these are things which reason 'forbids' (*apagoreuei*). Among many other supporting texts, I choose one more to quote in full, a citation of Chrysippus by Plutarch (*Comm. not.* 1069e): 'Chrysippus says: "What am I to take as the foundation of *kathēkon* and the material of virtue if I pass over nature and what accords with nature?"'

Chrysippus proposed that ethics should be founded on physics, on the *experience* of nature.[15] This experience reveals a divine sys-

---

[15] He also proposed that his moral theory was 'most in harmony with life and connects best with the ingrown preconceptions', *SVF* III.69. In trying to interpret the Stoics, we need to strike a balance between their genuine commitment to empiricism and their willingness to press moral intuitions to paradoxical conclusions, if necessary. Chrysippus wrote at least seven books on *kathēkon* and four on *lives* (livelihoods), cf. Brunt 1973 n. 11, 23ff.

tem of cosmic law, but that law is not to be interpreted as a mystery or a religious fiat devoid of all contact with the world as we find it. That would remove any intelligible sense from nature and experience. The laws of nature, I am suggesting, are just those rational principles which it is *our nature*, as individual persons, to understand and adopt – honouring parents, country, and so on. Our natures are parts of the rational community, as are our cities, imperfect microcosms to be sure, in the world as we find it, but capable here and now of performing at least some of the functions that reason dictates. The same general point can be made if we take Chrysippus here to be specifying first the necessary and then the sufficient conditions of human self-fulfilment. Disobedience to the general principles of rational conduct, as embodied in *kathēkonta*, is to put oneself outside that community to which one belongs by nature; and complete self-fulfilment – virtue and happiness – requires complete accord between the perfect rationality of the divine system itself and a person's own disposition. This last is only the wise man's achievement, for he and only he can have complete understanding of the system itself. But the system itself will be vacuous if it ignores the principles of which it is the system. If, in Cicero's words, the system can be described as 'the order and harmony of conduct' (*rerum agendarum ordinem et concordiam, Fin.* III.21), the only thing truly desirable ‖ for its own sake, we have every ground for viewing the wise man's moral insight as a systematic understanding and practice of *kathēkonta*. For that text presents this insight as something which develops out of kathekontic behaviour that is 'completely consistent with nature'.

The upshot of this discussion is that Chrysippus provides full endorsement for the kind of moral philosophy which MacIntyre approves. We have no reason to regard the functionalism of Epictetus or Panaetius as a different brand of Stoicism, catering for the needs of the ordinary person in social contexts which the sage, as 'world citizen', somehow transcends. The Stoics were as committed as Aristotle himself was to the moral scheme of MacIntyre's 'Aristotelian tradition' – 'untutored human-nature-as-it-happens-to-be, human-nature-as-it-could-be-if-it-realised-its-*telos* and the precepts of rational ethics as the means for the transition from one to the other' (p. 51). But their agreement to this scheme does not make the Stoics mere transmitters of 'the Aristotelian tradition'. Thanks to their remarkable and original concept of *oikeiōsis*, they thought they could show a coincidence between full self-realisation, perfect rationality, and moral virtue, starting from human nature-as-it-happens-to-be. The 'coincidence' is Platonic and Aristotelian, but the strategies are Stoic.

SELF-INTEREST AND THE STOIC COMMUNITY OF REASON

Oikeiōsis, the 'appropriation' or 'affective relationship' with which we are naturally endowed, has two faces or aspects – towards oneself and towards other human beings. The philological details are complex, but relatively clear thanks to recent studies. I propose to assume most of the results of those, in order to indicate the basic philosophical message of *oikeiōsis*.[16]

In an argument we may call 'the evolving constitution', *oikeiōsis* in relation to oneself is deployed.[17] The human infant, like other creatures, has an instinct from birth to pursue those things that suit its infantile constitution. This shows that it is naturally endowed with a concern for itself. Human beings are rational by nature, but their rationality evolves only gradually from infancy to maturity. An infant recognises that whatever accords with its infantile nature is valuable. But the same principle holds as reason develops. A person now comes to be concerned for her rational nature. The onset of rationality involves recognition that consistent moral conduct, rather than animal self-preservation, is what principally suits a rational nature. This shift of interest is the natural evolution of a rational being. Its now intelligent self-concern enables it to see that consistent moral conduct is what best accords with its nature.

This is an interesting argument. It starts from observable facts of infantile and animal behaviour. It then points out the further obvious fact that adult human beings have a range of interests for themselves that go well beyond what young children desire. Some of these interests may plausibly be called rationally desirable. But the argument suddenly concludes that only the moral life is truly desirable to a rational nature. Yet mature human beings do not normally regard the moral life as their only good. If that life is not

---

[16] See especially Pembroke 1971 and Kerferd 1972.
[17] I draw on D.L. VII.85–6. Cic. *Fin.* III.16–22, and Seneca, *Ep.* 121.6–15. For an excellent discussion, taking up problems I cannot pursue here, see Striker 1983.

normal, what authority do the Stoics have for calling it natural, especially when the opening steps of their argument seem to equate natural with normal?

Such a complaint misses the whole point of the argument. If human beings, as a matter of biological fact, identified their goal with a consistent moral life, ethics would ‖ cease to be necessary. The reason for specifying the moral life as our goal is to say that this is what we *should* pursue. But if we should pursue it, and don't, can it still be called natural? Certainly, if in fact the moral life is what actually suits mature human nature better than anything else. A law does not cease to be a law through non-observance. What the Stoics need to show is that human beings are so naturally constituted that nothing is better for them, more self-fulfilling, than living morally well. The fact that most people live as if this were false does not prove the Stoics wrong.

But have the Stoics shown that their *telos* is true of human nature? Not with this argument. Someone could accept its starting-points, and conclude that playing the piano is what suits rational self-concern, the full development of reason. Why should we suppose that consistency of moral conduct best suits a mature rational nature?

The Stoics go some way towards meeting this objection if we take account of the outward face of *oikeiōsis*. Start once again with the equation of natural and normal, but this time consider people collectively, from the outside as it were. This is Cicero's procedure in *Fin.* iii.62–8.[18] Parents' affection for their children, friendships between people, community life, he argues, give evidence of the fact that mutual attraction between human beings is something natural. Cicero means that we are so designed as a species that a well-ordered social life is naturally appropriate to us and not something imposed on us by external conventions. He continues: 'the Stoics hold that the world is governed by divine will; it is, as it were, a city and state, shared by men and gods, and each of us is part of the world. From this it is a *natural* consequence that we prefer the common advantage to our own ... furthermore, we are driven to benefit as many people as possible.'

As with the 'evolving constitution' argument, the conclusion does not seem to follow from the admittedly plausible claims about the

---

[18] For further evidence, cf. the articles in n. 16 above.

naturalness of social life. We may grant the naturalness of affection and some measure of human solidarity, without inferring that
we are *naturally* altruistic and benevolent. Cicero, however, represents the naturalness of these attitudes as a consequence of a
divinely organised world-government, of which we are all parts. Is
this a bald theological dogma? Or did the Stoics regard it too as a
statement which retains an intelligible connexion with the world
or nature in an empirical sense?

Chrysippus entitles us to gloss the proposition about divine world
government by reference to the 'community of reason'. That community of course, for a Stoic, is founded on the omnipresent perfection of god or cosmic nature. But it is not external to human
beings, for reason is *their* common property. A non-Stoic, who did
not accept Stoic theology, might be willing to grant that inferences
about human nature may justifiably be made from the fact that
reason is a property we share with our fellows. She might also be
willing to grant that reason is a faculty that recognises connexions
and relationships which, if they hold good at all, hold good trans-
personally, for rational beings in general. Now if mature human
beings are rational, and normally organise their lives in ways that
show some regard for one another, it is plausible to suppose that
some regard for one another is natural to rational beings. This can
supply a missing step in the 'evolving constitutions' argument. If a
person recognises that the full development of reason is *his* or *her*
natural good, that person would not consider playing the piano to
be that for the sake of which *everything* in life is to be done, the end
of *all* desires. The perfection of reason, as a concern for one's
rational self, must have ‖ regard to the life of human beings quite
generally. It cannot, as the common property of persons, have a
perfection exclusive to the individual. Reason is the natural foundation of our social life. So perfect reason will determine a perfect
moral life, a life of living well in society.

In some such way, I suggest, the Stoics would put their case to
MacIntyre. They would explain that the naturalness of their *telos*
is not to be taken to mean that it is normally recognised in full, or
is anything but arduous in the extreme. But nature does not make
us virtuous. It provides us with virtue as our *telos*, the ultimate
purpose and reason of our living. If nature's complete aims for us
remain unrecognised, that is the fault of our upbringing and of
the societies we inhabit.

Marcus Aurelius, who took this philosophy as his own art of living, most clearly reveals its relevance to MacIntyre's *After Virtue*. I pick out a few of his *Meditations*, which exemplify the moral scheme I have been discussing. It seems to me, though this is entirely an intuitive feeling, that they have a more obvious modern applicability than the *Nicomachean ethics*. 'If intelligence is common to us all, so too is reason which makes us rational beings; if so, that reason is also common which tells us *what to do or not to do*; if so, law is also common; if so, we are citizens; if so, we share in a political community' (IV.4)[19] Marcus tells himself to make *to koinō-nikon* his *telos* (XII.20). This, he says, is what is the leading element in the human constitution (VII.55). He tells himself to fit his life to his circumstances and truly to love his fellow human beings (VI.39). He speaks of us all as fellow-workers for a single goal (VI.42). The first thing that is specific to a person is benevolence towards other persons (VIII.26). He urges himself, when sleepy, to get up to do a person's work (V.1).[20]

This of course is not the whole of Marcus' philosophy, and only one central strand of Stoic ethics. Stoicism was not a secular humanism. (Nor, for that matter, were the ethics of Plato and Aristotle.) At the heart of the system lies a theory of natural theology. The popular image of Stoicism, as an attitude of dispassionate acquiescence to all external events, rests on the doctrine that everything which actually happens is providentially determined by immanent cosmic reason, identical to god. This idea, to which Marcus frequently appeals as buttress for his own equanimity, was the target of John Stuart Mill's famous attack on 'following nature', as an ethical principle, in one of his *Three Essays on Religion*.

Mill wrote: 'Not even on the most distorted and contracted theory of good which ever was framed by religious or philosophical fanaticism, can the government of Nature be made to resemble the work of a being at once good and omnipotent.'[21] Mill took nature in Stoic ethics to refer univocally to an externally observable criterion of good – the providential course of everything that happens. He completely omitted any consideration of the Stoics' theories of human nature, such as I have been describ-

---

[19] Cf. Cic. *Leg.* 1.23 and 33, cited by Farquharson 1944 *ad loc*. The sorites was a favourite form of argument in Chrysippus' writings.
[20] Further passages of the same tenor are V.6, 16, 22, 30; VI.40; VII.72.
[21] Mill 1969, vol. X, p. 389.

ing. By reducing 'following nature' to an obviously unworkable external criterion, Mill obscured the essential fact that nature in Stoic ethics is proposed as an internal criterion, the voice of reason, a teleological principle which exists in our nature in order to structure human life in the best possible way.

An extension of the same principle, admittedly, was presumed to be at work in events at large. Thus the 'common reason' is advanced not only as the objective ground of what we can and should do, but also as the cause of all happenings, outside our control, to which we should respond with agreement to their providential ordering. ‖

The Stoics thereby ran into difficulties and ingenious defences which Christian theology has made all too familiar.[22] Is such whole-hearted piety so essential to Stoicism that their conception of human nature would lose all point without it? Must the community of reason be at work in the earthquake and the genocide if it is also the objective ground of human well-being? These indeed are mysteries which I prefer not to penetrate. The essence of Stoicism seems to be organising one's internal resources – desires and feelings and judgements (cf. Epictetus III.2.2) – into a harmonious structure of rational principles and motives to action. This is the practical achievement promised by accommodating oneself to the community of reason. To engage sympathetically with that notion, it is only necessary to suppose that we are biologically structured as human beings with an inbuilt *telos*; and that that *telos* is our self-fulfilment or *eudaimonia* as well-reasoning men and women, living amicably together and performing those roles and tasks that are *ours*.

The Stoics thought that this could be deemed the goal that our nature as people requires. Perhaps they would be studied more widely today if they had not filled out this moral scheme with those unacceptable details by which they are popularly characterised – the relation of all goods to virtue, the identification of virtue with infallible perfection, the conception of emotional disturbances as signs of moral sickness, the comprehensive providence embodied in the world at large. Such doctrines, it may be said, are so essential to the Stoic system and to its supposed internal coherence that without them the philosophy would lose its whole *raison*

---

[22] I have explored some of these problems in Long 1968a, and Long 1986a, pp. 179–84.

d'être. Yet Panaetius, who was Head of the Stoa from c. 129 to 109 BC, may have had strong doubts about the first two, if not the third and fourth. His account of the kind of principles would-be Stoics should try to live by, on Cicero's evidence, paid little or no heed to any of them.[23]

I am not trying to outdo MacIntyre by offering neo-Stoicism as the philosophy for our time.[24] Nor do I wish to endorse the feasibility of a naturalistic ethical theory. But if naturalism is defensible in principle, it is hard to see how it could dispense with the kind of foundations the Stoics sought to provide.[25]

As a postscript, no would-be Stoic need stop practising the piano. The point of Stoic virtue, notwithstanding the heavy earnestness of some of our sources, is not abandoning ordinarily enjoyable and useful activities. The Stoic virtues are modes of understanding how to live well, mental dispositions, without any determinate content beyond general principles of the nature proper to being human. What they purport to give us is a particular outlook on the world, so that everything we do is describable by a virtue adverb – conversing, walking about, or whatever, *phronimōs*, 'reasonably' (in its full eighteenth-century sense). As they were honest enough to admit, a counsel of perfection; 'too much', as they wondered themselves, 'for human nature'?[26]

POSTSCRIPT 1995

My remarks in the later part of this chapter are discussed at some length by Engberg-Pedersen (1990, pp. 39–41). Describing the original paper as 'far more important than its title suggests' (n. 15, p. 241), he says (p. 39) that I 'see the issue here as being whether the criterion of goodness that is implied in the idea of 'following nature' is external or internal, but not in such a way that there is

---

[23] For recognition of the influence of Ciceronian Stoicism on Renaissance political thought, cf. Skinner 1978.

[24] This was the opinion expressed to me during the cold war by a Hungarian publisher, who had just encountered ancient Stoicism for the first time.

[25] Consider in this context Finnis' impressive study (1980). This book, like MacIntyre's, draws heavily on Aristotle, more lightly on Stoicism, which Finnis appreciates for 'its vision of order and reasonableness' (p. 377) but thinks 'perhaps exposed to Mill's objection' (p. 35 n. 39). I have suggested that the principal ethical significance of cosmic order is the universality of moral precepts for all members of the community of reason.

[26] Chrysippus in Plutarch, *Stoic. rep.* 1041f.

any intrinsic opposition between the two positions'. He takes me to have shifted from 'an external viewpoint' (in 'The logical basis of Stoic ethics' = chapter 6) to an 'emphasis on the internal view', referring to my remarks on p. 176, 'The essence of Stoicism ... inbuilt *telos*.' For Engberg-Pedersen, the move he attributes to me is in the right direction, but does not go far enough. He takes the key issue to be 'not whether the criterion of goodness is external or internal, but whether the reference to nature in Stoicism in *any* sense provides a criterion of goodness that is external to the way in which human beings themselves *take* things to have value' (1990, p. 41). To this question, he proposes an unequivocally negative answer

On p. 155 I have said why I do not agree with this interpretation. As I understand the Stoics, they take nature to be both internal to the individual person and external. (This was my position in 'The logical basis of Stoic ethics', where I never intended to suggest nature functions simply as an external criterion of goodness.) In the first case, nature manifests itself in the normative voice of the individual's impulse and reason; in the second case in the rational organisation of the cosmos. The challenge for us, as interpreters, is to articulate the two cases in such a way that they do justice to the Stoic intuition that 'our natures are parts of the whole' (D.L. VII.87). What I take this to mean is that self-reflection is demanded of us by our individual nature (with this Engberg-Pedersen fully agrees), but that, in addition, we can only fully comprehend our *telos* by perceiving how and where we fit within the rational organisation of nature (with this, it seems, Engberg-Pedersen disagrees.)

I do not take my position on nature in this chapter to have shifted significantly from the viewpoint I defended in 'The logical basis of Stoic ethics'. But Engberg-Pedersen is right to note a difference of emphasis. In 'Greek ethics after MacIntyre', in contrast with the other paper, I adduce a good deal of evidence from later Stoicism. This is because, like the later Stoics themselves, I am more concerned here with the ordinary person's rationality than with its ideal achievement in the wise man.

CHAPTER 8

*Stoic eudaimonism**

The history of ethics has moved on by some two thousand years
since Stoicism began to make its mark on the Roman Empire. If,
in the light of that history, we ask what kind of an ethical theory
the Stoics advance, an obvious answer is at hand. Like their Platonic and Aristotelian predecessors and their Epicurean contemporaries, the Stoics are eudaimonists. For them, as for these other
philosophers, ethics finds its official purpose not, or not primarily,
in justifying morality or in determining the grounds of a particular sphere of conduct labelled 'moral'. The sphere of Stoic ethical
inquiry is human life and conduct quite generally. In a manner
that looks thoroughly Aristotelian, with roots stretching back to
Socrates and Plato, the Stoics profess to be interested in an end
'for the sake of which everything is done but which is not itself
done for the sake of anything', 'the ultimate object of desire', 'the
summum bonum'. Nor do they disagree with other Greek philosophers on the term that characterises this objective. *eudaimonia* or
'happiness' is the *telos* set forth in Stoic ethics just as it is in Aristotle's ethical works. The Stoics, in other words, lay claim to being
philosophers who will tell us what happiness is and how happiness
is to be attained.

But this claim, if it is taken seriously, may seem to confront the
Stoics with two independent but equally powerful challenges. On
the one hand, 'happiness', as it is commonly ‖ thought to be represented in Stoicism, does not square well with the richness of
experience, positive emotion, and fulfilment of reasonable expectations that are well-acknowledged features of happiness in most
cultures. Stoicism has become a byword – witness our dictionary

---

* From a paper read at Boston University on 22 October 1987, as part of the Tenth Annual
  Boston Area Colloquium in Ancient Philosophy.

entries – not for happiness but for repression of emotion, indifference to pleasure or pain, and patient endurance. To be sure, Stoicism satisfies a number of conditions philosophers have deemed favourable to happiness – probity, a rational plan of life, internal harmony – but, this line of argument continues, it achieves invulnerability against ill fortune at the cost of emotional impoverishment and indifference to ordinary human experience. Its recipe for happiness, as a Ciceronian critic observed, would not even satisfy an unembodied mind (*De finibus* IV.27). Call this the 'impoverishment' objection.

The other critique confronts the Stoics with disingenuousness and pretence, or at best, self-deception and incoherence. It grants that they claim to be eudaimonists, but goads them with the objection that they misdescribe their ethical theory. Only superficially and in purely formal terms is 'happiness' the Stoic *telos*. What the Stoics are really recommending, according to this line of argument, is not the true route to happiness but a proto-Kantian moral outlook, in which happiness and morality are quite independent of one another. Stoic ethics, on this account, should be interpreted as an adumbration of the viewpoint that obedience to moral norms is categorical and absolutely binding on a rational agent irrespective of his happiness; such moral norms are expressions of a good which is *sui generis* and which has nothing to do with happiness, empirical data, or the outcomes of action, as ordinarily conceived. According to this challenge, the Stoics are of great significance for the development of ethical thought, but they are eudaimonists only nominally or in a sense that imposes intolerable strains on the coherence of their philosophy. Call this the 'disingenuousness' objection.

The spokesmen for these two objections are imaginary. They do, however, serve as rough approximations and exaggerations of tendencies commonly found in modern studies of ‖ Stoic ethics.[1]

---

[1] The 'impoverishment' objection is caustically stated by Jeremy Bentham 1834, vol. I, p. 300, cited by Irwin 1986a, p. 205; see also my remarks in Long 1986a, pp. 165–7. Striker 1983, pp. 165–7, suggests the Stoics would not have needed to argue that virtue is sufficient for happiness (which she regards as paradoxical) if they had not been constrained by 'their own and other contemporary presuppositions [which] seemed to demand that the final goal of life and the standard of value for actions should be one and the same thing, which had to be happiness'. For the 'disingenuousness objection', cf. Forschner 1986, p. 327, who finds tensions in Stoic ethics caused by their combining eudaimonism with 'was die kantische Tradition Moralität nennt'. One scholar who finds Stoic eudaimonism

It is timely to consider what precisely we should make of the Stoics' profession of eudaimonism.

As I proceed, I will follow the structure of this preamble. I shall argue first that the Greek ethical tradition, though a necessary component of the Stoics' eudaimonism, is insufficient to elucidate the contributions of physics and theology to their theory of the *summum bonum*. Then, I will consider, in terms of this more complex perspective, what defences the Stoics can offer against the 'impoverishment' objection on the one hand and the 'disingenuousness' objection on the other.

STOIC EUDAIMONISM AND ITS PLACE IN THE GREEK ETHICAL TRADITION

Eudaimonia, as its etymology indicates, is the name for a 'blessed' or 'god-favoured' condition, a condition in which a person's lot or *daimōn* is good. The term is normally and correctly translated 'happiness' – correctly because, as Gregory Vlastos has insisted, *eudaimonia* includes both the objective features of 'happiness' (attainment of good) and its subjective connotations (a profoundly contented state of mind).[2] Greek philosophers, it is true, devote more attention to characterising the formal and objective features of *eudaimonia* than to telling us what it is like, viewed from within, to be *eudaimōn*. Nor is *eudaimōn* ever used in Greek, like 'happy' in modern English, to describe transient moods or satisfactions. To call someone *eudaimōn* is to describe a person whose whole life is flourishing ‖ to the greatest extent available to human beings. But if *eudaimonia* is less psychological or subjective in its connotations than 'happiness', there is abundant evidence to show that the Greeks took a *eudaimōn* person to be subjectively satisfied with his or her life. If that were not so, it would be impossible to account for the importance all philosophers attached to emotional balance as a condition of *eudaimonia*. The Stoics cannot be rescued from the 'impoverishment' objection on the plea that their account of *eudaimonia* does not oblige them to do justice to the subjective requirements of happiness.

largely coherent and defensible is Irwin 1986a. I admire his treatment and agree with much of it. For reasons that will emerge later, however, I find his study too narrowly based on the Stoics' role as supposed respondents to Aristotle and insufficiently attentive to their physics and theology.

[2] Vlastos 1984, pp. 181–2; cf. also Kraut 1979, pp. 157–97.

If happiness is primarily located in the secure possession of goods that partly depend on chance – wealth, health, fame, family success – its attainment will be rare, especially in the ancient world, and partly outside human power. So it seemed to the earliest popular moralists of Greece. Long before Socrates and Plato, *eudaimonia* is being treated as either something well nigh impossible, or as a condition that depends less on fortune's whim than on a person's modest expectations and moral character. It is important to see that pessimists (who treat happiness as largely a function of good fortune) and revisionists (who have begun to internalise the goods of which happiness consists) were in general agreement about certain formal conditions essential to happiness – that it should be durable, complete and involve the possession of all or most things that are good for human beings.

The Stoics fully endorse all these conditions. Their doctrine that all the goods a person needs for happiness are internal and consist in a virtuous character might be interpreted simply as the most extreme version of what I just called the revisionists' conception of *eudaimonia*. The Stoics share with Socrates, Plato, Aristotle and Epicurus the doctrine that happiness is essentially a condition that depends upon a person's values, beliefs, desires and moral character. Where the Stoics stand alone is in their claim that happiness consists solely and entirely in ethical virtue and is thus completely independent of any of the 'goods' whose chanciness evoked the pessimism of the earliest moralists.[3] ‖

But here, I begin to anticipate. Before developing the Stoics' specific conception of happiness, we need to think more about the context already mapped out by their predecessors. A study of Plato's use of *eudaimonia* and cognate words reveals as uncontested features of the term the following features:

(a)   it is what everyone desires (*Euthydemus* 282a2);
(b)   it results from the acquisition of 'good things' / the absence of 'bad' things (*Symp.* 202c10; *Alcib.* 1 116b7; *Gorg.* 478c5);

---

[3] 'Stand alone' is right, I think, even though the Stoics themselves claimed Socrates as their precursor; see below. The Socrates of Plato's early dialogues holds that virtue is sufficient for happiness, cf. Irwin 1986a, pp. 87–8. Yet, as Irwin observes (pp. 90 n. 9, 105), this is entirely compatible with Socrates' taking the relation of virtue to happiness to be merely instrumental. I think Plato's text leaves it doubtful whether Socrates was interested in distinguishing between 'instrumentality', 'identity', or 'constitutiveness' as the relation of virtue to happiness. The Stoics, however, are insistent that virtue completely constitutes happiness, see the texts 60M, 61A, 63G in Long/Sedley 1987.

(c) it is what the gods have (*Symp.* 202c7);
(d) it is profitable (*Rep.* 1 354a6);
(e) it involves freedom to do what one wants to do (*Lys.* 207e2);
(f) it involves 'living well' (*Rep.* 1 354a1) or 'faring well' (*eu prattein*: *Gorg.* 507c4, *Charm.* 172a3);
(g) it is people's ultimate objective: no need to ask someone who wants to be *eudaimōn* why he wants this (*Symp.* 205a).

Plato's Socrates does not argue for these features of happiness, nor are they challenged by his interlocutors. We may take it that they specify features of happiness which would be generally endorsed by Greeks of the classical and Hellenistic periods. Aristotle appropriates them, as do the Stoics. In their ethics, as in Plato's, happiness is what everyone wants; it is everyone's ultimate objective; and the happy person (they would agree) is self-sufficient, and in possession of all the goods he needs for happiness.

The fact that the Stoics endorse all these features of *eudaimonia* shows that they do not wish to redefine the formal conditions of the concept. In claiming, as they do, that their ethical philosophy is in tune with people's preconceptions, they could refer to its endorsement of all these standard features of happiness.[4] But that expedient will carry no weight with those who attack Stoicism via the 'impoverishment' objection; for such people will say that ‖ their criticism is based on something different – for instance, the Stoics' restriction of the goods possessed by the happy person to the ethical virtues, or the Stoics' severance of pleasure from happiness.

Let us now consider features of *eudaimonia* which are not uncontested or formal properties of happiness, but ones which Greek philosophers seek to establish by argument. From Socrates and Plato onwards, all Greek philosophers offer proof of, or reasons for believing, the following two propositions. First, happiness is (either wholly or partly) a state and activity of the soul. Second, happiness (either wholly or partly) is generated by ethical virtue. Since ethical virtue is standardly regarded as an 'active state of the soul', and an active state of the soul deemed necessary to happiness is ethical virtue, the two propositions are mutually interentailing. For the purpose of evaluating the Stoics' eudaimonism, and responding to the charges of 'impoverishment' or 'disingenu-

---

[4] For Stoic appeal to 'common conceptions' or 'preconceptions', cf. 60b–g in Long/Sedley 1987.

ousness', we should acknowledge that they are not outlandish in linking happiness to an active state of the soul and, in particular, to ethical virtue. Today we may think that no philosopher has yet successfully proved that happiness is (wholly or partly) dependent upon ethical virtue. The Stoics, however, in defending that claim, could invoke Platonists, Aristotelians and Epicureans as their supporters.

So far, then, we find nothing distinctive about Stoic ethics either in its view of the formal conditions that *eudaimonia* must satisfy, or in its requirement that *eudaimonia* be connected with an active state of the soul and with ethical virtue in particular. Its distinctiveness begins to emerge once we attend to 'wholly or partly', the expression I had to include just now in order to establish agreement between Plato, Aristotle, Epicurus and Stoics on non-formal features of happiness. Of these philosophers it is only the Stoics who claim that happiness depends 'wholly' on an active state of the soul consisting in ethical virtue. To exhibit just some of the obvious differences between this position and rival accounts of happiness, we may observe that, for Plato (in some dialogues at least), pleasure as well as ethical virtue is a constituent of happiness. For Aristotle, external goods are necessary in addition to virtue and ‖ virtuous activity. For Epicurus, the state of the soul which actually constitutes happiness is pleasure; the state of the soul constituting virtue is treated as an essential instrument of happiness but not as something desirable *per se*, or as part of the content of happiness.

Within the Greek context I have been sketching, the Stoics appear to be eudaimonists whose distinctiveness chiefly consists in their economy, simplicity or parsimony. They agree with other Greek moralists that happiness is the secure possession of 'goods', but according to the Stoics the set of 'goods' is restricted to 'ethical virtue and what participates in this' (*SVF* 1.190, III.76): these are the only goods that there are. What marks the Stoics out, then, is their position that the goodness which constitutes happiness is ethical excellence, exclusively and homogeneously.[5] Thus the ancient debates, charted above all in Cicero, focus principally upon this issue. Opponents of the Stoics argue that happiness cannot be complete or perfect without the possession of goods additional to ethical virtue. The Stoics reply that ethical virtue is the only good,

[5] For good remarks on this, cf. Irwin 1986a, pp. 210–16.

and therefore the completeness of happiness *is* achieved by their doctrine. Opponents advance the 'impoverishment' objection. The Stoics reply that only on their theory can happiness be secure, guaranteed to be in our power, rendered self-sufficient, etc. – conditions that their rivals, with various qualifications, approve.[6]

I do not doubt that debates of this kind took place, and that Cicero's record of them is broadly accurate. But I also think that they oversimplify the issues, and tend misleadingly to represent Stoicism as an extreme version or perversion of Aristotelian eudaimonism.[7] Because, as I have been arguing, Stoic ‖ eudaimonism operates with so many of the standard ethical concepts, there is a strong temptation to read it as merely, or at least largely, a variant of or contribution to the familiar tradition. That is how Antiochus of Ascalon (Cicero's chief source and mentor) interpreted Stoic ethics, and I think T. H. Irwin's approach may be fairly so described. Was it all that Zeno, Cleanthes, and Chrysippus intended?

Various historical considerations make this improbable; but I think it is decisively ruled out for doctrinal reasons. Among the factors we need to take into consideration in accounting for the core of Stoic ethics there are two that seem to me to be primary: first, a radical intuition concerning 'nature' or the divine government of the world and the connexion of this government with human rationality; secondly, a belief that happiness, as conceived by the Socratic/Cynic tradition, more or less coincides with the natural and divine plan for human well-being. The second factor explains the Stoics' acceptance of eudaimonist concepts that are

---

[6] See especially Cicero, *Tusc.* v.40–1, 81–82 = 63L–M in Long/Sedley 1987.

[7] My own position on this issue is intermediate between Irwin's strongly Aristotelian reading of Stoic ethics (Irwin 1986a) and the belief of Sandbach 1983, p. 30, 'that all attempts to see Stoic ethics as a development from Aristotelian or Peripatetic thought have been unsuccessful', a conclusion criticised as 'too sweeping' by Rabel 1988, p. 145. Sandbach devotes most of his treatment of ethics to a critique of my article, Long 1968b. In that paper I wished to complicate the strands of influence on Stoic ethics by hypothesising a positive Aristotelian influence. I continue to find that a legitimate procedure, provided it is done with a clear eye on the full range of other antecedents; cf. my remarks in 1986a, pp. 109–13. Irwin, it should be said, is careful to note (1986a, p. 208) that Stoic arguments which he thinks are drawn from Aristotelian premisses 'may not have provided the Stoics themselves with their original reasons for believing their claims about virtue and happiness', but he declines to discuss Stoic 'arguments that might be derived from the place of human beings in cosmic nature', doubting their effectiveness for solving 'many problems about Stoic ethics'. Much of this chapter is an attempt to show why I think his doubts are unjustified.

ubiquitous in the Greek ethical tradition. But the first factor, the theocratic postulate, is largely new and alien.[8]

I should explain what I mean by these two factors. By the Socratic/Cynic tradition I refer to the doctrine that only one thing is good, namely knowledge or virtue, and only one thing is bad, namely ignorance or vice. From this, it follows, on eudaimonist ‖ principles, that the essence of happiness is knowledge or virtue, and the essence of unhappiness is ignorance or vice. Everything else is inessential, so far as happiness and unhappiness are concerned. This position, which I think Plato's Socrates virtually advances in the *Euthydemus* (278e3–281e5), was probably first formalised as a doctrine by the Stoics' Cynic precursors.[9] They, I assume, took Socrates to have proved that the so-called 'goods' – health, wealth, and the like – lack the attribute of 'necessarily benefiting' which is essential to any component of happiness.[10] Such misnamed goods are actually 'indifferent' since, taken by themselves, they no more benefit than they harm. It is only in conjunction with something else, i.e. knowledge, that they can be 'used well'; just as surely, in conjunction with ignorance they are 'used badly'. Goodness or badness, then, is entirely constituted by a person's knowledge/virtue or ignorance/vice.

This thesis – the univocity and homogeneity of goodness – was adopted and refined by Zeno and his orthodox Stoic followers.

---

[8] I let this remark stand even though Steven Strange 1989, p. 108 n. 7, commenting on my original paper, is quite right to call attention to the clear influence of the *Timaeus* on Stoicism and, one should add, the cosmology of *Laws* x. The chronology and extent of Plato's influence on early Stoicism is a subject that needs more careful study than it has so far received. I myself think that Chrysippus may have been the first Stoic to adopt a positive attitude to Plato as distinct from Plato's Socrates, cf. chapter 1, p. 19n. 43. The immanent or pantheist features of Stoic theology seem to have no informative Greek antecedents. Another way of making this point is to emphasise the difference between the centrality of 'nature' in Stoic ethics and its 'marginalised' status in the moral philosophy of Plato and Aristotle; cf. Laks 1989, p. 178.

[9] See also the virtually identical argument of *Meno* 87e–88e. In chapter 1, pp. 23–32, I have tried to prove that different interpretations of the *Euthydemus* argument underlie Zeno's controversy with the Cynicising Aristo over the scope of what has 'value' (*axia*). Since writing that paper I have had the benefit of reading Irwin's article (1986b). What Irwin calls 'Socrates' adaptive strategy' for happiness, i.e. adapting desires to suit any set of external conditions, seems to be a correct diagnosis of the *Euthydemus* argument and one which helps to show its appeal to the Stoics.

[10] Reference to the Cynics here has to be based not on explicit testimony but on the highly plausible assumption that the Stoic Aristo's hard line on the absolute indifference of everything except virtue and vice was pre-existing Cynic doctrine. For Stoic arguments along the lines of Socrates in the *Euthydemus* and *Meno*, see D.L. VII.101–5 = Long/Sedley 1987, 58A–B with discussion.

But before asking how it squares with their eudaimonism and the charge of 'impoverishment', we should consider its connexion with their specification of the *telos* (i.e. happiness) as 'living in agreement with nature'. Why do orthodox Stoics insist that Cynic doctrines, though 'a short-cut to virtue' (D.L. vii.121), are not sufficient to reveal the long road to happiness? If the Stoics can sustain their thesis that all you need for happiness is ethical virtue as conceived by Socrates and his immediate Cynic followers, why do they argue independently that this *telos* consists in 'living in agreement with nature'? ‖

This formula takes us directly to the first factor I mentioned – the theocratic postulate. In a well-known passage from his *On Ends* book 1, Chrysippus elucidated 'living in agreement with nature' as follows: 'Engaging in no activity which the common law is wont to forbid, which is the right reason pervading everything and identical to Zeus, who directs the organisation of reality. And the virtue of the happy man and his good flow of life consist in this: always doing everything on the basis of the concordance of each man's guardian spirit (*daimōn*) with the will of the director of the universe.'[11]

The context of this passage is the doxographer Diogenes Laertius' elucidation of an earlier statement he quoted from Chrysippus: 'Further, living in accordance with virtue is equivalent to living in accordance with experience of what happens by nature, as Chrysippus says in *On ends* book 1: for our own natures are parts of the nature of the whole. Therefore, living in agreement with nature comes to be the end, which is in accordance with the nature of oneself and that of the whole'; the passage cited above follows immediately.

This is far from a full account of what the Stoics had to say about virtue, but it shows with great clarity that this excellent character state, in their opinion, requires a knowledge of nature (i.e. Stoic physics and theology), and 'agreement' with nature (playing one's 'part' in the 'whole'). Proper emphasis on this point seems to me to be crucial if we are to have any prospect at this distance in time of understanding the core of Stoic ethics. What I have called the 'theocratic postulate' is *integral* to the Stoic con-

---

[11] D.L. vii.88 = Long/Sedley 1987, 63c. On this fundamental passage, see chapters 6 and 7, pp. 146 and 169.

ception of virtue, and to the reasoning that sanctions them in making virtue the sole constituent of happiness. It is because of 'nature's' law-like proceedings (on which much more below) that they think they are entitled to regard conformity with those proceedings (e.g. acquiescing without passion to everything that happens) as essential to virtue and happiness.

In a response to the first draft of this chapter, Gregory Vlastos wrote to me: 'So far as I can see the 'theocratic' principle changes one's conception of the relation of virtue to the universal order (it ‖ tells me that if I am virtuous my way of life is congruous with the order of the universe), but *does not change* either the *content of virtue* (courage, temperance, self-knowledge, justice are virtuous qualities regardless of whether or not I am a theist: they are virtuous also for atheists) or the *conception of happiness* (virtue remains the necessary and sufficient condition of happiness even if one does not believe in the theocratic principle).' As I understand them, the Stoics could not accept the latter part of these remarks. They agree, of course, with Vlastos' characterisations of the content of virtue and the conception of happiness; but the passage I quoted above should suffice to show that acceptance by an atheist of the formal points Vlastos mentions would not yield agreement with what a Stoic takes virtue and happiness to be. To live virtuously and to be happy as a Stoic, you need an understanding of nature which presupposes the truths of Stoic theology and physics.[12]

It should now be clear what I mean by the Stoics' theocratic postulate. Happiness – describable both as living in accordance with virtue and as living in agreement with nature – consists in obedience to something called Zeus, or divine and universal law. Happiness is a virtuous person's 'good flow of life', and a good

---

[12] I do not wish to imply that Stoicism, which is an exceptionally rich philosophy, can be summed up by my present focus on its theological perspective. There is no question, however, that Chrysippus took theology to be the crowning science; cf. Long/Sedley 1987, 26c, and see the good remarks by Kidd 1971, pp. 157–8, a reference Irwin (1986a) cites for its insufficiency in persuading him that we can learn much about Stoic ethics from their physics. Unquestionably there is more to learn about it than can yet be found in the modern literature. The important point is to discover why it is correct to describe Stoicism as Martin *et al.* (1988, p. 51) do as follows: 'The Stoics applied traditional philosophical values to the new individualism [i.e. of the Hellenistic world] and taught the taming of human passions by self-examination in order to effect a harmonious relation with the external order of things. True freedom was the moral freedom of a philosophical self-knowledge which recognized and conformed to an assumed orderly principle of the cosmos.'

flow of life requires harmonising one's own rational nature with 'the will of the administrator of the whole' – i.e. living as god the universal causal principle prescribes to those who share his rational nature.

We have now approached the territory of those who are inclined to accuse the Stoics of 'disingenuousness'. In the passage ‖ from Chrysippus, the Stoics appear to be saying that what is incumbent on a person is conformity of his will and conduct to universal moral norms. That sounds edifying, and historically interesting. But nothing in the passage shows why we should identify this 'life in agreement with nature' with happiness.

A good many of our Stoic cards are now on the table. On the one hand, the Stoics appear to be familiar eudaimonists but distinctive in their restriction of the requirements of happiness to ethical virtue – hence the 'impoverishment' objection. On the other hand, they appear to be connecting happiness, in a way as yet unclear, with obedience to a moral law that is divine and universally binding – hence the 'disingenuousness' objection. It is time to bring these two strands of their thought together, and to consider how this confluence bears on the challenges I posed at the beginning of this chapter.

STOIC EUDAIMONISM – INTERNAL AND EXTERNAL PERSPECTIVES

'Good flow of life' (*eurhoia biou*) was Zeno's definition of happiness.[13] The aquatic metaphor evokes regularity, unimpededness, and abundance – terms that fit such formal conditions of *eudaimonia* as completeness, stability, and self-sufficiency. Zeno also described the *telos*, and thus characterised *eudaimonia*, as 'living in agreement'.[14] He appears to have argued that since 'living in conflict' typifies unhappiness, 'harmony' or 'agreement' is essential to happiness (cf. Long/Sedley 1987, 63B). Thus we achieve happiness, 'a good flow of life', by 'living in agreement'.

'Living in agreement' with what? The authoritative Stoic answer, as we saw a few moments ago, is 'nature', where this includes both

---

[13] Stobaeus, II.77.21 Wachsmuth = Long/Sedley 1987, 63A.

[14] Stobaeus, II.75.11–12 Wachsmuth = Long/Sedley 1987, 63B. For what follows in the main text above, see the continuation of this passage. For discussion of what the Stoics meant by 'harmony', see chapter 9.

'human nature' and 'the nature of the universe'. These are big words, too big to be fully intelligible on their own. But already we have certain clues from Chrysippus about how they are to be understood. First, the two natures are so related that the 'human' is 'a part of' the universal one. The thought is not, or not merely, that our lives are unavoidably conditioned by the physical structure of the world. Human nature is 'a part ‖ of universal nature' in a much more comprehensive sense, a sense we could capture by expressing the relation as one of 'active participation', sharing in and contributing to the world's divine organisation. That thought in turn fits a second notion stated by Chrysippus – the notion of a community governed by law. We achieve life in agreement with nature by conforming ourselves to the rules prescribed by a deity who governs the universe according to right and rational principles.

The happy life, then, is represented as one in which we behave as members of a well-governed society. Nature in both its senses involves rules, and 'agreement with nature' requires obedience to these. A third notion present in this cluster of ideas is that of rationality. The Stoics think they have good reason to believe that 'rationality' constitutes the connexion that makes us humans 'parts' of god or universal nature. Indeed, it is precisely because we are rational that ethical principles present themselves to us as 'rules'; 'right reason' *is* 'law' (Cicero, *Leg.* 1.23), and, as Chrysippus told us above, identical to Zeus. This means that, in the Stoics' view, the world at large exhibits a structure and pattern of activity that is not merely intelligible but intelligent and prescriptive. As humans, we are not related to the world in a mechanistic or merely spatial and temporal way, but as one mind and will to another; for the world at large is a rational animal.

These are strange and difficult thoughts. Rather than elucidate them further at this stage, let me summarise as follows. In their reflections on happiness, the Stoics situate this state – what we all most want for ourselves – in 'a good flow of life'. They envisage this 'good flow' as a pattern of activity in which we 'agree with nature'. We achieve this agreement by conforming our minds and volitions to the legislative principles that 'reason', as embodied in the world animal, has determined to be right for the community of all rational beings.

To bring this cluster of ideas into a more tractable connexion

with thoughts on happiness and practical reason, we need to connect them with two fundamental Stoic beliefs about the world.
Suppose you have good grounds for believing that the world is
an entirely closed causal system, a law-like structure in ‖ which
nothing is random or in principle unpredictable. Suppose also you
have good grounds for believing that this system, though completely determinist, is not mindless but the life of a providential
deity who has organised the system so that it should be as good
as possible for its human members. From the first principle – the
determinist one – it follows that the state of the world at any one
time 'had to be' just as it is. There was no way, given the ante-
cedent conditions, that life would not be lush in California and
harsh in Ethiopia. From the second principle – the providential
and benevolent one – it follows that the state of the world at any
one time is the best possible. This may not be apparent from the
viewpoint of the Ethiopians, but if it were possible for a human
being to observe the global economy from the divine perspective,
reason would constrain him or her to acknowledge the fact.

The Stoics think they have equally strong grounds for subscrib-
ing both to determinism and to divine providence. These basic
facts about the world, as they interpret it, are probably the chief
explanation for Chrysippus' emphatic claim that 'There is no
other or more appropriate way of approaching the theory of good
and bad things or the virtues or happiness than from universal
nature and from the administration of the world.'[15] Determinism
alerts them to the recognition that there is an inevitable order
of things which includes our own histories, presents and futures.
Divine providence warrants them in believing that our lives have
a purpose within this design and that the divine causal principle
has been as benevolent as possible in equipping us to live well. In
order to develop a theory of happiness which does justice to both
of these principles, the Stoics need to show that the good for
human beings is entirely compatible with the way things are. If
unavoidable circumstances can imperil happiness, this casts doubt
on the effectiveness of divine providence. If divine providence
specifies a good for human beings which pays insufficient regard to
the way things are, this calls into question the rationality of the
natural order.

---

[15] Plutarch, *Stoic. rep.* 1035c = Long/Sedley 1987, 60A.

I lay stress on 'the way things are' because that expression seems to embrace the empirical generalisations the Stoics refer ‖ to by 'nature'. They invite us to look at the way things are, and to discover in them nature's system. Then, they invite us to perceive that system as a pattern whose parts fit together for the good of the whole (e.g. Marcus Aurelius v.8). 'The way things are' is both the microscopic and macroscopic structure of the world and also the foundation of all values.[16] To 'live in agreement with nature' is to live in the manner appropriate to the way things are for humans.

As has become increasingly clear over recent years, the Stoics derive their view of what is valuable and good for human beings by studying human development from infancy to maturity.[17] 'The way things are', it is unavoidable that young children should seek out from their environment those things that will make them flourish and feel contented – food, shelter, affection, and so forth – and avoid the opposites of these. We may conclude from this that such behaviour is natural and in accordance with the divine order of things. Young children are 'not yet rational'. Rationality develops only gradually, as language evolves through concept-formation founded on experience of 'the way things are'. Once maturity is achieved, the Stoics think that instinctive patterns of behaviour are superseded by the government of reason. Adult humans continue to be interested in things that will make them flourish and feel contented, and to avoid things that threaten their survival; but, in their case, this interest is mediated by and fundamentally modified by the fact that they form judgements and organise their desires as rational creatures (cf. Long/Sedley 1987, 57A, 59D).

'The way things are', according to Stoicism, you cannot be a mature person and not be governed by reason. Your reason probably is not the sound or fully effective governing-principle that it should and could be, and so you lack virtue and happiness. But it simply is a fact that your equipment for living a human life is your reasoning faculty since that faculty is what constitutes you as the kind of creature you have developed into. Even someone who radically misjudges the way things are acts under the direction of his reasoning faculty, albeit one that functions ‖ badly. Con-

---

[16] I have argued elsewhere that statements about 'nature' in Stoicism should be construed as *combining* statements of fact and value: see chapter 6, p. 147.

[17] See pp. 172, 261.

sequently, reasoning well is not merely necessary to the achievement of your end – happiness. Reasoning well, and the 'good feelings' (*eupatheiai*) that are its byproducts, completely constitute your end.[18] That is the way things are. Or, to put it in familiar Stoic language, living in agreement with nature *is* reasoning well.

This is one of the inevitable facts concerning the world. But it is a very special fact. Given the rational nature of yourself and the world, and given the fact that reasoning involves understanding, in exercising your rational faculties well, you actually understand nature. You become a 'student and interpreter', to cite Epictetus (*Discourses* 1.6.19 = Long/Sedley 63E), of the way things are. So in reasoning well, you live in agreement with universal nature – the nature of the world at large. But, by the coincidence of determinism and providence, reasoning well is the goal that the beneficent deity prescribed for human beings. So by reasoning well you understand and obey the laws laid down for the community of rational beings, and contribute your part to the world's rationality. We are back to the passage of Chrysippus cited on p. 187

What is the content of those laws? The Stoics would be out of step with 'the way things are' if they legislated a life for human beings and prescriptions for happiness which failed to fit a large part of common human experience and ethical tradition. In their complex theory of *kathēkonta*, 'proper functions', they developed a set of rules for 'living in agreement with nature'.[19] These rules take account of people's interests in health, appearance, family life, social activity and so forth. That is to say, the Stoics maintain that a mature human being has good reason to look after her health, be concerned for her appearance and reputation, be interested in the welfare of her family and society. The reasonableness of such concerns is an indication of their propriety and their agreement with a life in accordance with nature. Given the way things are, ‖ no one can be happy who disowns such concerns. Furthermore, human beings are frequently successful in pursuing these objectives. If that were not so, it would hardly be reasonable to treat such *kathēkonta* and obedience to them as grounded in our natures.

---

[18] For *eupatheiai* and the assessment of them as 'final goods', cf. Long/Sedley 1987, 60M, 65F.

[19] For the sources and brief discussion of them, cf. Long/Sedley 1987, section 59. For a good discussion, which bears on much that I say briefly in this paper, cf. Engberg-Pedersen 1986, pp. 145–83.

Is it not, then, only reasonable that human beings should *desire* the successful fulfilment of these objectives, and base happiness on their acquisition? The Stoics insist, and insist most strenuously, that this further inference is totally unreasonable. Unlike the Aristotelian, who says that successful outcomes make a difference to happiness, the Stoics maintain that they are 'preferable' but totally inessential. Reason would prefer that its efforts should be crowned with success, but the fact that an outcome is preferable does not warrant us in regarding its non-occurrence as unreasonable and therefore as something of which reason has been unreasonably deprived. Suppose you fall sick just as you are close to completing an important scientific experiment. You would, of course, have preferred to stay healthy. But it would be irrational to say that your sickness was unreasonable or something which retrospectively diminished the worth of what you actually tried to do.

A Stoic, then, will think it reasonable to pursue most of the same objectives as an Aristotelian, and he will agree that activities in pursuit of such goals are essential to happiness. But he locates the ethical value of these activities, and their relation to happiness, solely in their reasonableness – which is to say their agreement with human nature. How, then, are outcomes to be construed and evaluated? The answer to this should now be evident. Outcomes, to the extent that they fall outside the agent's control, are not his business or concern but that of universal nature. A person's involuntary sickness or other impediment is part of 'the way things are', but a part external to the nature of the person. The same holds good for what would popularly be called strokes of good fortune. Success or failure, in so far as they involve causes additional to the person, fall outside the scope of his rationality and happiness. ‖

But a little while ago we learned that 'agreement with nature' involves compliance with the divine organisation of the world. Does it not follow from this that even outcomes which are independent of a person's exclusive agency should be of concern to her, and, if of concern, have a bearing on happiness. After all, everything that happens, in the final analysis, is an expression of rationality in the universal sense.

For an answer to this question, we should return to the concept of happiness as 'a good flow of life'. Outcomes, the way the world actually is, concern the Stoic in the same way that the ocean concerns the navigator of a ship. His objective is to sail successfully through life. In order to do that, he needs to attend vigilantly to the state of the ocean and to act appropriately to this. Because he governs his life by rational principles, he does everything possible to chart a successful course, guiding himself by 'the way things are', i.e. his understanding of human and divine nature. He tries to avoid sailing in bad weather, but he accepts good and bad weather alike as unavoidable conditions of the way things are, and, because of his belief in providence, he does not discriminate between storm and calm in relation to his own happiness (cf. Marcus Aurelius v.8). Thus outcomes – the state of the world – do concern the Stoic's happiness but in a sense that negates the ordinary sense of concern. She is concerned to be undiscriminating in her attitude to outcomes, to regard success as no more a desirable result for the economy of the world than failure.

We are now in a position to see that the Stoics' eudaimonism is principally grounded in their beliefs about the relation in which human beings stand to a determinate and providentially governed world. As a route back to our original dilemma, it will be helpful to introduce Epictetus as a Stoic spokesman on the relation between this theological perspective and the ethical tradition on eudaimonism. ‖

EPICTETUS AND RESPONSE TO 'IMPOVERISHMENT' AND 'DISINGENUOUSNESS'

'What is it that every person pursues? To be in a good condition, to be happy, to do everything as he wishes, not to be frustrated, not to be put under compulsion' (iv.1.46). Epictetus' specification of the *summum bonum* is advanced as a factual claim, applicable without exception to all human beings. Notice the emphasis on 'freedom'. Freedom is already a dominant feature of happiness in the Greek ethical tradition. What accounts for its prominence in Epictetus is his Stoic conception of the way things are. Human beings cannot be 'free' if they pursue their natural desire for liberty on the false assumption that health or worldly success are just there for the taking. Our freedom, instead, depends on the recognition that we are unrestrictedly but exclusively free in the use of our minds – i.e. our thoughts, judgements, desires and outlook on the world.[20]

Epictetus represents this limited autonomy as a divine gift – the best that god could do for persons (1.1.7–13). Misfortune, as conventionally viewed, falls within its scope since happiness is a function of our autonomy:

God made all human beings with a view to their happiness, their good condition. To this end he gave them means, giving each person some things that belong to himself and others that do not. The things that are liable to frustration, removal, and compulsion are not his own, but those which are not liable to frustration are his own. As was right in one who cares for us and protects us like a father, he included the essence of good and evil among the things that are our own. (III.24.3)

This passage perfectly illustrates the convergence of determinism and providence I described earlier. Not only is happiness within the power of all human beings; it is also what we are made for and equipped to achieve by a deity whose benevolence is completely egalitarian and universalist. Happiness, then, is something objective, a good condition that is the same for all. Accordingly, it cannot depend upon a uniform allocation of other circumstances since they, quite patently, are not the same for all. Nor, given 'the way things are', could that unequal ‖ allocation be different from how it is. Determinism, then, constrains the Stoics to make happiness depend on 'the way things are', which includes many things that we cannot control. Divine providence justifies them in viewing 'the way things are' as inclusive of our own rationality and its sufficiency for happiness. Taken together the two perspectives offer an outlook whereby we treat everything that falls outside the mind's domain as an enabling, not disabling, condition for its exercise.

'The universe would truly be administered badly if Zeus were not concerned that his own citizens should resemble him, by being happy' (Epictetus, III.24.19). In what, then, does the happiness of Zeus consist? A Stoic will answer – in making the best possible, i.e. the most rational, use of the materials available for world-formation. Significantly, the Stoics use the same word for 'matter', *hylē*, in reference to 'accordance with nature', which is laid down

---

[20] For further discussion of Epictetus' concept of freedom, see my remarks in Long 1971c, pp. 190–2.

as the material of ethical virtue (Long/Sedley 1987, 59A). Micro-cosmically, a Stoic should develop a character which is the human equivalent to the divine organisation of the world. As the world consists of god and matter, i.e. a harmonious body, so a Stoic should apply structure and reason to the materials of her own existence. Or, as Epictetus phrases the point (Long/Sedley 1987, 63E), human beings are made by god to be students and inter-preters of the way things are.[21]

'Should' here signifies what is requisite for happiness. At all turns we have encountered happiness as the term the Stoics apply without apology to their recommended 'life in agreement with nature'. Is it an impoverished happiness, and is it disingenuous? ‖

CONCLUSION

I suggested, at the outset of this chapter, that a satisfactory account of happiness should include richness of experience, posi-tive emotion, and fulfilment of reasonable expectations. A test of Stoicism on these points will not be useful or even possible in iso-lation from their determinism and providence. If you reject these principles, you have no reason to agree with the Stoics that the world is a structure well ordered for human beings, and that the possibility of happiness is uniformly offered to everyone within the limits of the way things are. Let us, for the moment, accept these principles, and see how Stoic eudaimonism fares within such constraints.

'Richness of experience'. Common sense and humanity incline one to say that the congenital and material conditions of some people are too wretched to make it decent to talk of their oppor-tunity for happiness. I think a Stoic would accept this, but with a

---

[21] An anonymous reviewer of this paper invited me to say whether I think the 'theocratic postulate' takes the same form in Epictetus and Marcus as it does in the older Stoics. In the absence of nearly all verbatim material for Chrysippus and his predecessors, the question cannot be answered securely. All I can say here is that the ethical import of Epictetus' theology, as cited above, seems to me entirely in line with what we know of Zeno, Cleanthes and Chrysippus. Epictetus is consistently reticent on physics, and so we cannot say for certain how he viewed the relation between god and the world. He is, however, emphatic on the point that human beings are 'fragments' of god and have a 'part' of god within them, II.8.12. In the case of Marcus, we are on firmer ground. He regularly speaks of god, like Epictetus, in personal terms; but he also regularly identifies god with cosmic nature, e.g. VII.9, VIII.54, IX.1. I have little doubt that Epictetus had the same view.

qualification. He would agree that opportunities for happiness, to the extent that these depend on education, are not uniformly distributed. 'The way things are', external conditions prevent most people from understanding that happiness is completely in their power. But this does not negate the fact that Stoicism offers conditions for happiness that are optimal for people generally, in that they depend minimally on favourable circumstances. Really to believe yourself a fellow-citizen of Zeus – that is the key, the Stoic will say, to 'richness of experience', since it invites you to treat your own life as something that can make a vital contribution to everything that is good in the world.

'Fulfilment of reasonable expectations': an answer to this part of the 'impoverishment' objection has already been given. A Stoic will say that 'good flow of life' does include the fulfilment of all reasonable expectations since all you can reasonably expect is to achieve the good things that are within your power. To cultivate your rationality and to achieve harmony with your circumstances are reasonable expectations. There is nothing *reasonable* in expecting anything more. ‖

'Positive emotion'. This touches on a large issue, which I cannot discuss here in any depth. It must suffice to note that the Stoics claim such mental states as joy, cheerfulness and confidence to be 'final goods', i.e. constituents of happiness (see n. 18 above). They do not, then, ignore 'positive emotion' but maintain that it is a participant in or byproduct of ethical virtue – the disposition to reason well. A Stoic wise man is without the morbid emotions that characterise those with false conceptions of happiness. But his outlook on the world is not one that the Stoics themselves describe as 'resignation'. Rather, because he is in firm possession of all that is good, he derives positive emotion from his 'good flow of life'.

Now 'disingenuousness'. By arguments that I have already touched on, 'agreement with nature' or 'a good flow of life' coincides with the perfection of reason, and that in turn constitutes ethical virtue. The Stoic wise man is disposed by his virtue to perform all *kathēkonta*, i.e. to follow all the rules for proper conduct; and to perform them with full understanding of the unconditional demands they make on his nature as a rational being. He looks after his family, serves the interests of his country, keeps his promises, and so forth, because reason tells him that he should do these things. He does these things for their own sake, putting into practice his knowledge of what reason requires.

Undeniably, there is a resemblance between this account of what is ethically incumbent on human beings and the categorical demands of morality as conceived by Kant. But does that resemblance indicate any deep connexions between the two moral theories? According to Kant, 'there is nothing inconsistent with the wisdom of nature in the fact that the cultivation of the reason, which is requisite for [the production of a will that is good in itself], does in many ways interfere with the attainment of ... happiness. Nay, it may even reduce it to nothing, without nature thereby failing of its purpose' (*Metaphysics of Ethics*, transl. Abbott, p. 14). Kant can say this because he regards human nature, dualistically, as consisting of a physical aspect whose goal is happiness/pleasure, and a higher rational nature whose purpose is morality. ‖

The Stoics, if I am right, have no inkling of such dualism. In their theory, well-developed human nature is entirely unitary. As we develop from infancy to maturity, reason modifies our interests, values, and orientations, building upon, but not discarding, what was there at the outset. Well-developed human nature, though different from its immature predecessor, is an entirely self-coherent part of physical reality. Laws of nature apply to it just as they do to everything else.

Max Forschner (1986) has argued that the Stoics adumbrate Kant because they distinguish between conventional goods, like health, and moral goods (the virtues), deem both sets of goods to be natural to man, but treat only the latter as genuinely good and in conformity with man's rational nature. Hence, he implies, the Stoics really are proto-Kantians: what Kant regards as happiness falls outside the scope of rationality in both theories alike, and what the Stoics call happiness is really analogous to the life of Kant's higher nature.

Forschner's position would be plausible if the Stoics credited mature human beings with two natures, like Kant, and said that only one of these natures – the rational one – falls within the ethical domain. But that is not their theory. Rather, as we have seen, they think that human beings have only a single nature – a rational one, which is capable of conforming or failing to conform to the correct standards of rationality. The charge of disingenuousness mistakenly treats the Stoics' genuine eudaimonism as a misnomer for deontology.[22] In defence of the coherence of their ethics, the Stoics plead as follows.

To be sure, our ethics is a system which locates goodness solely in the proper functioning of reason. Hence we do resemble Kant in judging the moral worth of an action solely in terms of the agent's reasons and intentions, and not in terms of its outcome. But Kant arrives at this position by very different steps from ourselves, and even the points in which we seem to resemble one another need careful elucidation. Unlike Kant, we think that reason cannot function properly unless it consistently seeks to produce results which are 'in accordance with nature', i.e. agreeable to one's own normative condition and that of others. ‖ The legislative principles on which we act are grounded in empirical data – e.g. the naturalness of health, family affection, social cohesion to human beings. We think that well-functioning rational beings should do everything in their power to promote these states of affairs, and that happiness consists precisely in such efforts and in the mental states that accompany them. Thus the ethical life, as mandated by the benevolent deity, actually constitutes happiness.

Our critics are reluctant to take us seriously when we make this claim. That is because we deny that happiness requires us to possess or succeed in implementing any of the things we rationally seek to promote. But there is no incompatibility. Look at the way things are. Reason constrains you to agree that we should seek to promote all things that accord with our natures – our health, our family relationships, our life as citizens, etc. Equally, reason constrains you to admit that such objectives may sometimes conflict, requiring you to prefer one to the other, and that the final outcome of all such efforts is not something for which you are solely answerable or which can have any bearing upon the goodness of trying to promote such things. Consequently, we conclude that thoroughly rational beings will be content and happy entirely in the proper exercise of their rational faculties.

Our ethics only makes sense on the assumption that we are unequivocal eudaimonists. However, in order to find our position palatable, it is essential to recognise that we defend positions which are extremely contentious. First, determinism; second, divine pro-

---

[22] In a postscript to the second edition of his book, *Die Stoische Ethik*, Forschner has retracted his Kantian interpretation, in response to my critique of this position.

vidence; third, the availability of happiness to every normal person; fourth, the perfectibility of reason. If you reflect sufficiently on these four positions, and accept them, you will find that we offer an account of eudaimonism that is fully coherent and neither impoverished nor disingenuous. If you cannot accept them, you will do our ethics a disservice by assimilating it either to that of our Greek predecessors or to any of our modern successors. ‖

So much on behalf of the Stoics. The main argument of this chapter is that Stoic eudaimonism makes good sense if and only if one adopts a Stoic view of the way things are. If, as I have claimed, determinism and divine providence are crucial features of that view, any attempt to elucidate Stoic ethics which ignores these features will be broken-backed. I think this is why Cicero's accounts of Stoic ethics, which make little reference to what I call the 'theocratic postulate', are less successful than Epictetus and Marcus at conveying the emotional attractions of Stoicism. The latter are short on argument, but they do succeed in showing how Stoicism could give someone of their era a sense of being at home in the world.

As interpreters of ancient philosophy, we are strongly tempted to elide a doctrine such as divine providence which seems implausible, if not morally offensive (as I have argued in the past), and unhelpful for addressing any current philosophical concerns. I think there are ways of interpreting that doctrine which do not imply indifference to ordinary human interests or a complacent attitude towards eradicable evils, but that is not to the point here. Stoic ethics is worth our close study whether it illuminates moral philosophy in general or whether it does not. I do not say that their eudaimonism belongs with the latter, but rather that you need to be a Stoic to find their specification of happiness compelling.[23]

---

[23] In writing the original version of this chapter, I had the benefit of comments from Julia Annas, Alan Code and Gregory Vlastos. I am also very grateful to my commentator at Boston, Steven Strange, to the audience who discussed the paper and to an anonymous referee.

CHAPTER 9

The harmonics of Stoic virtue*

I

Stoic philosophers maintained that happiness consists in living harmoniously (ζῆν ὁμολογουμένως) or living in harmony with nature (ὁμολογουμένως τῇ φύσει ζῆν).[1] The shorter phrase was Zeno's original formulation of the ethical goal. He, or his Stoic commentators, glossed it as 'living in accordance with a single and concordant rationale (or ratio) – καθ᾽ ἕνα λόγον καὶ σύμφωνον ζῆν – since those who live in conflict are unhappy'.[2] The longer formula, 'living in harmony with nature', was developed by Zeno's successors (so we are told by Stobaeus, n. 2 below), because they took the shorter version to be an 'incomplete predicate':[3] i.e. the adverb ὁμολογουμένως lacked an expression indicating that with which harmony was to be achieved, and supplied it with the word for 'nature' (*physis*). This technicality, one may suspect, is a rather laboured explanation of the longer formula. 'Living harmoniously' is perfectly intelligible grammatically and semantically, especially in light of the observation that those who live in conflict are unhappy. Still, harmony is a relational notion, and Zeno must have intended his formula to be understood accordingly. It implies that the life so characterised has an orderly structure, that its con-

---

* This chapter was originally published in the 1991 supplementary volume of *Oxford Studies in Ancient Philosophy* commemorating A. C. (Tony) Lloyd on his seventy-fifth birthday. He died, alas, in 1994. I am deeply grateful for all that he taught me about ancient philosophy in a friendship that spanned over twenty-five years. Ptolemy, who makes a brief appearance here, was one of his favourites.
[1] For detailed discussion of this and other Stoic formulae for the goal of life, cf. Long 1967.
[2] Stobaeus II.75.11ff. (*SVF* I.179 = LS 63B). References to Stoic texts in this paper include, where possible, the corresponding excerpts in von Arnim's *Stoicorum Veterum Fragmenta* (*SVF*) and also those in Long and Sedley, *The Hellenistic Philosophers* (1987), abbreviated here as LS. My translations are normally taken over from this latter collection.
[3] Reading ἔλαττον ⟨ἢ⟩ κατηγόρημα as proposed in LS, note on 63B vol. II.

stituents are in agreement with one another and in agreement with everything else to which they are related. ‖

There is evidence to show that Chrysippus, in his use of the longer formula, was careful to exhibit both of these relationships: the internal – harmony with oneself, and the external – harmony with the world at large. His account of 'living in harmony with nature' makes this plain:

It is living in accordance with the nature of oneself and that of the universe, engaging in no activity which the common law is wont to forbid, which is the right reason [or 'correct ratio', *orthos logos*] pervading everything and identical to Zeus, who directs the organisation of reality. The virtue of the happy man and his good flow of life consist in this: always doing everything on the basis of the concordance (*kata tēn symphōnian*) of each man's guardian spirit with the will of the director of the universe.[4]

My purpose in this chapter is an analysis of what the early Stoics meant by a *harmonious* life or a life in *harmony* with nature. I want to investigate and speculate about their notion of harmony, a notion for which they had a variety of locutions, including the preposition *kata* with the accusative as well as such nouns as *homologia*, *akolouthia* and *symphōnia*.[5] The Stoic world is a systematic structure in which everything fits together according to a divine and rational plan. In proposing 'harmony' as a name for this structure, and 'harmoniously' as the mode of life appropriate to it, the Stoics, so I shall argue, intended to link their philosophy to the art which comes first to mind as the repository of consonance and concordance – music. By 'link' I mean that they sometimes chose language and thought-patterns which make reference to Greek musical theory and which need to be interpreted against the background of that theory. The paper offers evidence and argument for the hypothesis that Greek music provides important, and hitherto totally neglected, clues for interpreting some basic Stoic concepts.

---

[4] Diogenes Laertius vii.88 (*SVF* iii.4 = LS 63c), citing or paraphasing book 1 of Chrysippus, *Peri telōn*. For interpretation of the term *daimōn*, cf. note in LS, vol. ii, 63c. This fundamental passage is also cited on the following pages of this volume: 152, 169, 187. For a fine treatment of the link the Stoics drew between perfected rationality, and the harmony of nature, cf. Striker 1991, pp. 2–13.

[5] These nouns can be synonymous (cf. the equivalence of *homologia*, *harmonia* and *symphōnia* in Plato, *Symp.* 187b); but, as Andrew Barker points out to me, in technical harmonics *symphōnia* applies only to certain aesthetically special and structurally crucial relations, especially those of the fourth, fifth and octave.

In what follows I will first present some Stoic material which supports the hypothesis, directly or indirectly. Next I will make a brief foray into some Greek musical texts which seem to connect with, and to throw light upon, the Stoic material.[6] In the course of this later ‖ discussion I will consider how the hypothesis might illuminate the harmonics of Stoic virtue.

II

In the Stoic texts just presented the term *symphōnia* appears in conjunction with the term *logos*. This is entirely explicable on the assumption that *symphōnia* has its regular musical meaning, 'concord' (cf. n. 5 above). It is a commonplace of mathematical harmonics that *symphōnia* is a *logos*, a ratio between relatively high and low notes. Aristotle sometimes draws on this point, e.g. *De sensu* 3 439b25ff., where he uses an analogy with the ratios of concords to make a point about pleasing mixtures of colours. May we take the Stoics to be drawing a comparable analogy between musical and ethical harmony? If this suggestion is to stand, evidence will be needed to show that they envisaged some conceptual connexion between the two harmonies. The most obvious connexion to look for is numerical or quantitative since this is crucial to the notion of a ratio between sounds. For this, as we shall see in due course, there is excellent evidence. Another connexion that a proper analogy with music might seem to require is sound. Thus Aristotle observes (*Top.* iv.3 123a37) that *symphōnia* may be predicated of 'moderation' (*sōphrosynē*) but such a usage is metaphor since strictly all *symphōnia* pertains to sounds. This context is, of course, dialectical and Aristotle does not follow that rule in his own recourse to analogical use of *symphōnia* in the passage from *De sensu*. Still, if one thinks of purely instrumental music, unassociated with language, a close connexion between its harmonics and Stoic ethics would be tenuous at best.

In fact, song and word-rhythm as well as tonic pitch are integral

---

[6] I risk doing this in print only because Andrew Barker scrutinised an early draft of this chapter with great care, and sent me detailed comments and corrections for which I am enormously grateful. I have tried to keep my remarks about musical theory to the minimum which he would approve, relying heavily on his masterly volume (Barker 1989), and on what he has sent me in correspondence. For all speculations and errors I alone am responsible.

features of Greek musical theory. Harmony can pertain to vocal utterances, and though in a strictly musical context these will be sung rather than spoken, song would be an absurd connexion to look for in our hypothesised analogy.[7] A relevant connexion would be ‖ established if ethics in some sense as well as music involves an organised structure of sounds. Here it is pertinent to point out that the Stoics treated the vocal utterance of humans (*phōnē*) as the starting-point of dialectic or logic: 'It is articulated', as the Stoic Diogenes of Babylon said, 'and issues from thought' (D.L. VII.55 = LS 33H). In other words, the Stoics treated uttered language as the natural expression of reason. Given the references to *symphōnia* and *logos* mentioned above – living in accordance with a single and concordant *logos* and achieving concordance between one's guardian spirit and the world's administrator – a merely figurative allusion to music is too weak. The correct ratio that harmony in its musical sense manifests – concordance of high and low sounds – seems to function as the model for a mind that has its own correctly organised constituents, so that it is thoroughly in tune with itself and with external nature. If we substitute, for high and low sounds, verbalised thoughts and impulses, a theory is available for how the Stoics regarded a harmonious mental disposition: as exactly analogous to the well-tempered constituents of a musical scale. So much, in general terms, for the hypothesis to be explored.

In the mathematical or Pythagorean tradition of musical theory the notion of ratio, as expressed by *logos*, is crucial.[8] Aristotle reflects this when he characterises *symphōnia* in *Post. an.* 1 90a18–23: 'It is a ratio (*logos*) of numbers between the high-pitched and the low-pitched. Why does the high-pitched form a concord with the

---

[7] Originally, on the evidence of *De an.* III.2 426a27, I had supposed Aristotle to be committed to the position that the human voice is a συμφωνία τις, and he is so interpreted by Ross in his commentary *ad loc*. However, Barker 1981, pp. 248–66, has strongly objected to the coherence of this interpretation. He points out that Ross's reading, εἰ δ’ ἡ φωνή συμφωνία τις ἔστιν, though authorised by Priscian and Sophonias, is not that of the MSS, which reverse the words φωνή and συμφωνία. I find Barker's defence of the MSS reading attractive. None the less, the alternative shows that at least two ancient Aristotelians saw no difficulty in the thought that the human voice quite generally (doubtless in its modulations of pitch) is a harmonious sound; cf. Aristoxenus 18.12, 'For there is indeed said to be a kind of melody which belongs to speech, that constituted by the tone-patterns that occur in words, since tension and relaxation belong naturally to speech' (transl. Barker 1989, p. 138).

[8] Cf. Barker 1989, pp. 6–8.

low-pitched? Because the high-pitched and the low-pitched stand in a ratio of numbers.'[9] More on numbers later. What I want to emphasise at this stage, without introducing further technicalities, is the need to keep the sense of ratio or proportion to the fore when interpreting Stoic uses of the expression *orthos logos*. Familiar as we are with 'reason' as a central concept in ethics, it is all too easy to translate *orthos logos* by 'right reason', as if that expression ‖ were sufficient by itself to elucidate what the Stoics intended. Yet it is far from easy to specify precisely what they meant by prescribing rationality or 'right reason' as the foundation of living well.

In utilitarian ethics rationality characterises the most effective means for achieving the objective that maximises the good an agent can produce. In Stoicism, however, such means–ends reasoning is hardly the primary sense of an appropriately rational life. The utilitarian notion includes nothing comparable to the Stoic divinity whose organisation of the world constitutes the rational system of which each human being is an integral part – a rational system that pertains to ethics because, at the human level, it is conceptualised as 'the regularity and, so to speak, the harmony of conduct' (*rerum agendarum ordinem et, ut ita dicam, concordiam*, as Cicero expresses it on behalf of the Stoics (*Fin.* III.21 = LS 59D). Nor can the Stoics' *orthos logos* be suitably compared with reason as used in Kantian ethics. In Kant's usage the reason proper to a good will's determinations is entirely *a priori* and independent of events. Chrysippus, by contrast, explained living in harmony with nature as 'living in accordance with experience of natural happenings' (D.L. VII.87 = LS 63C). The primary contents of human rationality in Stoicism are derived from direct acquaintance with empirical events. The world fosters the acquisition of rationality, so the Stoics assume, because the world is a rationally ordered sequence of cause and effect. By attending to the evidence of this causal system, people gain insight into the workings of the divine *logos* that pervades everything.[10]

Zeno's account of harmony, with which I began, makes reference to 'a single and concordant *logos*' as the ground of harmo-

---

[9] Cf. Barker 1989, p. 71.
[10] For further discussion, cf. chapter 8 of this volume, p. 190, and also Long 1971b, pp. 95–6; 1971c, pp. 192–4; 1978b, pp. 308–11.

nious living. The expression is similar to Cleanthes' celebrated lines in his *Hymn to Zeus* on the divine administration of the world: 'You [Zeus] know how to make the crooked straight, to give order to the disorderly ... for thus you have harmonised (*synērmokas*) everything into one, good with bad, so that a single everlasting *logos* of everything is achieved.'[11] Cleanthes' *logos* seems to involve evaluative rather than quantitative order. None the less, what it betokens is evidently something balanced, proportional, ratio-like.

The *Hymn to Zeus* is permeated with echoes of Heraclitus.[12] The lines just cited recall his ‖ conception of the harmony of opposites and of the *logos* that constitutes the balance and measure in which all things stand to each other. While it is notoriously difficult to analyse the Heraclitean *logos* with any precision, one thing seems certain: a predominant sense of the term is 'ratio', 'proportion', 'measure'. In this connexion Charles Kahn has drawn attention to the importance of music for Heraclitus as a model of cosmic order. As he writes:

Music is a strikingly specific instance of unity and diversity ... The formal patterns of Greek music were regarded as familiar examples of a unity and 'agreement' that requires as its basis an objective diversity of sounds and tones ... If we see in Heraclitus' development of the theme of musical *harmonia* a reaction to Pythagorean ideas, there may be a direct connection between this emphasis on music and his conception of cosmic order in terms of 'measures' and proportion (*logos*).[13]

The Stoics' interest in Heraclitus, as an authority for their own philosophy, offers general support to the hypothesis that musical harmony should be to the forefront when we attempt to understand their notion of *orthos logos*. By itself, to be sure, that expression does not privilege music over other practices requiring precise, or relatively precise, numerical or quantitative discriminations, for instance mathematics, sculpture, medicine (see Appendix below). What needs to be stressed, before pressing the musical analogy further, is the fact that *orthos logos*, in Greek philosophical usage quite generally, connotes the presence, application or realisation of determinacy, proportionality, exactitude of quantitative or nu-

[11] *SVF* 1.537 = LS 541. A key text for music as the craft which reconciles opposites is Plato, *Symp.* 187; note especially the claim that the achievement of concord requires a good craftsman, 187d3.

[12] Cf. chapter 2 of this volume, pp. 46–52.

[13] Cf. Kahn 1979, pp. 284–5.

merical order. Hence 'right reason', though sometimes innocuous as a translation, is often too vague to capture the kind of correctness or rule or standard that is invoked. As is well known, Aristotle represents the 'mean' (intermediate between excess and deficiency) constitutive of ethically proper feelings and actions as 'the way the *orthos logos* states' (*EN* vi 1138b20), and in the *Eudemian ethics* (viii.3 1249a21–b6) he takes the 'standard' a virtuous man should apply in determining his choices to be analogous to the doctor's rule for judging the quantitative properties of health and healthy action. For my present purpose it is not necessary to ask how this relatively straightforward use of *orthos logos* relates to Aristotle's much more obscure use of the expression in his *Nicomachean* account of intellectual virtue. The point I want to make, by referring to Aristotle here, is his acceptance, without analysis or discussion, of the ‖ connexions between a well-balanced or well-proportioned state of affairs and *orthos logos*.

A further Stoic usage of the expression will be helpful to mention at this stage. In his account of the *telos*, based upon Chrysippus, Diogenes Laertius (D.L. vii.86 = LS 57A) specifies 'living correctly (*orthōs*) in accordance with *logos*' as the natural life for human beings: 'For *logos* supervenes as the craftsman of impulse.' Two important doctrines are involved here. First, rationality, as that which differentiates humans from other animals, is placed within the domain of craftsmanship or professional expertise. In a context concerning 'correctness' of action, the link between *logos* and *technē* by itself is unsurprising, but its full Stoic significance derives from the fact that their philosophy promises its practitioner 'a craft for the *whole* of life'. This point is made in a passage which draws an analogy between the craft of life and musicians:

As we say that the flute-player or the lyre-player does everything well, with the implications 'everything to do with flute-playing' and 'everything to do with lyre-playing', so the prudent man does everything well, as far as concerns what he does, and not of course also what he does not do. In their [the Stoics'] opinion the doctrine that the wise man does everything well is a consequence of his accomplishing everything in accordance with *orthos logos* and in accordance with virtue, which is a craft concerned with the whole of life.[14]

---

[14] Stobaeus ii.66.14–67.2 (*SVF* iii.560 = LS 61G).

The implication of this passage is that the wise man's craft of life is directly analogous to the musician's expertise; both of these impose correct structure on activities, the production of musical sounds and ethical conduct respectively.

The second doctrine presupposed by Chrysippus in his remark about *logos* as craftsman takes us into the domain of Stoic psychology: *logos* as the craftsman of 'impulse' (*hormē*). Impulse is the faculty which gives living beings above the level of plants their ability to initiate purposeful movements.[15] It constitutes their wants and aversions in response to awareness of objects in the environment or in response to their internal conditions. In non-human animals, impulse is non-rational and in children it is pre-rational. There can be no possibility of their impulses being commensurate or incommensurate with *orthos logos* since they lack rationality. In mature human beings, impulses have one or the other of these properties because they are, or are associated ‖ with, 'judgements' – correct or incorrect estimates of the value of objects. The mark of incorrectness is 'excess', hence such an impulse is called *pleonazousa*, one that 'goes beyond and disobeys the ruling *logos*' (*SVF* III.462 = LS 65J). Generically, the four cardinal passions sum up 'excessive impulse': pleasure and distress are impulses that exceed the actual advantages and disadvantages someone is experiencing, while appetite and fear go beyond the appropriate response to *anticipated* advantages and disadvantages (*SVF* III.391 = LS 65B).

From what has been said already about *orthos logos* we may take it as certain that it functions as the craftsman of impulses by moderating their excess and by making them commensurate with correct estimates of value. This much is implicit in the quantitative domain of the concept in its regular usage and confirmed by the Stoics' detailed analysis of the passions. But notions of balance, proportionality and harmony are not very informative for ethics without a model of their practical application. Aristotle provides a medical analogy, and the Stoics too made much of the parallelism between bodily and mental health. For Aristotle, with his well-known emphasis on the relative imprecision of ethics by contrast with theoretical science, medicine was a highly appropriate model. The Stoics, who like Plato were sticklers for an exact moral

---

[15] For the evidence on which this paragraph is based, cf. LS, sections 53, 65; and for further discussion in this volume, pp. 240, 268.

science, needed a craft analogy that would be isomorphic with
their conception of the harmonious life. So I turn now to consider
in more detail how music served them.

Aristo, one of Zeno's first associates, is reported to have said
that much training and struggle are needed to combat 'the whole
tetrachord, pleasure, distress, fear and appetite'.[16] In two succeeding verses, which almost certainly derive from Aristo, the passions
are said to 'pass into the innards and churn up people's heart'.
'Tetrachord' is a technical term of music, and the concept it
expresses is central to all Greek musical theory.[17] A tetrachord is
a sequence of notes spanning the musical interval of a fourth. The
combination of two pairs of tetrachords separated by a tone with
a further tone added at the bottom yields a double octave range.
By varying the intervals between the notes of each tetrachord the
various modes or harmonies are generated. How this, or anything
resembling it, fits Aristo's point is a question I postpone for the
present in order to focus simply on the term 'tetrachord'. Absent
from Plato, the word ‖ occurs only once in Aristotle's authentic
works, in a fragment of his *Eudemus* where Aristotle is explaining
harmonics.[18] It is a fair guess that the term is newish jargon even
though the musical structures it refers to must precede the formal
analyses using it that were made by Aristoxenus, the earliest musical theorist whose work survives in large quantity and an older
contemporary of the early Stoics. There seems to be no good reason why Aristo should use this word merely to indicate a set of
four things without any musical resonance. His usage encourages
us to look for further instances of musical terminology.

Aristo characterises the passions as 'the whole tetrachord'. What
of the Stoic virtues? As is well known, Stoic philosophers held
that individual virtues cannot be acquired in isolation from one
another. To be virtuous at all is to possess all the virtues, and cor-
respondingly with the vices.[19] A virtuous person must be prudent
and moderate and courageous and just. Moreover, only a person
of this disposition can perform a virtuous action, a *katorthōma*.

---

[16] Clem. Alex. *Strom.* II.20.108.1 (*SVF* 1.370). For the verse lines which follow Clement's
report, cf. Ioppolo 1980, p. 247 n. 14.

[17] For an admirably clear exposition, cf. Barker 1989, pp. 11ff.

[18] Fr. 25 Ross / Plutarch, *De musica* 1139b: ἐν γὰρ δυσὶ τετραχόρδοις ῥυθμίζεται τὰ μέλη.

[19] Cf. *SVF* III.243, 299 = LS 61F; *SVF* III.560 = LS 61G.

Various accounts of *katorthōmata* were given, which underline this feature of such actions.[20] They are 'perfect' or 'complete' proper functions (*kathēkonta*); they are everything done with *orthos logos*;[21] and, what is most interesting for the present inquiry, 'they contain all the *numbers* of virtue'. This expression is a standard one in Stoicism, though no other school that adopted the inter-entailment of all virtues appears to have used it. What does it mean?

In Cicero, *De finibus* III.24 (LS 64H), the Stoic spokesman Cato compares 'wisdom, the craft of life' with the arts of acting and dancing. Wisdom, he says, is like them and unlike the crafts of navigation and medicine in having its own performance as its end and not the attainment of an external objective; but it also differs from acting and dancing. The rightly performed actions of actors and dancers 'do not contain all the parts (*partes*) which constitute the expertise. But the right actions which the Stoics call *katorthōmata* contain all the numbers of virtue (*omnes numeros virtutis continent*). For wisdom alone [of all the arts] is occupied entirely with itself.'

Evidently 'containing all the numbers of virtue' is a property of morally right actions which can be inferred from wisdom's total self-containment. Provisionally we may characterise this self-containment as consisting in 1, completeness at any moment; 2, independence of ‖ any external conditions; and 3, closed systematicity. Can we say any more about the implications of the expression 'all the numbers of virtue'?

Judging from Stobaeus (*SVF* III.500 = LS 59K), 'having all the numbers' by itself, without the addition of 'virtue', was a familiar Stoic account of *katorthōma*. If this is shorthand, note should be taken too of Diogenes Laertius' report of the Stoics' analysis of 'beautiful' (*kalon*): 'They say that the perfect good is *kalon* from its having in full all the numbers required by nature, or [they say] that the perfectly symmetrical is *kalon*' (D.L. VII.100). Diogenes then immediately specifies the four cardinal virtues as the species of 'the beautiful' (*to kalon*). Seneca (*Ep.* 71.16) uses 'full' (*plenus*) as his gloss for the statement: 'virtue does not increase; it has its own numbers' (*virtus habet numeros suos, plena est*). Marcus Aurelius (III.1)

---

[20] For the evidence, cf. LS section 59, especially B4, J, K.

[21] Notice the etymological link between κατόρθωμα and κατ' ὀρθόν, the kind of verbal connexion Stoic philosophers were all too keen on exploiting.

exemplifies the mind's decline by the 'failure to make exact (*akri-boun*) the numbers of what is *kathēkon*';[22] and he has another instance of the expression which needs the full context in order to be appreciated.

If someone proposes the question to you, how is the name Antony written, will you utter each of the letters in a high-pitched way (κατεντεινό-μενος)? Suppose, then, they are angry, will you be angry in return? Will you not proceed gently (πρᾴως) to enumerate each letter? Here too, then, remember that every proper function (*kathēkon*) consists of a sum of certain numbers. These you must preserve without getting disturbed, and without showing hostility in return for hostility complete your project systematically. (VI.26)

Marcus draws an analogy between spelling out the letters of a name gently not excitedly, and performing the numerical sum that a proper function involves systematically and not disturbedly. More exactly, he uses a participle of the otherwise unattested verb κατεντείνομαι to contrast with πρᾴως, 'gently'. I translated κατεν-τεινόμενος 'in a high-pitched way'. The verb is an intensified form of ἐντείνω, which means 'stretch' or 'tighten'. Many crafts in Greek involve the correct application of stretching or tightening, for instance, archery, sailing, horsemanship; and two, in particular, where the appropriate tension needs to be exact, or in conformity with *orthos logos*, mathematics and music.[23] Nor is the verb ἐντείνω unknown to professional Stoic writers. Hierocles (in Stobaeus IV, p. 672 = LS 57G5) uses the phrase κατὰ τὸν ἐντεταμέ-νον. In its ‖ context this must mean 'in accordance with the well-tempered [i.e. virtuous] man'. 'Good tension' (*eutonia*) and 'lack of tension' (*atonia*) were terms by which Chrysippus delineated virtuous and vicious states of the soul.[24]

Investigation of the Stoic expression 'all the numbers' has introduced their recourse to the concept of tension. In their physical theory they used this to describe the vibrant movement of the *pneuma*, which functions like a musical string. Viewed macroscopi-

---

[22] For *akriboun* as something difficult to achieve in reference to 'all' (as distinct from some) virtue, see Aristotle, *Pol.* III.7 1279a40; and for its application to 'consummate musical execution', see Philodemus, *Mus.* p. 90 K.

[23] Cf. Plato, *Meno* 87a for ἐντείνω applied to inscribing a triangle in a circle; and *Phd.* 60d for putting words into verse, *Prot.* 326b for setting words to music.

[24] Cf. Galen, *Plac.* IV.6.2–3 (*SVF* III.473 = LS 65T).

cally, tension is that property of the divine *pneuma* or *logos* which makes it, in its interaction with matter, the universal principle of causation and dynamic coherence.[25] Viewed microscopically and ethically, tension is a property of the human soul, which is itself a fragment of the divine *pneuma*. When the soul's tension is of the right degree, it confers on its owner correct powers of judgement and action. Thus virtue and vice can be regarded as variant degrees of the soul's tension.

In musical theory tone or tension (*tonos*) may refer simply to raised or lowered pitch. Often, however, it refers to the character of a structure (e.g. a tetrachord) in which some crucial element has been raised or lowered irrespective of the pitch at which the whole structure is set. Thus in Ptolemy's *Harmonics* (1.12, 1.16) the 'tenser' genera are ones in which the intermediate notes of the tetrachord lie relatively high in relation to its fixed note boundaries. Andrew Barker, to whom I owe these points from correspondence, suggests that Plato's remark about the unacceptably 'relaxed' Ionian and Lydian modes (*Rep.* III 398e10) should be construed similarly.

A well-tuned or well-tempered scale has all its numbers or intervals consonant with one another. Given the connexions the Stoics posited between virtue and the right degree of the soul's tension, it is time to ask what contribution musical theory might have made to their use of the expression 'all the numbers'. Did they think of a virtuous character as directly analogous to the harmony of a musical scale? If so, what light could this shed on their concept of virtue and living in harmony with nature? ‖

III

It is reasonable to assume that the early Stoics will have been familiar with the basic structure of Greek harmonics, presupposed by but not invented by their musical contemporary Aristoxenus.[26] In what came to be called the Greater Perfect System, all Greek modes (Dorian, Lydian etc.) could be incorporated as species of a a double octave range, consisting of four tetrachords, with the two

---

[25] For the evidence and discussion, cf. LS section 47.
[26] A full account of what is summarised in this paragraph will be found in the Introduction of Barker 1989.

tetrachords of the central octave separated by a tone and with a further note added at the bottom at the interval of a tone below the lowest note of the lowest tetrachord. The fundamental difference between modes seems to have been the organisation of the intervals within an octave, so that a lyre-player would change modes by retuning the intervals between his strings without altering the overall pitch of his instrument, though the latter would become necessary if he were to modulate between modes in the course of a single composition.

Complications concerning relations between modes and pitch need not concern us here. The important point is simply to recognise the generic features of the system – its capacity to represent all harmonic musical relationships as a system of tones, half-tones, quarter-tones etc. In Pythagorean musical theory, though not in the system of Aristoxenus, mathematics, as distinct from auditory experience, explains harmonics. For the Pythagoreans, notes are conceived as numbers, and differences between notes, or intervals, as ratios of numbers – octave 2:1, fifth 3:2, fourth 4:3 etc.

The Stoics' explicit interest in numbers, and their hypothesised interest in a connexion between musical harmony and character (*ēthos*), require us to think that the musical theory on which they may have drawn was predominantly Pythagorean. Aristoxenus was cautious about correlations between musical structures and ethical dispositions (e.g. *El. harm.* 32.18ff.), and he categorically rejected mathematical ratios as the basis for expressing differences of pitch. But in any case, for the general kinds of musical interest one might plausibly attribute to the Stoics the Pythagoreans are the best sources, historically and conceptually. Among them we can count Plato, who had authorised links between musical harmony, ethics and cosmology in the *Republic* and *Timaeus*. There is also evidence that at least one leading Stoic, ‖ Diogenes of Babylon, shared Plato's beliefs in the significance of music in education.[27] As for the Pythagoreans specifically, Zeno wrote a work called *Pythagorica* (D.L. vII.4), the only work attributed to him in which another philosophical movement is named, though no details about its content are recorded.

If my general hypothesis is sound, we may take it as certain

---

[27] Diogenes' views on music are reported and criticised by Philodemus in his *De musica*. On this cf. Neubecker 1956 and Rispoli 1974, pp. 57–86.

that the Stoics were particularly inspired by Plato. Although Zeno seems to have advertised Socrates as his mentor rather than Plato, Chrysippus certainly drew heavily on Plato's cosmology as well as his ethics.[28] His borrowings from the *Timaeus* are obvious (cf. Long/ Sedley 1987, vol. I, p. 278), and it would be difficult to appropriate parts of that work, especially its doctrine of the world-soul, without sympathising with the harmonic theory that provides much of its details. But rather than argue my case via general affinity with Plato, I propose to invoke some passages from two later musical theorists, Ptolemy and Aristides Quintilianus. Each of these authors sets up correspondences between specific virtues and harmonic intervals (see below). Like all later philosophers with Platonic and Pythagorean sympathies, they could not avoid the general influence of Stoicism, whose trademark on the philosophical tradition was indelible by the first century AD. Even if they were not directly inspired by the Stoics in their manner of connecting music and ethics, the way they do this provides models for speculation about what the Stoics too could have done. So much by way of preliminaries to this section.

My hypothesis so far has rested heavily on the supposition that musical theory underlies the Stoics' expression 'all the numbers'. A quotation from Aristides Quintilianus helps to confirm this. Writing of the hexameter line (1.22), he says: 'The syllable, the foot and the metre are increased only up to the number six, because it is a perfect number and includes within itself all the ratios of concord (πάντας ἐν αὐτῷ τοὺς τῆς συμφωνίας λόγους).' By 'all the ratios of concord' Aristides must include 2 : 1, 3 : 2, 4 : 3, though just how his claim is meant to work remains unclear.[29] (Ancient numerology often ‖ borders on fantasy, especially in this author's efforts to make musical theory the key to understanding everything.) Such a passage, however, shows the supreme appropriateness of music as the craft to characterise a system in which numerical completeness is an all-or-nothing matter. A verse line with a false quantity or a musical scale with one interval defective is not marred by merely one blemish, while having everything else in order. The single numerical error is enough to wreck the whole harmony. I

---

[28] See chapter I of this volume, pp. 17–19.
[29] See Barker 1989, p. 450. The translation here and in my other musical excerpts is taken from his book.

have already written about the Greek tendency to treat uttered
language and musical harmony as categorically similar. Aristoxenus uses the composition of letters in proper order as analogous
to melodic intervals:

In speaking ... it is natural for the voice, in each syllable, to place some
one of the letters first, others second, third and fourth and so on for the
other numbers. It does not place just any letter after any other: rather,
there is a kind of natural growth in the process of putting together. In
singing, similarly, when the voice places intervals and notes in succession, it appears to maintain a natural principle of combination, and not
to sing every interval after every other, either when the intervals are
equal or when they are unequal. (27.2, transl. Barker 1989, p. 145)

Enough has been said for the claim that musical theory is the
most promising context from which to seek elucidation of the full
significance of the Stoic expression 'all the numbers'. To be sure,
the same expression is already found in Isocrates, *Busiris* 16, as a
mark of completeness quite generally: Isocrates there says that
'Busiris grasped all the numbers from which one might best organise public affairs'; compare English usage of 'factors' or 'measures'. In Isocrates, however, the relative clause establishes what
kind of numbers are applicable. His usage does nothing to elucidate what the numbers of virtue or of a right action in Stoicism
might be.

It seems obvious that one number supremely relevant to the
numbers of virtue, or the numbers that perfect a right action, is
four, i.e., the quartet of cardinal virtues – prudence, courage,
moderation and justice. Quite so. But why say 'all the *numbers* of
virtue', and not simply 'all the virtues' or 'the four cardinal virtues'? Some special kind of completeness seems intended by the
term 'numbers', and I now want to show why music is singularly
apt for understanding the Stoic virtues.

By the time of Chrysippus, if not earlier, the Stoics specified
'subordinate' virtues for each of the four cardinal ones. Thus, to
quote Stobaeus' account: 'To prudence are subordinated ‖ good
sense, good calculation, quick-wittedness, discretion, resourceful-
ness ... to justice, piety, honesty, equity, fair dealing', and similarly with courage and moderation.[30] These lists of subordinate

---

[30] Stobaeus II.60.18 = LS 61H; for discussion of the taxonomy of Stoic ethics recorded by
Stobaeus, see chapter 5 of this volume.

virtues are not presented as giving merely a sample of the relevant good states of character; they appear to comprise a comprehensive and definite number of these. Thus we may conjecture that 'all the numbers of virtue' probably refers both to the four cardinal ones and their subordinates, comprising in sum an absolutely definite number. The postulation of so many virtues gives point to the expression 'all the numbers'.

Next, consider how Stobaeus (II.63.6 = LS 61D), perhaps reporting Chrysippus, describes the interrelation of these virtues. He says: 'They all ... share their theorems and ... the same end. Hence they are also inseparable. For whoever has one has all, and whoever acts in accordance with one acts in accordance with all. They differ from one another by their own perspectives.' The point, as David Sedley and I explained it in *The Hellenistic Philosophers*, is this:

All the virtues [which are sciences, i.e. moral knowledge of some kind] have their theorems in common, but from differing perspectives. Each takes as its primary perspective the theorems governing its own special area of conduct: this is sufficient to differentiate it as a distinct virtue. But each takes as a secondary perspective the theorems governing other areas of conduct; and this is sufficient to guarantee that they have all their theorems in common, and hence are inseparable. (Vol. 1, p. 384)

This distinction between primary and secondary perspective enabled Chrysippus to retain the thesis of the virtues' inter-entailment while also acknowledging, as he did, that a virtuous man need not always be exercising his courage.[31] On this theory, every virtuous action will instantiate one specific virtue, from that virtue's primary perspective; that is to say, it will be describable as an action manifesting some specific knowledge, e.g., in the case of courage, the knowledge of what should be endured. From this perspective the action is one of courage rather than of justice etc. But, from the secondary perspective, a courageous act is also a just and prudent and moderate act because it also includes the knowledge specific to these virtues. In acting courageously, the virtuous man does nothing inconsistent with justice, moderation and prudence; were he to do so, he could not be said to act courageously. His courageous act, in other words, is entirely consonant with all the other virtues. ‖

---

[31] Cf. Plutarch, *Stoic. rep.* 1046e–f = LS 61F.

There is ample evidence to show that this kind of internal consistency was the hallmark of a virtuous character. Seneca contrasts it with the type of person who appears to act well in one sphere and yet does badly in another. Of the former he says:

He was always the same and consistent with himself in every action ... We perceived that in him virtue was perfected. We divided virtue into parts: the obligation of curbing desires, checking fears, foreseeing what has to be done, dispensing what has to be given. We grasped moderation, courage, prudence, justice, and gave to each its proper function. From whom, then, did we perceive virtue? That man's orderliness revealed it to us, his seemliness, consistency, the mutual concordance of all his actions (*omnium inter se actionum concordia*), and his great capacity to surmount everything. (*Ep.* 120.10–11 = LS 60E)

We are back to harmony. Supposing that the Stoics envisaged a virtuous character as directly analogous to a harmonic system, how might they have analysed the details? Given the four cardinal virtues and their subordinates, the most obvious model that comes to mind would draw on the four tetrachords and their constituent intervals. We could imagine this two-octave scale with its notes so tuned that they are appropriately pitched to make a Greek mode. The sum of cardinal and subordinate virtues actually exceeds fifteen, but no matter. We cannot expect the analogy to be exact in every detail. As it is, it could achieve a great deal that the Stoics wanted to explain.

First, the idea of definite ratios gives them a splendid model for the precise degree of the soul's tension that constitutes virtue as a whole. Secondly, the internal relationships of the notes, analysed in terms of the structure of each of the four tetrachords, provides an excellent analogue for the connexion of cardinal and subordinate virtues. As he plays, the musician is moving within the notes of one tetrachord, or ascending or descending to a higher or lower tetrachord. So, by analogy, the Stoic sage at one time is exercising this or that subordinate virtue in the domain of justice, and at another time displaying a subordinate Stoic virtue in the domain of courage. Thirdly, it accounts for the dual perspectives of the virtues. Just as the musician will fail if any of the notes in his mode is out of tune, so too virtue requires complete concordance between all its parts or 'numbers'. The individual note sounding at a given moment within the harmonic system needs to be concordant with all the other notes that are not being activated. So too what is primarily a courageous action must be secondarily a virtuous action quite generally, i.e. one in tune with all the other virtues. ‖ Fourthly, the conception of virtue as a harmony provides an illuminating analogy for the wise man's relationship with external nature as well as with himself. He may be pictured as someone whose character and actions are completely in tune with the causal system employed by cosmic nature.

The hypothesised model also presupposes that the constitutive tetrachords have the right form or ratios or 'tension'. When Aristo called the four cardinal passions 'the whole tetrachord', he was probably thinking of a musical structure whose intervals were of the wrong form, irrationally related to one another or 'too slack', recalling Plato's criticism of the Ionian and Lydian modes.

Obviously there is a high degree of speculation in what has just been said. However, the speculation is not idle. Both Ptolemy and Aristides Quintilianus undertake, each in his own way, to correlate virtues and musical structures. Ptolemy's account, though typically eclectic in its philosophical concepts, is heavily permeated with Stoicism, as Barker notes.[32] Aristides' treatment, which is much simpler, was scarcely original to him. I take his first since it provides the more economical model and one which the Stoics could easily have anticipated or borrowed from pre-existing Pythagorean musicologists.

Aristides (III.16) first takes a sequence of four tetrachords, and distributes the four cardinal virtues in the ascending order moderation, justice, courage and prudence. In other words he adopts the basic model that I just proposed for the Stoics. Secondly, he suggests that the double-octave range, analysed as three fifths, could accommodate justice and moderation as the first of these, courage as the second, and wisdom as the third and highest. His inspiration for this model is clearly Plato. The tripartite analysis depends upon the three parts of the Platonic soul, and Aristides is directly dependent on *Republic* IV 443d6–7: 'The just man harmonises the three parts [of the soul], just like the three intervals of a mode, high, low and intermediate, and including all intermediate intervals.' Since orthodox Stoics did not divide the soul into

---

[32] Cf. Barker 1989, p. 375. I have discussed Ptolemy's eclecticism in Dillon/Long 1988.

rational and irrational parts, they had no reason to adopt anything analogous to Aristides' second model.[33] For them the whole soul is rational, but its rational state is either 'correct' or ‖ 'incorrect'; in the latter case the soul's state 'exceeds' the proper rule of reason and is characterised by passion. They are more likely, then, to have favoured the first kind of model, treating the whole soul as a system either of correct ratios or as a structure marred by at least one incorrect ratio.

Aristides deals only with the four cardinal virtues. Ptolemy proposes a much more ambitious scheme (*Harmonics* III.5). Like the second model of Aristides, it is grounded in a tripartite division of the soul. Ptolemy correlates rationality with the octave, spirit with the fifth, and appetite with the fourth. He then enumerates three species of virtue for the appetitive part, starting with the virtue of moderation; four species of virtue including courage, for the spirited part; and seven species of virtue including wisdom, for the rational part. The number of virtues he chooses for each of the soul's parts correlates exactly with the number of notes in the octave, the fifth and the fourth. As for justice, he characterises this virtue (Platonically, of course) as 'a concord between the parts themselves in their relations to one another, in correspondence with the ratio governing the principal parts' (συμφωνία τίς ἐστιν ὥσπερ τῶν μερῶν αὐτῶν πρὸς ἄλληλα κατὰ τὸν ἐπὶ τῶν κυριωτέρων προηγούμενον λόγον). Unlike Aristides, Ptolemy for his scheme draws on the cardinal harmonic intervals instead of tetrachords. There was clearly no canonical way of correlating virtues with musical structures. Stoics, however, could have availed themselves of something like Ptolemy's approach, especially since it facilitates the incorporation of so many species of virtue. In concluding this chapter of his *Harmonics*, Ptolemy describes 'the whole condition of a philosopher as like the whole harmony of the complete [musical] system'. This is precisely what my hypothesis about Stoicism implies – the conception of a mind that is in complete harmony with nature as being directly analogous to a well-tuned musical instrument.

Ptolemy and Aristides are more Platonist than Stoic in their orientation, but, as has already been said, they could not avoid the influence of Stoicism. If this chapter's hypothesis is sound,

---

[33] For this crucial point, cf. LS 61B9–11 and section 65.

Stoicism will have encouraged their application of music to other areas of the world, but my thesis does not depend upon retrojecting their detailed schemes on the Stoics. I cite Ptolemy and Aristides here simply as paradigms, in order to show how music could be related to virtue in ways that the hypothesis requires. The Stoics were not musical theorists, and any analogy they drew with music will have been less elaborated than what we find in Ptolemy. None the less, I hope to have given reason for thinking that the analogy was important to them, in whatever way they worked it out, and that music was their principal craft analogy.

A final passage will show how easily the analogy could come to a ‖ Stoic's mind. Epictetus invokes the lyre-player as a paradigm to illustrate social discernment, autonomy and capacity to influence others rather than be influenced by them. 'Has any of you', he asks, '[in your dealings with people] the expertise of the lyre-player? When he takes up his lyre, the moment he touches the strings he can recognise those which are discordant and tune the instrument' (*Discourses* III.16.5). Epictetus' point is that people are either forced to become like those whose company they keep (since they lack the lyre-player's discernment and control of his strings) or they must have the power, which he says Socrates had, to convert those with whom they socialise to their own style of life – i.e. to make others harmonise with themselves.[34]

APPENDIX

I have argued that music is the craft analogy which was foremost in the Stoics' minds when they developed their account of virtue and its identity with the art of living harmoniously. Greek musical theory offers the best context for understanding such expressions as 'all the numbers'. In its structure as a dynamic progression of mathematically exact concordances, a musical mode or scale provides an excellent model for the wise man's actions in accordance with nature. It has not, however, been my intention to exclude the Stoics' use of other craft analogies. The interest of music, as a key to their thought, would not be reduced by their recourse to additional aesthetic or scientific models. Their concept of an 'art of life' would be decidedly odd if its terms of reference were too narrow to accommodate important features of crafts considered quite generally.

---

[34] The passage may be compared with one in Ptolemy's *Harmonics* (III.7) where he likens changes of souls in respect of external circumstances to harmonic modulations.

I make this point as a response to Adolf Dyroff, the only scholar who has previously investigated, in any depth, the expression 'all the numbers'.[35] In his book of 1897 (pp. 352–4), Dyroff proposed the Canon of the sculptor Polyclitus as the key to the Stoics' reference to numbers. How effective is this suggestion?

Polyclitus was famous for saying, in his work *Kanōn*, that: 'Excellence [in sculpture] is achieved little by little through many numbers.'[36] In what appears to be an allusion to this, Plutarch ‖ observes: 'In every work, beauty is the outcome of many numbers, so to speak, which arrive at a single measure (*kairos*) by the agency of some proportion and harmony.'[37] Dyroff, who does not mention the Plutarch reference, notes as a parallel to the first passage this saying attributed to the Stoic Hecato: 'Excellence is achieved little by little, but it is not a little thing' (D.L. VII.26). This saying, with its proverbial ring, hardly points to Polyclitus in particular, especially since it makes no reference to numbers. Diogenes, moreover, says 'some attribute it to Socrates'.

More to the point is Dyroff's reference to D.L. VII.90. There, in a general account of Stoic ethics, virtue is said to be 'quite generally, the perfection of anything, such as a statue'. From a passage in Galen we can infer that Chrysippus probably referred to Polyclitus' *Kanōn* in his account of bodily beauty, which he identified with the symmetrical arrangement of parts.[38] The same notion is applied to the soul in a context treating its analogies with bodily properties. The other two properties treated similarly are health and strength. Thus graphic art is given the same illustrative value as the arts of medicine and physical training.[39]

We can take it as certain, then, that sculpture in general was a craft analogy which the Stoics used, and as highly probable that Chrysippus supported his conception of beauty by reference to Polyclitus. None of this, however, gives sculpture the privileged position suggested by Dyroff. He fails to appreciate the enormous difference between 'many numbers', Polyclitus' rule, and 'all the numbers', the Stoic expression. What Polyclitus meant is open to conjecture.[40] If he had in mind a series of anatomical points, symmetrically related to one another, 'many numbers' would make sense: there might be more or less of them, depending on the size and shape of the work of art. 'All the numbers', as a practical

---

[35] A few years earlier Bonhöffer 1894, p. 215 n. 1, merely stated dogmatically that the image was derived from dancing, which is certainly not 'clear', as he claims from Cicero, *Fin.* III.24, the only justification he gives. In that passage (cited in my main text above, p. 211) wisdom, though first likened to dancing, is finally differentiated from it.

[36] Philo, *Mech.* 4.1 p. 49, 20 Schöne, cited in 40 B 2 DK. For the evidence on Polyclitus' *Kanōn*, and its interpretation, I have followed Stewart 1978, pp. 122–31.

[37] *Prof. virt.* 45c. Plutarch does not name Polyclitus here.

[38] *De plac.* v.448 Kühn (*SVF* III.472). Galen's reference to Polyclitus' *Kanōn* could be his additional comment; but in the context it reads more naturally as Chrysippus' own allusion.

[39] Stobaeus III.62.20–63.5. Similarly Cicero, *Tusc.* IV.30.

[40] For some good conjectures, cf. Stewart 1978.

prescription, would not be appropriate in such a fluid medium. We have seen why it fits music and Stoic ethics.

Finally, it should be noted that the key term of Polyclitus' *Kanōn*, on the available evidence, was *symmetria* – 'proportion'. The term has its uses in Stoic ethics and aesthetics, but their preferred word for harmony was *symphōnia*, which invokes music and not the visual arts. Emphasising action, as they did, the Stoics had good reason to prefer music to sculpture as their principal aesthetic model and craft analogy.

CHAPTER 10

Soul and body in Stoicism*

THE MIND/BODY (OR SOUL/BODY) RELATIONSHIP AND GREEK PHILOSOPHY

What a modern philosopher might call problems of the self and problems of personal identity take the form, in Greek philosophy, of questions about the human *psychē* and its relation to the body. In this chapter I propose to explore some of the ways in which the early Stoics approached such questions. The scholarly literature has not neglected the Stoic concept of *psychē*, but most of the discussions have focused upon detailed questions concerning the soul itself rather than its relationship to the body.[1] My procedure here will be designed primarily to illuminate that relationship. In the second part of the chapter, I will discuss the Stoic concept of 'uni-

* Versions of this chapter were presented to the Princeton University Ancient Philosophy Colloquium, in December 1978, and to a colloquy of The Center for Hermeneutical Studies of the Graduate Theological Union and the University of California, Berkeley, in June 1979. The latter, with responses from John M. Dillon, G. B. Kerferd, and David Winston, together with the discussion, was published in 1980 as *Colloquy 36* of the Center. I am grateful to the Editors, Edward C. Hobbs and Wilhelm Wuellner, for permitting me to publish this further version here. It is impossible to thank all those who have helped me with their comments, but I am especially grateful to my respondents named above, and also to Michael Frede and Josiah Gould. For the leisure to work on the subject I am greatly indebted to Princeton University where I worked as a Senior Fellow of the Council for the Humanities during the first semester of 1978–9, and to the Institute for Advanced Study, Princeton which gave me membership during the second semester of that year.
1 von Arnim 1903–5, vol. II, pp. 217–35, gives the fullest collection of evidence for *anima hominis* in Stoicism prior to Panaetius. Many texts in other sections of his vols. I–III provide further material (cf. the Index vol. IV), but his collection here, as elsewhere, is far from complete. In this chapter I shall be concerned with later Stoicism (Panaetius onwards) only incidentally. The most extensive modern treatment of the material is Bonhöffer 1890, whose entire book, from pp. 29ff., is a detailed discussion of evidence on 'anthropology and psychology' from early Stoicism as well as Epictetus. Briefer accounts, from a variety of perspectives, may be found in Bréhier 1951, Gould 1970, Long 1986, Pohlenz 1959, Rist 1969, Sandbach 1975, and Watson 1966.

fied bodies'; I will then bring *psychē* more fully into the argument by considering the nature of animal bodies and psychic functions; and finally I will make some brief remarks about 'rational souls' and their relation to (their) bodies.

For reasons that should become clear it is peculiarly difficult to characterise the Stoic position on the relationship between soul and body. But it may be helpful, as an introduction, to make some comparisons with the principal rival accounts that we have from antiquity, the Platonic, Aristotelian, and Epicurean. If one were to draw up a table or questionnaire and consider the similarities and differences among these four positions, the two extremes would be represented by Plato on one side and Epicurus on the other. Broadly speaking, one may call Plato a dualist and Epicurus a materialist. Plato and Epicurus are diametrically opposed on the question of the soul's relation to the body. Thus (1), Plato allows that Socrates, or Socrates' soul, can exist without the body that Socrates now happens to have. But Epicurus maintains (2): Socrates, or Socrates' soul, cannot exist independently of just that body which is Socrates' body. (3) According to Plato, Socrates, or Socrates' soul, is an incorporeal substance which can exist independently of any body. (4) Epicurus holds on the other hand that Socrates is an arrangement of indivisible bodies (atoms), some of which constitute his flesh, blood and bones, while others account for the vital powers of the body constituted by that flesh, blood and bones. (5) For Plato, Socrates, or Socrates' soul, is immortal. (6) But in the view of ‖ Epicurus Socrates is necessarily mortal, and his soul cannot survive the destruction of his body.

The Aristotelian and Stoic accounts, which are harder to describe briefly, fall between these two extremes. Aristotle's notion of the *psychē* as the 'form (or actuality) of a natural body which has life potentially', has proved attractive to some contemporary philosophers because it seems to them to avoid the pitfalls of dualism and materialism.[2] Certainly, if we ignore the status and duration of 'the active intellect', Aristotle seems to side with Epicurus at (2) and (6) above; for, if having a soul is to be an actually living body, it makes no sense to ask whether that form or actuality can exist

---

[2] This point is well brought out by Williams 1986. Two studies which illustrate Aristotle's apparent attractions are Barnes 1971–2 and Robinson 1978, who gives reference to many recent discussions of Aristotle's psychology. See also the stimulating and provocative book by Hartman 1977.

without the body of which it is the form or actuality. But there is little justification for treating Aristotle's psychology as a whole as if the 'active intellect' were only an embarrassing appendage. The 'active intellect' has no corresponding bodily potentiality, and it is explicitly said to be 'what it is only when separated, and this alone is immortal and eternal' (*De an.* III.5 430a22–3). Aristotle's account is most safely regarded as *sui generis* with some dualist and some materialist features.

It is rather the same, though for different reasons, with the Stoics. Unlike Epicurus, and Aristotle (without the active intellect), they would not accept (2) and (6) above. They would say that Socrates' soul, though not immortal, could and would survive the destruction of his body and thus it can exist independently of that body.[3] In this respect they resemble Plato. But against Plato they defend a version of (4) whereby Socrates here and now is entirely an arrangement of *two* things, each of which (in some sense awaiting clarification) is a body. If then it is helpful to speak of dualism in Stoicism, it is not a dualism of matter and incorporeal substance. For, given Stoic ontology, nothing can be truly predicated of Socrates which does not make reference to corporeal existence. In this respect the Stoics are at one with Epicurus. But at many points details of their position recall Aristotle so closely that we have reason to suspect his influence, an awareness of common problems, and Stoic attempts to improve upon him.

There is of course much common ground among all four philosophers. All of them accept the legitimacy of making a distinction between body and soul such that soul is the cause of intelligent life occurring within that part of space which is bounded by a normal human body. They all agree too in identifying the location of the principal activity of the soul with a particular region of the body.[4] What today would be called mental and moral attri-

---

[3] The evidence on the soul's survival is well discussed by Hoven 1971, who shows that probably all the leading Stoics posited survival of limited duration. The doctrine of periodic *ekpyrōsis* and reconstitution of the universe excludes any straightforward notion of immortality.

[4] The Stoic *hēgemonikon*, 'the principal part of the soul', is situated in the heart, which is also the primary location of the soul according to Aristotle in several different contexts; cf. Hartman 1977, pp. 138–9. For the Epicureans the *animus*, as distinct from the subordinate and pervasive *anima*, *media regione in pectoris haeret* (Lucret. III.140). In the *Timaeus* Plato localises 'the immortal reason in the head, the spirited part between the neck and the diaphragm, and the appetitive part in the belly (69d6ff.)', Robinson 1970, p. 106.

butes are universally regarded as attributes of the *psychē* as distinct from the body associated with that *psychē*; and to this extent notions such as personal identity and personality are 'psychic' rather than ‖ 'somatic'; which is not to say that they are uninfluenced or unmodified by the body's condition. Here there is room for considerable variation. It was also agreed, by all except the early Stoics, that the human soul itself admitted of a distinction between 'rational' and 'irrational' activities or states of consciousness. All except the Epicureans extended the possession of soul beyond terrestrial creatures and traditional gods. The entire world in Stoicism is an instance of the relation between body and soul; in Plato and Aristotle too the heavenly bodies are 'ensouled'.

THE SOUL AND 'UNIFIED BODIES'

If a modern philosopher claims that persons or human selves are bodies, we naturally take him to be denying dualism or the Cartesian concept of mind. Persons in Stoicism are bodies, but this statement by itself does not make the Stoics *materialists as distinct from dualists*. The Stoics had reasons, as we shall see, for insisting that the soul is corporeal; but those reasons fall within a general conceptual framework which denies that anything can exist which is not a body or the state of a body. Since persons do exist they must be bodies, according to Stoicism. The corporeality of the soul is not simply an empirical truth in Stoicism, though empirical reasons were given in its favour. It must be the case that the soul is a body or the state of a body, given the Stoic conception of reality. Accordingly the corporeality of the Stoic soul becomes an informative notion only when we ask what kind of a body, or real thing, it is taken to be, rather than by contrasting it with the Platonic or Cartesian conception of an incorporeal soul or self.

A human being, in Stoicism, is a composite of a *sōma*, in the sense (provisionally) of our saying that Heracles *has* a powerful body, and a *psychē* which is a body in some other sense.[5] More specifically he is an ensouled, rational and mortal body. More basi-

---

[5] A selection of texts: *bonum hominis necesse est corpus sit, cum ipse sit corporalis*, Seneca, *Ep.* 106.5 = *SVF* III.64, line 40; an 'animal' is οὐσία ἔμψυχος αἰσθητική, D.L. VII.143 = *SVF* II.633; ἐκ ψυχῆς καὶ σώματος συνέστηκεν (sc. ἄνθρωπος), Sextus Empiricus, *M* XI.46 = *SVF* III.96; the upshot of Philo's classification at *SVF* II.182 is man as 'body with soul, rational and mortal'.

cally he is a part of the universal stock of matter (*hylē*) pervaded through and through by a part of god (*theos*); or alternatively, he is a part of god pervading some part of the universal stock of matter. This last description of human beings is not, by itself, any ground for them to congratulate themselves on a special association with divinity. All things in the Stoic universe are combinations of god and matter, stones no less than humans. But if god and matter in association fail to tell us what is human about persons, that is no cause for immediate alarm. The Stoic god, in its constant conjunction with matter, can make rational beings as well as stones. But it is worth dwelling, initially, on the fact that persons are not different from any other discrete objects in their basic principles or constituents. Human beings no less than stones are subject to the laws of physics; they ‖ resist and offer resistance to other discrete objects, just like stones; human beings and stones are alike in having a shape and identity which persists over time. There is in Stoicism a great chain of being which tolerates no discontinuity or introduction of principles which operate at one level but not at another. The entire universe is a combination of god and matter, and what applies to the whole applies to any one of its identifiable parts.

But to speak of god and matter in conjunction is somewhat abstract for present Stoic purposes. God and matter are the fundamental Stoic *archai* – active and passive principles – but they are never found in dissociation from one another.[6] Even in the simplest state of the universe, before any cosmic cycle has commenced, something can be predicated of matter, namely fieriness. God always causes matter to possess at least this quality. Nor can god act without matter to act upon. The conjunction of god and matter always results in qualified matter (hence the possible description of god as 'matter in a certain state').[7] God and matter together constitute something that not only has mass or resistance to pressure, and that is extended in space, but something which has shape or form. Whether or not god and matter can, each by itself, be properly called bodies (as in the evidence they often are), it is certainly

---

[6] On the *archai* see especially Lapidge 1973, and Sandbach 1985, pp. 71–5.

[7] Some descriptions of god in relation to matter: 'matter is contemporaneous with god', god is 'the power which moves matter'; god 'pervades matter'; god 'is mixed with matter' or 'is in matter' or 'shapes each thing through the whole of matter' or 'is quality inseparable from matter' or 'is *logos* in matter': cf. von Arnim, *SVF* vol. IV (Adler) s.v. *theos*.

the Stoic view that every discrete body is matter pervaded and informed by god, and that each of these is necessary to its existence as a discrete body. The Stoics often described god as 'fire the craftsman' or as 'intelligent breath' (*pneuma*).[8] They also contrasted with the active principle thus described so-called 'inert elements', earth and water. Even though any one of these active or passive elements must itself, in the most basic analysis, be a combination of matter and god, it will be correct and helpful, for present purposes, to speak as though god is coextensive with *pneuma* and matter coextensive with the minimally qualified inert elements.

The justification for so doing is that the Stoics conceived wateriness and earthiness as 'transformations of fire' (or *pneuma*), and as such they are not instantiations of god *in propria persona*. The first-order distinction between god and matter gives rise to a second-order distinction between a rarefied active body, which is the nearest thing possible to pure god, and a dense passive body, which is the nearest thing possible to unformed matter. The distinction between body and soul, and the distinctions between all attributes or sets of things, are ultimately referable to the protean qualifications with which god informs matter.

This brief outline of the Stoic *archai* may help us to approach the difficult question, Is a human being or animal in Stoicism one body or two bodies?[9] The Stoics distinguished three kinds of bodies, or perhaps more accurately, ‖ four kinds, the fourth being a subdivision of the third: bodies composed of 'separated' parts (*diestōta*), such as an army; bodies composed of 'contiguous' parts (*synaptomena*), such as a house or a ship; 'unified' bodies (*hēnōmena*), such as stones and logs; and fourthly, or a subdivision of the last category, bodies unified and 'grown together' (*symphya*), namely, living things (*SVF* II.366 and 368, cf. *SVF* II.1013). 'Grown together' (*symphyēs*) is needed in addition to 'unified' to classify living bodies. Unity by itself does not point to life, any more than disjoined parts of an army signify something lifeless. Stones are like humans in being 'unified' bodies, and their unity is due to

---

[8] E.g. Aetius, *SVF* II.1027; Alex. Aphr., *SVF* II.310.

[9] For the question note also Plutarch's interpretation of the doctrine that 'each of us is two *hypokeimena*', one *ousia*, the other *poion* (supplying ποιόν with Zeller), *Comm. not.* 1038c = *SVF* II.762 with commentary by Cherniss 1976 *ad loc.*, and Dexippus *in Aristot. Cat.* p. 23, 25 Busse = *SVF* II.374. The passage needs detailed discussion, but the doctrine seems to me correctly understood by Dexippus as drawing a distinction between 'unqualified matter' (*ousia*) and ἰδίως ποιόν e.g. Socrates – i.e. in terms of the basic *archai*, *hylē* and *theos*.

the same cause. Both stones and humans are 'held together' by the *pneuma* which pervades all the rest of their matter. Stones are said to be held together or controlled by (or participate in) 'mere *hexis*' or '*hexis* alone' (*SVF* ii.988, 1013, 714), where their *hexis* consists in 'cohesive *pneuma*' or '*pneuma* that turns back to itself' (*SVF* ii.368, 458). Animals in general in as much as they are 'unified bodies' are also said in one text to be 'governed by a single *hexis*' (*SVF* ii.1013). But humans and animals in our evidence are generally differentiated from inanimate substances, such as stones, by reference to *psychē*. We see that the breath of god moves in different ways. In the stone it is mere coherence (*hexis*) but in the animal it is soul.

We shall need to ask whether the Stoics thought that animals participate in *hexis* as well as soul, or whether the soul univocally accounts for those features of animals (bones and sinews) which are analogous to the coherence of stones. A related point concerns plants. Stoic plants, unlike Aristotelian ones, do not have soul. Their powers of growth and reproduction are explained by *pneuma* which manifests itself as *physis* ('growth'/'nature'), a principle distinct both from bare *hexis* and also from soul (*SVF* ii.714–18). So the question arises of how functions of plants which animals also possess are analysed. Is *physis* a principle of life in the animal in addition to soul, accounting for its vegetative functions, or does the animal soul subsume the work of *physis* and account for everything that makes the body coherent and alive? Answers to these questions partly depend upon more basic interpretation concerning the concept of any 'unified body'.

The unity of any 'unified body', be it a stone, plant, animal, or human being, is explicitly attributed not to the form or arrangement or inseparability of its parts, but to one of its corporeal constituents, *pneuma*, and the 'cohesion' of 'tensional movement' this establishes throughout all the rest of the body. More generally, all 'unified bodies' are instances of 'complete blending' (*krasis di' holōn*). This technical expression refers to a form of compounding whereby 'two or even more bodies are extended through one another as wholes through wholes, in such a way that each of them ‖ preserves its own substance and qualities in a mixture of this kind ... For it is the special feature of things which are blended that they can be separated again from one another; and this can only take place if the things blended preserve their own natures in the mixture.'[10] Alexander of Aphrodisias, the source of this quotation or paraphrase of Chrysippus, observes that the Stoics cited the relation of soul and body as 'clear evidence' for such a kind of mixture: 'for none of the soul lacks a share in the body which possesses the soul. It is just the same too with the *physis* of plants, and also with the *hexis* in things which are held together by *hexis*. Moreover they say that fire passes as a whole through iron as a whole, while each of them preserves its own *ousia*.'[11] Alexander concludes this survey with the most general example of 'complete blending'; what is true of the 'unified bodies' just considered is true *a fortiori* of the elemental relation between the fine active pair of elements, fire and air (= *pneuma*), and the dense passive pair, earth and water. Fire and air wholly pervade the passive elements, but all four of them preserve 'their own nature and coherence'.[12]

It follows from this account that the soul/body relationship is a particular instance of a general principle in Stoic physics. It also follows that all so-called 'unified bodies' are at least two bodies: to be a unified body is to consist of at least two separately identifiable and separable bodies which are so blended that you cannot take a part of one of them, however small, without also, in that process, taking a part of the other(s).[13] But it would be a mistake to explain the 'unity' of 'unified bodies' as nothing more than a function of 'complete blending'. Two liquids, such as wine and water, can be 'completely blended', but they do not thereby constitute a 'unified body'. What we are concerned with is the unity of individual organic substances such as living creatures. If these are constituted by the 'complete blending' of cohesive *pneuma* and a passive body, the independent identity and separable existence of these constituents is not obviously analogous to that of wine and water. What body is left when you remove 'coherence' from a stone?

---

[10] Alex. Aphr. *Mixt.* p. 216.28–31 Bruns = *SVF* ii.473, p. 154.22–5.

[11] *Mixt.* p. 217.32–218.2 Bruns = *SVF* ii.473, p. 155.24–32. Todd 1976, p. 119, translates the first sentence in my quotation marks, 'for there is nothing in the body possessing the soul that does not partake of the soul' (οὐδὲν γὰρ ψυχῆς ἄμοιρον τοῦ τὴν ψυχὴν ἔχοντος σώματος. But word-order and the train of thought make it preferable to take οὐδὲν ψυχῆς as the subject of the sentence.

[12] *Mixt.* p. 218.2–6 Bruns = *SVF* ii.473, p. 155.32–36.

[13] Matter, according to Chrysippus, is infinitely divisible, D.L. vii.150 = *SVF* ii.482, as the doctrine of total blending requires, cf. Todd 1976, pp. 205ff.

More urgently, what is a human body in Stoicism when considered independently of the soul? We may hope to clarify this question by considering three possible answers.

1. *The body is the structure of bones, organs, blood and skin which contains the soul and which the soul, in turn, pervades.* This is the straightforward answer, but it can scarcely be correct in this formulation. For the body, as so described, has a definite complex structure: this means, according to Stoic physics, that the body is already an instance of 'complete blending', a compound structure generated by the interaction of *pneuma* and matter. But *pneuma* is the stuff of soul, and there is evidence that the Stoics ‖ supposed such bodily structures as bones to be due to the soul.[14] The body moreover is the body *of a living thing*. If then we take the body in this way, it appears that we are already invoking the concept of soul; we do not have an independently identifiable substance answering to body.[15] But this is what the soul/body relationship, as a mixture, requires.

2. *The body is matter in the form of earth and water.* This answer avoids the main difficulty in the previous one. Earth and water are not constituents of the soul, and so they are separately identifiable apart from soul. Moreover, these dense elements do provide most if not all the material of which the body consists. But this answer raises new problems. It seems to be simply false, or at least quite uninformative, to say that an animal's or a human being's body just is earth and water. Granted, the Stoics must regard a human being, like any other unified body, as a compound of the active shaping principle (*logos* = god = *pneuma*) and the passive material principle (*hylē* = earth and water). But that analysis is at a level of such utter generality that it seems quite inadequate to make a helpful distinction between the animal or human soul and the animal or human body. It is not earth and water without qualification that might serve to identify a living thing's body, but earth and water in a certain form. Yet that brings us back to the problems of the first answer.

3. *The body is earth and water informed by cohesive and vegetative (soul) pneuma, but not specific soul pneuma.* This third answer is a compromise between the two previous ones which seeks to keep their

---

[14] This will be cited below, and cf. Posidonius F28a–b Edelstein/Kidd 1972 for *psychikon pneuma* in bones.

[15] For an illuminating discussion of this kind of difficulty, cf. Ackrill 1972–3, pp. 129–32.

virtues and avoid their difficulties. I shall argue that it probably expresses the essentials of Chrysippus' position.

According to Sextus Empiricus some Stoics distinguished two usages of the term *psyche*: they applied it quite generally to 'that which holds together the whole compound', and specifically they used it to refer to the *hegemonikon* (*M* VII.234). For these Stoics, Sextus continues, it is only the soul in the latter sense which is invoked *when we say that man is composed of body and soul*, or that death is the separation of soul from body. This last point seems to recognise the difficulty of the first answer I considered above. Soul in the sense, 'that which holds together the whole compound', does not provide any informative way of distinguishing the body which a human being *has* from the 'unified body' which the human being *is*. But the Stoics need to be able to make that distinction in a relatively straightforward way if they are to justify speaking of a human being as a compound of body and soul, or to explain death as the separation of these. A more specific usage of soul is required in order to acknowledge that there is continuity as well as difference between the body which Socrates had ‖ when he was alive and the body which Socrates' soul has left behind.

The same distinction between two senses of soul is implied in a passage of Diogenes Laertius (VII.138–9). Referring to books by Chrysippus and Posidonius, he observes that *nous* pervades every part of the cosmos, just as soul (pervades every part) in us. 'But through some parts it is more pervasive and through others less so; for it passes through some parts as *hexis*, as through the bones and sinews; but through others as *nous*, as through the *hegemonikon*.' The basis of this distinction is of course the Stoic concept of *pneuma* and the different degrees of tension which characterise its movement. Since the soul itself is *pneuma*, and since *hexis* and *nous* are both functions of *pneuma* at different degrees of tension, it was possible for the Stoics to make soul responsible both for the form of the body (bones and sinews etc.) and for specifically psychic attributes. But they could only do so by distinguishing the soul as *hexis* (and, as we shall see later, *physis*) from the soul in the specific sense.

I conclude therefore that the Stoics must invoke the concept of soul in order to account for an animal body as an identifiable substance. But this is not open to the objections of our first answer,

once we cease to treat soul as an univocal concept. *Soul in general* is
responsible both for the body's form and for all vital functions. But
we can mark off the body from the soul by distinguishing between
bones and sinews (which are due to soul as *hexis*) and specifically
psychic attributes (which are due to soul as *hēgemonikon*). Thus both
the body and the psychic attributes are matter in a certain state.
But the nature of that 'certain state' depends upon the tension of
the soul *pneuma*.

   The point of decisive importance which will emerge more clearly
as I proceed is the Stoics' concentration on the specific usage of
soul, the soul as *hēgemonikon*. It is not the soul as *hexis* which differentiates an animal from a stone, for a stone too is governed by
hexis. That common pneumatic function indicates that both animals and stones have durable and individually identifiable bodies.
It does not indicate that stones are in some peculiar sense alive,
nor does it imply that an animal's bones and sinews are psychic
attributes. But bones and sinews are, for excellent reasons, attributed to the working of soul at the most general level. An animal
requires bones and sinews in order to live. The coherence of a
stone has nothing to do with life. Therefore the *hexis* of stones is
not a function of *pneuma* as soul, but the *hexis* of an animal must be
due to soul. This makes it clear that an animal's body is *matter
which has a form suitable for life*. I shall try to show in the next section
how the Stoics drew on the two conceptions of soul – the general
and the specific – in their account of the evolution of life in individual animals.[16] ‖

---

[16] I cannot attempt to offer here a comprehensive survey of existing treatments of the Stoic
concept of soul, but, to the best of my knowledge, the problem of identifying the body
and distinguishing between the two senses of soul has not been clearly recognised before.
A position with some resemblance to my own was briefly sketched by Ludwig Stein, as
Professor David Winston noted in his published comments on the earlier version of this
paper (see asterisked note above). Stein 1888, pp. 105–7, quoted Sextus, *M* vii.234 on
the two senses of soul and explained them as follows: 'hier wird also das ἡγεμονικόν in
einem gewissen Gegensatz zur ψυχή gesetzt, sofern es die Denk – und Empfindungs-
tätigkeit repräsentiert, während die Seele als Totalität mehr die physische Existenz des
Menschen ermöglicht' (n. 216). He maintains that what leaves the body on death is the
hēgemonikon, 'aber ein gewisser Grad von ψυχή ... muss selbst dem Leichnam noch inne-
wohnen, da er noch eine Form hat' (p. 107). Much of Stein's work is utterly perverse, but
he was more perceptive on this point than his critic, Bonhöffer 1890, pp. 105–6. Bonhöffer treats 'the soul which holds the whole compound together' as the *hēgemonikon* and
seven subordinate parts. But these, as we shall see, seem to have nothing to do with
explaining the form of bodily parts such as bones and sinews. For some analogous difficulties in Aristotle, cf. Mansion 1978.

THE SOUL AND ANIMAL BODIES

Having now clarified the Stoic distinction between the body and the soul, we may return to the question of their relationship, bearing the following points in mind: we are asking about the relationship between the body as an organic structure (held together by psychic *pneuma* in one sense of this expression) and the soul in its specific sense as *hēgemonikon* (plus seven subordinate parts, see below p. 242), or principle of specifically animal life; we already know that they must be related to one another as constituents of 'total blending', and that, accordingly, each of them has its own persisting substance; we also know (I think) that the soul, even in this specific sense, completely pervades all parts of the body, or at least, all parts where it is not already present as the principle of bodily form and coherence (*hexis*). In answer to the earlier question then, it seems to follow that all Stoic animals (things with soul) do consist of two bodies. They are compounds of what I shall call a flesh-and-bones body and a specific soul body. The specific soul body acts upon the flesh-and-bones body to make the compound of them both a sentient and self-moving being. The flesh-and-bones body contains the specific soul body and provides it with the bodily organs necessary for endowing the compound – the 'unified body' – with life as a sentient and self-moving being. From here onwards I shall conform with normal Stoic practice in using 'soul' to refer to *psychē* in the specific sense.

The Stoics argued formally for the corporeality of the soul; and the premisses of their arguments help to show how they interpreted the relationship between soul and body. Three principal arguments are attested, which I will call respectively, genetic, sympathetic, and contactual. The genetic argument, attributed to Cleanthes, rests on the premisses first, that offspring of animals resemble their parents not only in respect of bodily attributes but also in respect of the soul, where soul refers to passions, character, mental dispositions; secondly, resemblance and lack of resemblance are predicated of body, and not of incorporeals.[17]

---

[17] Nemesius, *Nat. Hom.* p. 76 Matthaei = *SVF* 1.518, p. 117.7–11, with the same argument attributed to him in Tertullian, *De an.* 25 = *SVF ad loc.* The force of Cleanthes' second premiss is obscure to me, since there seems no reason why two *asōmata* – e.g. in Stoicism, two equivalent or contrary statements – cannot be described as 'like or unlike' each other respectively.

Cleanthes' second argument is based on *sympatheia*: 'nothing incorporeal shares in the suffering of a body, nor does a body share in the suffering of an incorporeal; but soul suffers with the body when the body is sick and being cut, and the body suffers with the soul; the body turns red when the soul is ashamed and pale when the soul is afraid. Therefore the soul is a body.'[18] Aristotle of course instanced the same phenomena in arguing that anger, fear, etc., though *pathē* of the soul, are 'inseparable from the physical matter of the animals' (*De an.* 1.1 403b17), but he did not conclude that the soul as such must be a body. The third argument, 'the contactual' one, has ‖ its fullest form in Chrysippus: 'Death is separation of soul from body; but nothing incorporeal is separated from body; for an incorporeal does not even make contact with a body; but the soul both makes contact with, and is separated from, the body; therefore the soul is a body'.[19]

All three arguments assume that there must be a relationship of physical contact between the flesh-and-bones body and that within the body in respect of which an animal has sensations. So why not say that the soul is a part of the flesh-and-bones body – that sensation generally, and psychic attributes specifically, are nothing more than functions of the heart or the brain? The Stoics will not do this. They are willing to say that the soul is a physical part of the animal. But it is not a part or an organ of the flesh-and-bones body. The soul is a substance in its own right which permeates the flesh-and-bones body, and which leaves that body at death.[20]

The Stoics adopted this position, I suggest, not unthinkingly, nor out of respect for traditional Greek views or their own metaphysical assumptions. They supposed that an animal needs a body which is completely equipped with all the organs and functions of a flesh-and-bones body before its soul can come into existence, as the principle of specifically animal life for that flesh-and-bones body.

The soul cannot be an organ of the flesh-and-bones body because all bodily organs exist *before* the soul comes into being. The

---

[18] Nemesius p. 78 = *SVF* 1.518, p. 117.11–14.

[19] Nemesius p. 81 = *SVF* 11.790, p. 219.24–28.

[20] *Psychē* is a living creature; for it is alive and sentient (βούλονται δὲ καὶ τὴν ἐν ἡμῖν ψυχὴν ζῷον εἶναι. ζῆν τε γὰρ καὶ αἰσθάνεσθαι) Stobaeus, *Ecl.* 11 p. 65.1 Wachsmuth = *SVF* 111.306. The human soul is an offshoot (*apospasma*) of the cosmos *qua living creature*, D.L. vII.143 = *SVF* 11.633, cf. D.L. vII.156 = *SVF* 11.774, and for the soul's survival Hoven 1971.

seed in semen, like soul, consists of 'hot breath' which 'moves itself';[21] but the embryo which grows by the agency of this *pneuma* is not yet a *zōion*, an animal. Throughout gestation the seed *pneuma* 'remains *physis*'.[22] This means that an embryo belongs to the biological category of plants. Its mode of existence is adequately identified by 'growth' (*physis*).[23] As gestation progresses, the *physis pneuma* is said to become 'finer', and at birth this *pneuma* 'changes into soul' (or '*animal*'),[24] as a result of being instantly hardened by contact with the cold air outside. Forgetting about the fantastic embryology, we may note several further Stoic doctrines which well accord with this development from seed *pneuma* to soul *pneuma*. Like Aristotle they held that the heart is the first part of an animal to grow (Galen, *SVF* II.761) and that the heart in turn 'generates the other bodily parts'. The heart must owe its origin to the activity of the seed *pneuma*; and when the soul itself is fully developed the left ventricle of the heart is full of soul *pneuma*.[25] So there is a continuing relationship between *pneuma* and the heart both before and after an animal's birth.

The evolution of life for a rational animal passes through three stages each of which is identified by changes to a persisting *pneuma*. The seed changes to *physis*, the *physis* to soul, and the soul eventually becomes a ‖ rational soul. The differences from Aristotle are interesting. A Stoic animal's capacity to grow and to feed (Aristotle's nutritive soul, apart from reproduction) is not, as I understand the evidence, attributable to soul in its specific sense. The soul in this sense is not responsible for the basic bodily activities, and as we shall see, all of its so-called 'functions' (*dynameis*) have to do with sentient life. The body's growth and nutritive powers are due to the cohesive agency of *pneuma*, but *pneuma* prior to its changing from *physis* to *psychē*. What then about these vital functions after birth? An animal has to feed and go on growing. Are we to say that when *physis* changes to soul the new soul inherits the functions of 'causing growth', in addition to performing its work as the principle of sensation and locomotion?

[21] Cf. D.L. VII.158 = *SVF* II.741, Galen, *Def. med.* 94, vol. XIX Kühn, p. 370 = *SVF* II.742.

[22] Hierocles, *Elementa ethica* col. 1.12–15.

[23] Cf. Chrysippus ap. Plut. *Stoic. rep.* 1052f = *SVF* II.806; Galen, *De foet. form.* 3, vol. IV Kühn, p. 665 = *SVF* II.712.

[24] Hierocles, *Elementa ethica*, col. 1.21–2 μεταβαλεῖν εἰς ψυχήν; cf. Chrysippus ap. Plut. loc. cit., τὸ πνεῦμα μεταβάλλειν καὶ γίνεσθαι ζῷον.

[25] Galen, *De plac.* 1.6, p. 141 Müller = *SVF* II.897, p. 246.12–14, cf. Gould 1970, p. 126.

'Impression' and 'impulse', the basic psychic functions, are powers *added to* a pre-existing *physis*; and Philo, in one passage, describes soul as '*physis* which has also acquired impression and impulse' (*SVF* II.458). That seems a suitably Stoic account of soul as an animal's vital principle in the most general terms, but it does not easily accord with evidence for the soul in its standard, specific sense. Galen, for instance, distinguishes three kinds of *pneuma*: *hektikon*, *physikon* and *psychikon*, and says that it is the *physikon* which 'nurtures' animals and plants, and the *psychikon* which makes ensouled creatures sentient and capable of moving (*SVF* II.716). Clement of Alexandria maintains that 'non-rational animals' participate in *hormē* and *phantasia* (i.e. psychic faculties) in addition to *hexis* and *physis* (*SVF* II.714). Philo attributes bones to *hexis* and nails and hair to *physis* (*SVF* II.458). Galen again says that 'every plant is directed by *physis*, and every animal by *physis* and *psychē* together; if at any rate we all use the name *physis* for the cause of feeding and growth and such activities, and use *psychē* for the cause of sensation and self-movement' (*SVF* II.718). These texts are all mutually consistent, and entitle us to conclude that the dominant Stoic doctrine distinguished the *pneuma* which changes from *physis* to soul from the *pneuma* responsible for bodily coherence and growth after an animal is born.

Since there is no good evidence that soul in the specific sense does control digestion, bodily growth, etc., we should probably conclude that the functions of the Aristotelian nutritive soul (apart from reproduction) become functions of the *body* when an animal is born.[26] The idea would be that the growth of the body is now such that the heart etc. can control purely bodily functions without needing direction from the soul (cf. *SVF* II.708).[27] Presumably *pneuma* at the tension characteristic of *physis* must be present within

[26] Calcidius, *Ad Tim.* 220 = *SVF* II.897 p. 235.30–7 does appear to attribute to Chrysippus the doctrine that soul controls 'nutrition and growth' (*nutriendo, adolendo* line 33 of the *SVF* text). But he does not show how this could be a function of any of the soul's eight parts; perhaps he has conflated soul in the specific sense with soul as *pneuma* in general. Something similar may be implicit in an obscure passage of Philo, which survives through the Armenian translation, *Quaest. et solut. in Genesin* II.4 (*SVF* II.802). There the body is said to have its own *habitudo* (= *hexis*), but the coalescence of its constituents has a higher principle of coherence in the (all pervading) soul (*superior autem habitudo conexionis istorum anima est*).

[27] My interpretation thus differs sharply from the views of Bonhöffer 1890, p. 69 (cf. pp. 105–6) and Pohlenz 1959, vol. I, p. 87, who suppose that the soul which comes into being on an animal's birth takes over the functions of *hexis* and *physis*.

all bodily organs to maintain their form and functions, but this *pneuma* is no more part of the soul properly speaking than the *pneuma* which controls bones and sinews. Perhaps we can call it a persisting residue of the original ‖ *pneuma* which manufactured the living body.

The distinction between *physis* and *psychē* enabled the Stoics to unburden the soul from causing growth and nutrition; one can see why they want to do this. In the first place they need some way of distinguishing the flesh-and-bones body and its processes from mental functions. But, more importantly, they regarded the distinctive functions of animal life as sentience and locomotion.

Before discussing those functions I should like to compare the results of the last few pages with the conclusion of the second section of this chapter. There is an apparent contradiction in the evidence, which my analysis reflects. Earlier we had a distinction between soul as *hexis* accounting for bones and sinews (and bodily coherence generally), and the soul as specifically the *hēgemonikon*, accounting for psychic attributes. Now, with the later evidence, an animal's coherence (*hexis*) and growth (*physis*) are not attributed to its soul at all. The animal's soul is a principle additional to, and subsequent upon, a coherent, growing organism. The problem is probably to be resolved by means of the previous distinction between two senses of the word *psychē*. An animal does not have two souls, but its single soul can be treated as either all of its *pneuma* or only the most tenuous parts of that substance, depending upon what questions we are asking. All of the *pneuma* is responsible for an animal's being the kind of body that animals are; so in that sense all the *pneuma* is the soul. But what differentiates an animal from a plant and a stone is that its growth and coherence are for the sake of living a sentient and mobile life. It is a life of at least that degree of complexity which characterises everything that has soul. So, in this sense, only the *pneuma* which makes an animal sentient, mobile etc., is the soul.

PSYCHIC FUNCTIONS

We have seen the difficulty of making a distinction between the body of a living thing and its soul. But the Stoics were clearly on the right lines in using that hackneyed distinction for the important purpose of distinguishing between modes of life. Bodily processes are fundamental to an animal's life; but a different order of necessity is manifest in an animal's exercise of its senses. We may speak unkindly but correctly of someone who has sustained gross and irreversible brain damage, but whose bodily functions can continue to be made to work, as living the life of a vegetable. What we mean is that such a person cannot live a normal human life, and has perhaps, even, ceased to be a person. There is something in favour then of using the distinction between body and soul to isolate, as the soul, those vital functions ‖ which most sharply mark off animals from plants. More particularly, the Stoics' specific concept of soul makes the point that bodily processes – digestion and so forth – are not an animal's *governing principle*. What governs an animal, they said, is its soul, and that directs us to consider what an animal does, how it standardly behaves, as the key to understanding its nature.

The animal differs from the non-animal in respect of impression (*phantasia*) or sensation (*aisthēsis*) and impulse (*hormē*).[28] This is the standard Stoic view. Notice that these two functions of soul subsume Aristotle's *aisthētikon* and *kinētikon*. What it is to be a Stoic animal, most minimally, is to be a living body which is aware of itself and the external world, and more particularly, aware of itself reflexively as the subject of impulse. Awareness of, and impulse to pursue or avoid an external object, provide the necessary and sufficient conditions of animal locomotion. The fullest account of animal development is from the Stoic Hierocles, writing at about the time of Trajan on the foundations of Stoic ethics.[29] He begins his discourse with embryology.

As soon as an animal is born, he argues, i.e. from the first moment that it has a soul, it perceives itself.[30] He advances a series of arguments to support this thesis in opposition to those who say *aisthēsis* is just for recognising 'externals'.[31] The first psychic action of an animal is *synaisthēsis* of the body's parts and functions.[32] Evidence for this is, for instance, that birds perceive that they have wings, humans perceive that they have sense organs and that each

---

[28] Hierocles, *Elementa ethica*, col. 1.31–3; Philo, *SVF* II.844; Alex. Aphr. *SVF* II.1002 etc.
[29] Cf. chapter 11 of this volume. Hierocles' account is more compendiously repeated in Cic. *Fin.* III.16ff.; Aulus Gellius XII.5.7; D.L. VII.85–86, and with more detail in Seneca, *Ep.* 121.
[30] Col. 1.37–9.
[31] Col. 1.44ff.
[32] Col. 1.51, col. 2.1–3.

of these has its own functions: seeing, hearing, etc.[33] Furthermore, animals are immediately aware of a means of defending themselves.[34] The mechanism which explains self-perception appears to be 'tensional movement', the concept which explains the stone's coherence and the plant's growth.[35] In the animal 'tensional movement' is (in addition) the soul's mode of action. Hierocles maintains that the soul, because it is mixed with all the parts of the flesh and blood body, acts upon and is acted upon by them: 'For the body, just like the soul, offers resistance (*antibatikon*). And the *pathos*, which is a case of their simultaneously pressing together and resisting each other, is generated. From the outermost parts inclining within, it travels to the *hēgemonikon*, with the result that apprehension (*antilēpsis*) takes place both of all the body's parts and those of the soul. This is equivalent to the animal's perceiving itself'.[36] It is tempting to take this passage as giving not the paradigm account of sense-perception or any specific psychic act, but quite generally, as a description of the minimal conditions of any moment of sentient life. Hierocles does not say or imply that the *pathos* which results from contact between body ‖ and soul must be a result of some specific event affecting body or soul. The mere fact that body and soul are in constant conjunction is perhaps sufficient to constitute perception of *oneself*, where 'oneself' equals a living body. But Hierocles' main purpose is to demonstrate that feelings and sensations are psychic events such that the subject of them is aware that it is *his* body which is affected.[37]

Self-perception is not the only minimal condition of having a soul. Along with self-perception goes *hormē*, 'impulse', which also has the animal's own *systasis*, 'constitution', as its primary object from birth. Hierocles and Seneca adduce evidence from the behaviour of animals in support of this claim, e.g. tortoises' efforts to turn themselves back on to their feet, and young children's attempts to stand, even though they keep falling down, are not due to a desire to escape pain, but a desire to be in that state which they are con-

---

[33] Col. 1.51–61.
[34] Col. 2.3ff.
[35] Col. 4.27–38.
[36] Col. 4.44–53.
[37] I think this may include all that is meant by 'apprehension of all the soul's parts' (end of quotation in main text). But others have distinguished the soul's perception of itself from its perception of the body, cf. von Arnim 1906, pp. xxvi–xxviii and Pembroke 1971, p. 119. See further pp. 259–60 of this volume.

scious of as their own (natural) constitution.[38] An animal does not
know *quid sit animal, animal esse se sentit* (Seneca, *Ep.* 121.11).

The Stoics' emphasis on the self-perception of animals will
puzzle only those who think of non-human animals as Cartesian
automata. For we surely do want to say that animals see things
and feel pain, and if an animal sees things and feels pain then
some value must be assigned to the 'it' which sees and feels. If an
animal does not in some sense experience itself as the locus of its
seeing and feeling then we must surely deny that seeing and feeling can be predicated of it. What the analysis of such a self can be
it is naturally impossible to state in any but the most elementary
terms. The Stoics insist most strongly that animals are 'not rational'
(*aloga*). They lack the distinctively human quality of soul, but this
quality is regarded as a modification of the minimal soul, something which gradually develops in the human infant out of the
faculties which men and animals share.

We should not then think of rationality as an additional 'part'
of the Stoic soul. All mortal animals have the same eight psychic
parts. The soul of all animals is an *aisthētikē anathumiasis*, an exhalation of breath capable of perceiving (*SVF* 1.141, 2.778), and this
general definition seems to be consistent with its eight specific
parts. Five of these are the five senses; the remainder are voice,
reproduction and the so-called *hēgemonikon*.[39]

In dividing the soul into parts the Stoics were drawing attention
to its diffusion throughout the body and its multiplicity of functions. But the partition of the soul is not similar to the Platonic
model. What Plato distinguishes as reason, spirit, and appetite are,
in the Stoic soul, all activities of the dominant part, the *hēgemonikon*; the remaining seven parts, though physically attached to
the *hēgemonikon*, seem to be purely the instruments ‖ of its activity.
The Stoic soul is not fully analogous to the brain and the nervous
system; but the relationship of the *hēgemonikon* to the other seven
parts is obviously comparable, both spatially and functionally, to
the brain and the nerves which unite it with all parts of the body.

On this eight-part model, voice and reproduction resemble the
five senses in being *pneumata* stretching from the *hēgemonikon* to spe-

---

[38] Hierocles, col. 7.5–10, Seneca, *Ep.* 121.8, cf. Pembroke 1971, p. 119 with n. 28.
[39] For the evidence cf. *SVF* II.823–33.

cific bodily organs. The counting of voice and reproduction as distinguishable parts of soul became controversial. Panaetius rejected it (fr. 36 van Straaten), but his claim that voice should be regarded as a 'movement in accordance with impulse', and therefore a function of the *hēgemonikon*, does not seem to differ substantially from the earlier position (cf. D.L. vii.55). His predecessors also attributed voice to 'impulse', in the case of non-rational animals, or to 'thought' (rational impulse?) in the case of human beings; but they probably argued that though voice is a function of consciousness, the *hēgemonikon* needs to attach itself to the larynx and the tongue, just as its activity in sense-perception requires attachment to the sense organs.

They must also have been concerned to provide the human *hēgemonikon*, which is totally *logikon*, with the instrument for rational discourse (thought). Reproduction looks more puzzling, but only if we associate it on Aristotelian lines with the nutritive soul, as Panaetius seems to have done in explaining it as part of *physis* (fr. 86 van Straaten). Earlier Stoics did not of course claim that life at every level can only be transmitted through the soul's activity (the seeds of plants do not require a soul). What they thought was probably that animals do not reproduce without sensing and wanting a sexual partner, and more important still perhaps, that the soul itself must control the production of seed or female fluid which is to be capable of generating offspring which themselves will have soul.

But the most interesting concept is the *hēgemonikon* itself. I have mentioned its being located in the heart; just as the heart is said to be the source of other bodily parts, so probably the *pneuma* of the potential *hēgemonikon* in the embryo develops before other parts of the soul, which are described as its 'offshoots' (*ekpephykota*, *SVF* ii.836). The nutriment of the soul is said to be blood (*SVF* i.140), or 'the best blood' (*SVF* ii.781), with respiration also contributing (*SVF* ii.782–3). The Stoics grasped, however perversely, the vital relation between blood and respiration, and it is interesting that the soul's feeding requires an interaction between the heart and the *hēgemonikon*. This also confirms the suggestion that nutrition in general is a function of the heart, not the soul, and it shows most plainly that the heart is the vital centre of an animal. Destroy the heart and you destroy both the soul's food supply and its principal location. The importance of the heart to the unity ‖ of the animal helps to explain Chrysippus' strenuous efforts to defend it as the seat of the soul.

This discussion of psychic functions has been but a glimpse of a very large subject. I hope it has served, however, to bring out some general points of interest. The Stoics' anatomical knowledge was extremely rudimentary; but their conception of body and soul as two independent things which are 'completely blended' clearly induced them to explore the relationship between bodily organs and the psychic functions they regarded as supremely explanatory in an animal's life. Body and soul come together, most significantly, in the heart; but although the same conjunction is characteristic throughout the entire animal, it remains no more than a conjunction. Body and soul are not two aspects of a single substance. They are separate substances.

The soul is not the activity of the heart; the heart is not the cause of the soul. Their relationship exemplifies the unity of an animal, but an animal's unity as a living thing depends on a partnership between two distinct bodies. The closer one of these bodies, the soul, becomes to cosmic *logos* = god, so much less does it have in common with flesh and bones. For a whole complex of reasons the Stoics want to emphasise the kinship between man and god. But they cannot do this, without weakening the connexion between body and soul. Paradoxically, it seems, animals turn out to be better examples of 'unified bodies' than persons. This will become clearer as we consider the similarities and differences between their souls.

THE RATIONAL SOUL

No philosophers have emphasised more strongly than the Stoics did that rationality is *the* determinant of human life, and that it marks human beings off sharply from all other animals. And yet, as we have already seen, the human soul endows a human body with other psychic attributes which also belong to animals. This is not just a recognition of the uninteresting fact that human and other animals alike can see, hear, etc. The human soul was conceived by the Stoics as including the same parts and functions as the animal soul. What differentiates them is the presence or absence of *logos*: the growth and maturity of rationality are conceived as totally modifying the psychic parts and functions which, in themselves, are common to all animals including humans.

I think this point is established, or at least implied, by a seemingly authoritative text of Iamblichus. Writing of what must be the human *hēgemonikon* he treats it as the common *substrate* of four 'specific qualities' ‖ (*SVF* II.826). They are, in this order, *phantasia, synkatathesis* ('assent'), *hormē*, and *logos*. The oddity here is *logos*. It was basic Stoic doctrine that the entire human *hēgemonikon* is rational, through and through, yet here *logos* is but the last member of a quartet. The reason for this, I suggest, is that the first three 'qualities' pick out permanent dispositions of any *hēgemonikon*, animal or human. That is to say, the *hēgemonikon* is involved in every action of the soul in at least one of these three ways. The soul's seeing or hearing is not something independent of the *hēgemonikon*. It *is* the *hēgemonikon*, in its function as *phantasia*, the awareness of sense objects, reported to it as changes to the sense organs. Frequently too the awareness of a sense object will also be experienced as a *hormē* or *aphormē*, an impulse to pursue or avoid the external thing causing the stimulation of the sense organs. But such impulses will not serve as causes of action independently of 'assent', the third of the soul's basic qualities or functions.

There seems no good reason to question those few texts (Nemesius and Alexander of Aphrodisias, *SVF* II.979, 991) which explicitly attribute 'assent' to all animals; and the treatment of assent as a quality or faculty which can be named *independently of logos* (in *SVF* II.826 above) can best be explained on this assumption.[40] The assent of non-rational animals is presumably to be analysed as some kind of non-verbalised understanding or acceptance of the *phantasia* as a genuine awareness of an external object or bodily disturbance, which will give rise, often, to an impulse in accordance with the animals' *oikeiōsis*. Hence perhaps remarks in Stoic texts that animals have *simile quiddam mentis, unde oriantur rerum adpetitus* (Cicero, *ND* II.29), and the 'potential reasoning' of Chrysippus' dialectical dog (Sextus Empiricus, *PH* I.69).

---

[40] Cf. also Cicero, *Acad.* II.37 where Lucullus, speaking for the Stoicising Antiochus, claims that action, which distinguishes *animal* from *inanimum*, implies *sensus* and *adsensus*. I recognise that those who think assent must and can only be given to propositions may resist this claim. But the Stoics thought assent was given to *phantasiai* as well as to *axiōmata*. Perhaps *oikeiōsis* at all levels was thought to depend on assent, cf. Cic. *Acad.* II.38; and my remarks in Long 1986a, pp. 172–3.

If, as I suggest, any soul's activities consist in imaging, assenting and impulsion, then imaging, assenting and impulsion together pick out what it is to have a soul, or to be an animal.[41] This has interesting consequences for the soul of rational beings. *logos* is something which develops gradually in the human soul. The soul of an infant has only potential *logos*, and its behaviour is governed by an as yet non-rational *hormē*. Later '*logos* supervenes as the craftsman of impulse' (D.L. vii.86). The Stoic doctrine is not that *logos* comes into being as a new faculty to be set alongside impulse etc. What they claim rather is that the three psychic faculties which humans share with other animals *all* become modified, in human beings, by *logos*. There is evidence to support this in Stoic terminology. Human *phantasiai* (referring to all of them) are *logikai*.[42] The human *hormē* is also qualified by the same adjective, *logikē*.[43] As for 'assent' of human beings, its proper object is *lekta*, whose connexion with *logos* needs no demonstration.[44] *lekta* comprise, ‖ most importantly, the *meanings* of declarative sentences, alternatively called *axiōmata*. *noēseis*, 'acts of thinking', are described as *logikai phantasiai* (Galen, *SVF* ii.89).

All of this proves that the *logos* of the human soul is not one faculty, among others, but the *mode* of the whole soul's operation. Like other animals, human beings are creatures whose psychic attributes and behaviour can be analysed in terms of the three faculties, imaging, assenting and impulsion. But the human mode of imaging etc., is invariably a rational activity. There is another way of putting this which expresses, I think, the central insight of the Stoics: the human soul is a capacity for living as a language animal.[45] If I am right in my earlier interpretation of the soul in its specific sense, then the human soul does not animate the body in its structure as flesh and bones. It turns that structure into an instrument for perception, judgement and desire (here I refer again

---

[41] 'Imaging' is but one of many unsatisfactory renderings of *phantasia*. The noun expresses the state of 'being appeared to', but a translation needs to be wide enough to accommodate mental as well as sense impressions.

[42] D.L. vii.51 = *SVF* ii.61, cf. Kerferd 1978, pp. 252–3, who has convinced me that I was wrong to argue in Long 1971b, p. 83, that some human *phantasiai* might not be *logikai*.

[43] Stobaeus, *SVF* iii.169, cf. D.L. vii.86.

[44] Stobaeus, *SVF* iii.171.

[45] I have explored the implications of this more fully elsewhere; cf. Long 1971b and 1986a, pp. 123–5, 175–6.

to the three psychic faculties), where all three of these, even when mediated by the senses, are 'rational', in the sense that they belong to a creature whose life is irreducibly determined by its capacity to think and talk.

A soul's rationality, it seems, is a co-operative development of 'voice' and 'impression' (*phōnē* and *phantasia*). Both of these provide ways of distinguishing rational from non-rational souls. Human *phōnē* is 'articulate'; it issues from the heart and *hēgemonikon* and 'is despatched from thought'.[46] Human *phantasiai* differ from those of other animals in being capable of 'combination and transference', an obscure way of saying that human beings naturally make inferences and form concepts.[47] Language is the usage of significant sounds to express thoughts (*phantasiai*). But the expression of a thought in language is something *said* or *meant*, a *lekton* which is incorporeal, an abstraction from body.[48]

I allude, quite baldly I fear, to the doctrine of *lekta* here because it may raise new questions about the relationship between human soul and human body. Non-human animals according to the Stoics are granted some form of self-awareness, as we have seen, but *lekta* can have no part to play in their psychology. They do not say anything, and so their image of themselves cannot be linguistic or conceptual. A human being's soul, the Stoics probably supposed, regularly and naturally reacts to and governs the body by talking to itself; for this purpose it employs *lekta* which, so far from being reducible to body, are actually *incorporeal*. The human soul can describe its experience, and so it is not restricted to a uniform set of reactions to the body. It can literally govern the body because it can decide what description and value to give to ‖ its present, past or future bodily states.[49]

There appears then to be something irreducibly mental about the human soul, and this is due to its linguistic consciousness. The Stoics do not deny a necessary interaction between bodily states and conditions of the soul; that would be both implausible and

---

[46] D.L. vii.55 (Diogenes of Babylon) which is inconsistent with Sextus Empiricus, *M* viii.276, where birds are said to utter 'articulate cries'; Galen, *SVF* iii.894, quoting Chrysippus.

[47] Sextus Empiricus, *M* viii.276, cf. Long 1971b, p. 87 with n. 54.

[48] Evidence and discussion in Long 1971b, pp. 82–4.

[49] Other animals have only a most rudimentary concept of time, Cicero, *Off.* 1.11; Seneca, *Ep.* 124.17.

quite out of key with their conception of body and soul as 'totally blended'.[50] But I think they would say that no causal necessity links bodily changes and all of the soul's reactions to them. The soul has the capacity to give or withhold its assent to judgements about the body's condition and needs. So, while Stoics would no doubt admit that the soul cannot fail to be aware of an empty stomach, they would deny that that awareness automatically triggers a desire to eat. The hunger sensation and the desire to eat are separate states of the soul. The former is an unavoidable psychic reaction to the body; but the latter depends on the soul and the judgement that the soul makes. We could say that it is a relation between the soul or person and a proposition.

Such a distinction between body and rational soul is fundamental to Stoic ethics. Speaking strictly, the Stoics said that nothing good or bad can affect the body of a human being; good or bad, in the strict sense, can only be predicated of states of the soul and actions which are defined by the state of a soul. This doctrine is not a denial of bodily pain or pleasure, much less a denial that people may judge bodily pains to be bad and pleasures good. But the Stoics held that such judgements indicate a morally weak state of the soul since they confuse what is truly valuable (moral virtue) or harmful (moral weakness) with the condition of the body.

This attitude of emotional indifference to bodily pains and pleasures highlights the supposed independence and value of the soul. It explains the tendency to regard the essence of a human being, the real self, as identical to the *hēgemonikon*. Cleanthes allegedly called man 'soul alone' (*SVF* 1.538), and Epictetus sometimes treats the body as the mere container of the 'divine' soul or the ego.[51]

The dualist strain becomes still more evident when one reflects on the physical differences and functions of flesh-and-bones body and rational soul. If the *pneuma* which animates a plant-like embryo must be greatly refined in order to change to an animal soul, so much finer must be the *pneuma* of the rational soul. In its relation to the divine essence the human soul is the most rarefied of all bodies. Does this perhaps help to explain how a rational soul, while remaining corporeal, can be conscious of the incorporeal *lekta*? At any rate, its capacity for abstract thought represents some

---

[50] For useful discussions of the interaction cf. Lloyd 1978 and Rist 1969, pp. 37–53.
[51] Bonhöffer 1890, pp. 29–30; see further Rist 1969, pp. 256ff.

kind of transcendence over the purely corporeal which strictly is
the only kind of existence the Stoics recognised. When we recall
that the ‖ human *hēgemonikon* is credited with limited survival in
separation from the body, rising balloon-like from the corpse, the
dualism and the separation of body from spirit become evident
again.

So how are we to view soul and body in Stoicism? As I began by
saying, their relationship is an instance of the universal principle
of god pervading and giving form and energy to matter. The
series, *hexis–physis–*soul–rational-soul, gives us the means of classifying all 'unified bodies' as different manifestations of god's
interaction with matter. But god is only represented *in propria
persona* in the rational soul. Human beings share properties of
stones, plants and animals; what they share with stones and plants
accounts respectively for their bodies as coherent, growing entities; what they share with other animals, in addition, is the
capacity to behave as conscious and self-conscious bodies, but the
mode of all their consciousness is distinctively rational.

Physiologically speaking, human body and soul, during a person's existence, are interdependent and inseparable from one another. The body needs the soul in order to be a living *human* body;
the soul needs the body, out of which it originally grows, as its
location, partial source of energy (blood) and instrument for actu-
alising consciousness. But the soul's activities as mind – perceiving, judging, desiring etc. – though dependent on the soul's relationship with the body, are not reducible to or equivalent to that
relationship. Psychologically and morally speaking, persons for the
Stoics are states of rational consciousness, or, most literally and
accurately, 'intelligent warm breaths', which inhabit flesh-and-
bones bodies, and use them as instruments for their own life.

CHAPTER 11

Hierocles on oikeiōsis and self-perception*

There is a concept which has yet to make a firm mark on our modern map of the ancient philosophical landscape. The name of the concept in a literal English translation would be 'self-perception'. The Greek original consists of such phrases as ἑαυτοῦ αἰσθάνεσθαι, ἑαυτοῦ ἀντίληψις, and ἑαυτοῦ συναίσθησις. Cicero, on the only occasion that he gives a Stoic report of the concept, uses *sensus sui* (*Fin.* III.16). The concept of self-perception is remarkably interesting both historically and intrinsically. Nothing closely like it is to be found either in Plato or in Aristotle.[1] It was invented, I believe, by the Stoics. Vestiges of it also resonate in Stobaeus' report of what is probably the Stoicising ethical doctrine of the Academic Eudorus of Alexandria.[2] In our surviving

* This chapter is a lightly revised and annotated version of what I read at the international conference on Hellenistic philosophy, organized by K. J. Boudouris in Rhodes, August 1992. Reasons of space make it impossible for me to respond adequately to many of the comments made by conference participants, especially those on matters which go beyond the chapter's focus on the self-perception of animals. I am very grateful for all these contributions, and especially those made by Glenn Lesses, Dory Scaltsas, and Georgios Anagnostopoulos. I am also grateful for comments I received when I read a version of the paper at the Institute of Classical Studies in London.

[1] Aristotle uses the expression αὑτοῦ αἰσθάνεσθαι at *De sensu* 7 448a26, but the subject is clearly a human being not an unspecified animal (as in Hierocles), and the experience referred to is apperception. Aristotelians may well be Hierocles' target when he objects to those who 'think that αἴσθησις is given by nature [only] for the purpose of grasping external things' (col. 1.44–5). In an intriguing passage pointed out to me by Myles Burnyeat (D.L. III.15), Plato is credited by Alcimus with saying: 'How could animals have survived unless they grasped the Form (ἰδέα; sc. of survival) and had a natural intelligence (νοῦς) for this end?' This passage can be interestingly compared with Stoicism, in as much as it explains animals' self-preservation in terms of their natural faculty of cognition. However, the Platonic thesis credits animals with conceptual powers that go well beyond anything required by self-perception, as used by Hierocles.

[2] Stobaeus II.47.12: 'The subordinate end is that condition of an animal that is primarily appropriate, from the moment when it begins to perceive its constitution' (ὑποτελὶς δ' ἐστὶ τὸ πρῶτον οἰκεῖον τοῦ ζῴου πάθος, ἀφ' οὗ κατήρξατο συναισθάνεσθαι τὸ ζῷον τῆς συστάσεως). The term ὑποτελίς appears to have been coined by the early Stoic phi-

250

evidence only one Stoic philosopher treats of the concept at length and in depth. The name of the philosopher is Hierocles. His obscurity up to now probably explains why self-perception has attracted such little attention.

In a continuous chain of argument, which occupies some three hundred lines of a Greek papyrus, Hierocles seeks to prove the following thesis: All animals from the moment of birth perceive themselves continuously.[3] Hierocles' animals (which tacitly exclude fish and insects) include birds and reptiles as well as humans and other mammals. Self-perception, he argues, is both their primary and their most basic faculty. The context of his discussion, one might suppose, would be a scientific treatise on animal behaviour. Not at all. His argument about self-perception is the second step in a book entitled Ἠθικὴ στοιχείωσις, *Elements of ethics*.

This work first came to light in 1901 when a papyrus containing its opening pages was discovered at Hermopolis. The text came to Berlin, where it was rapidly edited and published by the greatest living expert on Stoicism, Hans von Arnim.[4] ‖ Arnim's edition appeared just too late for Hierocles to be mentioned in his standard work, *Stoicorum Veterum Fragmenta*, a fact which has contributed to Hierocles' subsequent inaccessibility. In addition, however, Arnim did nothing in his edition of Hierocles to suggest that the recovery of this fragmentary book was a major event. By damning his author with faint praise, Arnim did not encourage his readers to study Hierocles as a serious contributor to Stoic philosophy. The result is that Hierocles' *Elements of ethics* was scarcely read at all, even after its recovery, for several decades. That situation has begun to change, thanks to excellent pioneering work by several

losopher Herillus to distinguish the instinctual goal of animals in general from the goal aimed at by fully 'wise' persons (*SVF* 1.411). It is generally assumed that Stobaeus' immediate source is Arius Didymus, cf. chapter 5 of this volume, p. 127. For ultimate attribution of the passage to Eudorus, cf. Dillon 1977, p. 123.

[3] For a synopsis of Hierocles' main argument, see the appendix to this chapter. In the body of the chapter I generally refer to Hierocles by the sections of this synopsis. The synopsis itself includes at the end of each section a reference to the column and lines of the papyrus. A similar synopsis is printed in the Italian edition of the Greek text of Hierocles, Bastianini/Long 1992a. (For corrections to and later thoughts on this edition, cf, Bastianini/Long 1992b, which is a response to Delle Donne 1987/88, whose work was published after our edition was in final proof.) Many matters treated briefly in the present chapter are discussed at length in the commentary to our edition.

[4] Cf. von Arnim 1906. For bibliography of subsequent work done on the papyrus up to 1991, cf. Bastianani/Long, 1992a, 1992b.

scholars.[5] But the full measure of Hierocles' significance has yet to be taken.

His importance rests not only on the content of his work, but on the fact that it survives at all in legible quantity. Hierocles is, we can be virtually certain, the *Stoicus, vir sanctus et gravis* whom Aulus Gellius (*NA* ix.5.8) names as one of his contemporaries. The papyrus containing his book is datable by its handwriting to around AD 200 or a little earlier. Hierocles' life-time and our fragmentary copy of his work more or less coincide. Unlike the well-known moralising Stoics of the Roman Empire, Hierocles in this work writes like a professor and not a preacher.[6] His tone is dispassionate, his approach logical and systematic. He also writes like a lecturer who wants to hold the attention of his audience by lively anecdotes and stylistic embellishments. His *Elements of ethics* is the closest thing we have to an uncontaminated text-book or series of lectures on mainstream Stoicism by a Stoic philosopher. It is unique in its length, manner and direct witness to a Stoic professional at work.[7]

These things would be interesting even if Hierocles told us only what we already knew about Stoic doctrine from other sources. His philosophical importance rests on two things – the additional evidence he provides for basic Stoic concepts, and the methodology that he uses for establishing the foundations of Stoic ethics. Leaving the man on one side from now on, I return to the concept of 'self-perception'. What does Hierocles tell us about this concept? How does it feature in his argument? How, as historians of Greek philosophy, should we interpret 'self-perception'?

Hierocles approaches ethics as if he were doing geometry. He wants to establish a set of theorems which, by being appropriately organised, will take his students from an incontestable starting-point to deductions about the goal of human life. That final stage of his project is absent from our papyrus. At the point where the lacunae in the text begin to become extensive (numbered 7 in the

---

[5] Especially worthy of mention are Pembroke 1971, Inwood 1984 and Brunschwig 1986.
[6] In contrast to the papyrus text, the excerpts of Hierocles in Stobaeus (cf. Arnim 1906, pp. 48–63) involve more moralising than argument.
[7] The only other surviving Stoic work one might compare with the Hierocles papyrus is Cornutus' *Compendium of the Tradition of Greek Theology*, on which cf. Most 1989 and pp. 71–4 above. This treatise is clearly Stoic in its manner of interpreting the evidence of Greek religion, but it scarcely deals with the technical concepts of Stoic philosophy.

synopsis, p. 263) Hierocles has just completed his proof of a proposition about what earlier Stoics (cf. D.L. vii.84) called the 'first topic' of ethics. The name of this topic was *hormē*, 'impulse'.[8] Like his Stoic predecessors, Hierocles wants to lay a foundation for ethics with a theorem about a primal motivation which humans share with other animals. The theorem invokes the well-known Stoic concept of *oikeiōsis*, 'appropriating', 'owning' or 'coming to belong to'. What primarily motivates all animals, the Stoics argued, is a reflexive disposition of *oikeiōsis*: *self*-ownership or *self*-appropriation. This disposition manifests itself in the evident ‖ fact (see 6(ii) in the synopsis) that animals, from the moment of birth, behave in self-preserving ways. That pattern of behaviour shows, so the Stoics argued, that animals are innately motivated by love of what they primarily own – themselves.[9]

Self-owning sounds as strange in English, to convey self-loving, as οἰκειοῦσθαι ἑαυτῷ must have originally sounded in Greek. The Stoics took the word οἰκεῖος, which was the standard word for expressing the relationship between members of households and the ownership of property, and applied it (and related terms) to an animal's affective relationship to itself. Their concept of *oikeiōsis* involves the reflexive pronoun, ἑαυτός, but it would be a mistake to suppose that they took over a pre-existing concept of the self. What we today, thanks to the diffusion of modern psychology, may call '*the* self', was not part of everyday or even of philosophical vocabulary. Earlier Greek philosophers, of course, could express notions such as 'caring for oneself', or treating a friend as 'another self'; but in such cases the reflexive pronoun is not charged with the idea that there is something substantive – a self – which a philosopher might investigate in the way that he investigates the ψυχή.

Stoic *oikeiōsis* identifies selfhood (i.e. the perspective we today call subjective) as the foundation of any animal's life. By its reflexive formulation, 'self-belonging' characterises the disposition of care and ownership that an animal has in relation to itself. The

---

[8] For evidence and discussion of *hormē*, cf. pp. 145–7 in this volume.

[9] The relation of this primary *oikeiōsis* to social or other-regarding *oikeiōsis* (which is manifested by animals' love of their offspring; cf. synopsis section 8) is not explained by Hierocles in the extant portions of his text. In Bastianini/Long 1992a, I conjecture that Hierocles derived the secondary forms of *oikeiōsis* from an evolution in an animal's *phantasia* of itself (cf. synopsis section 7). For discussion of this issue in Stoic ethics generally, cf. Inwood 1984, Striker 1983 and Engberg-Pedersen 1990.

concept credits all animals with an identity that they love precisely because it is their own.

This much about *oikeiōsis* and the Stoic self we knew independently of Hierocles. We also knew from Cicero and from Seneca that *oikeiōsis* is not only a principle of self-motivation, but also a principle that implies and requires self-recognition. At the end of an argument of lightning brevity, Cicero concludes, on behalf of the Stoics, that newly born creatures could not desire anything unless they perceived themselves, and *therefore* loved themselves (*Fin.* III.16). Number 121 of Seneca's *Letters to Lucilius* is devoted to the question, whether all animals have an innate perception of their own constitution. Seneca answers the question positively, citing as evidence the fact that 'no animal has difficulty in handling its limbs ... They do this as soon as they are born. They begin life with this knowledge. They are born trained.'

It was a Stoic datum, then, that the self-love denoted by an animal's primary *oikeiōsis* implies and requires self-perception. We may restate their point by saying that an animal could not have an affective attitude towards itself unless it was aware of itself as something to be concerned about. Why that attitude should be positive and affectionate required a further Stoic argument that need not be pursued here.[10] The point I want to focus upon is self-perception as the foundation of primary *oikeiōsis* and therefore of Stoic ethical theory in general. If an opponent of the Stoics can cast doubt on self-perception as an animal's primary faculty, he can undermine their grounds for saying that animals are born with a self that they are concerned about. Self-perception is logically prior to self-love. ‖

It may well be that Hierocles writes at such length about innate and continuous self-perception because the concept needed defence against contemporary critics of Stoicism. Brad Inwood, in his excellent article on Hierocles (= Inwood 1984), has advanced this hypothesis. But Inwood himself, in my opinion, is mistaken to suggest, as he does (p. 155), that earlier Stoics, in contrast with Hierocles, 'had emphasized the desiderative rather than the perceptual basis' of *oikeiōsis*. *Oikeiōsis* does not *have* a desiderative basis.

---

[10] Hierocles (section 6(i) in the synopsis), like Chrysippus in D.L. VII.85, argues that it would be incompatible with nature's teleology for animals to have a neutral or negative attitude to themselves and their self-preservation.

It *is* an animal's desiderative basis, or rather, it is an animal's desiderative disposition, which has self-perception as its basis. That, I feel sure, had been the orthodox Stoic position long before Hierocles. His great merit, at least for us who have only a brief summary of Chrysippus' thoughts on the subject (D.L. vii.85), is the clarity with which he presents the logical relationship between self-perception and *oikeiōsis*.

Whether or not Hierocles' opponents are his contemporaries, he has two sets of them in view (papyrus col. 1.39–50), a fact not clearly registered by previous commentators.[11] One set of these denies that there is any such thing as self-perception. The other set accepts its existence, but not as a faculty that is present from birth onwards.[12] The structure of his argument is carefully designed so as to respond first to the real hard-liners – those who deny that there is any such thing as self-perception. Only after he has refuted these 'extreme simpletons' (as he calls them), does he turn to the task of proving the second point in two stages – first the continuity of self-perception, and second its originating at birth. By studying the progression of his argument, we can address my main question: What, in the Stoics' understanding of it, is self-perception?

In the first main part of his argument (4(i) in the synopsis), Hierocles argues that self-perception is proved by the way animals are observed to behave in relation to themselves and their environment. What answers to 'self' in the first half of this proof (4(i)(a) and (b) in the synopsis) are one, an animal's specific bodily parts together with their functions (e.g. a bird's wings or a human's sense organs), and two, an animal's specific equipment for self-defence (e.g. hoofs or horns). Hierocles claims that, in order to use these parts as they are seen to do, we must infer that animals perceive them. Here is our first clue, then, to the analysis of self-

[11] Although Inwood 1984, p. 158, recognises that Hierocles is responding to two sets of opponents, he generally speaks of them as a single group, 'who deny the existence of self-perception' (p. 157). That formulation is inappropriate for characterising the second set of opponents.

[12] In Bastianini/Long 1992a I conjecturally identify the first set of opponents with contemporary Peripatetics, and the second set with Academics such as Antiochus. Inwood 1984, who mainly refers to Hierocles' opponents as a single group, makes an excellent case for treating Antiochus (cf. Cicero, *Fin.* v.24, where 'self-recognition' is withheld from animals at birth) as the inspiration of Hierocles' opponents taken generally.

perception: the self that an animal perceives is the way its body is structured with a view to living its life as a bird or a bull etc.

In the third step of this proof (4(i)(c) in the synopsis), Hierocles identifies the self of self-perception by an animal's capacity to evaluate the strength or vulnerability of its bodily parts. For instance, snails protect their flesh by contracting into their shells, and tortoises behave similarly. In the fourth stage of this first proof (4(i)(d)), Hierocles reflects on the way one species of animal behaves in its encounters with another species. A lion is wary of a bull's horns but unconcerned about the rest of the bull's body; young chicks are not scared by a bucking bull (a conjecture in the text), but they run for safety at the approach of a ‖ hawk or a weasel. What is the bearing of such examples on self-perception? Hierocles' point, I take it, is that the discriminations one type of animal is seen to make, in reference to members of another species, imply a comparative assessment, and therefore perception, of its own powers and vulnerability *relative* to those of the others.

This is far from being all that Hierocles has to say about self-perception. But I propose to take stock of what we have so far. On the surface his initial argument is disarmingly simple. It presupposes no theoretical concepts about mind or body. The behaviour that he singles out is taken to be sufficient on its own to justify the attribution of self-perception to animals. As interpreters, we must be careful not to jump to any conclusions about self and perception that import ideas extrinsic to the material Hierocles adduces. In particular, we must be careful not to suppose that Hierocles is identifying an animal's self – the self of which it has perception – with what a post-Cartesian philosopher might call consciousness or mental states, i.e. thoughts, memories, emotions and so forth. Whatever self-perception is, Hierocles takes it to be present in some form from the very beginning of an animal's life. Initially at least, self-perception does not depend on any learning or experience. It appears in its primary manifestations to be non-conceptual, or at least pre-conceptual.[13]

<hr>

[13] Several people have asked me whether an animal's self-perception, in my understanding of it, involves propositional content, concepts and belief (*doxa*). These are not questions that Hierocles addresses. He sometimes says that what an animal perceives is *that* something is the case (e.g. col. 3.2–6), and Seneca does so too (cf. *Ep.* 121.21). However, I am not convinced that such formulations are intended to inform us about the animal's psychology, from the animal's own perspective. Arguments for and against attributing propositional content to animal perception are interestingly marshalled by Sorabji 1990, pp. 307–14.

We have seen what it most basically involves – a sensory relationship between those parts of an animal which are vital to its survival or specific way of life and the animal as an organic whole. In terms of what I previously said about *oikeiōsis*, this account of self-perception fits very neatly. *Oikeiōsis* is an animal's innate disposition to be concerned about and motivated by what belongs to itself. What it perceives in self-perception, is precisely its relation as the whole animal it is to what it owns – its specific bodily parts and their functions. However, Hierocles cannot, without cheating on his argument, borrow from *oikeiōsis* in order to explain self-perception. His case for *oikeiōsis* relies on self-perception. He must, as he does, try to establish the latter independently of the former.

None the less, the concept of belonging or ownership, which links self-perception to *oikeiōsis* retrospectively helps to clarify the self that is perceived. What an animal perceives, in perceiving itself, appears to be what belongs to it as its constitution.[14] It perceives the parts and functions which make it the animal that it is.

When I first started thinking about self-perception, I treated it as an *ad hoc* concept which the Stoics had recourse to because of their ignorance of neurology and genetics. It remains true that the examples of self-perception adduced by Hierocles cover behaviour which, as moderns, we have been accustomed to calling instinctual. But self-perception too is instinctual, on the Stoics' own findings. The question I want to ask is whether there is a modern concept, sufficiently similar to self-perception, that we can use as a means of testing the scope and explanatory power of the Stoic notion. Is it still reasonable today to suggest that instinctual behaviour involves a sensory or cognitive relationship between the ‖ animal, in its identity as an organic whole, and its specific parts?

In his book, *The Man who Mistook his Wife for a Hat* (1987), the neurologist Oliver Sacks describes the case of a young woman who, as a result of a spinal lesion, lost all control of her body. In due course, by the use of vision, she was able to recover some mobility. Yet years later, he writes (p. 51): 'She continues to feel ... that her body is dead, not-real, not-hers; she cannot appropriate it to herself.' This passage caught my attention because its language

---

[14] What Hierocles calls an animal's self-perception Seneca (*Ep.* 121) terms *constitutionis suae sensus*. We are probably to take it that there is no significant difference between these expressions, but it would have been helpful if each author had explained the precise connexion between 'self' and 'constitution'. See further Brunschwig 1986, pp. 136ff.

is so similar to the Stoic concepts of self-perception and *oikeiōsis*. Sacks' patient had lost the capacity to feel her body as something that belonged to her.

There is a modern term for what she had lost – 'proprioception'.[15] The term was invented by the great neurologist Charles Sherrington, as a name for what Sacks calls (p. 43): 'that continuous but unconscious sensory flow from the movable parts of our bodies (muscles, tendons, joints), by which their position and tone and motion are continually monitored and adjusted'. In his book *The Integrative Action of the Nervous System* (1906), Sherrington distinguished what he called the 'extero-ceptors' of smell, vision and hearing, from the proprioceptors which he located both in the head and in the body generally. He stressed the fact that, though proprioception and exteroception are distinct functions, they habitually work together in an animal's behaviour. As he puts it (p. 344): 'The locomotion of an animal impelled by its eye towards its prey involves cooperation of the labyrinth [the proprio-ceptive organ in the head] with the retina.'

Proprioception is a form of perceiving. Sherrington writes (p. 343) of 'our muscular sensations' which 'contribute to perceptions of the relative flexions or extensions of our limbs'. Proprioception covers reflexes of attitude and posture, and reflexes of movement. The animal behaviour surveyed by Hierocles and by Seneca – inverted tortoises turning themselves upright, bulls lowering their horns etc. – is exactly similar to cases mentioned by Sherrington. He points out that a frog whose proprioceptive mechanism is working, unlike one whose spinal cord is not intact, reverts to the upright position if inverted. Another of Sherrington's examples that recalls Hierocles is 'the steady flexed posture of the frog directed toward a fly' (p. 344).

Despite the scientific history that separates the Stoics' self-perception from proprioception, the two concepts are remarkably similar in what they seek to explain. Like modern neurologists, the Stoics are interested in the principle that enables animals to function internally as well-organised wholes, coordinating their movements and ensuring that the deployment of their bodily parts is

---

[15] The following remarks about proprioception are adapted from my commentary in Bastianini/Long 1992a. Brunschwig 1986, p. 137, is the first scholar to have observed that the kind of awareness the Stoics called self-perception is what 'nowadays we should call proprioceptive'.

appropriate to their environment. Loss of proprioception, according to Sacks (1987, p. 52), involves 'loss of the fundamental organic
mooring of identity' or loss of 'our sense of *ourselves*; for it is only
by courtesy of proprioception ... that we feel our bodies as proper
to us, as our "property", as our own' (p. 43). Shades of primary
oikeiōsis again.

What do I want to conclude from the striking affinities between
proprioception and self-perception? Not, of course, that the Stoics
were proto-neurologists ‖ but that their concept of self-perception
is as technical and theoretical in its scope as proprioception. We
should interpret self-perception not as a naive projection of human
consciousness on to animals, but as registering the fact that there
is something that it is like to be a bat (let us say, with acknowledgement to Thomas Nagel's famous article of that title)[16] from
the bat's perspective – something that is felt and perceived within
the organism itself.

Although the Stoics were not neurologists, their conception of the
psychē and its parts is functionally similar to that of the brain and
the central nervous system. What correspond in Stoicism to nerves
are fine stretches of *pneuma*. These interpenetrate all other parts of
the body, making those parts receptive to the 'command-centre' in
the heart, and transmitting information about them back to the
'command-centre'. In the next stage of his argument (section
4(ii)(a) in the synopsis), where he deals with the continuity of self-
perception, Hierocles draws on this Stoic model of the soul/body
relationship.

This is the one place in his text where he advances his own definition of self-perception. It occurs as the conclusion to an elaborate account of the continuous interaction that takes place between
an animal's *psychē* and its body (col. 3.56–4.53). Hierocles identifies
the *psychē* as a 'faculty of perception'. Because the *psychē* interpenetrates all the rest of the animal (we may think again of the
nervous system), it is capable of responding perceptively to every
condition of the animal's body. This interaction between body
and *psychē* generates a *pathos* (the modern analogue of this would
be a neural signal), which is conveyed to the command-centre of
the *psychē*. The result of this, Hierocles says, 'is a perception of all

[16] 'What is it like to be a bat?' in Nagel 1979, pp. 165–80.

the parts, both those of the body and those of the *psychē*: and this is equivalent to the animal's perceiving itself'.[17]

At first glance one is puzzled by the expression 'all the parts'. Hierocles needs to say 'all' in order to set up his equivalence with 'self', but does he not beg the question in proposing that what an animal perceives of itself at every moment is 'all' its parts? Why not say it perceives 'some' part of itself? In addition, are there not times when an animal perceives none of its parts – for instance when it is asleep? These challenges would be in order if Hierocles were claiming that an animal is always focusing with reflexive awareness on all of its parts. But that interpretation is excluded. In the next step of his argument for the continuity of self-perception (4(ii)(b) in the synopsis), Hierocles argues that self-perception persists without interruption during sleep. Waking consciousness, then, or focusing on something is not necessary to self-perception. We are to think of it, generically, as an invariant disposition, generated by the continuous interaction between body and *psychē*.

Since self-perception is lifelong and need not involve waking consciousness, we are reminded once again of the receptive and reflexive functions of proprioception. Just as proprioception involves a continuous monitoring of the body, so Hierocles' animals continuously perceive *all* their parts. What an animal's continuous self-perception involves, I suggest, is not necessarily noticing or being conscious of anything at all, but being always in a disposition to monitor every ‖ part of itself as its own property and special concern.

That minimalist interpretation of self-perception is quite compatible with the thought that self-perception intermittently involves self-awareness as well as self-monitoring. When they are awake, of course, animals do notice things. In noticing things by means of their sense organs, they also, according to Hierocles, perceive themselves, i.e. the way they are affected by what they see, hear and so forth (cf. 4(iii)(c) in the synopsis). Self-perception, he argues, regularly accompanies all other kinds of perception. Here, I suggest, in the interaction of sensory perception (exteroception) and self-perception (or self-monitoring), the animal gets the self-image (*phantasia* of itself) that it responds to with *oikeiōsis* – concern for itself (cf. 6(i) in the synopsis). For example, a dog sees

---

[17] ὡς ἀντίληψιν γίνεσθαι μερῶν ἀπά[ν]των τῶν τ[ε τ]οῦ σώματος καὶ τῶν τῆς ψυχῆς· τοῦτ[ο] δέ ἐστιν [ἴσ]ον τῷ τὸ [ζῷον αἰ]σθάνεσθαι ἑαυτοῦ. See also p. 241 above.

a bone *as* something it wants to belong to itself, or it smells a snake *as* something it does not want to belong to itself.

The Stoics, fortunately as I think, were not troubled by Cartesian dualism and its legacy concerning human consciousness. Descartes regarded non-human animals as automata or organic machines. The Stoics saw them as autonomous organisms, not conscious as we are, but responsive to themselves as self-perceivers. As such, human infants and young animals have a great deal in common. The Stoics were also untroubled by Christian ideas about differentiating humans from animals in terms of an immortal soul. They were thus open to the thought we may be just recovering – that animal behaviour can teach us something about ethics and the common needs of all animal species, including ourselves. There is a story to be told about how self-perception in a human being evolves from its 'proprioceptive' foundations into the capacity to perceive oneself as a rational agent. Hierocles probably told it, but unfortunately the papyrus breaks off just as it reaches the human animal.

On the basis of Hierocles' text we are in no position to know how he connected rudimentary self-perception, as an attribute of all animals, to the ethical concepts that pertain specifically to humans. Here, to conclude, are a few reflections and speculations on this point.

The Stoics, it seems, walk a fine line between emphasising continuity and difference between human and non-human animals. In crediting all animals with self-perception and self-love, they claim that these capacities are the foundations of animal life quite generally. This should imply (given the Stoics' teleological interpretation of nature) that every normal animal, including humans, is equipped at birth with all that it needs in order to begin to orient itself successfully as the kind of animal that it is. Continuity also obtains at the parental or social level, since self-regarding *oikeiōsis* is complemented in maturity with a further *oikeiōsis*: to care for offspring (section 8 in the synopsis). However, these continuities between human and non-human animals have to be reconciled with the fact, as the Stoics see it, that mature human nature is utterly distinctive in ‖ virtue of its rationality. Hence, what self-perception and self-love can and should mean, for rational humans, must be radically different, in crucial respects, from their counterparts in other animals and in 'not yet' rational infants.

Continuity and difference are reconciled, I suggest, because the animal model of self-perception identifies only the starting-point of a human self. Non-human animals do well in their non-rational ways; they are designed to perceive and appropriately use their bodily parts. Human beings, on the other hand, are designed to evolve from such concerns into thinking animals, who prefer mental to bodily well-being. What mature human beings perceive, in perceiving themselves, is a constitution that involves capacities for thought and includes desires that are shaped by reasoning. Unlike the other animals, humans have to decide what their nature, as so constituted, requires. The necessity for such decision makes it possible for humans to misuse their rationality, so that they love parts of themselves that are animal rather than distinctively human. Thus Epictetus observed (*Discourses* 1.6.20): 'It is wrong for man to begin and end where the non-rational animals do. He should rather begin where they do and end where nature has ended in our case.' As a dog, we might say, sees a bone as something that it wants to belong to itself, so the human being who has an understanding of ethics *should* see justice as something he wants to belong to himself.

A mature human self differs from the dog's self because 'should' does not enter into the dog's self-perception. It enters the human's because human reason partly manifests itself prescriptively, giving normative direction to the impulses that manifest a person's self-concern and other-directed behaviour. However, this discontinuity between humans and other animals does not undermine the interest of looking at psychological attributes which they all share. There is something to think about in the proposal that the 'proprioceptive' capacities which enable other animals to monitor their lives are what we, as humans, start from and can shape by reflection and training into ethical dispositions.

APPENDIX: Synopsis of Hierocles' *Elements of ethics*

1. The best starting-point for ethics is an animal's *prōton oikeion*. When does an animal's life begin? Not as a foetus but at the moment of birth. At that moment the foetal *physis* changes into *psychē* (col. 1.1–30).

2. *aisthēsis* and *hormē* are the defining attributes of an animal. An exposition of an animal's *aisthēsis* is essential for knowledge of its *prōton oikeion* (col. 1.30–7).

3. As soon as an animal is born, it perceives itself (col. 1.37–50).

4. Proof of 3:

 (i) Animals perceive themselves, as evidenced by the fact that:
   (a) Animals perceive their specific parts (col. 1.51–2.3).
   (b) Animals perceive their equipment for self-defence (col. 2.3–18). ‖
   (c) Animals perceive which of their parts are weak and which of them are strong (col. 2.18–3.19).
   (d) Animals perceive the powers in other animals (col. 3.19–52).
 (ii) Animals perceive themselves continuously, as shown by:
   (a) The continuous interaction of their souls and bodies (col. 3.52–4.53).
   (b) The fact that they perceive themselves even during sleep (col. 4.53–5.38).
 (iii) Animals perceive themselves as soon as they are born, since:
   (a) Continuous self-perception implies self-perception from the beginning of life (col. 5.38–43).
   (b) No time for the beginning of self-perception is more plausible than the beginning of life (col. 5.43–52).
   (c) Perception of external things begins at birth, and presupposes self-perception (col. 5.52–6.10).
   (d) Self-perception is prior to the perception of anything else (col. 6.10–24).

5. As soon as it is born, an animal has *oikeiōsis* to itself and its constitution (col. 6.49–53; 7.48–50).

6. Proof of 5:

 (i) An animal must have an attitude of affection for the *phantasia* of itself that it has (col. 6.24–49).
 (ii) Animals under all circumstances seek to preserve themselves (col. 6.53–7.48).

7. As an animal develops, its mode of *phantasia* becomes more refined (col. 7.50–8.27).

At this point the papyrus becomes practically illegible for about thirty lines.

8. When mature, animals have four kinds of *oikeiōsis*, which include affection for their offspring as well as for themselves (col. 9.1–10).

Lacuna of two columns.

9. Man is a social animal (col. 11.14–19).

CHAPTER 12

Representation and the self in Stoicism*

The Stoics philosophised about the mind, but they did not treat the philosophy of mind as a division of inquiry separate from their interests in logic, physics and ethics, the official 'parts' of their philosophy. Attention to this point is essential for any sympathetic understanding of their significant contributions to what *we* call 'philosophy of mind'. For example, their arguments and theses about the pneumatic nature of the mind and its faculties, though historically interesting and intelligible, are unlikely to impress those who know the philosophical tradition since Descartes. The Stoics distinguish the mind and the soul (of which the mind is a part) from the body, but they take the soul itself to be corporeal. Do they, then, attempt to combine materialism and dualism? That would be a seriously anachronistic interpretation. The Stoics did not face the philosophical issues that we characterise by these alternatives. They wanted an account of the soul which would distinguish it from flesh, blood, bones and sinews, and at the same time explain the soul/body relation as a physical interaction. Hence they identified the soul with 'breath' (*pneuma*) that completely interpenetrates every part of the flesh, blood, bones and sinews.[1]

Notwithstanding their 'materialism', the Stoics seem to have seen no problem in theorising about psychological faculties and states *as if* the mental could be analysed as a domain of its own. In

---

* In writing this chapter, I have benefited from comments by Stephen Everson, and also from the discussion a version of it received at the meeting of the Scottish Association for Ancient Philosophy in Edinburgh, July 1989.

[1] In chapter 10 of this volume I offer an interpretation of how the Stoics viewed the relation of soul to body. For the basic evidence on early Stoic psychology and philosophy of mind, see Long/Sedley 1987, sections 39 and 53. There is much useful material, especially for Epictetus, in Bonhöffer 1890. At the end of this chapter I argue that the Stoics can be presented with a mind/body problem of the familiar type.

this they were surely right. A thought or an emotion is a mental event, whatever may be its actual relation to physical processes and structures. Like Aristotle (*De anima* 1.1, 403a29), the Stoics held that emotions can be non-reductively described ‖ in two ways: they are both judgements, the mental analysis, and 'swellings' and 'contractions', the physicalist analysis.[2]

In this chapter I focus upon an aspect of Stoic thought to which questions of 'mind' as distinct from 'body' are largely irrelevant. What I want to argue is that the Stoics were primarily interested in the mind and its faculties for the light that such inquiry could shed upon the self. The self is a psychological and ethical concept. What we may loosely call Stoic 'philosophy of mind' is most creative and distinctive in the tools it provides for understanding and shaping our individual selves. This also happens to be a subject for which our evidence is not fragmentary and tendentious, as is so often the case in the study of Stoicism. The *Discourses* of Epictetus, transmitted by Arrian, contain a powerful philosophy of the self, unsystematic in presentation, but thoroughly clear in its general direction. In the first part of this chapter I will discuss the mental faculties which provide the Stoics with their innovative approach to the self. In the second part, I will seek an answer to the question, Why does Epictetus typically characterise a Stoic's purpose as 'making correct use of representations' (*phantasiai*)?

As a preliminary, let me explain what I mean by a philosophy of the self. In recent years a new subject of inquiry has begun to burgeon – the conceptualisation and history of the individual or person.[3] It is a subject that infiltrates the conventional disciplinary boundaries of philosophy, psychology, anthropology, history and literary criticism; its special concern is 'representation'. By 'representation' I mean the way in which individual human beings perceive themselves, or what it is for them to have a first-person outlook on the world or first-person experience. The self in this sense is something essentially individual – a uniquely positioned viewer and interlocutor, a being that has interior access of a kind that is not available to anyone else.

A self of this kind, it may seem, is always with us. But selves have

[2] Cf. Long/Sedley 1987, vol. 1, p. 420.
[3] The bibliography is already huge. I have found the following particularly helpful: Rorty 1976, Carrithers *et al.* 1985, Martin *et al.* 1988, and especially Taylor 1989.

histories, and what their representation consists in is not something culturally or conceptually constant. Christianity, Romanticism, Marx and Freud are some of the many influences that have helped to shape ways in which we Westerners view ourselves, what we take ourselves, in first-person reflection, to be. A number of contemporary scholars have begun to recognise the significance of Stoicism among early sources of the modern self. Thus Charles Taylor writes: ‖

The [Stoics'] singling out of ... assent is one source of the developing notion of the will, and there is already an important change in moral outlook in making this the central human faculty. What is morally crucial about us is not just the universal nature or rational principle which we share with others, as with Plato and Aristotle, but now also this power of assent, which is essentially in each case mine.[4]

Taylor is quite right to comment as he does on the novelty of Stoic assent, within the tradition of ancient philosophy, and its contribution to the notion of a strictly personal or individual identity and commitment. No less novel and significant, however, is the role that the Stoics assign to *phantasia*, 'representation'. In their philosophy, unlike that of their predecessors, 'representation' encompasses the entire life of the mind. This is best interpreted, so I will argue, as a new focus on consciousness, on the individuality of the perceiving subject, as the fundamental feature of the mental. Once this is understood, we see why the Stoics attached such ethical importance to control and correct use of representations.

REPRESENTATION (PHANTASIA) IN STOICISM

The term *phantasia* makes its main historical entry as a Platonic term of art with reference to Protagorean relativism.[5] Plato uses *phantasia* to pick out the different 'appearance' or 'perception' that one and the same entity may generate in a pair of observers. It is important to keep this original sense in mind when considering subsequent uses of the term. *Phantasiai* are necessarily individual experiences, appearances *to individuals*. This is not to say that they

[4] Cf. Taylor 1989, p. 137.
[5] *Theaetetus* 151c. This will not be Plato's first use of the word if those manuscripts which include it at *Republic* 382e preserve the right reading.

must pertain to a subjective and private sphere as distinct from the observable and public domain, or that there cannot be type-identity between the *phantasiai* of a group of individuals. Realist philosophers, no less than sceptics, relativists and subjectivists, must make room for *phantasiai* in their philosophies of mind. The point is simply that any post-Platonic philosopher who wished to refer to individual experience of any kind – the way things appear to the individual subject that experiences them – had *phantasia* available as the appropriate term.

As one studies Stoicism from its fragmentary Zenonian origins down to the continuous *Discourses* of Epictetus and the *Meditations* of Marcus Aurelius, it becomes evident that *phantasia* has a centrality that it lacks in Plato and Aristotle.[6] No doubt the Stoics were influenced in their use of it by these predecessors, especially Aristotle. But Stoic *phantasia*, though recognisably || Aristotelian in certain respects, is not to be accounted for solely as his legacy. By the end of the *De anima*, it is true, *phantasia* has assumed an importance not even hinted at early in Aristotle's treatise: it enters importantly into Aristotle's account of perception and thought, desire and action, true and false belief, and imagination. Some of the Stoics' work on *phantasia* might be viewed as a tidying-up of Aristotle, turning what is disjointed in his account into a unitary notion.[7] But I think that would be a superficial interpretation of the material. We need to understand the Stoic concept in its own terms, and so my future references to Aristotle will have that end in view.

In Stoicism psychology and ethics are intimately related. The Stoics begin their reflections on both of these subjects by considering the common properties of humans and other animals.[8] Human beings are animals, albeit 'rational' ones. Their animal nature is evidenced by the fact that they have a 'soul', where soul signifies agency, or a creature's capacity to cause itself to move

---

[6] For the primary evidence of the concept in early Stoicism, cf. Long/Sedley 1987, section 39.

[7] See especially *De anima* III.10 433a9, 433a20, 433a27, 433b29, and *EN* VII.8 1150b28. These passages show that Aristotle could have anticipated most of the work the Stoics assign to *phantasia*, but I do not think that he did so in any systematic way.

[8] Cf. D.L. VII.85–6 = LS 57A, and, much more fully, Hierocles, *Elements of ethics*, cols. 1–6, edited by Bastianini/Long 1992. For Hierocles, see also chapter 11 of this volume, and Inwood 1984.

about in the world. The self-motion of animals is due to the conjoint operation of two faculties, *phantasia* and *hormē*, 'impulse':
'They [i.e. animals] are moved by themselves when a representation occurs within them which calls forth an impulse.'[9] Possession of a representational faculty and an impulsive faculty is what
distinguishes every animal or ensouled creature from plants and
inanimate beings.[10]

Approaching the Stoics via Aristotle's psychology, we might be
inclined to say that their account of animal nature is merely a ter-
minological variation of his position. For Aristotle, possession of
aisthēsis, the faculty of sense-perception, differentiates all animals
from plants, and he insists that *aisthēsis* is always accompanied by
to orektikon, the appetitive faculty ‖ (*De an.* II.3 414b1).[11] Substitute
to orektikon for *hormē* and *aisthēsis* for *phantasia*, and we can translate
the Stoic terms into their Aristotelian equivalents. To this I would
reply: little will be distorted by the former substitution but a great
deal by the latter. *Aisthēsis* in Aristotelian usage signifies particular or co-operative activities of the five senses. What the Stoics
subsume under the 'representational faculty' includes impressions
mediated by the five senses but is not confined to these. According
to Chrysippus, 'the first thing appropriate to every animal from
the moment of birth is its own constitution and the consciousness
(*suneidēsis*) of this' (D.L. VII.85 = LS 57A). Hierocles, a Stoic professor of the Roman Imperial period, argues at length (see n. 8
above) that the first object of an animal's *aisthēsis* is not anything
external to an animal's body but *the animal itself*. He seeks to prove
that animals continuously perceive their bodily parts and their
specific powers from the moment of birth, and that such self-
perception is a precondition of their perceiving anything else (col.
6.2).

This is a very striking claim. In addition, Hierocles argues that

[9] Origen, *De principiis* III.1.2–3 = LS 53A. The fullest study of the Stoic psychology of
action is Inwood 1985.

[10] There is no agreed translation of *phantasia*, and no single modern word is entirely apt.
'Appearance', 'impression', 'presentation' and 'representation' are the English renderings most commonly adopted. In Long/Sedley 1987, 'impression' is consistently used,
but the Humean connotations of this term may mislead. For this chapter I find 'representation' the most effective word, and I have modified the translations taken from LS
accordingly.

[11] Unlike the Stoics, Aristotle equivocates on the question whether all animals possess *phantasia*; cf. Hicks 1907, note on *De an.* II.2 413b22. That is sufficient by itself to show how
differently he regards this faculty.

an animal must perceive itself *before* it perceives anything else (col. 6.21) These are not Aristotelian doctrines, and I suspect that Aristotelians are Hierocles' target when (col. 1.45) he objects to people who think *aisthēsis* is 'for the sake of perceiving externals'.[12] In using *phantasia* rather than *aisthēsis* as the name for an animal's perceptual faculty, the Stoics emphasised their difference from Aristotle. On their account of the mind, sense-perception is not a faculty in its own right, so to speak, but a sensory 'mode of representation' (*phantasia*). Likewise, in the case of humans, thought is not an independent faculty, but a non-sensory mode of representation. For Aristotle, on the other hand, *phantasia* stands for the capacity to visualise (hence the common translation, 'imagination') and this, he argues, 'is different from both perception and thought' (*De an.* III.3 427b14). Without entering into the notorious complications of Aristotle's concept of *phantasia*, it seems clear that he has no interest in reducing all states of awareness to 'representations' *simpliciter*, which would make *phantasia* superordinate rather than merely contributory to perception, thought and other mental faculties. His philosophy of mind does not place a unitary consciousness at the centre of an animal's life. This was ‖ the Stoics' contribution, and one which decisively marks off their philosophy of mind from all that went before.

The Stoic supposition that all animals perceive themselves and do so from birth onward is a subject for study in its own right.[13] The point that needs to be emphasised now is simply this: in making self-perception basic to animals' life, the Stoics are saying that, in order to live at all, any animal must have some representation of itself, some sense of itself as the subject of its own experiences, cat-like, dog-like etc. This self-perception is not something unrelated to sensory operations. Rather, it is a prerequisite of them, and accounts for the fact that the seeing or hearing taking place in that body over there is that creature's seeing or hearing as distinct from your or my seeing or hearing.

---

[12] Aristotle, of course, recognises that 'we perceive that we perceive' (*De an.* III.2), but this reflexive consciousness need not imply self-consciousness (cf. Kosman 1975), or a sense of one's organic unity, which seems to be what the Stoics mean by an animal's 'perception of itself'; cf. Inwood 1984, pp. 174–7, for stimulating remarks on the Stoic soul–body compound's awareness 'of itself as a whole'. My main disagreement with Inwood has to do with the novelty he ascribes to Hierocles. I think that Hierocles' emphasis on self-perception was standard Stoic doctrine.

[13] See chapter 11 of this volume.

The Stoics' intuition concerning self-perception is directly relevant to another distinctive feature of their philosophy of mind –
their concept of the *hēgemonikon* (see LS 53H, K–M). This term picks
out the soul's 'commanding part', located in the heart, the centre
of an animal's body. What this part of the soul commands or governs is all that we would call today sentient, conscious and purposed life as distinct from automatic bodily processes.[14] The
'commanding part' of the soul has distinct functions of its own,
which most basically include the pair already mentioned, *phantasia*
and impulse (*hormē*). What it does not have is distinct 'parts'.
In other words, that which is the subject of *phantasia* is also the
subject of *hormē*. It is one thing, what we may call the animal's
self or mind, to which things appear and which responds to such
appearances or representations with desire or aversion. *Phantasia*
and *hormē* do not constitute a division of the soul into distinct parts,
potentially capable of conflicting with one another. There is no
subject or ego over and above the *hēgemonikon*, no place for a self
that has separate, quasi-Platonic constituents, a desiring part and
a cognitive part. The *hēgemonikon* provides the Stoics with the concept of a unitary self, actively engaged as a whole in all moments
of an animal's experience.

A concern to emphasise the unity of the experiencing subject is
a further reason, we may presume, why the Stoics treat *phantasia* as
the mental faculty encompassing all objects of awareness. Applying the notion to human animals, we may take it as a Stoic datum
that my sensing something white, my awareness that what is hurt-
ing is my leg, my recollection of someone's birthday, my current
thought of Socrates, and my reflection on ‖ the square root of
two, are all alike in being representations, appearances of something to me.[15]

If the representational faculty covers all of these mental states,
what mental states fall outside its scope?[16] The answer, I believe, is

[14] In chapter 10 of this volume I argue that the Stoics restrict the scope of the soul's 'commanding part' to the functions distinctive of an animal's sentient mode of life. The
evidence suggests that they treated all purely organic functions – breathing, digestion,
growth etc. – as activities controlled by the heart, which needs no direction from the
soul's 'commanding part'.

[15] Our evidence does not tell us much about the ways the Stoics distinguished one type of
representation from another. But see LS 39A, and also 39B, where 'imagination' and
'figments' are marked off from the general class of *phantasiai*.

[16] For this use of the term 'mental state', see Wollheim 1984, p. 33: 'Mental states are epi-
sodic or transient phenomena'. Wollheim distinguishes them from 'mental dispositions',

none. As I understand the Stoics, they classify all occurrent sensations and feelings, recollections, imaginations, and all transient thoughts as 'representations'. There is no other faculty in virtue of which mental states can appear to the self that has them.

At this point we should take note of the canonical definition of *phantasia*: 'A representation is an affection (*pathos*) in the soul, which reveals itself and its cause.'[17] Much could be written concerning the elucidation of the difficult expression, 'reveals itself'. Let me briefly say that I take 'reveals itself' to signify the fact that any *phantasia* is experienced as such, i.e. it is experienced as an awareness or perception of the object (its cause) that it reveals; 'reveals itself' is an attempt to capture the reflexive or phenomenological aspect of representations. The source of this definition proceeds to illustrate it by the example of seeing something white; but we should not be misled by this example into treating sense-perception as anything more than the paradigm case of representations. The Stoics, like Aristotle, maintain that representations can be of sensory or non-sensory objects. They also claim that all our concepts (*ennoiai*) are *phantasiai*; that memory is a 'store' of them; and that they enter into the causal account of everything we do.[18]

As a *pathos*, a representation is passive; it is an instance of our being affected, 'stamped', or imprinted in such a way that we are made aware of something – e.g. in the case of seeing, of something white; in the case of pain, of an unpleasant disturbance to my leg; in the case of fear, of something dangerous. That of which we are made aware, or that of which the representation is a representation, is described as the 'cause' of the representation, i.e. whatever it is that brings about the representation of something white, of a painful leg, of something dangerous etc. Frequently the relation of this cause to the content of the representation will be ‖ completely isomorphic. A white house within my line of vision will

(such as knowledge, belief, emotions, desires, virtues and vices, characterising these as 'persistent phenomena, which manifest themselves intermittently') and 'mental activities' such as thinking a thought, 'by means of which we bring about mental states or bring dispositions into being or initiate bodily movements'.

[17] Aetius IV.12.1 = LS 39B: ἐνδεικνύμενον αὐτό τε καὶ τὸ πεποιηκός. Some MSS read ἐν αὐτῷ instead of αὐτό τε but the latter reading is supported by Sextus Empiricus, *M* VII.161 αὐτοῦ ἐνδεικτικόν.

[18] Cf. D.L. VII.51 = LS 39A4; Plutarch, *Comm. not.* 1084f = LS 39F; Philo, *Leg. alleg.* 1.30 = LS 53P; Stobaeus II.86.17 = LS 53Q; Cicero, *De fato* 42 = LS 62c8.

normally cause me to see that there is a white house there. But as
with the English expression, 'I have the impression that ...' representations are not necessarily veridical. Appearance and reality
may not coincide. The appearance of its cause that a representation mediates – for instance the appearance of a bent stick that
a straight stick reveals through water – will not always justify a
judgement to the effect that such and such is really the case. As is
well known, the Stoics claimed that only certain representations –
kataleptic ones – give unmistakably sound evidence concerning their
causes.

Representations, then, can be false or misleading. Yet, whatever their veridical status, they always present something to the
'commanding part' of the soul (*hēgemonikon*), which constitutes the
mind in Stoicism. In other words, the Stoics view the mind, in
one of its basic operations, as a receptor which is constantly being
occupied by a sequence of representations. They take it that the
external world and/or one's internal condition continuously acts
upon the mind, and thereby provides it with some definite content
or object(s) of awareness.[19] The significance of this point for their
deeper intuitions will become clear when we compare and contrast
their view of the difference between human representations and
those of other animals.

In addition to the representational faculty, all animals have the
faculty of impulse; and, as I said at the outset, the conjoint operation of these two faculties explains the purposive movement of
animals. Even at the purely animal level, it seems, the Stoics would
want to say that representations are thick with individual content;
one thinks of the distinction they drew between the willing dog
tied to a moving cart and the recalcitrant dog that is dragged
instead (*SVF* II.975 = LS 62A). The way things appear to a creature – the representations it has – depends not only upon the things
in question but also upon the kind of creature that it is and the
kind of training and habits that it has. Now the Stoics insist that
animal impressions are 'simple', in contrast with human impressions.[20] By 'simple' they mean that animals do not synthesise and
conceptualise their experience. The 'commanding part' of their

[19] The 'continuity' of an animal's self-perception is a conclusion for which Hierocles argues
at length; cf. chapter II of this volume, pp. 260, 263.
[20] Cf. Sextus Empiricus, *M* VIII.275–6 = LS 53T.

souls is non-rational. That of adult human beings, on the other hand, is not only rational but rational through and through. The orthodox Stoics firmly reject the standard Platonic division of the human soul into a rational 'mind' and an irrational part or parts responsible for sensing, appetite and passion.[21]

The Stoics' insistence on the complete rationality of the human *hēgemonikon* is a further indication of their commitment to a unitary view of the ‖ mind. They do not deny that humans can act or think 'irrationally', but they insist that irrationality is a defect of reason itself and not the manifestation of a different part of the mind that makes a person inattentive to reason. What makes adult human beings rational through and through is the fact, as Stoics see it, that all their experience is mediated by concepts and language. Thus, applying the point I stated above, how things appear to a rational animal will necessarily depend upon the kind of language user that it is; or, to put it another way, on the kind of concepts that it has. Or, to put it in Stoic terms, for every rational representation there is a *lekton*, a 'sayable', which will articulate the representation in propositional form: S is P.[22]

Along with the development of language and rationality there develops in the human soul a third faculty in addition to those of representation and impulse, the power of giving or withholding 'assent' (*synkatathesis*) to representations.[23] The term means 'casting a vote' or 'committing oneself'. As a faculty, assent functions as a power that can mediate between representations and impulses. Representations, as we have seen, are thought-contents, for instance, the way things look, smell, appeal to us, repel us etc. As thought-contents, representations naturally claim our attention since awareness normally involves attentiveness. The faculty that answers this claim is assent. Representations, considered simply as the fleeting contents of the mind, are not judgements; rather they should be regarded as potential judgements: 'That looks like my

---

[21] Two of the principal testimonies are Plutarch, *Virt. mor.* 440e, 446f = LS 61B and 65G; cf. Long 1986a, pp. 175–7.

[22] Cf. D.L. VII.49 = LS 33D; D.L. VII.63 = LS 33F; Seneca, *Ep.* 117.13 = LS 33E; and see p. 283 below.

[23] It is a matter of controversy (cf. Inwood 1985, pp. 72–91) whether non-human animals are endowed by the Stoics with a rudimentary kind of assent, but that question need not concern us here. If, as I myself believe, non-human animals do have such a faculty (cf. chapter 10 of this volume, p. 245, and Long/Sedley 1987, vol. I, p. 322), it is of too rudimentary a kind to affect the profound difference the Stoics posited between the representations of adult humans and those of other animals.

hat', as distinct from 'There's my hat'; 'I have the impression that
it would be good to go to the beach', as distinct from: 'It would be
good to go to the beach.'

A representation, once it has occurred, cannot be revoked or
erased from my life. But, according to Stoic theory, the occurrence of a representation does not impel me to act accordingly.
The impulse to do so is up to me because it depends on what I do
with the representation, i.e. whether I assent to it or not. The
Stoics' intuition that assent is an essential faculty of the human
soul draws attention to their interest in the self, the first-person
perspective, what each individual does with his experience. Any
representation is a part of my experience, but I can make it *mine*, –
my outlook, or belief, or commitment – or *not mine*, by giving or
withholding assent.

We should note that the role of assent in this account of life and
action is restricted to acceptance or rejection of the representation. Assent does not generate ‖ the thought-content itself. The
role of assent is judgemental, interpretative, and volitional. Like it
or not, I had the thought, let us say, that it would be good to go to
the beach. Because there are many other things that I ought to be
doing, I may pause to consider whether in fact it would be good to
go to the beach. I may well wish I had not had that representation.
Perhaps I say to myself, I must try in future to avoid such experiences. However, because of the kind of values and beliefs and
habits I have had up to now, I find myself having such representations from time to time.

We are getting close to the point where I can introduce Epictetus. Before doing so, I should sum up the principal ideas necessary
for understanding the importance he attaches to our making correct use of our representations.

A representation is anything at all that 'appears' to us, anything
that constitutes an instance of our awareness. Plainly representations cover an enormous range of thought-contents, but that range
for any individual will not be completely unrestricted. The representations that we receive as individuals from external and internal stimuli are powerfully determined by a wide range of factors –
our natures as human beings, our experience as particular persons,
our beliefs, desires, foibles, education, and so forth. We could
express this point by saying that representations will characteristically include general and particular elements. As putative judge-

ments, they are amenable to description in public discourse, in forms that will be intelligible to other persons. Yet, as appearances to *this* individual, they have an irreducible particularity – they are mental affections of this and only this person. There will, in many cases, be an objectively true proposition that a person assents to in assenting to this or that representation. Yet, what it is for that person to assent to this or any other proposition will remain something unique, nor will the individual content of anyone's representation be fully specifiable in any proposition. To put it in a form that is most helpful for approaching Epictetus – how to deal with the representations that one has is a matter for each person's individual decision.

EPICTETUS ON THE CORRECT USE OF REPRESENTATIONS

Epictetus repeatedly insists that an ethically good life is equivalent to making correct or proper use of representations (for instance, *Discourses* I.1.7, II.1.4, II.22.29, IV.6.34). In the first discourse of Arrian's collection, he says that this is the one and only faculty that the gods have put in our power (1.1.7 = LS 62K). What does he mean by this faculty? He glosses it in a number of ways. It is our reasoning faculty, the only faculty we have that can have cognisance of itself as well as everything else. It is our desiderative and ‖ impulsive faculty. It is our capacity to give or withhold assent. It is our *prohairesis*, or moral character. It is the faculty that tells us whether or not to do something, that passes judgement on the truth and value of anything of which we have a representation.

This faculty – let us call it *prohairesis* for short – is the essential self, as Epictetus conceives of this, the bearer of personal identity. 'You are not flesh nor hair, but *prohairesis*: if you get that beautiful, then *you* will be beautiful' (*Discourses* III.1.40). A person's *prohairesis*, or moral character or faculty of assent, is a function of reason, a state of the soul's 'commanding part'. Yet because the role of reason that preoccupies Epictetus is the individual's autonomy and responsibility, he identifies himself not with reason *simpliciter*, 'but with the practical application of reason in selecting his commitments, in keeping his emotional balance, his serenity, by not extending himself to goals and values that lie beyond his control'.[24]

[24] So Kahn 1988, p. 253.

As Charles Kahn, the author of these quoted remarks, also observes, 'The Platonic–Aristotelian identification of the person with the intellect offers no basis for a metaphysics of the self in any individual sense. Epictetus, on the other hand, identifies himself with something essentially personal and individualised.'

We can understand Epictetus' detachment of himself from his flesh and hair. And from what has been said before, we can understand why Epictetus chooses assent or *prohairesis*, and not representations themselves, as the locus of the persisting self. If my representations are up to me to interpret, accept or reject, there must be a 'me' to which they appear and an 'I' which reacts to them – a subject that is identifiable precisely by the representations that it receives and by what it does with them. Even non-rational animals, as we have seen, are credited by the Stoics with something analogous. In what follows I want to explore Epictetus' account of this 'subject', or what he takes the self-perception of humans to consist in.

Epictetus distinguishes the goal of humans from that of other animals by reference to their differences in respect to representations:

God had need of animals' making use of their representations, but of our attending to their use. For this reason it is sufficient for them to eat and drink and rest and procreate ... For us, on the other hand, to whom he has also given the power of attending to things, these animal activities are no longer sufficient ... God introduced man as a student of himself and his works, and not merely as a student, but also as an interpreter of these things. (*Discourses* 1.6.12–20 = LS 63E)

The correct use of impressions, then, is a 'hermeneutic' activity. As rational beings, Epictetus is saying, we are not constituted as creatures who can act satisfactorily if we simply allow representations to determine our ‖ conduct – eating simply because attractive food appears, running away simply because danger is evident. To function well, to live as our nature requires, we need to reflect on and evaluate the appearances that the world and our internal states generate in us. We should note the stress on 'need to'. Epictetus is well aware of the fact that representations often overwhelm people and constrain them to act without proper reflection. His discourses are packed with analysis – psychoanalysis one is tempted to call it – of the conditions under which this may happen, and of what may be done to resist such representations (cf. II.22.5, III.12.11, II.22.6).

But since any representation is what appears to me or to you, is it not the way you or I take things – a full manifestation of the self, in other words? The advice to interpret representations looks suspiciously like trying to bolt the stable after the horse has left. If my beliefs and desires, which make me the kind of person I am, are an influence on the kind of representations to which I am subject, it is also the case, as the Stoics acknowledged, that representations have helped to generate my beliefs and desires.[25] The causal relation works both ways. Hence the *prohairetic* 'faculty of using impressions', unless it is a transcendental 'ego', seems more likely to reinforce them than be capable of acting as their judge. Against any such transcendentalism, it may seem, is the Stoics' stress on the mind's unity. As we have seen, they reject the Platonic model of a mind divided into rational and irrational faculties. On their view reason, whether soundly or perversely, is at work in all aspects of the mind's activity.

Interestingly, Epictetus, and also Marcus Aurelius, do not evade this problem but face it very squarely. Marcus says: 'Your mind will be just like the repetition of your representations; for the soul is coloured by its representations' (*Meditations* v.16). Epictetus asks: 'Why do we assent to anything?', and answers: 'Its appearing that it is the case' (*Discourses* 1.28.1). Note 'appearing', *phainesthai*. Epictetus' point is that we are predisposed to assent to any representation whose thought-content appears to us to be true. He then asks: 'What do we have in the case of actions that corresponds to truth or falsehood?', and answers: 'The proper and the improper, the advantageous and the non-advantageous, the autonomous and the non-autonomous' (*Discourses* 1.28.5). The implication is that we are predisposed to assent to whatever appears to us to be proper and in our interests and in our power. Epictetus then asks: 'Is it impossible for someone to think that something is in his interests and not to choose it?', and answers that it is impossible. He ‖ illustrates this thesis by interpreting the famous lines of Euripides'

---

[25] Cf. the processes of concept formation described at D.L. VII.53 = LS 39D; Aetius IV.11.1–4 = LS 39E.

Medea (1078–9): 'I understand the evils I intend to do, but passion is stronger than [or "in charge of"] my reflections.'[26] According to Epictetus, Medea's words illustrate the fact that she regards gratifying her anger and avenging herself on her husband as more in her interests than saving her children. He imagines someone responding: 'Yes; but she is deceived', and replies: 'Show her clearly that she is deceived and she will not do it; but until you show her, what does she have to follow except what appears?', i.e. her representation of what is more in her interests.

Epictetus, like Socrates, denies *akrasia* – the possibility of doing something that you genuinely believe to be worse than what you ought to do. Medea, he says, deserves pity not anger. According to his analysis, it was impossible for Medea, given her character, not to prefer revenge to the life of her children. He generalises the point as follows (*Discourses* I.28.10): 'The measure [i.e. the standard or rule] of every person's action is what appears', and offers a startling example of its application:

The *Iliad* is nothing but a representation (*phantasia*) and the use of representations. Paris had a representation of abducting the wife of Menelaus, and Helen had a representation of following him. If Menelaus had had the representation that it was an advantage to be robbed of such a wife, what would have happened? We would have lost not only the *Iliad* but the *Odyssey* as well.

These passages illustrate the problem I raised a few sentences ago. On the one hand, Epictetus says that a good life consists in using one's representations correctly, and that this is a faculty that human beings possess. This thesis suggests that we are able to take stock of our representations, interpret their content, and accept or reject courses of action that they propose. It implies that responsibility, praise and blame, rest not with our representations but with the use that we make of them. On the other hand, Epictetus also says that people cannot fail to act in accordance with their representation of what is dominantly in their interests. He speaks of representations as being good or bad (*Discourses* I.28.10). His examples of Medea and the figures of the *Iliad* impute to people whose ethical principles are unsound corresponding representations that induce their assent. Their horse has already bolted. What correct

---

[26] Medea's self-analysis was plainly a Stoic topos. For an interesting discussion of Chrysippus' approach to it, cf. Gill 1983.

use could Medea have made of the representation that she should prefer revenge to her children's life?

The tension between these points of view is undeniable. Yet it is a tension which needs to be recognised and addressed in any serious ethical inquiry. ‖ The two viewpoints I have just identified in Epictetus' thought correspond to a standing problem for ethical psychology. On the one hand we hold people responsible for wrongdoing, on the presumption that it was in their power to resist unethical impulses – our version of the requirement to use representations correctly. At the same time our theories of upbringing, education and social welfare are strongly influenced by the belief that people's desires and interests, and hence their representations or occurrent mental states, are strongly shaped by the kind of world they are offered. To the question, 'Is blame or pity the more appropriate response to the wrongdoer?', Epictetus answers 'pity' (*Discourses* 1.28.9).

Epictetus lets the tension emerge, but he does not leave matters there. To resolve it, to the extent that it can be resolved, he advances his own version of living 'an examined life'. I want briefly to consider two of his principal recommendations, both of which turn on resources he thinks anyone can employ in 'using representations'. As I run through these, the reader may find it helpful to imagine Medea listening.

First, he suggests various ways in which we can detach ourselves from our representations. For instance, instead of immediately assenting to a representation, we can engage it in dialogue, saying: 'Wait for me a bit, representation; let me see who you are and what you are about, let me test you' (*Discourses* 11.18.24–6). Representations of wrong courses of action are prone to give us attractive pictures of what will follow for us if we act upon them. We should forestall such pictures by opposing to the first representation 'a fair and noble one', which will give us the incentive to chuck out its predecessor. Alternatively, offered the representation of something pleasurable, we should first reflect on the duration of the pleasure and then compare that to the time subsequent to the pleasure and the possible self-revulsion we shall experience during this later time (*Encheiridion*, 34).

Both of these strategies incorporate the two viewpoints I mentioned above, but in ways that seek to resolve the tension between them. Epictetus is not saying that we can ever act independently of representations. He preserves the thesis that people always act on the basis of what appears suitable to them (as Medea does), but insists that action need not be based upon first impressions. Once we have learned that first impressions do not always present us with what, on reflection, we really want for ourselves, we can use that knowledge to produce alternative representations and thus enlarge the scope of what it is open to us to do.

But Medea might say that she has no such knowledge. Epictetus has a response to this objection which introduces the second recommendation I want to discuss. Like earlier Stoics, he holds that all human beings normally develop into persons who have 'preconceptions' (*prolēpseis*) of what is good ‖ and bad. This does not mean that they have correct understanding of basic ethical truths, but rather that it is part of human nature to acquire such concepts as the profitability of what is good, the desirability of one's own happiness, and the identification of happiness with the possession of what is good (cf. *Discourses* 1.22.1). Where human beings typically go wrong, according to Epictetus, is in the way they fit or fail to fit representations of particular circumstances to preconceptions. Medea can be asked to consider whether her intention to kill her children accords with her general views of what is good for her, i.e. whether her current representation coheres with her preconception of her own well-lived life.

This test – one of consistency – will be ethically inefficacious if a person finds no discrepancy between his or her current representations and long-term beliefs and aspirations. The Stoics, however, would not be impressed by this objection since they take internal conflict or inconsistency to be the hallmark of unhappiness.[27] Unhappy persons, on their view, fail to get what they want or get what they do not want. In other words, their desire for happiness is constantly at odds with their immediate impressions of what they should seek or avoid. If happiness is a consistent life, free from disappointment and frustration, and if happiness is every one's long-term goal, it makes excellent sense to invite unhappy persons to interrogate their representations and ask whether their impulse to pursue this or that objective matches up with their desire for happiness.

It should now be clear why Epictetus identifies ethical sensibility

---

[27] Cf. Stobaeus II.75.11 = LS 63B1.

with the correct usage of representations. As thought-contents quite generally, the sequence of representations is the process of a human life that is available to introspection. Because representations are states of the reasoning faculty and reason can reflect on itself, we can subject our representations to scrutiny and interpretation. We can ask what they tell us about our characters and what our characters tell us about them. Marcus Aurelius exhorts himself to cultivate the practice of constantly discovering 'What precisely it is that is generating your representation, and to disclose it by analysing its cause, material, reference, and necessary duration' (*Meditations* xii.18).

There are striking similarities here and in much else that I have been saying to the views of a contemporary philosopher whose work is strongly influenced by psychoanalysis. I refer to Richard Wollheim in his book *The Thread of Life*. Justifying self-examination against the strictures brought against it by Kierkegaard, Wollheim writes:

Self-examination is an activity that is distinguishable from leading our lives ... but it must go on even as we lead them ... Though self-examination does ... require us to look into the past, it is the only alternative to a more baneful relation to the past to which we are otherwise ‖ condemned. If we show ourselves unprepared to learn, or to try to learn, from the past in the way in which self-examination asks us to, we shall be forced to live in it.[28]

This is what Epictetus' Stoicism is all about. Our representations are our selves, at the level of momentary consciousness. But they are not all that we are. Unlike non-human animals we are not simply recipients and users of our representations but 'students and interpreters of them'. Our natures are such that we fashion our own selves, and correct self-fashioning requires the interrogative and reflective task I have been describing, which is the work of each individual's assent or *prohairesis* or moral character. A committed Stoic will also use representations as the means of testing and training his character. He can represent imaginary situ-

---

[28] Cf. Wollheim 1984, p. 163. See also Foucault in Martin *et al.* 1988, p. 37: 'He [Epictetus] wants to watch perpetually over representations, a technique which culminates in Freud.' Foucault calls Epictetus' concern with control of representations 'a kind of permanent self-examination' (p. 38). This explains Epictetus' constant use of dialogue, monologue, personal pronouns and reflexives. Invented conversations provide him with the way of exhibiting the self to itself.

ations by which to check his reactions to things or confront those of his beliefs and desires which are not yet fully in tune with his ethical principles. Having the 'correct use of representations' as his decisively human faculty, he takes responsibility for the way the world impinges upon himself.

Some of the material I have drawn on for this chapter might suggest that Epictetus is feeling his way towards the idea of 'a subject that is not identical with any set of its experiences, memories or traits, but is that which *has* all of them, and can choose either to identify with them or to reject them as alien'. This formulation, by Amélie Rorty, is intended to signify 'the view of the person as the "I" of reflective consciousness, owner and disowner of its experiences' as influenced by the development of philosophy and culture since Descartes.[29] Stoicism is certainly an important part of the prehistory of this development, but Epictetus' conception of the self has no vestiges of a free-floating ego. In order to be at all, he suggests, we need a persisting view of ourselves, a bottom-line representation or narrative which is called into play whenever an 'I' is called upon to register and evaluate new experience.

The faculty of assent, though it includes the power of reflective consciousness, is not a noumenal self or observer, detachable from all experience, nor is it merely a monitor of representations. It constitutes a person's moral identity, and, as such, it is a character formed by experience, a disposition to make or decline to make specific commitments and choices. The content of these is given in representations. It is representations that provide selves ‖ with the viewpoints which they can select as appropriate to who they are, or reject as inappropriate. The Stoic self of Epictetus is constituted not by assent *simpliciter* but by the way assent uses representations.

Throughout this chapter I have been talking about one aspect of Stoicism, the access that individuals have to their own experience, a person's use of representations. Any creative discussion of Stoic philosophy requires a distinct focus, but there is always a risk of distortion by omission or emphasis since the system was peculiarly holistic. Two points in particular have an importance that I have barely hinted at in the main argument.

[29] Cf. Rorty 1976, p. 11.

The first concerns human beings generically. Responsible, though they take each of us to be, for the way we relate to or 'appropriate' the world, the Stoics insist that we are endowed with natures which make us 'parts of the whole'.[30] There is a normative way of living, a rational life 'in accordance with nature', which we are genetically equipped to understand, as our reason and experience develop, and which specifies what we should all seek as moral agents. Stoic self-fashioning is not a case of making up one's own values, but learning to take the norms of nature as one's own.

A second determinant of the self is that set of circumstances which characterises one's unique position in the world – one's nationality, gender, age, family relationships, status, profession and personality. The Stoics developed interesting categories for analysing individuals along these lines.[31] These roles or *personae* fall outside the scope of this chapter, but they are obviously central to a person's use of representations. For, as Epictetus makes plain, representations will typically involve our picturing ourselves in one or more of these roles, for instance, Medea as dishonoured wife and as mother. Epictetus invites someone to consider 'who you are' by running through a sequence of 'designations' – human being, citizen of the world, son, brother etc. (*Discourses* II.10). For each designation he offers a normative account, a representation of how someone so entitled should conduct himself. The idea is that, in order genuinely to be what one is (son, citizen etc.), each person must internalise a set of rules that constitute that role.

There is also a further dimension, too large to be fully developed, and too large to be omitted altogether. According to the Stoics all representations that befall normal adult humans are 'rational'. As Michael Frede has shown, this means that such representations presuppose concepts and make the mind conceptualise their object in a certain way.[32] The ‖ Stoics acknowledged this point by associating 'sayables' (*lekta*) with rational representations. *Lekta* specify the propositional content of these representations; they are the

---

[30] Cf. D.L. VII.87–9 = LS 63C. This fundamental text is treated at length on pp. 145–9 of this volume.
[31] Cf. Gill 1988 and chapter 7 of this volume, pp. 164–6.
[32] Cf. Frede 1987, pp. 68–71.

way we describe the objects that are presented to us.[33] And here lies an intriguing problem.

Phantasiai are physical structures – modifications of the corporeal mind. *Lekta* are incorporeal. It is a basic axiom of Stoic metaphysics that bodies cannot affect non-bodies, or non-bodies bodies (Nemesius 78.7 = LS 45c). So, it would seem, there can be no straightforward causal relation between *phantasiai* and the propositions that state our conceptualisation and interpretation of them – no straightforward causal relation between my representation of *p* and *p*. The only surviving Stoic answer to this problem is quaint and obscure. According to Sextus Empiricus, the Stoics said that *lekta* influence the mind not, as bodies do (for instance something white), by direct contact, but at a distance; they are likened to a trainer who may stand back and invite his pupils to imitate his movements instead of manipulating their limbs directly. Representations are not generated 'by' *lekta* (by their direct agency) but they can none the less 'result from' them.[34]

The problem that concerns Sextus Empiricus is how the Stoics can account for the representation of something incorporeal, such as a proof. But I think we are entitled to use this passage as a basis for speculating about the relation between any representation and its corresponding proposition.

Epictetus constantly emphasises the fact that the way things affect us depends upon how we describe them:

You say, 'I don't like leisure, it is solitude'; 'I don't like a crowd, it is confusion.' Instead of talking like this, if circumstances bring you to a state of spending time alone or with just a few, call it peace and use the situation in the right way. Talk to yourself, train your representations, work at your preconceptions. But if you fall in with a crowd, call it games, a festival, a holiday, try to celebrate with the people. (*Discourses* IV.26)

In this passage Epictetus invites someone to redescribe his experience, to *re*-present or replace 'solitude' with 'peace' and 'a crowd' with 'a festival', i.e. to fit a different *lekton* to the situation of which

---

[33] Cf. Long 1971b, pp. 82–4, and Long/Sedley 1987, section 33.

[34] Sextus Empiricus, *M* VIII.409 = LS 27E. The Greek originals of 'by' and 'result from' are ὑπό with the genitive and ἐπί with the dative respectively. The latter is familiar in the expression ἐφ’ ἡμῖν, 'in our power'. For further discussion of the question of how incorporeals can play any part in the world, cf. Long 1976b and most recently Brunschwig 1994, pp. 159–69.

the person is aware, to dispose himself differently to that situation. Applying the passage from Sextus Empiricus, we should say that the way persons view their situation (cf. Medea from above) will depend on the *lekton* they select as the paradigm appropriate to their set of beliefs and values. *Lekta* will 'result in' representations, not because they are the actual source of what we perceive or think but because they are the way we are disposed to interpret that source. Epictetus insists ‖ that 'the correct use of representations' is 'in our power'. It is reasonable to suggest that what is in our power is a *lekton* or description, and that this is 'our' individual contribution to our representations. In that case, the mind's freedom from constraint, so strongly emphasised by Epictetus, gains a (transcendental?) dimension that scholars of Stoicism have tended to overlook. Persons are not constrained by incorporeal *lekta* to experience their representations in one determinate set of ways. Rather, it seems, it is up to them to decide what *lekton* matches their situation, what precisely they are experiencing, and how they should evaluate that experience. If this is on the right lines, the Stoics may have room for a stronger sense of free will than is normally admitted. Epictetus' injunction to use representations correctly gains a useful conceptual resource in the causal gap which the self or assent fills between *phantasiai* and *lekta*.

Yet, as so often in philosophy, a solution in one area generates problems in another. The corporeal mind of the Stoics must have access to the incorporeal *lekta*, but the process by which it does so remains a mystery.[35] Since only minds can have access to *lekta*, there is an aspect to the Stoic self which raises the familiar dualist problems of mental and physical after all. It is tempting to conclude with the thought that the Stoics find themselves in this position precisely because they discovered the mind to be the centre of *consciousness*. We still don't know what consciousness is, but it should be clear from this chapter that it is what the Stoics meant by 'representation' or *phantasia*.

---

[35] Problems about the mind's relation to *lekta* are further discussed in chapter 10 of this volume, pp. 247–8.

Bibliography

Ackrill, J. L. (1972–3) 'Aristotle's definitions of psuche', *Proceedings of the Aristotelian Society* 63: 119–33

Annas, J. E. (1992) *Hellenistic Philosophy of Mind* (Berkeley/Los Angeles/London)

(1993) *The Morality of Happiness* (Oxford)

(1994) 'Plato the Skeptic', in Vander Waerdt 1994a, pp. 309–40

Arnim, H. von (1890) 'Über einen stoischen papyrus der Herculanensischen Bibliothek', *Hermes* 25: 473–95

(ed.) (1903–5) *Stoicorum Veterum Fragmenta* (Leipzig) (= *SVF*)

(1924) 'Kleanthes', Pauly–Wissowa, *Realencyclopädie der klassischen Altertumswissenschaft*, 11.1, cols. 558–74

(1906) *Hierokles. Ethische Elementarlehre. Berliner Klassikertexte*, vol. IV (Berlin)

Arnold, E. V. (1911) *Roman Stoicism* (London)

Barker, A. D. (1981), 'Aristotle on perception and ratios', *Phronesis* 26: 248–66

(1989) *Greek Musical Writings: II Harmonic and Acoustic Theory* (Cambridge)

Barnes, J. (1971–2) 'Aristotle's concept of mind', *Proceedings of the Aristotelian Society* 72: 101–14

Barnes, J., Brunschwig, J., Burnyeat, M., and Schofield, M. (edd.) (1982) *Science and Speculation* (Cambridge/Paris)

Bastianini, G., and Long, A. A. (1992a) 'Hierocles', in *Corpus dei Papiri Filosofici Greci e Latini (CPF)* I, vol. I** (Florence), pp. 268–451

(1992b) 'Dopo la nuova edizione degli *Elementi di Etica* di Ierocle Stoico', *Studi* cxxix of Accademia Toscana di Scienze e Lettere (Florence), pp. 221–49

Bentham, J. (1834) *Deontology*, ed. J. Bowring (London/Edinburgh)

Bonhöffer, A. (1890) *Epiktet und die Stoa* (Stuttgart)

(1894) *Die Ethik Epiktets* (Stuttgart)

Boyancé, P. (1967) Review of Giusta (1964, 1967), *Latomus* 26: 246–9

Brancacci, A. (1981) 'La filosofia di Pirrone e le sue relazioni con il Cinismo', in *Lo scetticismo antico*, ed. G. Giannantoni (Naples), vol. I, pp. 213–42

Bréhier, E. (1951) *Chrysippe et l'ancien Stoicisme*, 2nd ed. (Paris)

Brink, C. O. (1956) 'oikeiosis and oikeiotes: Theophrastus and Zeno on nature in moral theory', *Phronesis* 1: 123–45

Brunschwig, J. (ed.) (1978) *Les stoiciens et leur logique* (Paris)

  (1986) 'The Cradle argument in Epicureanism and Stoicism', in Schofield and Striker 1986, pp. 113–45

  (1994) *Papers in Hellenistic Philosophy* (Cambridge)

Brunschwig, J., and Nussbaum, M. (edd.) (1993) *Passions and Perceptions* (Cambridge)

Brunt, P. A. (1973) 'Aspects of the social thought of Dio Chrysostom and of the Stoics', *Proceedings of the Cambridge Philological Society* 199 (NS 19), 9–34

Buffière, F. (1956) *Les mythes d'Homère et la pensée grecque* (Paris)

  (ed.) (1962) *Héraclite: Allégories d'Homère* (Paris)

Burnet, J. (1930) *Early Greek Philosophy*, 4th ed. (London)

Caizzi, F. D. (1964) 'Antistene', *Studi Urbinati* 1: 25–76

  (1966) *Antisthenis Fragmenta* (Milan)

Carrithers, M., Collins, S., and Lukes, S. (edd.) (1985) *The Category of the Person* (Cambridge)

Cherniss, H. (1935) *Aristotle's Criticism of Presocratic Philosophy* (Baltimore)

  (ed.) (1976) *Plutarch's Moralia XIII*, 2 vols. (Cambridge, Mass./London)

Cooper, J. (1975) *Reason and Human Good in Aristotle* (Cambridge, Mass.)

Cortassa, G. (1978) 'Note ai *Silli* di Timone di Fliunte', *RFIC* 106: 140–6

Covotti, A. (1897) 'Quibus libris vitarum in libro septimo scribendo Laertius usus fuerit', *Studi Italiani di Filologia Classica* 5: 65–97

Crönert, W. (1906) *Kolotes und Menedemus* (Leipzig)

Dawson, D. (1992) *Allegorical Readers and Cultural Revision in Ancient Alexandria* (Berkeley/Los Angeles/London)

DeFilippo, J. G., and Mitsis, P. T. (1994) 'Socrates and Stoic natural law', in Vander Waerdt 1994a, pp. 252–71

Deichgräber, K. (1938) 'Bemerkungen zu Diogenes' Bericht über Heraklit', *Philologus* 93: 12–30

De Lacy, P. (1948) 'Stoic views of poetry', *American Journal of Philology* 69: 241–71

  (1977) 'The four Stoic *personae*', *Illinois Classical Studies* 2: 163–72

Delle Donne, V. (1987/88), 'Per una nuova edizione dei "Principi di etica di Ierocle stoico (P. Berol. 9870)', *Annale dell'Istituto Italiano di Studi Storici* 10: 113–44

Diels, H. (ed.) (1879) *Doxographi Graeci* (Berlin)

Dillon, J. (1977) *The Middle Platonists* (London)

Dillon, J. M., and Long, A. A. (edd.) (1988) *The Question of 'Eclecticism'. Studies in Later Greek Philosophy* (Berkeley/Los Angeles/London)

Döring, K. (1972) *Die Megariker* (Amsterdam)

  (1979) *Exemplum Socratis. Studien zur Sokratesnachwirkung in der kynisch-stoischen Popularphilosophie der frühen Kaiserzeit und im frühen Christentum. Hermes Einzelschrift* 42 (Wiesbaden)

Dragona-Monachou, M. (1971) "Ο "῾Υμνος στὸ Δία" Καὶ τὰ "Χρυσὰ "Επη"", *Philosophia* 1: 329–76

(1976) *The Stoic Arguments for the Existence and the Providence of the Gods* (Athens)

Dyroff, A. (1897) *Die Ethik der alten Stoa* (Berlin)

Edelstein, L., and Kidd, I. G. (edd.) (1972), *Posidonius*, vol. 1: *The Fragments* (Cambridge)

Engberg-Pedersen, T. (1986) 'Discovering the good: *oikeiosis* and *kathe-konta* in Stoic ethics', in Schofield and Striker 1986, pp. 145–84

(1990) *The Stoic Theory of Oikeiosis. Moral Development and Social Interaction in Early Stoic Philosophy* (Aarhus)

Farquharson, A. S. L. (1944) *The Meditations of Marcus Aurelius*, 2 vols. (Oxford)

Finnis, J. (1980) *Natural Law and Natural Rights* (Oxford)

Forschner, M. (1986) 'Das Gute und die Güter. Zur Aktualität der stoischen Ethik', in *Aspects de la philosophie héllenistique, Entretiens sur l'Antiquité classique*, vol. XXXII (Fondation Hardt, Vandœuvres/Geneva), pp. 325–59

(1995) *Die stoische Ethik: über die Zusammenhang von Natur-Sprach-u. Moral philosophie im altstoischen System*, 2nd ed. (Stuttgart)

Fortenbaugh, W. W. (ed.) (1983) *On Stoic and Peripatetic Ethics. The Work of Arius Didymus*, (New Brunswick/London)

(1984) *Quellen zur Ethik Theophrasts* (Amsterdam)

Fraser, P. (1972) *Ptolemaic Alexandria*, 3 vols. (Oxford)

Frede, M. (1974) *Die stoische Logik* (Göttingen)

(1987) *Essays in Ancient Philosophy* (Oxford/Minneapolis)

(1989) 'Chaeremon der Stoiker', *Aufstieg und Niedergang der Römischen Welt* 2.26.3: 2067–103

Fritz, K. von (1972) 'Zenon von Kition', in Pauly–Wissowa, *Real-Encyclo-pädie der klassischen Altertumswissenschaft* x², cols. 83–121

Frye, N. (1967) *The Anatomy of Criticism: Four Essays* (New York)

Giannantoni, G. (1983–85) *Socraticorum Reliquiae*, 4 vols. (Naples)

Gigante, M. (1976) *Diogene Laerzio*, 2nd ed., 2 vols. (Rome/Bari)

Gill, C. J. (1983) 'Did Chrysippus understand Medea?', *Phronesis* 28: 136–49

(1988) 'Personhood and personality: the four-*personae* theory in Cicero, *De officiis* I', *Oxford Studies in Ancient Philosophy* 6: 169–99

Giusta, M. (1964, 1967) *I Dossografi di Etica*, 2 vols. (Turin)

Glucker, J. (1978) *Antiochus and the Late Academy* (Göttingen, 1978)

Gould, J. (1970) *The Philosophy of Chrysippus* (Leiden)

Graeser, A. (1972) 'Zirkel oder Deduktion? Zur Begründung der stoischen Ethik', *Kant Studien* 63: 213–24

(1975) *Zenon von Kition, Positionen und Probleme* (Berlin/New York)

Grote, G. (1885) *Plato and the Other Companions of Socrates*, 3 vols. (London)

Guthrie, W. K. C. (1962) *A History of Greek Philosophy*, vol. I (Cambridge)

Hahm, D. E. (1983) 'The diairetic method and the purpose of Arius' doxography', in Fortenbaugh 1983, pp. 15–38

Hartman, E. (1977) *Substance, Body, and Soul. Aristotelian Investigations* (Princeton)

Hegel, G. W. F. (1971) *Vorlesungen über die Geschichte der Philosophie* (Frankfurt)

Henrichs, A. (1968) 'Philosophy, the handmaiden of theology', *Greek, Roman and Byzantine Studies* 9: 437–50

(1974) 'Die Kritik der stoischen Theologie im PHerc. 1428', *Cronache Ercolanesi* 4: 5–32

Hicks, R. D. (ed.) (1907) *Aristotle's De anima* (Oxford)

(1910) *Stoic and Epicurean* (London)

(1911) 'Heraclitus', in *Encyclopaedia Britannica*, 11th ed. (New York) vol. x, pp. 944–5

Hilgruber, M. (1989) 'Dion Chrysostomos 36 (53) und die Homerauslegung Zenons', *Museum Helveticum* 46: 15–24

Hirzel, R. (1882) *Untersuchungen zu Ciceros Philosophischen Schriften*, 3 vols. (Leipzig)

Hoven, R. (1971) *Stoïcisme et Stoïciens face au Problème de l'au-Delà* (Paris)

Inwood, B. (1984) 'Hierocles: theory and argument in the second century A.D.', *Oxford Studies in Ancient Philosophy* 2: 151–84

(1985) *Ethics and Human Action in Early Stoicism* (Oxford)

Ioppolo, A. M. (1980) *Aristone di Chio e lo stoicismo antico* (Naples)

Irwin, T. H. (1986a) 'Stoic and Epicurean conceptions of happiness', in Schofield and Striker 1986, pp. 205–44

(1986b) 'Socrates the Epicurean', *Illinois Classical Studies* 11: 85–112

Kahn, C. H. (1964) 'A new look at Heraclitus', *American Philosophical Quarterly* 1: 189–203

(1969) 'Stoic logic and Stoic logos', *Archiv für Geschichte der Philosophie* 51: 158–72

(1979) *The Art and Thought of Heraclitus* (Cambridge)

(1983), 'Arius as a doxographer', in Fortenbaugh 1983, pp. 3–14

(1988) 'Discovering the will: from Aristotle to Augustine', in Dillon and Long 1988, pp. 234–59

Kerferd, G. B. (1967) Review of Giusta (1964, 1967), *Classical Review* 17: 156–68

(1972) 'The search for personal identity in Stoic thought', *Bulletin of the John Rylands Library, University of Manchester* 55: 177–96

(1978a) 'What does the wise man know?', in Rist 1978b, pp. 125–36

(1978b) 'The problem of synkatathesis and katalepsis', in Brunschwig 1978, pp. 251–72

Kerschensteiner, J. (1955) 'Der Bericht des Theophrast über Heraklit', *Hermes* 83: 385–411

Kidd, I. G. (1971) 'Stoic intermediates and the end for man', in Long 1971a, pp. 150–72

(1978) 'Moral actions and rules in Stoic ethics', in Rist 1978b, pp. 247–58

Kindstrand, J. F. (ed.) (1990) *[Plutarchus] De Homero* (Leipzig)

Kirk, G. S. (1959) 'Ecpyrosis in Heraclitus: some comments', *Phronesis* 4: 73–6

(1962) *Heraclitus. The Cosmic Fragments*, repr. with corrections of the 1954 ed. (Cambridge)

(1955) 'Some problems in Anaximander', *Classical Quarterly* 49: 21–38

Kleve, K. (1983) 'Scurra Atticus. The Epicurean view of Socrates', in *Suzetesis. Studi sull'Epicureismo Greco e Romano offerti a Marcello Gigante*, ed. G. P. Carratelli, 2 vols. (Naples)

Kneale, W. and M. (1962) *The Development of Logic* (Oxford)

Kosman, L. A. (1975) 'Perceiving that we perceive: *On the soul* III, 2', *Philosophical Review* 84: 499–519

Kraut, R. (1979) 'Two conceptions of happiness', *Philosophical Review* 88: 157–97

Laks, A. (1989) 'Commentary on J. Annas, Naturalism in Greek ethics: Aristotle and after', in *Proceedings of the Boston Area Colloquium in Ancient Philosophy*, vol. IV, ed. J. J. Cleary and D. C. Shartin, pp. 172–86

Lamberton, R. (1986) *Homer the Theologian. Neoplatonist Allegorical Reading and the Growth of the Epic Tradition* (Berkeley/Los Angeles/London)

Lapidge, M. (1973) 'Ἀρχαὶ and στοιχεῖα': a problem in Stoic cosmology', *Phronesis* 18: 240–78

Lassalle, F. (1858) *Die Philosophie Herakleitos des Dunklen von Ephesos* (Berlin)

Lincke, K. (1906) 'Xenophon und die Stoa', *Neue Jarhbuch für Philologie* 17: 673–91

Lloyd, A. C. (1971) 'Grammar and metaphysics in the Stoa', in Long 1971a, pp. 58–71

(1978) 'Emotion and decision in Stoic psychology', in Rist 1978b, pp. 233–46

Lloyd, G. E. R., and Owen, G. E. L. (edd.) (1978) *Aristotle On Mind and the Senses* (Cambridge)

Lloyd-Jones, H., and Parsons, P. (edd.) (1983) *Supplementum Hellenisticum* (Berlin/New York)

Long, A. A. (1967) 'Carneades and the Stoic telos', *Phronesis* 18: 59–90

(1968a) 'The Stoic concept of evil', *Philosophical Quarterly* 18: 329–43

(1968b) 'Aristotle's legacy to Stoic ethics', *Bulletin of the University of London Institute of Classical Studies* 15: 72–85

(1970) 'Stoic determinism and Alexander of Aphrodisias *De fato* (i–xiv)', *Archiv für Geschichte der Philosophie* 52: 247–68

(1971a) (ed.) *Problems in Stoicism* (London)

(1971b) 'Language and thought in Stoicism', in Long 1971a, pp. 75–113

(1971c) 'Freedom and determinism in the Stoic theory of human action', in Long 1971a, pp. 173–99

(1976) 'The early Stoic concept of moral choice', in *Images of man in ancient and medieval thought. Studies presented to G. Verbeke* (Louvain), pp. 77–92

(1978a) 'Timon of Phlius: Pyrrhonist and satirist', *Proceedings of the Cambridge Philological Society* 204 (NS 24): 68–91

(1978b) 'The Stoic distinction between truth and the true', in Brunschwig 1978, pp. 297–316

(1978c) 'Sextus Empiricus on the criterion of truth', *Bulletin of the University of London Institute of Classical Studies* 25: 35–49

(1980) 'Stoa and Sceptical Academy: origins and growth of a tradition', *Liverpool Classical Monthly* 5.8: 161–74

(1981) Review of Döring 1979, *Classical Review* 31: 298–9

(1982) 'Astrology: arguments pro and contra' in Barnes 1982, pp. 165–92

(1985) 'The Stoics on world-conflagration and everlasting recurrence', in *Southern Journal of Philosophy* 23 suppl., 13–38

(1986a) *Hellenistic Philosophy. Stoics, Epicureans, Sceptics*, 2nd ed. (Berkeley/Los Angeles/London; 1st ed., London 1974)

(1986b) 'Diogenes Laertius, Life of Arcesilaus', *Elenchos* 7: 429–49

(1988) 'Ptolemy on the Criterion: an epistemology for the practising scientist', In Dillon and Long 1988, pp. 176–207

(1990) 'Scepticism about gods in Hellenistic philosophy', in M. Griffith and D. Mastronarde (edd.), *The Cabinet of the Muses* (Atlanta)

(1992) 'Finding oneself in Greek philosophy'. *Tijdschrift voor Filosofie* 54: 257–79

(1996) 'Theophrastus and the Stoa' in *Reappraising the Sources for Theophrastus*, ed. M. Van Raalte and J. Van Ophuijsen (New Brunswick/London)

Long, A. A., and Sedley, D. N. (1987) *The Hellenistic Philosophers*, 2 vols. (Cambridge)

Longrigg, J. (1975) 'Elementary physics in the Lyceum and Stoa', *Isis* 66: 211–29

McDiarmid, J. (1953) 'Theophrastus on the Presocratic Causes', *Harvard Studies in Classical Philology* 61: 1–156

MacIntyre, A. (1967) *A Short History of Ethics* (1967)

(1981) *After Virtue* (Indiana/London)

Madvig, J. N. (ed.) (1876) *M. Tulii Ciceronis De finibus bonorum et malorum*, 3rd ed. (Copenhagen)

Maier, H. (1913) *Sokrates* (Tübingen)

Mancini, A. C. (1976) 'Sulle opere polemiche di Colote', *Cronache Ercolanesi* 6: 61–7

Mansion, S. (1978) 'Soul and life in the *De anima*', in Lloyd and Owen 1978, pp. 1–20

Marcovich, M. (ed.) (1967) *Heraclitus* (Merida)

(1965) 'Herakleitos', Pauly–Wissowa, *Realencyclopädie der klassischen Altertumswissenschaft* Suppl. x, cols. 246–320

Martin, L. H., Gutman, G., and Hutton, P. H. (edd.) (1988) *Technologies of the Self: A Seminar with Michel Foucault* (Amherst)

Mates, B. (1961) *Stoic Logic*, 2nd ed. (Berkeley/Los Angeles)

Meerwaldt, J. D. (1951) 'Cleanthea I', *Mnemosyne* 4: 38–66
(1952) 'Cleanthea II', *Mnemosyne* 5: 1–12

Meineke, F. (1859) *Mützells Zeitschrift* 13

Mill, J. S. (1969) *Essays on Ethics, Religion and Society* = vol. x *of The Collected Edition* (Toronto)

Mondolfo, R. (1958) 'Evidence of Plato and Aristotle relating to the ekpyrosis in Heraclitus', *Phronesis* 4: 75–82
(1972) *Eraclito, Testimonianze e Imitazioni* (Florence)

Moore, G. E. (1903) *Principia Ethica* (Cambridge)

Moraux, P. (1968) 'La joute dialectique d'après le huitième livre des *Topiques*', in Owen 1968, pp. 277–312

Most, G. W. (1989) 'Cornutus and Stoic allegoresis: a preliminary report', *Aufstieg und Niedergang der Römischen Welt* 2.36.3, pp. 2014–65

Nagel, T. (1979) *Mortal Questions* (Cambridge)

Neubecker, A. J. (1956) *Die Bewertung der Musik bei Stoikern und Epikureern* (Berlin)

Owen, G. E. L. (ed.) (1968) *Aristotle on Dialectic. The Topics* (Oxford)
(1986) *Logic, Science and Dialectic. Collected Papers on Greek Philosophy* (London/Ithaca)

Pearson, A. C. (1891) *Zeno and Cleanthes* (London)

Pembroke, S. G. (1971) 'Oikeiosis', in Long 1971a, pp. 114–49

Pfeiffer, R. (1968) *History of Classical Scholarship. From the Beginnings to the End of the Hellenistic Age* (Oxford)

Philippson, R. (1937) 'Zur Psychologie der Stoa', *Rheinisches Museum* 86: 140–79

Pohlenz, M. (1959) *Die Stoa. Geschichte eine geistiger Bewegung*, 2nd ed., 2 vols. (Göttingen)

Praechter, K. (1901) *Hierokles der Stoiker* (Leipzig)

Quilligan, M. (1979) *The Language of Allegory: Defining the Genre* (Ithaca)

Rabel, R. J. (1988) Review of Sandbach (1983), *Journal of the History of Philosophy* 26: 144–5

Richardson, N. J. (1975) 'Homeric professors in the age of the sophists', *Proceedings of the Cambridge Philological Society* 201 (NS 21): 65–81

Rispoli, G. M. (1974) 'Filodemo sull musica', *Cronache Ercolanesi* 4: 58–86

Rist, J. M. (1969) *Stoic Philosophy* (Cambridge)
(1978a) 'Zeno and the origins of Stoic logic', in Brunschwig 1978, pp. 387–400
(ed.) (1978b) *The Stoics* (Berkeley/Los Angeles/London)

Robinson, H. M. (1978) 'Mind and body in Aristotle', *Classical Quarterly* 28: 105–24

Robinson, T. M. (1970) *Plato's Psychology* (Toronto)

Rorty, A. (ed.) (1976) *The Identities of Persons* (Berkeley/Los Angeles/London)

Rusten, J. S. (1985) 'Interim notes on the papyrus from Derveni', *Harvard Studies in Classical Philology* 89: 121–40

Sacks, O. (1987) *The Man who Mistook his Wife for a Hat* (New York)

Sandbach, F. H. (1971a) 'Ennoia and prolepsis', in Long 1971a, pp. 22–37

    (1971b) 'Phantasia kataleptike', in Long 1971a, pp. 9–21

    (1975) *The Stoics* (London)

    (1985) *Aristotle and the Stoics*, Cambridge Philological Society, suppl. 10

Scheffler, S. (1983) Review of MacIntyre (1981), *Philosophical Review* 92: 443–7

Schenkeveld, D. M. (1976) 'Strabo on Homer', *Mnemosyne* 29: 52–64

Schofield, M. (1983) 'The syllogisms of Zeno of Citium', *Phronesis* 28: 31–58

    (1984) 'Ariston of Chios and the unity of virtue', *Ancient Philosophy* 4: 83–96

    (1991) *The Stoic Idea of the City* (Cambridge)

Schofield, M., and Striker, G. (edd.) (1986) *The Norms of Nature. Studies in Hellenistic Ethics* (Cambridge/Paris)

Sedley, D. N. (1973) 'Epicurus, On Nature book XXVIII', *Cronache Ercolanesi* 3: 5–83

    (1976) 'Epicurus and his professional rivals', *Cahiers de Philologie* 1: 122–59

    (1977) 'Diodorus Cronus and Hellenistic philosophy', *Proceedings of the Cambridge Philological Society* 203 (NS 23): 74–120

    (1993) 'Chrysippus on psychophysical causality', in Brunschwig and Nussbaum 1993, pp. 313–31

Sherrington, C. (1906) *The Integrative Action of the Nervous System* (Cambridge)

Shields, C. (1994) 'Socrates among the Skeptics', in Vander Waerdt 1994a, 341–66

Siebeck, H. (1873) *Untersuchungen zur Philosophie der Griechen* (Halle)

Skinner, Q. (1978) *The Foundations of Modern Political Thought*, vol. 1 (Cambridge)

Solmsen, F. (1968a) 'Cleanthes or Posidonius? The basis of Stoic physics', in F. Solmsen, *Kleine Schriften* (Hildesheim)

    (1968b) 'Dialectic without the Forms', in Owen 1968, pp. 49–68

Sorabji, R. (1990) 'Perceptual content in the Stoics', *Phronesis* 35: 307–14

Stein, L. (1888) *Die Erkenntnistheorie der Stoa* (Berlin)

Steinmetz, P. (1986) 'Allegorische Deutung und allegorische Dichtung in der alten Stoa', *Rheinisches Museum* 129: 18–30

Steinthal, H. (1890) *Geschichte der Sprachwissenschaft*, 2nd ed., 2 vols. (Berlin)

Stewart, A. F. (1978) 'The Canon of Polykeitos: a question of evidence', *Journal of Hellenic Studies* 98: 122–31

Strange, S. K. (1989) 'Commentary on Long' (= chapter 8 of this volume), *Proceedings of the Boston Area Colloquium in Ancient Philosophy, vol. 4 1988*, ed. J. J. Cleary and D. C. Shartin, pp. 102–12

Striker, G. (1983) 'The role of oikeiosis in Stoic ethics', *Oxford Studies in Ancient Philosophy* 1: 145–68

    (1991) 'Following nature: a study in Stoic ethics', *Oxford Studies in Ancient Philosophy* 9: 1–74

    (1994) 'Plato's Socrates and the Stoics', in Vander Waerdt 1994a, pp. 241–51

Tate, J. (1929) 'Cornutus and the poets', *Classical Quarterly* 23: 41–5

    (1930) 'Plato and allegorical interpretation [2]', *Classical Quarterly* 24: 1–10

Taylor, C. (1989) *Sources of the Self* (Cambridge, Mass.)

Tieleman, T. (1995) Review of Engberg-Pedersen 1990, *Mnemosyne* 48: 226–32

Todd, R. B. (1976) *Alexander of Aphrodisias On Stoic Physics* (Leiden)

Usener, H. (ed.) (1887) *Epicurea* (Leipzig)

Vander Waerdt, P. A. (1991) 'Politics and philosophy in Stoicism', *Oxford Studies in Ancient Philosophy* 9: 185–211

    (ed.) (1994a) *The Socratic Movement* (Ithaca)

    (1994b) 'Zeno's *Republic* and the origins of natural law', in Vander Waerdt 1994a, pp. 272–308

Van Straaten, M. (ed.) (1952) *Panaetii Rhodii Fragmenta* (Leiden)

Verbeke, G. (1949) *Kleanthes van Assos* (Brussels)

Vlastos, G. (1955) 'On Heraclitus', *American Journal of Philology* 76: 337–68

    (1984) 'Happiness and virtue in Socrates' moral theory', *Proceedings of the Cambridge Philological Society* 210 (NS 30): 181–213

    (1985) 'Socrates' disavowal of knowledge', *Philosophical Quarterly* 35: 1–31

Wachsmuth, C. and Hense, O. (1884–1912) *Ioannis Stobaei Anthologium*, 5 vols. (Berlin)

Watson, G. (1966) *The Stoic Theory of Knowledge* (Belfast)

Wehrli, F. (1928) *Zur Geschichte der allegorischen Dichtung Homers in Altertum* (Basel)

Weinstock, S. (1927) 'Die Platonische Homerkritik und seine Nachwirkung', *Philologus* 82: 121–53

White, N. P. (1979) 'The basis of Stoic ethics', *Harvard Studies in Classical Philology* 83: 143–78

    (1983) 'Comments on Professor Long's paper' (= chapter 5 of this volume), in Fortenbaugh 1983, pp. 67–74

Williams, B. (1986) 'Hylomorphism', *Oxford Studies in Ancient Philosophy* 4: 189–200

Wollheim, R. (1984) *The Thread of Life* (Cambridge)

Zeller, E. (1892–1909) *Die Philosophie der Griechen in ihrer geschichtlichen Entwicklung*, 4th ed., 5 vols. (Leipzig)

Zuntz, G. (1958) 'Zum Kleanthes Hymnus', *Harvard Studies in Classical Philology* 63: 290–8

Index of subjects

Index of names

Index of passages cited